Knowledge, Ideology, Reproduction

Historical Materialism Book Series

The Historical Materialism Book Series is a major publishing initiative of the radical left. The capitalist crisis of the twenty-first century has been met by a resurgence of interest in critical Marxist theory. At the same time, the publishing institutions committed to Marxism have contracted markedly since the high point of the 1970s. The Historical Materialism Book Series is dedicated to addressing this situation by making available important works of Marxist theory. The aim of the series is to publish important theoretical contributions as the basis for vigorous intellectual debate and exchange on the left.

The peer-reviewed series publishes original monographs, translated texts, and reprints of classics across the bounds of academic disciplinary agendas and across the divisions of the left. The series is particularly concerned to encourage the internationalization of Marxist debate and aims to translate significant studies from beyond the English-speaking world.

For a full list of titles in the Historical Materialism Book Series available in paperback from Haymarket Books, visit: www.haymarketbooks.org/series_collections/1-historical-materialism.

Knowledge, Ideology, Reproduction

The Scholastic Apparatus in Louis Althusser and the Althusserian School

Giacomo Clemente

Translated by
Fabio Gironi

Haymarket Books
Chicago, IL

First published in 2025 by Brill Academic Publishers, The Netherlands
© 2025 Koninklijke Brill NV, Leiden, The Netherlands

Published in paperback in 2026 by
Haymarket Books
P.O. Box 180165
Chicago, IL 60618
773-583-7884
www.haymarketbooks.org

ISBN: 979-8-88890-793-1

Distributed to the trade in the US through Consortium Book Sales and
Distribution (www.cbsd.com) and internationally through Ingram
Publisher Services International (www.ingramcontent.com).

This book was published with the generous support of Lannan
Foundation, Wallace Action Fund, and the Marguerite Casey Foundation.

Special discounts are available for bulk purchases by organizations and
institutions. Please call 773-583-7884 or email info@haymarketbooks.org
for more information.

Cover art and design by David Mabb. Cover art is a development of
Construct 46, Kathleen Kersey for Morris & Co. Arbutus / Malevich drawing,
paint and wallpaper on canvas (2006).

Printed in the United States.

Library of Congress Cataloging-in-Publication data is available.

Contents

Foreword   VII
Acknowledgments   XXVIII

Introduction   1

1 Pedagogical Function and Class Struggle: On the Genesis and Structure
   of 'Student Problems'   13
       Introduction   13
   1   Technical Division and Social Division   15
   2   The Pedagogical Function   22
   3   *'Just because we are stepping onto a train it doesn't mean we know how
       to drive it!'*: On the Genesis of 'Student Problems'   26
   4   Knowledge as a Commodity: André Gorz on the Contradictions
       within (Academic) Capital   43
   5   Knowledge as a Commodity: J-P. Milbergue on the Internal
       Contradictions of the (Capitalist) University   54

2 The School Does Not Exist: Scholastic Mythology and Ideological
   Reproduction in Pierre Macherey   68
       Introduction   68
   1   The School and the Text: Representation and Synecdoche   75
   2   The Mechanisms of Fiction: Generation by Reduction and
       Pedagogical Separation   84
   3   The Mechanisms of Fiction: Functioning by Pedagogical Analogy as
       an Act of Ideological Belief   88
   4   Five Hypotheses about School Apparatuses   93
       4.1   *First Hypothesis*   94
       4.2   *Second Hypothesis*   96
       4.3   *Third Hypothesis*   96
       4.4   *Fourth Hypothesis*   98
       4.5   *Fifth Hypothesis*   99
   5   Culture and Ideology: Roger Establet   101
   6   On the Ownership of the Means of Expression (and the Genesis of
       the Class-Based School): Michel Tort   120

3 'Schools'   137
    Introduction   137
    1   *Schools I*: The Ideological Representations of the School and their
        Theoretical Identification   150
    2   *Schools II*: The Characteristics of the School-Form as a Social
        Form   163
    3   *Schools III*: Schooling and Wage Labour   177
    4   Schooling and the Reproduction of Labour Power   182
    5   Once Again on Wage Theory: The Wage-Form and the Notions of
        'Labour' and 'Qualification'   189
    6   Schooling as a 'Technical' Criterion for Measuring 'Qualification' and
        as a Principle for Establishing Individual Attitudes   201

4 Outlines of the History and Geography of Class-Based School
    Education   214
    Introduction   214
    1   On the Historical-Geographical Differences in the Establishment of
        Schools in Three Capitalist Countries   219
    2   The *école préparatoire* and the *école progressive* as Ideological Forms
        of the Class-Based School   224
    3   On the Historical Processes of Formation of the Class-Based School:
        The Antediluvian Forms   226
    4   The Transition Phase: A Look at the French Case   236

    Afterword   245

    References   253
    Index   258

Foreword

Of the many puzzling, or at least under-explained, postulates in 'Ideology and the Ideological State Apparatuses', one of Althusser's most widely read works, few have been as systematically overlooked as his assertion that the educational system or the 'scholastic apparatus' (*appareil scolaire*) is dominant over all the Ideological State Apparatuses proper to modern capitalist societies. It is finally more fundamental than the political State Apparatus by which the bourgeoisie as a class imposes its rule by means of 'the regime of parliamentary democracy combining universal suffrage and party struggle', as well as the cultural or religious apparatuses that perpetually present the capitalist order as simultaneously the best and the only possible world. If the domination of the scholastic apparatus appears 'paradoxical', as Althusser writes, it is only because in what he calls the concert of the ISAs, 'one Ideological State Apparatus certainly has the dominant role, although hardly anyone lends an ear to its music: it is so silent! This is the school'.[1] Thus, the dominant ISA is also the most silent, as if its silence were the necessary condition of its dominance, allowing it the freedom to operate unheard. While Althusser provides a brief explanation of the function of the educational State Apparatus, comparing it to the place of the Church under feudalism, his explanation raises more questions than it answers, particularly concerning the precise meaning of 'ideology' and 'ideological'. His argument abruptly ends and the essay continues, perhaps in anticipation of the reader's questions, with an account of ideology as Althusser understands it. Education never again appears: it has been restored to the silence proper to it.

Only now, a half-century later, has this music been made audible and intelligible: Giacomo Clemente's book, *L'apparato scolastico in Louis Althusser e nella scuola althusseriana*, demonstrates in intricate detail the extent to which both the theory and practice of education, from primary school to the university, were essential to Althusser's theoretical and political development from the early fifties to the period of the 'late Althusser', even when this element of his thought itself proceeded silently and inaudibly. Clemente very carefully reconstructs the often complex and contradictory relations between debates about and within the *apparato scholastico* and Althusser's theories of theory or philosophy. He does so, moreover, with an extraordinary thoroughness, by examin-

---

1 Althusser 1995, p. 175.

ing the published and unpublished texts that Althusser devoted to concrete controversies in the university involving both pedagogy as well as curriculums and situating them in the context of broader discussions carried on by such figures as André Gorz (the unnamed adversary Althusser addresses in 'Student Problems') and Pierre Bourdieu, among others. To his credit, Clemente treats Althusser's work as inseparable from the collective projects in which he was engaged with his current and former students, all of whom had written on educational questions early in their careers, and had agreed to produce together a study of *l'école* shortly after the events of May 68. The participants in this collective project read the work of French educational reformers, from Jules Ferry to Célestin and Elise Freinet, the proposals and critiques that emerged in the aftermath of the Russian Revolution (above all, those of Krupskaya who sought to address the effects of the division between intellectual and manual labour on the concrete forms of proletarian democracy), as well as Freire and various documents from the Chinese Cultural Revolution on the work of transforming the universities. They also engaged with the work of Bourdieu and Passeron (*Les hérités* and *La reproduction*) in ways that stimulated the development of the notion of ideology the Althusserians shared.

Clemente's detailed account of the collective project whose aim was to produce a theory of the *apparato scholastico* as outlined in the ISAs essay and whose members included Balibar, Macherey, Michel Tort, Christian Baudelot, and Roger Establet shows that the very failure of the group to produce the definitive work to which they had already given the title *'L'Ecole'*, itself produced a series of theoretical effects, both immediate and deferred, the power of which we are just beginning to appreciate. Clemente shows the development of Althusser's ideas through an examination of his early interventions aimed at countering concrete proposals for reform by governmental bodies, as well as those made by students, even entering the discussion of the correct demands of the PCF's student organisations, to the collective project that marked a break with Althusser's earlier approach to education and to ideology in general that emerged in the aftermath of 1968. Clemente's study is full of discoveries, a knowledge of which is necessary to any comprehensive understanding of Althusser's work: it is nothing less than a map of a previously little-known part of Althusser's thought, as well as that of his colleagues, especially Balibar and Macherey.

The fact remains, however, that for many readers the idea that education, a field that occupies a very low place in the hierarchy of academic disciplines (one of the forms of its silence), could nevertheless have played an important part in the development of Althusser's philosophical thought, will prove difficult to accept. Did not Rancière assert a version of this thesis in the service of his condemnation of Althusser's 'lesson', writing as if Althusser's entire theory existed to justify the current form of the university with its pantheons of experts, specialists, and geniuses set apart from the masses?[2] Indeed, Clemente's book allows us to appreciate the extent to which Rancière's critique captures something of Althusser's notion of education in the period leading up to the seminar on *Lire le Capital*, including its bearing on the science/ideology opposition and the notion of Theory (with a capital T). But Clemente also shows that this was no more than the beginning of Althusser's sustained reflection on the educational system, a process whose development was neither linear nor continuous. Because Althusser literally lived and worked within what he came to call the *appareil scolaire*, the École Normale Supérieure, his experience of political and social conflicts was often mediated through this institution (as well as that of the PCF with its proletarian base). Administrative measures, both proposed and enacted, affected him and compelled him in some cases to respond to them; moreover, it was through this institution that he felt the effects of class struggle, especially the reforms imposed by the capitalist class to 'streamline' higher education, that is, both to reduce costs and to weaken or eliminate those disciplines whose contribution to the reproduction of capitalism was in doubt. Even more striking was the impact of successive student mobilisations on the direction of his thought, provoking him to contest their demands, even as he was increasingly marked by their struggles.

Althusser published his first significant reflection on education, *L'enseignement de philosophie'*, in the June 1954 issue of *Esprit*. His immediate objective is to protest a proposed reform that would eliminate a philosophy requirement for students in 'the experimental sciences', on the grounds that science professors could best teach the philosophy relevant to their field as part of their courses. While Althusser defends the requirement that all university students take a course entirely devoted to philosophy as part of their general education, he feels compelled to defend philosophy itself against the prevailing antipathy. He notes that following the war, various idealisms emerged within philosophy: Hegel read as tragedian and Husserlian phenomenology and existentialism, with their emphasis on human freedom, and a transhistorical human condition. And while he admits that these philosophies threaten the progress of knowledge with their rejection of 'intellectual rigour and scientific honesty', he holds that it would be a mistake to regard them as heralding the end of philosophy or its dissolution into the field of literature. Not only should we

---

2   Rancière 2012.

not hesitate to defend philosophy, more importantly, we should recognise that *'la philosophie se défend. Il existe aujourd'hui un front de résistance tacite, des marxistes aux rationalistes, aux idéalistes classiques, et jusqu'à certains phénoménologues, qui refusent de voir la philosophie déchoir dans la «littérature», se couper de la science, ou disparaître comme théorie général'.*[3]

Even in this very early text, Althusser insists that philosophy is the site of perpetual conflict, a 'struggle between tendencies', and that its greatest achievements are products of this struggle, the defence of science against the constant innovations of a multitude of adversaries. What many of philosophy's critics regard as the decline of philosophical thought is merely the temporary balance of forces internal to it: *'La lutte de la philosophie contre ses menaces internes est donc inséparable de la lutte des tendances à l'intérieur de la philosophie: elle est inséparable de la lutte pour la rigueur de la réflexion et de la méthode, de la lutte pour le respect et l'intelligence de la réalité positive. Ce n'est pas cette lutte qui condamne la philosphie: elle en fait la grandeur'.*[4]

The crisis of philosophy, for Althusser, is the attempt, in the name of modernisation, to render philosophy superfluous without saying so in the name of professional training. The reformers argue that the knowledge of philosophy necessary to a given discipline, whether mathematics or history, will be taught by a mathematician or historian, who is thereby presumed to be sufficiently familiar with the philosophy of mathematics or the philosophy of history to incorporate it into their courses: *'on tenait, dans les hautes sphères de la rue de Grenelle, la philosophie pour un luxe anachronique, que la France pouvait s'offrir aux temps de sa splendeur, mais qu'elle devait sacrifier aux rigueurs de la nécessité'.*[5]

Le front de resistance tacite, however, must also oppose the tendency to turn the required philosophy course into an exercise in creative writing (that is, fiction or poetry) or in the art of rhetoric. Philosophy's vocation, according to Althusser, is critical reflection on the present and the elaboration of a theory capable of defending the acquisitions of science and of protecting scientific practice from exploitation for non-scientific ends. While Althusser's conception of the struggle between tendencies in philosophy, that is, the opposition of idealism and materialism, is quite crude relative to his later theorisation of philosophical practice (rigorous and systematic thought versus fragments of personal experience taken as universal), even more striking is his defence of

---

3   Althusser 1954, p. 860.
4   Ibid.
5   Althusser 1954, p. 862.

the traditional *enseignement* with its assumptions of expertise combined with the class-bound dilettantism that Bourdieu and Passeron would soon identify and denounce.

Ten years later, and shortly after the conclusion of the Algerian War and the mass radicalisation in opposition to it, Althusser published 'Student Problems', in many ways an updated version of the earlier text. This time, however, the 'liberal conception of the university' had to be defended not from the ministry of education, but from the students themselves. The national student union, the UNEF, once focused primarily on financial support for students, went through a process of radicalisation with the commencement of the Algerian War. The PCF's failure to support independence for Algeria and its rejection of the strategy of *insoumission* (draft refusal) alienated the Communist student group, the UEC, which led to internal divisions and ended its claim to represent the left among students. With the end of the war in 1962, the national student union, the UNEF, once again turned to *syndicalisme*, but of a far more ambitious type than before. From 1962–64, the organisation produced a set of demands as part of a proposal to transform the French university system, the *Manifeste POUR UNE RÉFORME DEMOCRATIQUE DE L'ENSEIGNE-MENT SUPERIEUR*.[6] Althusser's 'Student Problems' is a direct response to this Manifesto, the first version of which had appeared a few months before his intervention, particularly its concrete proposals for the reform of both the content and the form of instruction at the university level.

The Manifesto openly rejected both '*le modèle de l'université libérale, qui se voulait indépendante aussi bien du pouvoir politique que des nécessités économiques*' and '*l'université technocratique*',[7] oriented exclusively to the production of graduates suited to the demands of the market. Its emphasis on the outmoded and irrelevant content of many courses, from the sciences to letters, together with its critique of the discrepancy between what students learned and what they would be expected to know after graduation, however, seemed to Althusser to establish the needs of the economy at any given time as the norm according to which a given course could be judged 'old-fashioned'. Such an orientation was antithetical to the training in reflection and criticism that, from its origins in the medieval cities, the university had provided, according to Althusser. In fact, he defends a rather idealised (and idealist) notion of the university as an *Imperium in Imperio* in Spinoza's sense, as if, against everything

---

6   *Manifeste POUR UNE RÉFORME DEMOCRATIQUE DE L'ENSEIGNEMENT SUPERIEUR* (1964). https://www.institut-tribune-socialiste.fr/wp-content/uploads/1964/11/64-09_manifestensei g.pdf.

7   *Manifeste*, p. 4.

he later argues in the ISAs essay, it is a space of freedom that plays no role in the reproduction of the capitalist order, and that the existing means of the production and transmission of knowledge within it are 'necessary' and unchangeable. He does not effectively respond to the argument in the Manifesto that *'Il va de soi que les «franchises» dont jouit actuellement l'Université, quant à la nomination de professeurs et assistants, à l'utilisation des locaux, etc. et les institutions qui les défendent, assemblées et conseils de faculté, d'université, ne doivent pas être abandonnées aux attaques du pouvoir. Toutefois l'autonomie de l'université, est bien autre chose que ces simples franchises, qui ne sont actuellement que des alibis à une perte réelle de pouvoir de l'université sur son propre domaine et à une diminution de son importance, tant sur le budget de l'Etat que dans la société'.*[8]

Further, the students, influenced by the work of André Gorz (particularly, *Stratégie ouvrière et néocapitalisme*) and the concept of *autogestion*, or self-management, assert that *'A long terme, les étudiants affirment avec force leur volonté de participer à la gestion de leur faculté. Dès à présent, ils protestent contre l'absence de tout droit syndical étudiant et revendiquent la reconnaissance de la section syndicale de faculté'.*[9] In response, Althusser introduces the distinction, central to his essay, between the technical and the social division of labour: the first is necessary in an objective sense, necessary to the existing technologies, the existing instruments and means of production; the second is necessary only to class domination and the extraction of surplus-value. This distinction allows him to reject the students' demands:

> Through the knowledge taught at university passes *the permanent dividing line between technical and social divisions of labour, the most constant and profound of class divisions* ... Now, what is remarkable is that in the case of the university the *social division of labour*, and therefore *class domination*, comes *massively* into play, but not only – or even mainly – where student and non-student theorists look for it. It comes *massively* into play, and in a 'blinding' way (which doubtless is why one does not always 'see' it), in the very *object* of intellectual work; *in the knowledge* the university is commissioned to distribute to the students.[10]

The *Manifeste* further questioned the function of the student-professor relationship, both its inequality and the ways that this relationship rested on a

---

8   *Manifeste*, p. 14.
9   *Manifeste*.
10   Althusser 2011, p. 13.

set of individualising rituals and practices. The examinations and the different modes of performance expected of the individual student were organised in a series of competitions that not only made every student the adversary of every other, but produced inequalities that further undermined any form of cooperation. The instructor/professor was set apart from the students so as to judge the degree to which they have acceded to the norm or deviated from it in a hierarchically divided space in which the right to speak or to remain silent is unequally distributed. Moreover, faculty, too, were expected to compete against each other in their scholarly work: they learned very quickly that achievement without recognition was as detrimental to professional advancement as recognition without achievement. The mutual individualisation of student and teacher through various relays and mechanisms would be described by Foucault a decade later, in *Surveiller et Punir*. In fact, Althusser himself both before and after 'Student Problems' was engaged in the production of a concept of '*le sujet d'imputation*' that would become the interpellated subject by 1969–70, as if Althusser's ability to integrate the students' critique was deferred to the time when the student-worker revolt provided an irrefutable demonstration of its truth.[11] In 'Student Problems', however, Althusser reduces these complexities to a simple confrontation with a subject who possesses knowledge and a subject who lacks it: 'The pedagogic function has as its object the transmission of a determinate knowledge to subjects who do not possess it. Therefore, the pedagogic situation is based on the absolute condition of an inequality between a knowledge and a lack of knowledge'. It is worth mentioning that Althusser's practice in no way corresponded to his theory: none of his contemporaries could be said to depend so completely on collective theoretical labour, on thinking with others. Althusser became Althusser only when he and a group of students formed a 'community of thought', as Macherey called it, that in a way resembled the transmission of knowledge from teacher to student. We might even suggest that when it came to reading Marx's *Capital*, he had adopted the students' view that '*il ne peut être question de séparer ce que l'on enseigne de la façon dont on l'enseigne. L'UNEF se refuse à considérer les méthodes de travail comme de simples techniques plaquées sur un contenu*'.[12]

Clemente shows in great detail the ways in which the student radicalisation entered the lecture hall, calling into question not only Althusser's notion of pedagogy but ultimately some of the 'axioms', as one student called them, of his theoretical positions. 'Student Problems' was not only a critique of the

---

11   Althusser 1996.
12   *Manifeste*, p. 16.

UNEF's demands as laid out in the *Manifeste*; it was also a direct outgrowth of Althusser's decision to invite Bourdieu and Passeron to hold a seminar at the ENS on the topic of '*théorie et méthode en sciences humaine*'. Althusser's introductory lecture, together with the initial presentations by Bourdieu and Passeron, appeared to some of the students present to ignore the emerging critique of the student-professor relation and the traditional roles and rituals that characterised French academic life. Bruno Queysanne, a member of the UEC (the PCF's student group) and later a specialist in the theory and history of architecture, wrote to Althusser after the event to express his shock and anger at the uncritical restaging of what he argued was not simply a mode of communicating knowledge but an organisation of space and a disposition of bodies, the site of ritualised movements and a liturgy of speech acts. In other words, the struggle in which he and others had participated (a strike at the Sorbonne, at which he was a student, a few months earlier) had revealed, but in a way not entirely intelligible to him or to Althusser, that domination was exercised not simply through the content of what was taught or in the style of the communication, but in the ritualisation of movements and voices whose uniformity and regularity are lived as natural and necessary. For Queysanne, '*la disposition de la salle, le nombre de participants, la maniere légère avec laquelle tu traitais des principes*' sufficed to signify the failure to grasp '*l'autoritarisme Classique*' that was irreducible either to the knowledge transmitted or to the allusions and turns of phrase that perpetuate class differences within the otherwise free space of the liberal university. Finally, only what Althusser would later call the mass ideological revolt of the students, a revolt whose intelligence he resisted until May 68, could lead him to the discovery of the concept of the Ideological State Apparatus as the condition of intelligibility of the institution of the university. This concept existed in the practical state in the very actions by students that Althusser initially regarded as threatening the production of knowledge. In an unsigned text published in *Cahiers marxistes-leninistes*, Balibar notes that the argument of Bourdieu and Passeron casts doubt on any notion of students as the proletariat of the academic realm, a notion '*qui faisait des étudiants dans leur ensemble des prolétaires esclaves de ces maîtres capitalistes que seraient leurs professeurs. Les vraies scissions passent au sein du «milieu étudiant» lui-même et on n'y retrouve pas par hasard, avec une faible marge d'approxima-tion, les scissions des classes de notre société*'.[13] While proposals for educational reform had long cited the effects of class differences among students, Bourdieu

---

13   Anonymous [Etienne Balibar], *Les Héritiers*, par P. Bourdieu et JC Passeron, notes de lec-ture, *Cahiers marxistes-leninistes* 3, 28–48.

and Passeron furnished 'non la simple constatation d'une inégalité et de sa correspondance générale avec une inégalité scolaire (économiquement fondée), mais
la description du mécanisme de l'inégalité'.[14] Balibar neither questions their use
of quantitative methods, nor does he dispute the results these methods have
returned. Instead, he examines 'leur propos et la pertinence des questions qu'ils
posent'.[15]

Balibar defends the positions Althusser articulates in 'Student Problems', but
reformulates the terms of the argument. The 'freedom' of the liberal university
that allows it to function as an *Imperium in Imperio* where critical thought
is by definition always possible, is replaced by the far more limited and conditional notion of the relative autonomy of the university. For Balibar, as for
Althusser, this complicates any attempt to establish by analogy a causal connection between the worker-capitalist relation and that of student-professor.
It discourages the search for resemblances or homologies and compels us to
take the 'reality' of the university as irreducible and determinate. Balibar then
returns to the distinction between the technical division of labour, whose
necessity derives from the acquisitions and contemporary activity of science
(or the sciences), and a social division of labour that represents a continuation
of extra-academic class divisions within academia. Because the necessity of the
technical derives from the objectivity of a science, it is not susceptible to reform
based on moral norms, but changes only in response to the imperatives pre-
scribed by the science in question. The adequate study of a science can only
take place according to the forms of the technical division of labour proper to
it, which in turn, exists only in the university: 'il s'agit de se les approprier pour
pouvoir éventuellement transformer le contenu (idéologique). L'autodidactisme
est le plus grand ennemi de l'organisation politique léniniste'.[16]

But neither Balibar nor Althusser appears to acknowledge the aporia that
this position produces: how does one demarcate the technical division of
labour at a given moment from a purely social division of labour in their constantly changing practical and institutional existence? Both seem to suggest
that the actual state of instruction pertaining to a given science is necessarily
determined by the rational activity of the science itself and that this instruction
will change only when and if the science itself undergoes change. This position
deprives instruction of any autonomy in relation to the science, while granting
it complete autonomy in relation to the reality of the social and political world.
And while Althusser counters student demands for a more collective approach

---

14   Ibid.
15   Ibid.
16   Ibid.

to education with the argument that it is the content of what is taught, not the form in which this content is conveyed that matters, he nevertheless insists that the pedagogical forms through which the knowledge of biology is transmitted are determined by the science itself and cannot be changed. Neither Althusser's position nor its reversal by Rancière ten years later allows us to grasp the problem posed, but overlooked, by Balibar of the reality specific to the university and of the reality or materiality of ideology itself in all its forms.

It is not easy to explain the chasm that lies between the Althusser who could defend the 'liberal conception of the university' and its 'technically necessary' hierarchies in the 1964 essay, 'Student Problems', and the Althusser who, by 1970, regarded the school as a factory that produced ideology, as other factories produce cars or machine parts. Clemente's work not only makes visible and intelligible the caesura that separates two distinct ways of thinking about education in Althusser's work, a caesura determined by the events with which it was roughly contemporaneous: the great struggles opened by May 1968, and before that, in 1966, the Chinese Cultural Revolution (with its critique of the Chinese university and the rejection of the subordinate place of students within it) and the sudden emergence of Maoism in France (in which a number of Althusser's students played a significant role). To use Althusser's own terminology, not only did practice precede theory and critique take flight only after insurgency, but the mass ideological revolts of the Chinese Cultural Revolution and May 68 represented the new theory in the practical state. We should note that Althusser wrote his brief and unsigned text on the Chinese Cultural Revolution within weeks of the Declaration of Central Committee of the Chinese Communist Party on August 8th 1966 in which the famous 16 points of the Cultural Revolution were laid out. Despite the fact that one of the points involved the need 'to transform the old educational system and the old principles and methods of teaching' and with a thoroughness that made the demands of French student movement seem very modest, Althusser accorded the Chinese Cultural Revolution a historical significance that compelled him to rethink the concept of ideology, and with it, the very notion of the school.

> Le P.C.C. déclare que ce sont les organisations de masse de la jeunesse, principalement de la jeunesse urbaine, donc avant tout des lycéens et étudiants, qui sont actuellement à l'avant-garde du mouvement. C'est une situation de fait, mais dont l'importance politique est évidente. D'une part, en effet, le système d'enseignement en place, ou la jeunesse est formée (il ne faut pas oublier que l'Ecole marque toujours profondément les hommes, même pendant les périodes de mutations historiques) était en Chine le bastion de l'idéologie bourgeoise et petite-bourgeoise. D'autre part, la jeunesse, qui n'a

pas fait l'expérience des luttes et guerres révolutionnaires, constitue, dans un pays socialiste, un point très sensible, où se joue une partie d'avenir capitale. La jeunesse n'est pas révolutionnaire du seul fait de naître dans un pays socialiste, ni de grandir dans les récits des exploits de ses ainés. Si malgré toutes les énergies de son âge, elle se trouve, du fait d'une carence politique, abandonnée dans un désarroi ou un «vide» idéologiques, elle est alors livrée en fait aux formes idéologiques «spontanées» qui ne cessent de peupler ce «vide»: idéologies petites-bourgeoises et bourgeoises, soit héritées du passé national, soit importées de l'étranger. Ces formes trouvent leurs points d'appuis naturels dans le positivisme, l'empirisme et le technicisme «apolitique» des savants et autres spécialistes.[17]

It is surprising indeed to read Althusser's list of the '*idéologies petites-bourgeoises et bourgeoises, soit héritées du passé national, soit importées de l'étranger*' that have emerged or re-emerged in post-revolutionary Chinese academia: '"apolitical" positivism, empiricism and technicism of scientists and other specialists'.[18] In a single phrase whose significance for the development of Althusser's thought concerning education and the notion of ideology in general is easily overlooked, he has rejected the arguments advanced in 'Student Problems'. The distinction between the technical and social division of labour which, Althusser had argued, established the teacher-student relation and the individual nature of research as objectively necessary and inalterable, now, according to his own analysis, was among the bourgeois ideologies that promoted a restoration of capitalism. The Chinese Communist Party's denunciation of 'scholar-tyrants' who under the cover of 'purely academic discussion' claimed that truth and reason are above political conflict in order to create the ideological grounds on which to argue in favour of a gradual return to capitalism, would soon enough be applied to Althusser himself. Rancière, the most effective of Althusser's critics, used Althusser's own reading of the Cultural Revolution to portray him as a scholar-tyrant who appealed to science in order to impose a philosophy of anti-revolt on his students.

The Cultural Revolution allowed Althusser to see not only what was invisible to him when he wrote 'Student Problems' in early 1964, namely the objectively materialist character of the objectives of the student movement, but also the extent to which his own intervention had failed, nullified both by the force

---

17   Anonymous [Louis Althusser], 'Sur la révolution culturelle', *Cahiers marxistes-leninistes*, 5–16, https://adlc.hypotheses.org/archives-du-seminaire-marx/cahiers-marxistes-leninis tes/cml14-sur-la-revolution-culturelle.

18   Ibid.

of its own contradictions; this self-nullification, in turn, produced a theoretical void quickly filled with the apologetic ideologies that Althusser otherwise opposed. Without the public acknowledgement of his own errors that would later become a trademark of Althusser, the specific combination of the French student struggles and the Cultural Revolution allowed him to think critically about the material existence of the university, rather than defend its current forms as necessary, a gesture designed to exclude any inquiry into their political function. Althusser now faced the reality to which he had often alluded, but never truly examined: that unlike Spinoza or Marx, he wrote and spoke from within a particular apparatus with the rituals and liturgies that determined what must be said, what could not be said, and, perhaps most importantly, what was sayable, but only at a greater or lesser cost to the speaker. The imprecision of concepts such as 'the educational system' or 'academia' would soon be replaced by 'the educational apparatus', a rudimentary notion to be sure, but one whose very rudimentary character made it capable of preventing both theoretical regression to the earlier conceptions and a theoretical voluntarism for which it would figure as the foundation.

May 68 solidified Althusser's turn in relation to student struggles. In a letter to Maria Antonietta Macciocchi, written in March 1969, he develops a lengthy critique of the role of students in the May events, above all, their relations to the workers' struggles, going so far as to deny the existence of a student movement in any true sense of the term and asking why instead of going to the factories to support the workers, students did not ask them to come to the occupied universities to 'teach them' how to organise a successful occupation. Although he hardly mentions the role of the PCF and its affiliates, much of what he writes concerning the concrete struggles is a defence of its line composed in the workerist idiom of *L'Humanité*. At a certain point, however, he ceases to reduce the student movement to petit-bourgeois pseudo-Marxism and discovers other causes than class position:

> It is not terribly difficult to find evidence for the impact of the international anti-imperialist class struggles on the birth and development of this Movement. To name only the most significant, let us remember the effect on young students and intellectuals of the war in Algeria, the Cuban Revolution, guerrilla war in Latin America – where 'Che' met a heroic but politically costly death – the prodigious and victorious struggle of the Vietnamese people against the aggression of the world's greatest military power, the Chinese Cultural Revolution, the violent revolt of black Afro-Americans in the large cities of the US and the Palestinian resistance. These anti-imperialist struggles have met with an extraordinary

receptivity among the contemporary youth of our countries, including young workers (let us not forget that in France it was the proletarian and peasant youth who were mobilised for the Algerian war, that it was they who paralysed Salan's 'putsch' and made his officers hesitate and that they have not forgotten this lesson).[19]

The 'combined effect' of the great anti-imperialist and anti-racist struggles internationally and a massive rejection of bourgeois ideology, Althusser argues, has led to a mass ideological revolt fought on a new terrain of struggle: the educational system. On the basis of these observations, Althusser advances the following hypothesis:

> that the Movement of the young students and intellectuals, on both a national and international level, must be considered as an *ideological revolt* (N.B.: an ideological revolt is not, in and of itself, as the students too readily believe, a political revolution) *which first attacks the apparatus of the educational systems of the capitalist countries*.[20]

The key word here, the single word that signals a kind of 'rupture' with all Althusser's previous thinking about the 'educational system' is of course 'apparatus'. It is with this term that Althusser brings all the lofty ideas and ideals concerning education down to earth, that is, confers upon them the materiality that alone allows them to operate and to produce effects. The concept of apparatus allows us to identify the features of the 'vast battlefield' on which the mass ideological revolt takes place, the uneven distribution of positions within it, and the advantages and disadvantages proper to each of them. And just as in the Church, which Althusser will soon announce has been replaced by *L'école* as the dominant ISA, the effects of subjection are obtained not by means of ideas, but by ideas existing in the actions and disposition of bodies: 'kneel down, move your lips in prayer and you will believe'.

The result of the theoretical discovery made possible by the May revolt, and the student struggles that preceded it, was the project Clemente describes in detail, and with unfailing precision, on the basis of a wealth of material in *l'archive Althusser*: the attempt by Althusser and a particularly distinguished group of former students (Balibar, Macherey, Establet, Baudelot and Michel Tort), to produce a theory of what they called *l'apparato scolastico*,

---

19   Althusser 2018.
20   Ibid.

a fundamentally different object than 'education', that opened both a new field for research according to which the terrain of struggle could be understood as something more than a battle of ideas. The spatial arrangements, separating or compacting, excluding or confining individuals, assigning places according to hierarchies of authority, organising greater or lesser visibility and audibility, the modes of surveillance and discipline, all could now be examined, not as natural, inescapable forms of any conceivable educational system, and thus politically neutral, but as means of a simultaneous subjection and subjectivation of individuals. The emergence of these practices as objects of study did not replace or distract from the imperative to understand how the educational apparatus reproduced class inequalities; on the contrary, they were shown to be means (among others) by which they were reproduced.

Balibar has provided an account of the circumstances that led Althusser in 1969 to write the manuscript he initially intitled 'De la superstructure', published posthumously as *Sur la reproduction*, that confirms that by this time, he saw the school and education as forming the central mechanism in the reproduction of the division between intellectual and manual labour (drawing in part from Durkheim) and thus of class relations. The group of former students described above were already engaged in a collective project on the French educational system, both examining empirical data and rereading such figures as Durkheim and Bourdieu, as well as the more practically oriented works of Célestin Freinet and Krupskaya (both of whom addressed the problem of the overcoming of the division of intellectual and manual labour in relation to the Russian Revolution of 1917). Althusser proposed a contribution to this project that, whatever his initial intentions, attempted to provide its theoretical foundation. While the collective project ultimately foundered, Clemente shows that the work that preceded and followed it around the question of education and its apparatus, and that has been strangely neglected or dismissed even by scholars of Althusser, represents, despite, or because of, its ultimate failure to cohere into a unified school of thought, an essential moment in 'Althusserian' thought that has something to contribute to theory today.

Near the beginning of *Sur la reproduction* Althusser affirms his break with the positions expressed in 'Student Problems', asserting that 'the purely "technical" division of labour is just a facade for a very different kind of division, the social division of labour, which is an effect of the division between classes'.[21] Now, Althusser understands the idea of a necessary technical division of labour,

---

21   Althusser 1995, p. 65.

one of the justifications of the existing arrangement in schools, as an extension of the division between 'manual labour and intellectual labour', to which
Marx refers from *The German Ideology* on.[22] While Althusser describes Marx's
formulation as 'crude', he insists that it refers to what is 'produced by all class
societies'. It is still produced, and increasingly produced, by modern capitalist class society, despite the 'spectacular progress of science and technology'
and the growing numbers of 'intellectual workers' in new categories, such as
'researchers', whom we shall discuss when the time comes. That is why Marx
was on the mark when he said that socialism should 'abolish the distinction
between manual and intellectual labour'.[23]

This process of separating and dividing students is not an expression or
representation of the prevailing division of labour into manual and intellectual, workers whose tool is the body and those who work with their intellect,
but is part of this division; such a process cannot be understood as operating
through ideas or the propagation of the pseudo-knowledge that exists to justify
it. Instead, the means of separation and division proper to the *appareil scolaire*
are material in every sense of the term, involving techniques of individualisation, as well as enclosure, and the disposition of bodies in both space and time,
precisely the phenomena described a few years later by Foucault in *Discipline
and Punish*. In fact, Althusser, in *Sur la reproduction* articulated a concept that
was central to the published extract and that in fact illuminates the ideological work of the *appareil scolaire*, although Althusser nowhere acknowledges
this: the concept of the interpellation of the individual as subject. School is
the place where individuals are subjected through practices of coercion often
subtle, but sometimes actively violent, that is, they must be rendered docile
(meaning 'teachable', derived from the Latin verb *docere* – to teach), in order to
made into a subject, a being responsible both causally and legally for his or her
actions. The double process of subjection and subjectivation, however, to take
his analysis further than he does, does not produce a universal subject but a universal hierarchy of subjects produced by the division of labour, itself always the
site of class struggle. This latter point is key: the very fact that the educational
system, despite Althusser's lapses into functional explanation, is understood as
an apparatus rather than as the institution of the transmission of knowledge
whose material existence is no more than a setting or backdrop, represents the
break (*coupure* or *rupture*) that makes possible both a knowledge of the role of
the school in the reproduction of capitalist social relations and a knowledge of
the mechanisms (the practices and rituals) by which it operates.

---

22   Althusser 1995, p. 64.
23   Althusser 1995, p. 63.

The body of the student is as a much a target as the mind; not simply ensuring sufficient exercise to reinvigorate the mind, but the daily, hourly, surveillance of the body: the extent and frequency of its movements, a division of such movements into the productive and unproductive, the ration of mobility to immobility, in short, a surveillance that induces self-surveillance and a discipline that is finally realised in self-discipline. The fact that it has proven very difficult to challenge the organisation of time in education, to reduce the periods of relative immobility imposed on the child, the reason 6–8 hours somehow appears normal and natural, and any effort to reduce this time seems an encouraging of idleness, derives from the usually unstated assumption that such disciplining of the body prepares most students for the drudgery that awaits them. For the majority of children, such discipline, in addition to the acquisition of basic skills in math and reading, together with an idealised narrative of their nation's history, constitutes their education. Others, a few, continue on, destined for intellectual labour, not only better trained in the use of language, but to varying degrees, equipped with a knowledge of basic logic and rhetoric, as well as history, political science, etc. Fewer still will become specialists: scientists, social scientists, scholars of philosophy, art, literature, etc.

Althusser alludes to this reality, not simply to demonstrate the function of the *appareil scolaire*, or to stress the inequality that it necessarily produces, but even more to evoke the urgency of transforming education in the course of the cultural revolutions that followed both the Russian Revolution of 1917 and the Chinese Revolution of 1949:

> That is why Lenin's desperate insistence on the need to establish a new, polytechnic school education (it unfortunately had small success), which would, moreover, combine manual labour in real production with intellectual labour, was – and is – so important. That is why it seems to us that the news reaching us through what we can gather about certain experiments of the Cultural Revolution (mandatory training periods in basic production units for 'intellectuals' of all orders, 'controlled' shakeups in the distribution of different manual and intellectual jobs among the producers, a real upgrading of jobs involving only implementation to posts of great authority and responsibility) has something to do with the class struggle against the radical determination, in our country, of the 'technical division of labour' by the 'social division of labour'.[24]

24   Althusser 1995, p. 65.

Overcoming the division of labour, or at least reducing it to the greatest extent possible, was, for Lenin, the unavoidable condition of any genuine proletarian democracy. Workers had to have as much time as possible away from work to continue their education and participate in the management of the Soviet republic, even as an increase in production was a pressing necessity. The obvious answer was the polytechnic: a merging of production and education by increasing labour force participation, so that all would work part-time in order for everyone to have time for 'education', now understood as a lifelong endeavour. In accordance with the notion of proletarian democracy, the emphasis was placed on the self-education of groups and individuals, rather than on instruction by experts. Everyone would be teacher and student simultaneously. Krupskaya argued that mathematics and the physical sciences could be learned best in the context of workplace in which the theoretical and practical were united. As Althusser noted, however, the difficulties faced by the early Soviet republic prevented the realisation of these projects. The failure to overcome the division of labour weighed heavily on the development of the USSR. The question of the school also emerged as the central unresolved problem of the 1949 Chinese revolution, a source of inequality and thus dissatisfaction that increasingly threatened the gains of the revolution. Together, these developments, together with the struggles in the French university that culminated in May 1968, seemed to Althusser to establish the centrality of the *appareil scolaire* as the means of production of the division of intellectual and manual labour.

Baudelot and Establet's *L'école capitaliste en France* (1971) was the only publication to issue directly from the *L'école* project or, more precisely, from the failure of the participants to agree on the conclusions to be drawn from their research. It was here that the rudiments of the notion of *appareil scolaire* advanced by Althusser were finally sketched out. Moreover, Baudelot and Establet attempted to justify his argument that this ISA was dominant in relation to the others, and not just because it was the apparatus through which the mass of the population passed, and where they were inoculated against anti-capitalist (socialist or communist) ideas. They were among the very few in the years following the publication of '*Idéologie et les appareils idéologiques d'état*' to articulate the degree to which the conception of ideology that emerged from this essay differed from what had been understood by the term previously. Althusser, they argued, had shown that ideology, if the term is to be useful, cannot be understood as ideas: ideology '*n'existe pas en dehors des pratiques dans lesquelles elle se realise*'.[25] Accordingly, the notion of submission to bour-

---

25   Baudelot and Establet 1971, p. 273.

geois ideology can no longer be understood as something like acceptance of the ruling ideas; instead, this submission 's'effectur par la soumission de chaque instant à un ensemble de pratiques qui constituent le 'ritual matériel' de l'idéologie bourgeoise'.[26] In the case of the *appareil scolaire*, ritual extends beyond the classroom, where it takes the forms of the division of roles between student and teacher, examinations and writing exercises, but also exists in the material links between school and family (another ISA, according to Althusser), such as the report card (*carnet de notes*) in which grades (*notes*), as Baudelot and Establet argue, presented to the parents, serve as a form of compensation or reward for a student's labour. Competition for grades mimics the operation of the market: the achievements of a student, like those of a worker, are attributable solely to the effort and ambition of each individual. Success or failure are the outcome of free and fair competition, the results of which are attributable only to the individual student.

Baudelot and Establet further underscore the coercive function of the rituals proper to the *appareil scolaire*, from homework to the forms of discipline applied to recalcitrant students and the incentives offered to those who obey. These measures constitute the form in which bourgeois ideology is communicated, but they cannot be separated from its content, that is, its ideas, theories and themes. In *L'ecole capitaliste*, it is noteworthy that the preferred term for the process of the transmission/imposition of the dominant ideology is one Althusser tended to avoid: inculcation. In French as in English the term suggests what is popularly known as 'brainwashing', that is, the process through which an individual is compelled through coercive and manipulative means to adopt beliefs opposed to those he or she held previously. Baudelot and Establet, however, add something to the meaning typically assigned to the term, by recalling its literal meaning in Latin, that of 'treading down' or 'treading in', as in a foot pressing something into, or imprinting itself on, the ground through the direct application of force. In this way, they not only capture the materiality of the pedagogical means of instruction, the force that must accompany the act of teaching, given the resistance that instruction always encounters. The fact of resistance in turn signals that the *appareil scolaire* is the site of struggle (the ideological class struggle) in which practices of resistance and refusal counter the disciplinary strategies on which the supremacy of bourgeois ideology rests. The struggle against bourgeois ideology is not simply reactive, as if it were still captive of that ideology by remaining its mere negation. Again in contrast to Althusser, Baudelot and Establet speak of a separate and distinct

---

26   Ibid.

proletarian ideology immanent in the acts of resistance carried out by students (and occasionally teachers), whose dispersed and divergent manifestations are the effects of a strategy rooted in the collective memory of the working class.

The *appareil scolaire* does not produce class inequality as a result, the outcome of a long series of tests and trials whose conclusion is with few exceptions decided in advance. If this were the case, the authors argue, a comprehensive reform of the educational system could be changed to produce a different result. The division into the two networks or tracks occurs within the *appareil scolaire* and operates from 'the first day of their schooling'.[27] This division is 'the means and principle of its functioning', a fact that for Baudelot and Establet has a fundamental political significance.[28] The demand for *'l'allongement de la scolarité obligatoire'* which they recognise will at least postpone for a time the ordeal of 'direct exploitation in its most savage forms' will not two distinct networks (*reseaux*) corresponding to the division of manual and intellectual labour (and thus to the two primary antagonistic classes in society).[29] Students are separated by means of evaluations (both academic and psychological), examinations, and grades, as well the individual records of behaviour and disciplinary actions, that is, through material practices that produce material results. Certainly, the themes characteristic of bourgeois ideology and its tendency to adopt the guise of 'truth', 'knowledge', 'culture', and 'good taste', are what are most immediately visible and, as such, the most common objects of critique.[30] It is, however, the ideology silently practiced in the *appareil scolaire*, incarnate in its rituals and liturgies, that concerns Baudelot and Establet. We find it in the various forms of individualisation that define the *appareil scolaire* that together mask the collective, class, effects of their practices and allow the claim that treating every student as an autonomous, free and equal, individual is the realisation of the ideals of French republicanism. They cite the example of the imposition of the 'rigid norms' of the French language through 'coercive practices:' students are assessed and judged (and therefore individualised) according to the degree to which they deviate from its stylistic norms.

But the very functioning of the *appareil scolaire* also produces friction, that is, resistance, above all, when the attempt to inculcate bourgeois ideology collides the material forms of proletarian ideology. The children of workers diverted to the *Collèges d'enseignement technique* have devised means of subversion in many ways analogous to the forms of resistance typical of industrial workers.

---

27   Baudelot and Establet 1971, p. 270.
28   Ibid.
29   Baudelot and Establet 1971, p. 273.
30   Baudelot and Establet 1971, p. 272.

Baudelot and Establet cite a well-known study by the US sociologist, Donald Roy, on the practice of 'goldbricking' (*freinage ou coulage*) on the shop floor, whereby workers give the appearance of working diligently, while in fact conserving their energy for pursuits outside of work.[31] Students, they argue, use similar tactics to avoid concerning themselves with subjects they regard as meaningless (because these subjects are explicitly committed to the inculcation of bourgeois ideology) but which they are obliged to study. Does this mean that everything that is taught at school is 'ideological', even mathematics, physics, biology, etc.? The authors reject as 'metaphysical' the idea that what is taught must be either simply bourgeois ideology or genuine knowledge. The first is absurd: the reproduction of capitalism depends on genuine knowledge, above all, in the sciences. The second, however, is equally untenable: the primary function of school is the separation and classification of individuals in accordance with the prevailing division of labour. Pedagogical methods, whatever their differences, are designed to achieve this end, with the result that the transmission of knowledge is always subordinated to the process by which what Althusser called the interpellation of individuals takes place.

While the analysis outlined in *L'école capitaliste* clearly represents an attempt to develop the basic notions Althusser proposes in the ISAs essay, there are certain points of disagreement or perhaps rectification. The idea of proletarian ideology is one of these. While Althusser never uses the phrase, which in certain ways leads the concept of ideology in a new direction, his assertion that ideology has a material existence opens the possibility of speaking of a proletarian ideology that exists in the acts, practices and even rituals or counter-rituals of the proletariat. Understanding the educational system as an apparatus which in turn is less a mechanism than a condensation of unceasing class war, leads Baudelot and Establet to explain the tactics and strategies at work. Because bourgeois ideology is always only dominant and cannot entirely exclude proletarian ideology, it is compelled to engage in repression, subjection and deformation (*refoulement, asservissement, et travestissement*), for example, speaking of manual labour in archaic and idealised forms: the worker as solitary craftsman, as much artist as artisan.[32] According to such a representation, the worker is dedicated to his craft, with neither the time nor the inclination to engage in politics which, in turn, never intrudes into his workshop. Working-class youth, confronted with such myths and perfectly aware of the discrepancy between them and the reality of capitalist production, rebel either by disrup-

---

31   Baudelot and Establet 1971, p. 175.
32   Baudelot and Establet 1971, pp. 274–6.

tion of the everyday order or by simply quitting school: it is not theirs and no reform can change its fundamental character.

Baudelot and Establet conclude with the example of the Chinese Cultural Revolution and the campaign to create a genuinely new university or perhaps a model of education not that will no longer serve as a refuge for bourgeois ideology, above all, its insistence on the separation between manual and intellectual labour that preserves privileges and allows the rejection and disparagement of ideas that arise from the proletariat on the grounds that 'truth is above politics'. Because the direction of the Cultural Revolution is determined by the initiative of the masses themselves 'who have been invited to undertake the work of criticising, discussing and remaking the educational system',[33] the Chinese are in the process of discerning 'the first organic forms that will put an end (after a very long process) to the division between manual and intellectual labour, that is, to the material and ideological basis of the existence of classes'.[34] They will do this by implementing the notion of the 'polytechnic' as it was originally understood: the unification of the process of production and the process of learning. The fact that the conditions for its realisation did not exist in either the Soviet Republic or the People's Republic of China should not prevent us from continuing to reflect on the problems that led to its formulation.

The process that led Althusser from his initial considerations on the educational system to the concept of the *appareil scolaire* was anything but continuous; on the contrary, it was marked by the interruptions and reversals that are the surest signs of the power of his thought, the power both to affect and to be affected. Althusser's thought was profoundly affected by the struggles around him, including those waged by students, that made the reality of what could only be understood as an Ideological State Apparatus visible and available for knowledge. Giacomo Clemente not only demonstrates the importance of education in the development of his theory but explores the complex network of discussions and debates within which Althusserianism took shape. His book is a model for all those who seek to grasp the singular force of Althusser's theses, known and as yet unknown, that continue to surprise us with their capacity to illuminate realities once covered in darkness.

Warren Montag

---

33   Baudelot and Establet 1971, p. 318.
34   Baudelot and Establet 1971, p. 319.

Acknowledgments

The present study is the outcome of research that I carried out at the *Institut Mémoires de l'édition contemporaine* (IMEC) in Normandy. I take this opportunity to thank the Institute, and in particular the Director General, Mme Nathalie Léger, as well as the library staff for being so kindly available to me, in particular the Director of the collections, Mme Sandrine Samson.

I would like to thank the translator of the book, Fabio Gironi, as well as Dave Mesing for his work in the revision of the text.

In the text, I will quote my own translation of the unpublished archival documents that I have consulted, as well as my own translation of all the texts published in French that have not yet been translated in English; finally, Althusser's works that are available in English will be quoted from the published translations.

Introduction

The sixth issue of the journal *Esprit*, published in June 1954 with the special title of 'Réforme de l'enseignement', includes a short article: 'L'enseignement de la philosophie'. The author was a thirty-six-year-old *agrégé de philosophie*, Louis Althusser.[1]

More a political than theoretical intervention, the article begins with a simple empirical premise: 'today the teaching of philosophy is a problem'.[2] In the first instance, therefore, the aim of the article is to bring some clarity: that is, to disabuse those who are engaged in the educational process (and, in particular, philosophical education), as well as everyone else (since that problem is now 'in front of the general public'), of the mistaken hypotheses that hinder a correct theoretical grasp of the 'problem'.

The first hypothesis to be discarded is that the teaching of philosophy is in a state of crisis because philosophy itself is in a state of crisis. Althusser explicitly claims that *'the crisis of the teaching of philosophy is not, today, the effect of a crisis of philosophy'*. It is undeniable that immediately after World War II, the development of certain currents of thought (or ways of thinking) had the effect of undermining 'the internal balance of the philosophical universe'. These new ideas, as an expression of their own time ('it is no coincidence that these spiritual revolutions coincided with the tragedy of the pre-war period, and of the war itself'),[3] immediately revealed both a regeneration (of that philosophical universe) and *therefore* a deterioration (of the elements that previously defined it). According to Althusser, this is precisely what happened in France. Husserlian phenomenology and existentialism, on the one hand, and Marxist philosophy on the other, *executed* (in the sense of a death sentence) this transition: they have caused the 'end of the extraordinary prestige of the philosophy of Léon Brunschvicg and [the] decline of the influence of Alain and of Bergson'.[4] But this act of disruption did not simply banish traditional residents of that space. Indeed, the new currents that appeared on the philosophical scene engendered a conflict, since it is in the nature of idealism in general (of which phenomenology is a dominant component) to occasion a struggle: either because of a certain 'simplicity' or 'vulgarity' of those self-referential exercises

---

1 Althusser 1954.
2 Althusser 1954, p. 858. On the general question of the teaching of philosophy, see Illiterati 2007.
3 Althusser 1954, p. 859.
4 Althusser 1954, p. 858.

called phenomenological descriptions; or due to existentialism's break with 'the great classical rationalist tradition' (due to its emergence out of a phenomenological matrix); or again because of those pragmatist-positivist tendencies that turn philosophy into a mere a technical exercise, expunging every 'theoretical virtue' – so that *this time* idealism is a 'danger' for philosophy.[5] Thus, Marxists and rationalists, 'classical idealists', and even 'certain phenomenologists' form – within this renewed 'philosophical universe' constituted by the whole of its (executive and therefore conflictual) elements – 'a resistance front'.

Whether the aim is to exile the traditional figures who occupied the philosophical scene (as in the case of Brunschvicg, etc.) or to try to do so along with those who had previously sanctioned such an exile (as it was for the exponents of the phenomenological currents, banished by Marxists etc.), the fact remains that *philosophy defends itself*. This is a crucial point. Seen from another angle – that of the continuous and *essential* reconfigurations of the philosophical field – Althusser's argument exposes what has just been mentioned regarding the horizontality of all its articulations that, occasionally through conflict, represent the constitutive factor of philosophy: a field that can never be constituted once and for all. In short, Althusser suggests that if the contemporary crisis of philosophical teaching is not the effect of a crisis of philosophy itself, it is because *philosophy lives in a perpetual state of crisis*: its components, being real forces, *are by definition critical*, if we use the term 'critical/criticism' to suggest both a rejection of theoretically unacceptable philosophical beliefs (which are therefore exiled) and the critical conditions of a patient who is about to die (and who therefore can be exiled) or who, although seemingly healthy, is nonetheless doomed because different historical conditions will eventually engender the germination of new philosophical nomenclatures (a way of saying that philosophy is, in a sense, always contemporary). Althusser is clear about this: 'if philosophy is "a child of its time"', it follows that 'new philosophies and new concepts' should always arise in new historical conjunctures, and it was precisely the contradiction between 'real problems' and the old philosophical scene that caused 'the end' of Brunschvicg's 'philosophical kingdom'.[6] In brief: the philosophical universe is, by definition, in a state of (perpetual) upheaval, and if contemporary philosophy, after the exile of the old guard, finds itself in a state of crisis because of the struggle between Marxist materialists and phenomenological idealists,

---

5   Althusser 1954, p. 860.
6   Althusser 1954, p. 859.

this 'crisis' is nothing but a normal crisis. These are battles that philosophy fights against itself, and they reflect the social struggles of our times: far from condemning it, on the contrary they prove the actuality and the vitality of philosophy.[7]

There is also a second hypothesis that should be discarded: the claim that the crisis of philosophical teaching would be the effect of a lack of vocation among students. In other words, the 'problem' is not *the effect of a disaffection of students towards higher studies in this discipline*.[8] Instead, to find the reason for this disaffection we should once again consider what philosophy *is* (for Althusser) or, better still, we should examine the particular status of the (all too human) content of its statements. Althusser asks:

> is it not because of its being a universal discipline, because it allows us to think the totality and the interconnection of the cultural and human problems of a world in which [students] deeply experience the crisis, and because it therefore responds to the concerns and intellectual needs of our students, that philosophy enjoys such prestige among them?[9]

In other words, philosophy should not be concerned with the crisis of philosophical teaching, because philosophy is always in a state of crisis, and students are also unconcerned about it, as they remain attracted to philosophy.

Althusser's thesis is thus as follows: *the origin of the problem of the teaching of philosophy should be sought in the placement assigned to philosophy by public authorities*.[10] The example of secondary education is revealing. If, at the beginning of the twentieth century, all students in secondary education 'concluded their course of studies with a year of philosophical teaching', then with the development of the exact sciences we have witnessed the eclipse of philosophy's dominion (due to the introduction, first, of a class of elementary mathematics 'which takes half of the students from the philosophy class' and then an experimental sciences class that clearly involves 'a new reduction of the actual students of the class of philosophy'). If we add the subsequent division 'of the philosophy class in four sections', the game is over: by expropriating the dominion of philosophy and transforming all final-year classes 'into classes of professional training', politics ultimately leads to the 'triumph of professional

---

7   Ibid.
8   Althusser 1954, pp. 860–1.
9   Althusser 1954, p. 861.
10   Ibid.

specialisation and immediate utilitarianism over theoretical and general culture. *Logically, philosophy must be the victim of such a triumph*.[11]

The breakdown of philosophical knowledge (which here represents true knowledge) and the multiplication of terminal teachings as merely instrumental to the exteriority of training (i.e., *to labour power*: politics reduces students to the status of future 'subordinates or workers') have disastrous effects on what the education process itself *must* represent. This is an interesting problem that, in this introductory context, assumes a particular strategic value. Indeed, Althusser's text says something else than what it explicitly declares, for it tells us *about what it omits*: in his exposition of the 'problem' of the teaching of philosophy Althusser is also telling us something about *teaching in general*. On this point, three theses can be identified.

First, there is only *one* educational process (and it should return to being one) because it should have only one conclusion (philosophy, functioning as a general theory, must have the character of a dominant discipline, and should this character be lost, it must strive to retrieve it: it is necessary to outline 'a project for the future that, by means of a truly renewed teaching open to all young people, *will make philosophical teaching compulsory for all secondary school students*'.[12] The implication of Althusser's strategy is clear, and we will return to it later: *to call for a defence of philosophy means to call for a defence of education as a whole, and vice versa*).

Second, the educational process, by its very nature, is (and should be) *apolitical*, because politics is precisely that which corrupts its *natural* function (far from being defined through the exteriority of education, the educational process is, assuming the very nature of its terminal component, an *essentially cultural process*. Politics 'wants to prohibit the mass of young people in our country from accessing general culture').[13]

Finally, the educational process, by its very nature, is (and should always be) *democratic*, since it has a *unifying objective* (if there is a singular objective and a singular educational process, then *the object of the educational process should also be singular*. This is a unity that rejects any 'anti-democratic policy' insisting on the exteriority of a professionalising function that would reduce education to a 'programme of cultural Malthusianism', divisive in the same way that students are divided into various final-year professionalising classes).

In short: politics should stay out of the process of the transmission of knowledge, and it should not interfere in the business of a community without

---

11   Althusser 1954, p. 862.
12   Althusser 1954, p. 864.
13   Althusser 1954, p. 862.

politics such as the one engaged in the educational process. The truth of this process is that of theory and general culture, and if a political program, conditioned by external needs, has now entered the halls of that secular Church that is the school, philosophy must once again regain control of the knowledge that was submitted to those extrinsic needs (only philosophy can save 'secondary education from the threats of specialisation and premature professional training').[14] Unity, independence from politics, democracy – these are notions that, if reflected by the internal principle of philosophy as a general culture, are anything but 'philosophically' irrelevant (we will see why I use quotation marks here in a moment). This is not because of what they are (or what they have represented in the tradition), as we might suppose, but rather *because of what they claim to be, located in the (ideological) discourse of a specific social sector.* Indeed, for my project in this book, the strategic value of Althusser's text on the teaching of philosophy does not lie in what it documents (since the question of the crisis of higher education, especially in the French context, is now totally irrelevant to us). Rather, the presuppositions behind this text allow us to appreciate the critical distance that, at a certain moment in time, Althusser himself (and the group of his young students) takes *vis-à-vis the meaning of his own theoretical claims.*

This allows me to clarify the purpose of this work. The following is a historical and philosophical reconstruction of the theses formulated by Louis Althusser and his students *about the educational processes of the class-based school, and its function.* My analysis is primarily based on two groups of writings, most of which are still unpublished, and therefore have no established interpretive tradition. These two groups can be divided into two distinct historical phases. In order to emphasise its specificity, I will examine each historical phase as if it were a conclusive moment of theoretical reflection.

The first phase is defined by the little-known article 'Student Problems' [*Problèmes étudiants*], which Althusser wrote in January 1964. Chapter 1 will be dedicated to an analysis of this text, and my aim will be to elucidate its genesis and to present its reception (above all, by Jean-Pierre Milbergue, through two versions of a text published in 1965 titled *La signification politique des rapports pédagogiques dans l'Université française*). Althusser's essay was written in the wake of the serious allegations of authoritarianism that Bruno Queysanne had made against him, on the occasion of the inaugural lecture dedicated to 'Théorie et Méthode en Sciences Humaines', which Althusser delivered in December 1963 during the seminar led by Pierre Bourdieu and Jean-Claude Passeron

---

14   Althusser 1954, p. 864.

(later published, in 1965, with the title *Rapport pédagogique et communication*). At the core of 'Student Problems' lies the issue of a certain *pedagogical function* that, within the framework of a materialist epistemology (essentially, the one presented in his 'On the Materialist Dialectic'), is what allows for the vertical transmission (moving from those who know to those who do not) of scientific generalities (i.e., the contents of true knowledge).

I will dedicate the rest of my inquiry to the second historical phase, which marks a radical break with the first (by admission of Althusser himself who, in his *Sur la reproduction*, repudiates the excessively technical and theoretical approach he adopted in 'Student Problems'). At this stage, in line with the formula included in the famous 1970 text 'Ideology and Ideological State Apparatuses',[15] it is necessary to address *the question of the relationship between the school apparatus and the reproduction of capitalist relations of production*. To this end, I examine the large number of Althusser's unpublished typescripts and manuscripts – still neglected by the secondary literature – linked to an unfinished collective research project titled 'Schools' [*Écoles*]. The first important document belonging to this project, dated 10 March 1968, is Pierre Macherey's 'Les mythologies scolaires', which I will analyse in the second chapter. The last, dated 3 November 1969, consists of three notes on the geography and the history of the formation of the class-based school co-written by Macherey and Christian Baudelot, which I will turn to in Chapter 4. The 'Schools' project as a whole was the outcome of a collaboration between Althusser himself and above all, Étienne Balibar, Pierre Macherey, Michel Tort (who, from this unfinished work, drew inspiration for his *Le Quotient intellectuel*, published in 1974),[16] Roger Establet, and Christian Baudelot (whose *L'école capitaliste en France*, published in 1971, was inspired by his participation in 'Schools').[17] Only the first three chapters of 'Schools' are still available to us, and the third chapter of this book will be dedicated to their analysis.

The present work will reveal how the educational process, far from representing an object of mere occasional interest, was considered a crucial issue by both Althusser and the *groupe Spinoza* in general, one that is wholly decisive if the aim is understanding the real powers behind the functioning of social reproduction.

In this sense, the importance of this study is necessarily twofold. From an historical point of view, the aim is to shine a rather unusual light on Althusser's work, focusing on what can be defined, at the moment only generically, as a

---

15   In Althusser 2014.
16   Tort 1974.
17   Baudelot and Establet 1971.

'pedagogical question'. In this sense, reconstructing the theoretical guidelines that underlie the two historical phases I mentioned above allows us to *complicate* the theoretical role that the scholastic institution plays for Althusser – *alongside* and *beyond* his 1970 theses on the ideological apparatuses of the state (according to which the school system represents the dominant ideological apparatus of capitalist modes of production), which still represents the primary theoretical reference point for the articulation of this problem. On the other hand, such an historical reconstruction has unavoidable theoretical repercussions: it goes to supplement and deepen some of Althusser's more strictly philosophical theses (in particular, those presented in 'On the Materialist Dialectic' and 'Marxism and Humanism'). This is an original theoretical vantage point, since these repercussions attribute a substantial value to Althusser's 'pedagogical discourse', furthering our understanding of his core philosophical theses.[18]

I now want to briefly return to Althusser's 'L'Enseignement de la Philosophie' since, on closer inspection, this text hides a final, fundamental assumption. Once the homology between philosophy and general theory is established (embedded into the educational process, philosophy is a 'school of *theory*' and a 'theoretical and general culture', that is, a 'universal discipline' that reflects upon 'totality' by means of 'method' and 'rigour of reflection'), then *to say that philosophy exhibits a theoretical generality is to make a philosophical claim*. In other words, it could be said that the thesis that outlines the validity criteria of a philosophical proposition is necessarily a statement that – *in the very act of that theoretical outlining* – becomes a valid philosophical proposition. An additional assumption, that is nothing more than a game of mirrors and self-referentiality: Althusser justifies his claims (as an act of enunciation) by virtue of what he claims (as enunciated), and, simultaneously, what he claims (as enunciated) is justified by virtue of his claiming it (as an act of enunciation). Philosophy is both the *subject* and the *object* of enunciation: as an object, it is the content of the theoretical claim (that philosophy is the dominant element of the educational process); as a subject, it represents its validating factor. The truth-value of Althusser's thesis is, once again, found at the level of its self-referentiality. But this is the point I want to emphasise: being a text on the

---

18   For example: Jacques Rancière in his polemical 'Sur la théorie de l'idéologie Politique d'Althusser' (Rancière 1973) appraises the reactionary features of Althusserian epistemology (in *For Marx*, the philosophical thesis) on the basis of the ideas expressed in 'Student Problems' (the pedagogical thesis) which, therefore, is taken to represent the factual implication of that general thesis.

teaching of philosophy, that self-referentiality implies a *philosophical legitim-isation of philosophy within the (elective) place of its transmission (here, the con-text of secondary education)*. This is as if to say that the professional philosopher (that is, the professor), besides being involved in the educational relationship, is also the *theoretical subject* of its enunciation. The professor (of philosophy) enunciates their (dominant) position, and this position can only be enunciated by the professor (of philosophy): in other words, *they are present in what they enunciate and what they enunciate is present within them*.[19] The professor, qua professional philosopher, justifies their own position, and they alone can, due to their being a professional philosopher, justify this position by performing their function.

Identifying this further assumption allows me to formulate a simple ques-tion, whose answer *silently runs through the analysis performed by Althusser and his group*, especially in the context of 'Schools': what is their position *vis-à-vis* the claims they make in that work? What kind of theoretical propositions do they adopt? Are they philosophical propositions? Pierre Macherey (who was present when 'Schools' was written), gives us an important and, in some ways, disconcerting clue, seemingly rejecting the kind of theoretical stance that was adopted by Althusser in 1954. I will quote in full a passage which precisely explores the relationship between philosophy and the university (considered as a theoretical object of philosophical propositions and, *simultaneously*, as an elective space for the production of those propositions: once again, it is a game

---

19   On the relationship between philosophy and philosophy as a profession (that is, between philosophy and philosophy of the professor), see Althusser 2017, pp. 18–19: 'If you ask them: "But then why don't you consider yourselves philosophers? Who, in your opinion, deserves to be called a philosopher?", they will all answer, in unison: *"Philosophy teachers, of course!"* And they are absolutely right. Except for people who, for personal reasons – that is to say, for pleasure or their own benefit – continue to read philosophers and "do philosophy", the only people who deserve to be called philosophers are in fact the ones who teach philosophy. Naturally, this *fact* throws up a first question or, rather, two. 1. Is it really by chance that *philosophy* is so closely bound up with teaching and those who teach it? All indications are that it isn't; for, after all, the marriage of philosophy and teach-ing doesn't just go back to our philosophy classes, it doesn't date from yesterday. At the very beginnings of philosophy, Plato taught philosophy, Aristotle taught philosophy ... If this marriage between philosophy and teaching isn't due to chance, it must express a secret necessity. We shall try to find out what that necessity is. 2. Let us take another step. Since, *or so it seems*, philosophy isn't much use in everyday life, as it doesn't pro-duce knowledge and has no concrete applications, we may well wonder: what earthly purpose does it serve? We can even ask ourselves the following strange question: might it be that *the one purpose philosophy serves is the teaching of philosophy*, and nothing else? And if the only purpose it serves is the teaching of philosophy, what might that mean?'

of mirrors and self-referentiality). Although Macherey does not speak directly about schools, or higher education, or the educational process in general, the core issue remains the same:

> Can philosophy be useful? Should we expect it to tell the truth about the university? After all, the university is where philosophy claims, by virtue of its propensity to tell the truth about everything, to occupy its rightful place, bringing together in a single formula the appeal to 'defend the university' and that to 'defend philosophy'. The defensive tone of these claims leads to the suspicion that they are appealing to an already lost cause. They take for granted that they represent a last stand and, more worryingly, a kind of retreat or retrenching, thereby turning the university into a bunker or a ghetto and, by reflection, endowing philosophy with undue privileges. This retrenching into itself is exemplified by the effort to perpetuate an idea towards which both the university and philosophy would converge, once they are brought back (do I need to specify it?) to their *pure* essence. I will make it bluntly clear: we must beware of philosophers who reflect about, or advocate for, the university by trying to bring it back to its idea or essence – identifying their being philosophers with the promotion of this essence – turning ideas and essences into most profitable commercial resources and making themselves entitled to exploit their countless possibilities. Playing on the kinship of the word 'university' with the word 'universality' – the latter designating precisely the type of reality that, defined by its global character, they have appropriated – they have no difficulty in transforming the historical reality of the thing that is the university (with all the impurities which, being a thing, it contains, and with the modifications to which it has been subjected) into an immaterial and timeless ideality. The immateriality and timelessness which they assign to the university guarantees its character as an indestructible unity: in this form, it is disposed and destined to be preserved and perpetuated. And this suffices to justify its 'defence', presented as a return to an idea or essence which, positioning oneself from the point of view of truth, would be unthinkable to betray. And so, the philosopher presents himself as the best defender of the faith that is due to them.[20]

These are harsh and powerful words, which clearly formulate a novel and definitive ban. One might ask somewhat rhetorically: is it not precisely the philo-

---

20   Macherey 2011.

sophical standpoint itself, and its mode of discourse, that produces its other presuppositions, such as unity, general culture as an internal principle of formation, and lack of political engagement? A novel and definitive ban, I said: indeed, it is precisely the philosophers who must stay away from the educational process (here, the university), because as soon as they speak of its universality (that is, of its immaterial and timeless ideals), they speak ideologically. In sum: a correct theoretical analysis is *not* a philosophical analysis. Everything that Althusser and his group say about the 'pedagogical question' *does not refer in any way to a philosophy of education* (and what is questioned is precisely the idea of education as a specific mode of ideologising). The analysis of the educational process performed by Althusser and his group, in fact – starting from 'Student Problems' (a text published shortly after 'On the Materialist Dialectic' and just before 'Marxism and Humanism'), but even more clearly in 'Schools' (which, apart from its positive claims, also contradicts the ideas expressed in 'Student Problems') – is part of an attempt to renew historical and dialectical materialism, whose theoretical grounds will be outlined by Althusser and his colleagues in the process writing the texts that I will examine in this work.[21]

What Balibar claims about Marx's theoretical thought also applies to the theses presented in 'Schools':

> Marx's theoretical thinking presented itself, at various points, not as a philosophy, but as an alternative to philosophy, a *non-philosophy* or even an *antiphilosophy*. And it has perhaps been the greatest anti-philosophy

---

21   On this point, for example, already in *For Marx*'s preliminary Remarks on the terminology, one reads of a terminological difference: 'Theory (with a capital T)', although synonymous with 'Marxist "philosophy" (dialectical materialism)', does not correspond to the term of 'philosophy' because philosophy, ultimately, is ideology (because ideological is its function). Althusser writes that 'Engels felt the need to encapsulate the difference between ideological philosophies and Marx's absolutely new philosophical project in a terminological distinction. He proposed to register this difference by designating Marxist philosophy by the term *theory*' (Althusser 2005, p. 162). This is a genuine *leitmotiv*, and variants of Althusser's thesis on the ideological function of philosophy (think of the famous formula contained in his 1973 response to John Lewis, according to which philosophy 'is, ultimately, class struggle in theory'), can be found as far as *Philosophy for Non-Philosophers*. Here, for example, we read that 'All past philosophies known to us ... acted "on command" in the dominant class's (or classes') service, working on the "raw material" of the ideology determinant for that class ... If every philosophy unfolds on class theoretical bases and unifies the existing ideological elements as the dominant ideology, for the dominant class's benefit, it is easy to see why philosophy produces not knowledge, but only a weapon in a fight. A weapon is a weapon: it produces nothing but the power of victory' (Althusser 2017, p. 180).

of the modern age. For Marx, philosophy as he had learnt it, from the tradition which ran from Plato to Hegel, including more or less dissident materialists like Epicurus or Feuerbach, was in fact merely an individual undertaking aimed at interpreting the world. At best this led to leaving the world as it was; at worst, to transfiguring it.[22]

Starting from the analysis of the chapters of the 'Schools' that are available to us (as well as some preparatory texts made for this unfinished work, such as Macherey's 'Les mythologies scolaires'), I will use the term *true-factual propositions* to designate the ideological propositions, and the term *theoretical propositions* to indicate the theoretical (or 'philosophical' in the Marxist sense) ones. The reason for the first definition will become clear in the course of my analysis. Here it will suffice to mention the fact that the ideological character of those propositions, by explicit declaration of Althusser (in an unpublished text on 'Les Grand Illusions de l'École', written in 1968), is given by a particular illusion (that is, by a particular representation) – an illusion whose epistemological singularity is produced by the fact that the abstract nature (in the sense of separateness) of its conclusions is produced by means of an immediate (empirical) proximity. It is called a *philosophical illusion*.

∴

In the passage we examined above, Macherey speaks of a sleight of hand of philosophical discourse, produced by the affinity between the words 'university' and 'universality', the latter being a peculiar mode of its way of speaking. This sleight of hand is also identified by Balibar (indeed he was also present when 'Schools' was drafted, or, better, he was *the most* present), in an article titled 'Sub specie universitatis':[23]

> 'University' and 'universality' can be translated into the same Latin word *universitas*, as they both involve an idea of totality, of leaving no exception, nothing that is irreducibly outside (*universitas rerum, universitas generis humani, universitas studiorum*). We know that universities were created indeed with an ambition (which they have striven to retain) of leaving no significant realm of knowledge and even no interest of mankind out of their course of studies, and it seems that, in modern times,

---

22   Balibar 1995, p. 2.
23   Balibar 2006, p. 4.

philosophy as a reflection on universality has been not only associated to this project, but primarily involved in its definition and implementation.

Universality – University. Let me stress this point, to be absolutely clear: the fact that we are talking about the university and not about educational processes in general does not change in any way the meaning of the question that I am interested in exploring. Indeed, we will see how the university, the supreme stage of education – in the context of that authentic metaphysical cosmology that is the school system, seen from the point of view of its ideological representation – plays the role of an unmoved mover. Universality, university, philosophy and its elective space: an ideological communion that suffices to integrate a reflection on its nature, i.e., a 'critical reflection on its present and future', with an examination of 'the norms, standards, and discursive models that philosophy owes to its academic institutional location'.[24]

In short, the present study can be conceived, at least programmatically, as moving beyond the field of Althusserian studies. Based on the ideological assumption of a link between philosophy and the university, and configured as an historical reconstruction of an anti- or non-philosophical theory of the educational processes in general, this book represents a premise (and, in some ways, the only possible premise) for an anti-philosophical or non-philosophical theory *of philosophy itself*.

---

24   Balibar 2006, p. 6.

Pedagogical Function and Class Struggle: On the Genesis and Structure of 'Student Problems'

Introduction

A revised draft of an unpublished text originally written in 1963 and titled 'Le communisme et le étudiants', 'Student Problems' appeared in January 1964 in the *points de vue* section of issue 152 of the communist journal *La nouvelle critique*.[1] This issue was titled 'Les étudiants'. Althusser wanted to intervene in the debate that was then underway in the student world, particularly involving the UNEF[2] (which, after the Algerian War of 1956, put demands on the specific conditions of student labour at the forefront of its agenda) and the UEC.[3] An epigraph is included directly under the title. Its opening four lines proclaim: 'The following text has no other objective than to define as precisely as possible the theoretical grounds on which the analysis of student problems can be developed'.[4]

It may be useful to keep in mind that this article was written during the period that the texts later included in *For Marx* were composed. Indeed, 'Student Problems' was published only four months after 'On the Materialist Dialectic' (August 1963) and five months before 'Marxism and Humanism' (June 1964). Given the convergence of some crucial theses inherent to the science–ideology couple, it is reasonable to wonder why 'Student Problems' was not included in *For Marx*. Most likely, this had nothing to do with the *j'accuse* that appears in *On the Reproduction of Capitalism*, since by then the political context had radically changed in comparison to 1965, when *For Marx* was published.[5]

---

1 ALT2. A2-03.03.
2 Union nationale des étudiants de France.
3 Union des étudiants communistes.
4 Althusser 1964, p. 80. Translator's note: The English translation of 'Student Problems' does not contain the entirety of the original essay. When translating from the original essay, I will reference the French version of the text (Althusser 1964).
5 I am referring to Julien Girval-Pallotta's thesis, presented in the context of the seminar 'Mouvements étudiants et luttes sociales', held on 7 November 2009 and available at: https://grm.hypotheses.org/files/2013/01/GRM3.RC_.Pallotta.pdf

The only reference to this text in Althusser's work appears in a footnote in *On the Reproduction*, which was written at least five years later,[6] in the context of the distinction between the technical and social division of labour. Indeed, it is in 'Student Problems' that this distinction first becomes operative. If the 'technical division' corresponds to 'all jobs whose existence is exclusively justified by the technical necessities that define the mode of production at a given moment in its development in a given society', then the purpose of the 'social division' is 'to ensure the work process of the society *in the forms of class structure and domination*'.[7] Later on, the function of this distinction (which at this level indicates a *real* distinction – technical and social divisions are distinct but separate – and not a *modal* one: these divisions, although distinct, both fall within the framework of the same division, so that referring to one already implies a reference to the other, as Rancière pointed out in a 1973 text, to which we shall return later) will be made clear.

For the moment it will suffice to highlight the presence of the distinction between technical and social division, which Althusser first formulated in 1964. The footnote reads as follows: 'We here rectify the "technicist" and "theoreticist" tendency that marked some of the arguments in ["Student Problems"]'.[8] Here it is as if Althusser means to say: both the distinction and the identification of the two divisions are correct, and that is why the former must be maintained. However, this identification needs to be adjusted in the light of its development. It is no coincidence that in *On the Reproduction of Capitalism*, in a political context (that of May 1968) that is absolutely crucial for the reformulation of the 'technicist' and 'theoreticist' tendencies contained in his 1964 text, Althusser labels any attempt to consider this distinction real as an 'ideological imposture', since 'all the forms in which the putatively "technical" functions of the division of labour are carried out, are direct or indirect effects of the dominant relations of production'.[9] This is tantamount to saying that the technical division of labour, far from being defined according to a society's degree of development, already depends on its social purposes – that is, on the reproduction of the relations of production that determine it. The immediate implication here is that the technical division is *already* placed within the form of the division into classes. A technical division is already a social division. There are thus technicist and theoreticist tendencies – but why? Let us dive into the substance of Althusser's text.

---

6   The typewritten text in which this footnote appears, and that is the basis of the critical edition of the volume, is undated.

7   Althusser 2011, p. 11.

8   Althusser 2014, p. 34 n. 19.

9   Althusser 2014, p. 36.

1   Technical Division and Social Division

The theoretical principles placed at the level of scientific theory, which aim at understanding the university as a proper object of inquiry, as noted above, are those of the technical and the social division of labour:

> Marx applied these principles in the analysis of capitalist society. They are valid for the analysis of all human societies (in the sense that social training [*formation*] relies upon a determined mode of production). They are valid *a fortiori* for a particular social reality like the university, which belongs for obvious reasons to every modern society, capitalist, socialist or communist.[10]

As I mentioned, the technical division corresponds to the place that the labour process assigns to an individual, according to the degree of development of a society at any given time. Its level of application to the university, then, 'consists of undertaking the *pedagogic training* [*formation*] of future technical, scientific and social cadres of the society, and of participating in creative scientific work [*travail scientifique créateur*]'.[11] Scientific work, pedagogical training, technical division of labour – these categories imply one another, since pedagogical training (the transmission of knowledge), based on the technical division (by competences), is itself the basis of scientific work (which is creative).

Althusser seems very far from the more famous formulation contained in his 1970 text on the apparatus, where the school represents the privileged ideological apparatus of the state. In 'Student Problems' – in relation to the class domination of the social division, and by virtue of its technical division – Althusser refers to the university as a 'privileged' site within the social formations in which independence, individualism, and freedom cannot be reduced to the formally identical qualifications of bourgeois individualism:

> Traditionally the university represents 'liberal' values: critical spirit, freedom of scientific research and discussion, and so on. These do not, as some people dangerously say, spring from bourgeois individualism, but from genuine scientific values. It would be a serious mistake to confuse the liberty every scientific activity needs, as the very air it breathes, as the

---

10   Althusser 2011, p. 11.
11   Ibid.

basic condition for all scientific research, with the ideology of economic and political 'liberalism' of the bourgeoisie.[12]

Althusser thus introduces a crucial thesis here: 'for Marxists, it is *not* the *form* in which knowledge is either transmitted or absorbed or discovered that constitutes the "decisive link", but the *quality of the knowledge* itself'.[13] The quality of the knowledge and form in which knowledge is transmitted, assimilated, etc., means that knowledge is seen as the *object* of transmission and the pedagogic function is the *form* of its transmissions. Thus, form on the one hand, and content on the other. Any ambiguity must be removed from this statement. What looks like indifference towards form is not, in fact, aimed at form in general: it is rather an indifference dictated by the fact that 'Marxists' – precisely because they make the scientificity of knowledge their priority – are indifferent to the fact that this scientificity must be guaranteed by a well-determined pedagogical training. This is a pedagogical mediation that, precisely because it is based on the technical division of labour, makes the university the place of qualifications that are formally identical to those of bourgeois individualism:

> to oppose *collective* forms to the well-grounded individual or liberal forms of scientific research; to condemn the latter as if they were manifestations of the bourgeoisie's 'liberal' or 'individualist' ideology; these are very dangerous points of view, as much from the pedagogic as from the political and ideological standpoint.[14]

Clearly, the question of form is all but indifferent. In a footnote Althusser specifies that 'in the problem posed by teacher/student activity' it is '*content* (knowledge) which is dominant, and the *form* subordinate'.[15] Once again, this does not mean that the form is indifferent. On the contrary, the pedagogical function, grounded in the technical division of labour, seems to represent the *ratio essendi* of the transmitted object, that is to say, that *an adjustment relationship* must be established between form and content (Althusser uses the term *correspondance*) which finds in the form of the transmission the condition of validity of the transmitted object. More precisely, the form is at once *conditioned* (subordinate to the object, which has the dominant position) and *necessary* (that is, essential to the validation of the scientific quality of the

---

12   Althusser 2011, p. 12.
13   Althusser 2011, p. 12.
14   Ibid.
15   Althusser 2011, p. 15 n. 1.

transmitted object). It is the *form* of the transmission that assigns the value of scientific truth to the *content*, precisely because of the latter's dominant position. Althusser is very clear about this:

> Is the knowledge distributed a true *science*? [this question indicates the overriding concern with content, the 'quality of knowledge itself']. If yes, then its distribution really corresponds to *technical* necessity, and then the pedagogic function is essentially healthy, even if its *forms* [a subordinate concern, relative to form] are relatively 'old' and need reforming.[16]

For now, it will suffice to point out that *the pedagogical function corresponds to technical necessity, seen as a formal condition for the scientific validation of knowledge as a transmitted object.* Is the transmitted object scientific? If so, then the technical division of university labour, which grounds pedagogical training, is really operational and 'essentially healthy', while assuming a relatively 'old' morphology (later I will return to this strange clarification pertaining to the 'old' forms of the pedagogical function). So much for the technical division.

On the other hand, if it is true that, *a fortiori*, the principles guiding the analysis of the technical and the social division can be applied to every determinate social reality, when we turn to social division and class domination, then in the context of the university, things take place 'in very special conditions'.[17] Although it represents a place of freedom and critical inquiry – forms, as we have seen, that cannot be reduced to those of bourgeois individualism – the university also contains an internal tension. *This tension does not concern the form of teaching, which depends on the technique of transmission, but rather pertains to knowledge as the object of intellectual labour.* Althusser writes that:

> What is remarkable is that in the case of the university the *social division of labour*, and therefore *class domination*, comes *massively* into play, but not only – or even mainly – where student and non-student theorists look for it.[18] It comes *massively* into play, and in a 'blinding' way (which doubtless is why one does not always 'see' it), in the very *object* of intellectual work; *in the knowledge* the university is commissioned to distribute to the students.[19]

---

16   Althusser 1964, p. 89.
17   Althusser 1964, p. 85.
18   Here Althusser is probably referring to the student analyses of the 'qualitative' reformulation of the pedagogical relationship.
19   Althusser 2011, pp. 12–13.

These categories also apply to the technical division. There, quality of knowledge as content and form of its transmission; here, the form of transmission (an object of the students' theoretical work) and knowledge as a means for the enforcing of class domination. These categories are placed in an inverted relationship: there, the object was guaranteed by the form of its transmission; here, the object is transmitted in accordance with class politics, regardless of the form of its transmission or, more precisely, with no heed to a specific form that would validate its scientific content: 'The social division of labour is therefore only technical in the sense that it reflects the mode (social, political, ideological) of domination in the social work process.'[20] Thus, Althusser asks: 'Is the knowledge distributed a pure ideology? As in certain subjects and courses? If yes then education is in the service of an ideology, and therefore of a class policy, *even if the "forms" of teaching are very "modern"*'.[21]

Ultimately, the same categories appear in both the technical and social division: *form* (of transmission) and (transmitted) *content*. On the one hand, in the technical division, the quality of scientific knowledge is guaranteed by the form of its transmission: the technical division of pedagogical training is adequate to the transmitted content, a scientific content validated by that form. On the other hand, in class domination, the object of knowledge is transmitted without regard to the form of its transmission, that is, irrespective of the determinacy of a form that would sanction its scientific value: the social division of university labour acts directly on the object, without guaranteeing its formal process of validation.

Again, on the one hand the emphasis is on the *form* as that which warrants the quality of a *content*; on the other hand, the emphasis is on *content*, regardless of any *form* that could guarantee its scientific value. On the one hand, technical division; on the other, social division. On the one hand, scientific knowledge; on the other, ideological knowledge.

This is Althusser's central argument: 'through the knowledge taught at university there passes *the permanent dividing line between technical and social divisions of labour, the most constant and profound of class divisions*'.[22] For Althusser, knowledge thus has two faces: either knowledge is scientific knowledge, or it is ideological knowledge. It is either true knowledge or false knowledge. We can make three observations on this point:

1.   The first is related to *the science–ideology pair*. Knowledge is defined in many ways. There is scientific knowledge and there is ideological know-

---

20   Althusser 2011, p. 11.
21   Althusser 2011, p. 13.
22   Ibid.

ledge. If, in general, the science–ideology pair marks the dividing line of class struggle for Althusser, it also marks the dividing line of class struggle within the thing that is the university, since this couple, in what is taught within the university, is defined by the *permanent dividing line between technical and social divisions of labour*.[23] To wonder why 'Student Problems' wasn't included in *For Marx*, then, was no idle question (indeed, in a letter to Bruno Queysanne to which I shall refer later, and which can be considered as the moment in which the theoretical core of 'Student Problems' was first formulated, Althusser explicitly links the question of the pedagogical function to his 'On the Materialist Dialectic').[24] Although maximalist, *For Marx*'s fundamental thesis can be made explicit by saying that ideology (or philosophy, or humanism, or Hegel) is the opposite of science (or epistemology, or a certain Marxism, or a certain Marx), and *vice versa*. 'Student Problems', then, seems to represent the factual explication of this general thesis. Through a programmatic writing that, in fact, finds its *raison d'être* in providing strategic-operational lines to the student movement, Althusser intends to show if not the place of production, at least one of the places of real production of scientific generalities. On this theme, it is worth considering a very uncompromising and pertinent text written by Rancière, 'On the Theory of Ideology: The Politics of Althusser'. This essay was translated into French in 1973 but originally (and very significantly) written for an Argentine magazine in 1969, during the aftermath of the events of May 1968. Indeed, in this article Rancière identifies a close connection between the Althusserian general thesis that ideology is the opposite of science and 'Student Problems' in order to show how this text is the factual transposition of a general thesis (for Rancière, the transposition of an attitude that is ultimately metaphysical and, therefore, revisionist): 'Student Problems' and 'Marxism and Humanism', according to Rancière, 'are devoted to deducing the political consequences of the theory of ideology'.[25] The profoundly ironic aspect of the claim that the university would be one of the places of the production of scientific statements, lies in the fact that – as Mladen Dolar says in relation to Lacanian discourse (the discourse of the university is not the discourse of science and science does not appear in Lacan's theory of discourses) – Marx, just like Freud (who, with Galileo or Spinoza, is

---

23   Ibid.
24   Cf. 872ALT/142/6, pp. 1, 2, 7, 8; ALT2. A40-04.03 (A), p. 6.
25   Rancière 1974.

among the main thinkers Althusser links to the production of a scientific generality) could produce knowledge outside the university context.[26]

2. Following from the first, the second observation concerns *the separation between the social and technical division of labour*. The 'permanent dividing line between technical and social divisions of labour' runs through knowledge.[27] This is a division that is not simple distinction, because, if science and ideology, as seen in (1), are qualitatively opposite domains, then the technical and the social division of labour are irreducible, just as the various forms taken by knowledge are irreducible. Althusser's crucial theoretical move is therefore to emphasise how these principles are separate since they introduce an irreducible dichotomy within knowledge. At this stage of Althusser's thought, this means that scientific discourse, understood as opposed to ideological discourse, remains an option – guaranteed by a certain pedagogical training based on technical division – that is achievable from within the domain of the university. Therefore, the university is not merely an ideological target but the very place of class division: 'through the knowledge taught at university passes *the permanent dividing line between technical and social divisions of labour, the most constant and profound of class divisions*'.[28] In order to stop considering the university as a place of class division, and to construe it as an apparatus of class domination, it was necessary *to make the division of labour not separate but distinct*. In other words, it was necessary to turn the technical and social division into *modal* (and not real) divisions within the division of labour itself in general, since its separation implies the possibility of the transmission of a knowledge which, being non-ideological, is *already* so to speak on the side of the revolution. And this is indeed what seems to be happening, starting with that 1969 footnote in *On the Reproduction of Capitalism* directly referring to 'Student Problems' precisely for what pertains to the distinction between technical and social division, and in which the rectification of 'technicalism' and 'theoreticism' has, as its immediate implication, a redefinition of the university. The university should now be seen as a place where knowledge *as such* is articulated through a system that is the very *raison d'être* of bourgeois ideology (its Ideological State Apparatus).

3. Lastly, this means that, in this text, knowledge is still seen as *indifferent to its place of production*. Althusser here details what we could call

---

26   Cf. Dolar and Clemente 2017, p. 245.
27   Althusser 2011, p. 13.
28   Ibid.

a syntactic theory of knowledge: a sort of orthopaedics of the modes of transmission that is *indifferent to where the objects transmitted are produced*. There is a sort of specific attention paid to the formal correctness of the statement (*form*), which guarantees the scientific validation of the object (*knowledge*), regardless of the positioning of the place of enunciation (*university*). And this is not at all undermined by the fact that Althusser also speaks of the social division of university labour (in fact, in relation to the division within knowledge in general, the problem does not arise on the side of class domination – i.e., false knowledge – but rather pertains to the possibility of the transmission of non-ideological knowledge – that is, scientific knowledge). Rancière, in the text cited above, goes on to argue that:

> there is no ideology in the University which could be the Other of science. Nor is there a science which could be the Other of ideology. The University does not teach "science" in the mythical purity of its essence, but a selection of scientific knowledges articulated into *objects of knowledge*. The transmission of scientific knowledges does not proceed from the concept of science. It forms part of the *forms of appropriation* of scientific knowledge and these are *class* forms of appropriation. Scientific theories are transmitted through a system of discourse, traditions and institutions which constitute the very existence of bourgeois ideology.[29]

Therefore, knowledge – even scientific knowledge, and even when considering the correspondence with its mode of transmission – bears the mark of its factual placement and is influenced by the forms of appropriation that, in the case of the university are '*class* forms of appropriation'. This thesis clearly echoes those of another crucial text published in 1964, the same year as 'Student Problems'. Of course, I am referring to Bourdieu and Passeron's *The Inheritors: French Students and Their Relations to Culture*. In that book, the two sociologists famously argue that academic success is grounded in 'cultural heritage' as well as those attitudes towards study ('amateurism') which, disguised as natural qualities by the postulate of formal equality ('charismatic ideology'), are the effect of a specific social origin. More precisely, *a reproductive circularity of culture* is here at stake – I am not referring to the 1970 text on reproduction, but to an essay penned by Bourdieu alone, *La transmission de l'héritage culturel* [The Transmission of Cultural Heritage], written in 1966.[30] On the one hand,

---

29   Rancière 1974, p. 6.
30   Bourdieu 1966.

inequality *vis-à-vis* culture is the principle of inequality *vis-à-vis* the school system: a bourgeois origin allows a student to enjoy the 'cultural privilege' that lies behind scholastic success (that is, pedagogical communication is a function of the culture that the user owes to his or her social origin). On the other hand, however, inequality *vis-à-vis* the school system is the principle of inequality *vis-à-vis* culture: the training imparted in schools facilitates the assimilation of the codes of use of the objects of knowledge (that is: the culture of the user is always related to pedagogical communication).

2   The Pedagogical Function

Let us continue with the analysis of Althusser's text. The university is the place of two distinct and separate divisions. In other words, it is the place of a class division that divides knowledge: on the one hand, scientific knowledge (coming from the corresponding technical division) and on the other, ideological knowledge (coming from social division, regardless of the modes of transmission, i.e., coming from a technical division functional to that type of transmission). It can be seen how, in the use Althusser makes of them, Marxian principles are still placed on an abstract level since, for now, we know *that* a technical division is necessary but we do not know *which* pedagogical training corresponds to it: 'since this knowledge calls directly into question the pedagogic function on which the university is based, it is necessary to provide an objective analysis of the latter'.[31]

Althusser is very clear about this point (which defines the content of Part III of 'Student Problems'): 'the pedagogic function has as its object the transmission of a determinate knowledge to subjects who do not possess it'.[32] This means that *knowledge is peculiarly divisive as it is based on an essential inequality, defined by the position that the subjects take in relation to it* (that of those who know and those who do not). The scientific validation of an object of knowledge, therefore, is established by a pedagogical training that is structured by a relationship of vertical disparity: 'the pedagogic situation is based on the absolute condition of *an inequality between a knowledge and a lack of knowledge*'.[33]

This crucial claim makes it possible to outline a topology of knowledge, one which for Althusser is inscribed in the very line of class division. At one level, knowledge – according to the incidence of the double division of labour in

---

31   Althusser 2011, p. 14.
32   Ibid.
33   Ibid.

general – is determined by the difference between science and ideology. At another level – that of the pedagogical function as an expression of the technical division – knowledge is placed in a relationship of inequality that makes non-knowledge (rather than false knowledge) the other of knowledge (of scientific knowledge, not knowledge in general). On the one hand, there is a relationship internal to knowledge *in general* (a relationship that is expressed by a line of *division*: class division). On the other hand, there is a *specific* relationship between knowledge and non-knowledge (a relationship that is expressed as a substantial *inequality* which makes sure of the scientific possibility contained as a separate part within knowledge in general).

There are two noteworthy consequences. First of all, Rancière's critique of Althusser – according to which, by means of a (metaphysical and therefore reactionary) twist, Althusser contradicts himself (first knowledge is the place of a division, then, in the pedagogical function as defined by the division between those who know and those who do not, knowledge 'has the status of science', thus justifying 'the eminent dignity of the possessors of knowledge'[34]) – does not seem to be formally correct, since the knowledge that is transmitted within the pedagogical function is a specific translation of the scientific knowledge that is contained in knowledge in general.

Secondly, the fact that 'the famous pupil–teacher, lecturer–student, relationship is the *technical expression of this fundamental pedagogic relationship*'[35] shows, on the basis of this topography of knowledge, that for Althusser the true placement of class division is not to be located in the pedagogical – teacher–pupil/professor–student – relationship as had been described by the theorists of the UNEF. Consider, for example, 'Naissance d'un syndicalisme étudiant', a paradigmatic text of the student movement published in *Les Temps Modernes* in February 1964. Here Marc Kravetz writes that 'essentially what the student learns at the University is passivity and submission'.[36] Class division is not located within this unequal relationship since the latter (which is based on the technical division) is on the side of scientific knowledge, as it is opposed to ideological knowledge (which is based on the social division). This relationship opens a space that, determined by the productive practice of scientific generalities, (technically) excludes the ruling class's influence on the object of knowledge.

It is precisely on this theoretical basis that Althusser intends to establish a dialogue with the theorists of the UNEF (from a theoretical point of view

---

34 Rancière 1974, p. 7.
35 Althusser 2011, p. 14.
36 Kravetz 1964.

close to the exquisitely 'quantitative' positions of the PCF): Althusser's intervention, that is, *is defined by a theoretical (topographical) strategy that shifts
the axis of class division from the vertical and unequal pedagogical relationship to the content of knowledge in general.* This is why any attempt to under-
mine this relationship (guided by 'democratic' ideals of self-education – in
this sense, the relationship between Althusser and the *Groupe de Travail Universitaire* is bound to be rather ambiguous) inevitably leads to an inaccurate
conception of scientific work (of its transmission techniques), and therefore to
ideological errors (due to unscientific production) and ultimately to political
mistakes (wrong strategic alliances): 'no pedagogic questions, which all presuppose unequal knowledge between teachers and students, can be settled on the
basis of *pedagogic equality* between teachers and students'.[37] So, for example,
for students

> it is erroneous to transfer a demand (for equal representation) from one
> sector where it is objectively justified (the coordination of activities) to
> a sector where it is not justified (the coordination of syllabuses and of
> properly pedagogical institutions).[38]

In a passage that deserves to be quoted in full, Althusser argues that:

> [students] also risk alienating the goodwill of their professors, who are
> thus unjustly treated with suspicion in their own pedagogical activity,
> and whose knowledge is held to be superfluous. They may even alienate
> them *politically*, to the point of transforming possible allies and comrades
> in struggle into enemies of the political or trade-union cause that the
> students defend. By retarding their scientific training, students who con-
> tent themselves with 'participationist' methods, through which they give
> themselves the 'democratic' illusion of knowledge, will get stuck for a long
> time in a half-knowledge – that is, in a state that does not give them the
> weapons of scientific learning.[39]

It is easier, then, to understand the meaning of that strange clarification regarding the 'old yet reformable forms' of the 'healthy' pedagogical function, which
Althusser had included in the context of his argument for the correspondence of the pedagogical form (conditioned and necessary) with the scientific

---

37   Althusser 2011, p. 14.
38   Althusser 2011, pp. 14–15.
39   Althusser 2011, p. 15.

object. This is because, for Althusser, arguing for the need of the technical division does not translate into anything other than the classical form of transmission of knowledge, that is, the form in which knowledge is the object of a relation of acquisition. Any 'reformability' of this relationship, something that Althusser seems to consider possible, must be based on a technically undemocratic relationship. Further, it is significant that, for Althusser, the relationship of scientific collaboration between researchers, which makes the laboratory completely different from the university, effectively negates the pedagogical relationship.[40]

∴

These are Althusser's arguments: the goodwill of professors; pedagogical anti-democraticism seen as productive of a genuine science opposed to semi-science; an apology on behalf of the professor as guarantor of a space of validation external to the place of production of ideological generalities (in other words, the professor as the one who establishes a vertical technical relationship that specifies the scientific possibility of knowledge in general); a line of class division within knowledge in general; a break produced by the pedagogical function as a technical expression of the division of labour; and, finally, hinting at revolution: 'It is no accident that a reactionary bourgeois or "technocratic" government prefers half-knowledge in all things, and that, on the contrary, the revolutionary cause is always indissolubly linked with knowledge, in other words *science*'.[41]

Rancière, in the text I have already quoted from, writes some scathing lines on this topic:

> Speaking in their name, defending their authority, Althusser quite naturally adopts the class position expressed in revisionist ideology – that of the labour aristocracy and the cadres. ... At this point, the Althusserian theory of ideology functions as the theory of an imaginary class struggle to the profit of a real class collaboration, that of revisionism. The transformation of Marxism into opportunism is complete.[42]

---

40 Althusser 1964, pp. 92–3.
41 Althusser 2011, p. 15.
42 Rancière 1974, p. 37. On this matter see also Rancière 1991.

3   *'Just because we are stepping onto a train it doesn't mean we know how to drive it!'*: On the Genesis of 'Student Problems'

In a 2008 interview, Peter Hallward asked Rancière if the ENS *normaliennes* who were involved in the theoretical formulations of the *Cahiers pour l'Analyse* had reinforced the distinction between theory and practice by doing so. This is a distinction that not only runs parallel to that between the ENS and the University but, above all, to a gesture of appropriation of the former with respect to the latter. Hallward's question, of course, is only tangential to my inquiry. However, I am particularly interested in Rancière's answer:

> In the UEC circle at the ENS there were very active people and at the Sorbonne there were students who were very committed to theory, in particular the philosophy group. In *La Leçon d'Althusser* I talk a little about these students, who were very active, who criticized Bourdieu when he came to the École, etc., and wanted to promote collective forms of work. *They were critical of the organization of knowledge, they anticipated many of the questions that emerged in 68.* And Althusser intervened to denounce this 'ideological' drift amongst the young in the most violent terms. He insisted on the fact that the students were there to learn, to acquire the science that would deliver them from their petit-bourgeois ideology. It is science that must direct politics, etc.; the legacy of this insistence is the article Althusser wrote against the students at the end of 1963.[43]

Three theses can be extracted from this important passage:
1.   'Student Problems' represents the theoretical peak of both a historical (1963 anticipates many of the issues of 1968) and a political (i.e., critical promotion) conjuncture.
2.   Such a conjuncture, based on a desire to reorganise the techniques of the transmission of knowledge, concerned the theoretical (or ideological) formulation of collective intellectual labour practices.
3.   Both the formulation and the theses of 'Student Problems' are based on a preliminary division (from the Althusserian point of view) between theoretical and political practice. Thus, the 'ideological' aspect of student formulations would be determined (again, from the Althusserian point of view) by an inversion of the relationship between theory and politics (triggering an affirmative circularity that would allow students to produce

---

43   Hallward and Rancière 2012, pp. 260–1.

a correct scientific theory of education, on condition that they acquire 'the science that would deliver them from their petit-bourgeois ideology' within a pedagogical function that is the opposite of what they proposed, and that can only be politically produced). In short, if it is true that 'it is science that must direct politics', then the opposite is not true since, by so doing, a scientific theory would fall into an 'ideological drift'.

It is precisely in his 1974 *Althusser's Lesson* that Rancière delves into this matter. Here is another passage that deserves to be quoted in full:

> This theoretico-political conjuncture crystallized in Althusser's intervention against the syndicalist left. Two events provoked his reaction: the student strike led by the FGEL in November 1963 whose main – and notable – slogan was, 'Sorbonne to the students', and the intervention by FGEL's secretary, Bruno Queysanne, during the inaugural lecture of Bourdieu and Passeron's seminar at the École Normale Supérieure. In Queysanne's intervention, in his questioning Bourdieu and Passeron about the political status of a sociological research project about academic learning that protracted the authoritarian division of academic labour, Althusser recognized his enemy: here was leftism, the subordination of science to politics, the aggression of illiterate politicians against researchers. In the students' questioning of the privileges of knowledge, Althusser saw the resurgence of the obscurantism of proletarian science, and against this threat there was nothing to do but state in no uncertain terms that the scientific knowledge of an object has nothing to do with its political transformation.[44]

Clearly, these two passages overlap: we find a reference to 'Student Problems', to the organisational demands of the division of intellectual labour (the slogan 'Sorbonne to the students' is merely its political elaboration), and to the stakes linked to the subordination of theoretical practice to political practice, that is, to the resurgence of bourgeois science and proletarian science as names of a *gauchist* ideological politics.

They overlap indeed, with the exception of one point that is only briefly hinted at in the interview ('[the students] criticized Bourdieu when he came to the École'). There is here a new clarification that should be examined in greater detail, which concerns the role of Bruno Queysanne.

---

44   Rancière 2011, pp. 39–40.

∴

Indeed, through analysing the relationship between Queysanne and Althusser, it will be possible both to reconstruct the genesis of 'Student Problems' and to improve our understanding of its core theoretical elements. This is what happened: in early December 1963, probably on Friday the 6th,[45] Althusser gave his introductory lecture 'Théorie et Méthode en Sciences Humaines' at the seminar organised by Bourdieu and Passeron, later published in 1965 with the title *Rapport pédagogique et communication.*[46] In summary, the central theoretical move of Althusser's intervention could be defined as *a dehumanisation of the Human Sciences* (later, talking about the relationship between Althusser and Bourdieu in the three-year period that runs from 1963–1966, we will see in more detail the move to which this strategy belongs). A narrow understanding of the Human Sciences aside (informed by their mere *status quo*, that is, regardless of the general logic underlying any factual determination), the main presupposition is that the question of their definition can only be raised within the university, as a specific region of its enunciation: 'there is a broader definition which is in search of itself, that which is inscribed in the title of the Faculty of Letters and Human Sciences'.[47] On the one hand, *Letters*, on the other, the *Human Sciences* – and it is 'the juncture of the two terms' that 'poses the problem'.[48] By raising the problem of their relationship, the university employs the former to delimit the field of application of the latter, establishing a vertical relationship. It is as if to say that the 'and' that joins together the two and makes up the name of the Faculty does not combine two qualitatively equivalent elements, but rather establishes and defines the order of the problem (and, above all, the direction of their relationship): the Faculty 'considers that the Human Sciences must cover the field of what used to be called Letters'.[49] How? By questioning and rejecting the implicit categories of that domain. This, structured by *rhetoric* – which, in producing literary objects (it is a 'knowing how to speak' and a 'being able to appreciate those who speak'), is a technique for consumption and reproduction (knowing how to understand and to appreciate those who speak is the condition for being able to reproduce literary objects, and to be able to speak) – is essentially dominated by aesthetic, ethical, and religious categories:[50]

---

45   As indicated in a letter from Althusser to Queysanne, to which I will refer below.
46   Bourdieu, Passeron, and de Saint-Martin 1965.
47   ALT2. A40-03.01, pp. 1–2.
48   ALT2. A40-03.01, p. 2.
49   ALT2. A40-03.01, p. 2.
50   ALT2. A40-03.01, p. 4.

It is quite obvious that works of art are conceived as a means of aesthetic enjoyment – it is their beauty that interests us – and are equally received, if you like, as a lesson in practical morality ... When Montaigne reads Plutarch, he simply compares the life experience of a man with his own experience, and he compares it, and then he draws an equation from it: that's the *Essays*. ... So, it is at once dominated by aesthetics, by morality, and by religion – which is a form of morality, indeed it is the form in which morality presented itself during a very long period of human history.[51]

Here Althusser questions aesthetic, ethical, and religious categories. In other words, he rejects rhetorical production and reproduction as a structure that, albeit partially, covers the production 'by man in his human activity as a man'[52] (this is, essentially, the Faculty of Letters): a negation of humanistic categories (*les Humanités*) that defines the type of relationship presupposed by the components of the name Letters and Human Sciences. To dehumanise the Human Sciences, to remove the human from that which is human is ultimately *to do* science. The Human Sciences, then, must make the domain of Letters scientific ('You can see that this is not science at all'[53]). And the problem posed by the name of the Faculty – clearly, the act of posing the problem *already* opens the space for a structured conflict – concerns, again, the (scientific) subsumption of those specific categories: 'these Humanities, these Letters, become Human Sciences, become a science',[54] or again, 'this is the project which is at work in the simple expression: Human Sciences, in the expression Faculty of Letters and Human Sciences'.[55] In short: 'Someone who, today, wants to make a science of culture ... would obviously and *a priori* be obliged to renounce these categories, that is to say that he would be obliged to question all the implicit categories that dominate this domain'.[56]

Hence sociology, if it wants to belong to the Human Sciences (and it *must* do so on the basis of a programme),[57] must *turn itself* into a science (Althusser's talk was meant to be a self-contained intervention, as shown by the lines of continuity with 'Philosophie et sciences humaines', from July 1963 – after all, it was

---

51   ALT2. A40-03.01, pp. 5–6.
52   ALT2. A40-03.01, p. 3.
53   ALT2. A40-03.01, p. 6.
54   ALT2. A40-03.01, p. 7.
55   ALT2. A40-03.01, p. 8.
56   ALT2. A40-03.01, p. 6.
57   'The programme has not yet been completed, it has only just begun to be completed and there is still a huge area to cover'. ALT2. A40-03.01, p. 10.

the opening of a seminar organised by two sociologists). Sociology must occupy this position and contribute 'to cover[ing] the old domain which used to be called Letters-Humanities'.[58] It must turn itself into a science on the basis of its generalised definition (starting from the definition of what a science is) and the overcoming of its real determinations, whether they concern an 'abstract and general theory', or an 'ethnology' or an 'empirical sociology'.[59] That is to say, it must overcome its *de facto* status: 'if we compare this idea of a science to the current state of sociology, we immediately realise that there is no adequacy',[60] with the exception of Bourdieu and Passeron, who Althusser places precisely among those 'who today want to make a science of culture'.[61]

For our purposes, this Althusserian thesis is already extremely interesting. Could this intervention represent a preliminary and programmatic version – a *Théorie* and a *Méthode* – of a new conflict of the Faculties after the one inaugurated by Kant? (It is no coincidence that Althusser himself, in addition to using this definition, considers the Faculties of Law and Medicine as dealing with all those objects that can be properly considered human products).[62] Should we not consider this a real re-actualisation of the conflict of Faculties, based on the theoretical assumption contained in 'Student Problems' that through technical mechanisms of scientific validation, the university still represents the place of transmission of non-ideological objects (thus making 'Student Problems', so to speak, the pragmatic side of the questioning of humanistic – and therefore ideological – categories that is articulated in 'Théorie et Méthode en Sciences Humaines')? In virtue of this re-actualisation, and on the basis of the double division of labour in general, could we not define Kant as an Althusserian *ante-litteram* (qualifying the conflict as anti-ideological; we could ask whether the technical and social division of university labour can be made to correspond to the Kantian division between *lower* and *higher* faculties) and Althusser as a Marxist Kantian (considering his thought as a re-actualisation of Kantian theoretical stakes – *to construct an ethics for the unity of knowledge* – and of its systematic disposition)? In fact, was it not Kant himself who, *before* Althusser and *with* Althusser, structured the university by means of a topology of knowledge (what else is conflict, if not a localized conflict)? And is it not

---

58 ALT2. A40-03.01, p. 10.

59 Cf. ALT2. A40-03.01, p. 11.

60 ALT2. A40-03.01, p. 28.

61 ALT2. A40-03.01, p. 6.

62 'Obviously there are other human productions which do not belong to the Faculty of Letters, but which are still human, namely, Law which belongs to the Faculty of Law, Medicine which belongs to the Faculty of Medicine' ALT2. A40-03.01, p. 3.

Althusser who, *after* Kant and *with* Kant, showed that within the university knowledge is transmitted through the categories of the division of labour in general?[63]

Whatever our assessment of the theoretical relationship between Althusser and Kant on the problem of the university, the historically relevant point lies elsewhere. Althusser was attacked by Bruno Queysanne who, in a letter dated 8 December 1963, criticised both the didactical form and the theoretical 'lightness' of his *première séance* of the seminar in which he participated, invited by Althusser himself. It is when attending this lecture, moreover, that Queysanne attacked Bourdieu and Passeron on the authoritarian form of their teaching, which they employed 'in its most sophisticated form'.[64]

Althusser's intervention also provoked a discussion among the students in the seminar, as shown by references to the critique of the universalist attitude of ethnography (the 'particular nature of the primitive society would authorise Mauss to speak of any social fact as a total social fact, the whole being entirely present in the part'),[65] documented in the account of the questions raised by Althusser during the 10 January 1964 seminar, in turn prompted by some observations made by Godelier and Milner.[66]

---

63   'Whoever it was that first hit on the notion of a university and proposed that a public institution of this kind be established, it was not a bad idea to handle the entire content of learning (really, the thinkers devoted to it) by mass production, so to speak'. Kant 1979, p. 23. For a precise historiographical reconstruction of the Kantian text, see Landolfi Petrone 1997. For a theoretical analysis of the same work, see Bertani and Pranteda 2003.

64   Cf. Queysanne's letter, cited below.

65   ALT2. A40-03.04, p. 2.

66   Godelier and Milner's observations can be summed up with the question: 'Is it not necessary to relate to their real conditions of validity a certain number of concepts which one would risk using [outside these precise conditions] in other different conditions, without asking oneself whether, as the conditions change, the validity of these concepts is also affected? This question raises the problem of the relationship of ethnology to its original object (primitive societies) on the one hand, and the problem of the validity of the ethnological approach and of ethnological concepts – or of concepts inspired by ethnology – outside their original domain, and in particular in modern societies, on the other', Ibid., 1. An impossible transposition, that of ethnological categories from the field of primitive societies to that of modern society; an impossibility that invalidates the very epistemological structure of ethnology which, despite having the advantage of producing theories within the 'thing which it analyses' (ALT2. A40-03.01, p. 14), would refer, for modern societies, to a false concept of totality. Hence Althusser's critique of ethnographic universalism (of the universalism of 'everything in the part'): 'In this case one can no longer think of the general essence of the social whole through only one of its parts, none of its parts being, in the strict sense, *"pars totalis"*, for if the totality has not disappeared, it is the structure of the totality that has changed radically', ALT2. A40-03.04, p. 3.

On 8 December 1963, Queysanne writes a critical letter to Althusser. In reply-
ing, Althusser writes two different letters: one private, the other public. The
private letter is dated 11 December 1963. The other, an undated open letter, was
probably written in December 1963 (as further testified to by some references
contained in J.-P. Milbergue's own open letter, written in the same month). To
put it starkly, the private letter is an extended, and theoretically stronger, version of the open one.

As mentioned, J.-P. Milbergue also joined in the debate, and responded to
Althusser's open letter with his own, titled 'Réponse à la lettre adressée récem-
ment par Althusser à Queysanne'[67] (an extended version of which was later
published, in 1965, in *Les Temps Modernes*, with the title 'La signification politique des relts pédagogiques dans l'Université française'). Georges Lapassade
also wrote his own response to Althusser in an open letter dated 13 January
1964 and,[68] most importantly, with a polemical text titled 'Eloge du révisionnisme: À propos de la lettre d'Althusser à Queysanne, et des problèmes posés
par le travail du C.E.R.S'.[69] Let us take a closer look at Queysanne's letter.

> Dear comrade, or dear master, or sir – I don't really know how to consider
> myself anymore and, as Bourdieu said, the logic of the discourse requires
> a beginning, and the first step can very well be arbitrary.
>
> Dear comrade, I am writing to you to clarify my position regarding your
> seminar, to which you were kind enough to invite me. I went there expect-
> ing a research group. In the background there was this idea of 'the first
> year of sociology', so I thought that the working methods would not be
> traditional ones. Moreover, I was strongly motivated since the proposed
> subject concerned the University, which is our primary concern at the
> UNEF and at the UEC. But when I saw the layout of the room, the num-
> ber of participants, and the casual treatment you gave to methodological
> principles, I was shocked! (ENS students who know me well will tell you
> how much I am conditioned by affective considerations). When Bour-
> dieu and Passeron started their duet [XXX], otherwise called 'ideal genesis
> of their research' or 'pedagogical experience in a laboratory', I wondered
> where we were going, and what we wanted to accomplish. But when, in
> the end, they took on the garb of the teacher who dictates the subject
> to be discussed next, and who assigns reports to do, their kindness and
> the camaraderie with which they organised the work of others appeared

---

67   Cf. ALT2. A40-04.03 (D).
68   Cf. ALT2. A40-04.03 (C).
69   Coll. *La contemporaine*, 4Delta 1183/8.

to me as a most refined form of classical authoritarianism. We were not heading towards any novel terrain ...

Hence my cries, my concept-borborygmi [*concepts-borborigmes*], and my anger at the end – all the more violent because I felt that it wasn't shared by the others. And my grave tactical mistake. The one that consisted, as you saw very well, in presenting myself as a rival 'master'. In other words, by taking the role of the critic of the University as opposed to the three of you, who were its avowed representatives (more or less, at that time ...), I validated the University/non-University dialectic. Accepting this dialectic in these terms did not mean leaving the University: it only meant defending the son against the father while remaining within the same family structure. It would have been enough for me to pronounce the word of 'collective researcher' [*chercheur collectif*] in opposition to that of 'research master' [*maitre de recherche*] that I denounced. Then my criticism of the master would have appeared to target the model of the master, and not just the three of you. And, even at this first stage of my critical approach, I would not have appeared as a negativist. The next time I'll do better.

I also made another mistake. That of taking your theoretical introduction seriously. And my criticism was as superficial as your presentation. But this does not prevent me from telling you:

– that it is not enough for me to know that you think of 'justifying for twenty hours' the didactic exposition of your thought. Already in your article on materialist dialectics I did not understand the meaning of your axiomatics of production (GI, GII, GIII). I did not understand the analogy between conceptual labour and economic labour. I did not understand this unitary, Cartesian way of speaking about science. Also, for now I question the value of your justification insofar as it does not [xxx] the presentation [*expose*] that you make of it. (In particular I did not recognise your critical approach in your description of ethnology. But perhaps I have no sense of humour).

– that you thought it was appropriate to begin with a theoretical presentation of the task to be fulfilled. Even if you didn't take this presentation seriously, it seems to me to be indicative of the importance that is to be granted to the reflection on the method of method, in other words on the conditions of possibility of theoretical research about the human sciences, that is to say the understanding of a theory by means of a provisional method invested in a research project on the University. Now it seems to me that the very articulation of this problem was passed over in silence during the first session. The method of research was not critically presented. It only appeared as a 'work plan' [Which may well be modified by the students, if they can (*dixit* Passeron)!!!].

You were stressing the importance of asking the right questions, but the questions you were asking, or the ones that Bourdieu and Passeron asked in their 'ideal genesis of their research', were immediately presented as the right ones. In other words, we are witnessing a rigged intellectual psychodrama, because everything seems to have been heard beforehand. The research project that is being proposed to us is nothing but a travesty. And I am not willing to play this game.

So, tell me what my game is. This is precisely the answer I don't want to give. For that would mean accepting the status of master. (Although there's at least one 'participant' in the seminar who has proposed that, next to the Althusser-Bourdieu-Passeron seminar, there should also be a Queysanne seminar!). My game could not possibly be a university game, with masters and students. This relation seems to be undesirable even at the level of a classic research project, and it is certainly out of place in the context of a research project that presents itself, from the beginning, as non-classical. But is the Althusser seminar a non-classical research seminar? I ask myself this question, and I don't think I can presently answer it. The act itself of inviting non-normalist militants [*militants non-normaliens*] is non-classical, but not admitting to having done so is very classical. The atmosphere of the seminar is that of a research group, but it has the structure of traditional teaching. So, I am entitled to wonder if the Althusser seminar isn't simply structured as classical teaching.

I think that to answer this question in the seminar itself, with the participation of all its members, would be the first step towards a seminar as I understand it.

The second step would be to determine whether only the masters and their 'chosen' disciples (e.g., Walter) are to be researchers, or whether the seminar as a whole is to share the task of research.

The third step will be taken when the field of research has been explicitly and collectively determined. Will it be for the lecturers [*maitre-chercheurs*] the seminar participants considered (or constituted?) as a representative sample of the School? Or will it be for the seminar-researcher-collective [*séminaire-chercheur-collectif*] the whole of the School, that is to say, itself and all that constituted the reality of the École Normale Supérieure in 1963–64?

This third step implies the choice of the university-object, and that the method and theory of inquiry on this object will be constituted on the way.

The fourth step would be a reflection on the first three steps and the updating of the principle – so far still implicit – that a reflection on the sociology of the University cannot be carried out by academics as such. In other words, a seminar on the sociology of the university that questions its own structure would have at least one uncritical element in its approach And, therefore, it could not be carried through to the end. But I thought that this was your project. You will thus understand my violent surprise when, during last Friday's session, I saw the seminar take a non-critical path. See you soon, certainly next Friday. Be sure of my militant friendship.

Bruno Queysanne[70]

Clearly, Queysanne's argument in this letter revolves around a critique of the division of university labour. He offers an explicit critique, with regard to the posture of Bourdieu and Passeron ('their kindness and the camaraderie with which they organised the work of others appeared to me as a most refined form of classical authoritarianism'), as well as a self-critique targeting his self-inclusion in university dialectics ('Accepting this dialectic in these terms did not mean leaving the University: it only meant defending the son against the father while remaining within the same family structure'). But he also puts forward a theoretical critique, through the identification of four steps leading to a definition of 'a seminar as I understand it' (which will lead to an analysis that cannot be conducted by 'academics as such').

Far from considering Queysanne's thesis as a viable theoretical option, the radicality of the Althusserian response, dated 11 December, consists in *neutralising it on the level of its very elaboration*, by presupposing a division between theoretical and political practice, their relationship of separation and mutual presupposition: 'Think what you like, but in Marxist theory, truth is essential to any political action: scientific truth, which is the only rigorous and authentic form of knowledge'. In making use of 'On the Materialist Dialectics' – which, as Althusser constantly repeats in both versions of the letter, evidently represents the theoretical presupposition of his thesis – he offers a sort of *Organon* against the 'the sophistry of the university'. It is here that, far from being inessential, Queysanne's claim turns out to be very significant: 'Already in your article on materialist dialectics I did not understand the meaning of your axiomatics of production (GI, GII, GIII)'.[71]

---

70   ALT2. A40-04.03 (B).
71   ALT2. A40-04.03 (A), p. 7.

Although seemingly straightforward, Althusser's thesis, as he reveals it in his private letter to Queysanne, is actually quite complex. It can be broken down into six points:

1. Queysanne, disregarding the division between practices – that is, lacking a Theory[72] (which makes him, essentially, an anti-dialectic materialist) – betrays an erroneous conception of theoretical practice: 'your idea of science and scientific research does not correspond to reality'.[73] More precisely, instead of analysing the general conditions of objectivity of scientific research (to work on ideological generalities with 'theoretical' generalities in order to produce scientific generalities), Queysanne considers as constitutive *the very forms* that structure research, although these, as we have already seen, are not to be considered indifferent. However, in relation to the object that, in a *conditioned* relationship, is in a dominant position, they are also *necessary* for the validation process.

2. Queysanne's reformulation of the division of intellectual labour is to be understood as a consequence of this theoretical lack, which can therefore classifiable as ideological (*gauchiste*: 'your *idea* of science in the domain of the Humanities ... is basically grounded on the identification of the theoretical practice of a sociological or historical science with a political practice').[74] This, in other words, is tantamount to saying that the forms within which a research is carried out constitute the *conditions of impossibility* of the search for its general conditions of objectivity (in an ideological domain, that is: to misuse the university – to make an *immediately* political use of it – implies badmouthing the university, because it assumes a *mediated* theoretical standpoint).

3. Scientific practice, which only pertains to generalities, is exercised in solitude: 'my "research", which, in order to simply exist, had to be exercised *in the very forms of solitude*, of "individualism" as you say a bit carelessly (Marx was alone when he wrote *Capital* and Lenin was alone when he wrote *Mat*[erialism] and *Emp*[irico-criticism]: not just theoretically *alone*, complete "individualism", but worst of all *politically alone*, absolutely alone)'.[75]

---

72 Obviously, I am referring to the definition of Theory given by Althusser in Althusser 2005, p. 168: 'I shall call Theory (with a capital T), general theory, that is, the Theory of practice in general'.

73 ALT2. A40-04.03 (A), p. 3.

74 ALT2. A40-04.03 (A), p. 5.

75 ALT2. A40-04.03 (A), p. 6.

4. Following the third point, scientific practice shows how the university, as an object of research, is the place of the vertical transmission of generalities. It is precisely here that Althusser's letter represents a 'proto-' version of 'Student Problems', but with a caveat: he explains how 'people of all ages can meet, sometimes, inside the University (it provides the premises and the electricity, but not yet, alas, the soviets! for they will come from elsewhere, if they will ever come) and more often outside: some to teach what they know about Lenin, and others to learn what the former know. This pedagogical situation – fortunately! – goes far beyond the University'.[76] The pedagogical situation, the relationship between those who know and those who do not, goes beyond the university situation: 'Knowledge and ignorance are categories that (fortunately!) go far beyond the University'.[77] That is to say, the definition of the university itself, by removing the specificity of a discourse that is posited as immediate, strips away the halo of mystique around the university seen as an original place. It is as if for Althusser, the university at first limited itself to organising a situation that overcomes it and therefore precedes its existence. This is an organisation, however, that far from being ineffective, somehow also places the university in an utterly irreducible position with respect to formally equivalent situations: its structuring – responding to a technical division of scientific validation and to the establishment of a specific discourse, like that on the political conjuncture – *takes place, so to speak, after everything else. The university has a beginning but not an Origin.*

5. The university is *both the subject and the object of generality*. As an object, it is a generality of theoretical practice (the pedagogical function is the product of theoretical research); as a subject, it is the place of the transmission of generalities (based on the specificity of the pedagogical function produced by theoretical practice).

6. Thus, compared to other generalities, the university has, so to speak, a rather unique position. If the university is the place of the transmission of generalities and if, on the other hand, it can itself be subjected to the

---

76 ALT2. A40-04.03 (A), p. 4.

77 Ibid. According to Queysanne, Bourdieu and Passeron simply repeat, in most refined ways, the forms of intellectual authoritarianism. Althusser, therefore, can only defend them on the basis of this point: 'B. and P. are there. And that's why they do this course: to teach the students what they've discovered. (and some of the professors we invited, some of the sociologists who were in the room the other day and you're a "student" when you've learned something from someone, whatever the age ratio). That's it'.

labour of theoretical practice (that is, it can itself be a generality) then it – *qua* subject – represents the place of its own (*qua* object) technical explication (a reflective circularity for *which the pedagogical function is said while being practiced*).

This singularity is suggested by Althusser himself in his open letter: 'the teacher formulates the theory of the pedagogical situation, of the necessity of the pedagogical situation, and exposes it to those who are subjected to this situation, i.e., himself and his students'.[78] This is an important clarification: the teacher, in addition to being involved in an unequal relationship (he is among those 'who are subjected to this situation'), is also *the theoretical subject of his or her own enunciation* (the one who theoretically demonstrates its 'necessity'). And the teacher takes on the role of subject of enunciation due to *his or her being a teacher, due to his or her involvement in this unequal relationship that, theoretically produced in the forms of individuality, places him or her in a position of superiority*. According to an affirmative circularity, it is the teacher who states his or her position, and this can only be stated by a teacher. He or she is present in what he or she states, and what he or she states is present within him or her. The teacher justifies his or her position, and only he or she can do so, merely by performing his or her function.

This can then be stated in a seventh and final point, which follows from the previous ones. In a way, this is the only *genuinely* political point (it implies a theoretical justification of the relations of force on the basis of these very relations and *vice versa*):

7.   The teacher is *both subject and object of the pedagogical function*. As an object, he is the *active part* of a situation that, structured as a relationship of inequality, subdues him or her along with his or her subjects. As a subject is the *subject of enunciation*, since the pedagogical function has a vertical structure with respect to knowledge and this determines, knowledge being an object, the subject's position of superiority. This can only be stated through a tautology: 'The teacher is responsible [for the theory of the pedagogical function] as a function of the division of roles in the pedagogical situation, i.e., in the pedagogical situation the teacher is a teacher because he is *ahead of the game* in terms of knowledge'.[79] Ultimately this means that *the roles are always justified from within the division of roles itself*. This is a circular definition where, in this specific case, *the need for the teacher's role is stated as the teacher practices this role, made*

---

78   872ALT/142/6, p. 5.
79   872ALT/142/6, p. 5 (first italics added by me).

theoretically necessary by the teacher: 'I have *never* met ... *any student who was theoretically* or scientifically able to formulate this theory of the pedagogical situation'.[80] And this is because, once again, the student, like the professor, is involved in the same tautological circularity, albeit *from the opposite direction*. The student cannot formulate a theory of the pedagogical situation precisely because he or she is a student, and if she or he were able to formulate it that would mean that 'that as far as knowledge is concerned he is already capable of being a teacher although, from the administrative point of view, she is not yet part of the teaching staff'.[81]

In his open letter, Althusser again identifies the flaw that, in his opinion, undermines Queysanne's critique. As should be expected, he points to a confusion between theoretical and political practice, although these may involve the same object:

> In this respect I am *absolutely categorical*, so listen carefully. Scientific (or theoretical, i.e., research) practice on the following object – the structure of the University (in all its implications) – cannot in any case, on pain of a very serious theoretical and political fault, be confused for even a single moment with any other form of practice on the same object, in particular that of a trade union, or an ideological/political practice of transformation of this concrete object.[82]

Once again, for Althusser this division represents the necessary condition for the elaboration of a theory: the condition for the correct positioning in front of an object, which can be object of different practices. Ultimately, Queysanne, in addition to producing a false scientific theory (i.e., an ideological theory: he notes that formulations about the pedagogical situation of the UNEF and the EUC which, although 'brilliant ... are not scientific ... [and] are not really coherent except at the level of ideology, in the Marxist sense of the term')[83] also promotes, *for this very reason*, an *unfounded politics* (because it lacks a theoretical foundation: as we read at the conclusion of Althusser's private letter, 'a politics, even an enthusiastic and a deeply lived one, which is based on errors ... will be doomed to some spectacular successes but ultimately to a deep failure').[84]

---

80   872ALT/142/6, p. 6.
81   872ALT/142/6, p. 5.
82   872ALT/142/6, p. 8.
83   872ALT/142/6, p. 6.
84   ALT2. A40-04.03 (A), p. 7.

Therefore, it is in Althusser's open letter that a theory of the university structure is given a stronger theoretical form, almost fully formalised if compared to
the general indication about those who know and those who do not, which
is contained in the private version. This is a formulation that, and this is crucial, 'plays' with categories that have a direct link with those that a month
later, in January 1964, will again be mobilised in 'Student Problems'. Here, with
respect to the modal qualification of the technical division, Althusser, as we
have seen, writes: 'the pedagogic situation is based on the absolute condition
of an *inequality between knowledge and the lack of knowledge*'.[85] This, then, is
how Althusser formulates the point in his private letter to Queysanne:

> This *situation*, the only situation on which the search for valid forms of a
> *pedagogy* can be based, is an academic situation, you will say. Yes, if we get
> rid of all the rest (which is a lot), it is the only authentic truth that exists
> in any pedagogical enterprise: the objective distance between *knowledge*
> [*savoir*] and *non-knowledge* [*non-encore-savoir*]. Pedagogy – pedagogical
> practice – must begin from this distance in order to *reduce it*, and it can-
> not be considered as already reduced at the beginning![86]

As in 'Student Problems', the pedagogical situation is presented as explicitly
containing a relationship of inequality, characterised by an objective distance.
In the open letter, Althusser more precisely identifies three modes of transmission, thus articulating what can in fact be defined as a 'theory of transmission
(scientific, pedagogical or ideological)'.

In the first mode, the transmission takes place in a situation of (scientific)
equality. Here, the emphasis is placed in the first instance on the scientific qualification of the transmitted object and, only by virtue of the possession of this
object, on the subjects of the transmission (on their disposition). The equality of the subjects of the transmission is therefore *conditioned*, in formal terms,
by the transmitted object (equality is, so to speak, a necessary effect determined by the position of the object of knowledge). For this reason, this mode of
transmission could be defined as a *scientific situation of substantial equality*, its
substantiality being determined by the scientific nature of the *content* of the
situation (the form of equality is conditioned, its content is unconditioned).
Althusser writes:

---

85   Althusser 2011, p. 14.
86   872ALT/142/6, pp. 2–3.

> You should know that in scientific matters what constitutes a scientific
> discussion (and not a pedagogical dialogue) is a certain equality of know-
> ledge between the interlocutors: they have in common what can be called
> the "state of the question" regarding that particular science.[87]

In the second mode, the transmission takes place in a situation of (pedagogical)
inequality. Here, the emphasis is placed, in the first instance, on the scientific
qualification of the object transmitted and, only by virtue of the scientific
nature of this object, on the specific technique of its validation (the object, once
again, is placed in a dominant position, while the technique of its transmission
in a necessary and conditioned one). For this reason, this mode of transmission
could be defined as *a pedagogical situation of substantial inequality*, where the
substance of this inequality is determined by the scientific nature of the *content* of the situation (the form of inequality is conditional, its content unconditional). It is verticality in the face of knowledge that, in this transmission,
determines its placement in a pedagogical situation rather than a scientific one,
as if to say that, although the transmitted object is qualitatively equivalent to
that transmitted in a situation of substantial equality, it conditions the terms of
its transmission – and, therefore, the subjects of the situation – in a completely
different way. Althusser writes:

> If, indeed, there is too great a (provisional) *inequality of knowledge* be-
> tween the participants, that is not science, but pedagogy; and those who,
> being in a pedagogical situation, want to believe that they are in a 'sci-
> entific' situation are either playing with the situation ... or are being
> played by the situation, or again are fooled by their illusions.[88]

In the last mode, the transmission takes place in a situation of (ideological)
equality. What differentiates this from the first modality is that the emphasis
here is placed, in the first instance, on the subjects of the transmission (i.e.,
on their configuration) and, only by virtue of their division of labour, on the
(not scientific) qualification of the transmitted object. This is precisely what
Althusser means, as we mentioned before, when he objects that Queysanne
considers 'the forms in which it [scientific practice] is exercised as *constitutive*' – the forms, far from defining the general conditions of theoretical objectivity, are the 'forms of organisation, exchange, etc. ... in short forms of "parti-

---

87   872ALT/142/6, p. 3.
88   872ALT/142/6, p. 3.

cipation" between researchers'.[89] Hence, this mode of transmission could be defined as an *ideological situation of formal equality*, where the formality of the situation is determined by the indifference relative to the transmitted object or – and this is entirely equivalent – by the merely formal priority that the subjective disposition has over the object of knowledge (the form of equality is unconditioned, the content is conditioned). Althusser writes:

> [There is] another situation, where the condition of a scientific discussion is *formally* realised – *the equality between the knowledge of the participants* – in the case where the participants are roughly of the *same level of knowledge*: [this is a] condition, which, if it is not more rigorously defined (this shared level of knowledge must be the current scientific level: the current scientific consensus, and not of an *outdated* state) can also cover therefore, apparently, and illegitimately justify the following factual situation: there can also exist an equality of knowledge that is simply an *equality in non-knowledge*, either a partial ignorance, or a 'knowledge' that takes itself for knowledge, while being mere ideology.[90]

The abstract symmetry between scientific transmission and ideological transmission (because it is determined by a different relationship between form and content) can therefore be further specified as follows: the form of transmission is ideological if – the object of knowledge being indifferent – it is the product of a political practice that declares the pre-eminence of the form of transmission. It is pedagogical if, giving priority to the object, it is the 'transcendental' instance of a scientific validation. Finally, it is scientific if, based on the preliminary identification of an object placed on the 'current state of the question', it is the consequential instance of a scientific transmission.

This means that the situation that is hidden or mistakenly understood (because it is 'a knowledge that takes itself for knowledge') by the ideological situation of formal equality requires, in order to be resolved, reference to the substantiality of a pedagogical situation. In order that it can reach, at best, the substantiality of a scientific situation pedagogical practice must in fact start from an objective 'provisional' distance, only to then 'reduce it'.

This entire argument can be summarised by the following thesis: *the illusion of formal (ideological) equality must be replaced by substantial (pedagogical) inequality, eventually leading to substantial (scientific) equality.*

---

89   872ALT/142/6, pp. 1–2.
90   872ALT/142/6, pp. 3–4.

In conclusion, therefore, we can see that Rancière's ideas we examined at the beginning of the section have been confirmed.

Indeed, 'Student Problems' is a theoretical construction motivated by a historical conjuncture that called for a political redefinition of the relations of intellectual labour. Presupposing the division between theoretical and political practice, this text is the product of the former relating to an object that can also be examined by the latter. It is a product in which the 'technical division' and the 'social division' – which, as we have seen, are theoretical principles defined by the 'knowledge of Marxist-Leninist scientific theory'[91] – represent nothing more than the theoretical emergence of a theoretical practice. This is what the epigraph of the essay declares: 'the following text has no other objective than to define as precisely as possible the theoretical bases on which the analysis of students' own problems can be developed'.[92]

4   Knowledge as a Commodity: André Gorz on the Contradictions within (Academic) Capital

In the closing lines of his open letter, Althusser indicates what kind of relationship the communist students of the UEC *should* have with those of the national student association (UNEF), to which the former belong. Here it is not a question of reactivating historical relations of force that are irrelevant, but rather of highlighting the return and, above all, the developments of theoretical claims that have been operational in the past. Indeed, UEC members *should*, as Marxists, be responsible for the elaboration of the theoretical grounds for UNEF students, in order to guide its party line in a relationship that, as Althusser will say in 'Student Problems', follows 'the relations that the Party (or a communist organisation) should have with an organisation for economic struggle (the union)'.[93] The conditional tense must be used. In fact, as we learned from Althusser's reply to Queysanne, that is not how things happen:

> To be honest with you, I believe that the theoretical error that you make – confusing the theoretical practice of a science with other practices (including the political practice based on this science) – is at the heart of the theoretical errors implied in the current ideology of the UNEF, and in

91   Althusser 1964, p. 80.
92   Ibid.
93   Althusser 1964, p. 104.

the 'theory' that the comrades of the UEC put, in fact, at its service. Yes, I say at the service of the ideological errors of the UNEF itself (which to my knowledge has, if I dare say, well the right to be mistaken, since the theory of the UNEF is not the Marxism).[94]

Since the division of practices is a Marxist thesis or, which amounts to the same thing, since the politics that is implied by the relation of their distinction and presupposition is a Marxist one, a UNEF militant can be forgiven an ideological error. But the same cannot be said of the UEC position (particularly Queysanne), precisely because as a Marxist, a UEC member should have a clear understanding of how a 'scientific technique' works. What Althusser hopes for is basically a kind of Marxist (Althusserian) 'return to the fold' of (theoretically confused) Marxist students:

> It is only natural that the UNEF is mistaken (man being by nature an ideological animal: I could develop this scientific formula in a whole book).[95] What is not 'natural' is that the UEC is mistaken about the theoretical validity of the 'theoretical' system that it objectively puts at the service of the ideology of the UNEF. Because the UEC has a scientific theory at its disposal, better, it was constituted in order to apply ... this scientific theory, it has therefore absolute duties towards this scientific theory ... *absolutely overriding* duties, I mean absolutely overriding theoretical duties, i.e., which must, for theoretical reasons – including political reasons based on this absolute theoretical priority (in the Leninist sense of the absolute primacy of theory) – *trump all other priorities*, and in particular those which are simply the consequence of an ideological following, the forms of priority that the UEC, in fact, grants to *the strategy* of the UNEF to its own ideological, economic (student salary) and 'political' objectives of the UNEF, 'the Sorbonne to the students', a totally aberrant slogan, from the point of view of the Marxist theory, but that tens of thousands of people and some hundreds Marxists could contemplate during days in the open air, floating, yes floating, like the 'floating' theory that supports this banner, and if not all the other banners of the UNEF, at least several of them, yes floating in the open air and in the open sky, i.e., *in the utopia and in the theoretical emptiness itself.*[96]

---

94   872ALT/142/6, p. 9.
95   Dedicated, perhaps, to the Ideological State Apparatuses?
96   872ALT/142/6, pp. 9–10.

The passage is quite self-explanatory. For the UEC the objective should be to reverse the trend, i.e., to find the disposition to reverse ideological relations into truly political relations. It is a question of filling a vacuum, illuminating and guiding the political path because such a path is scientifically determined. It is therefore a question of replacing ideological objectives with more urgent scientific duties, and among these (and this is the crucial point) some specific objectives should be discarded: both economic (student salary) and 'political' ones ('The Sorbonne for the students'). This question too, although appearing as a mere occasional reference, is theoretically reformulated in 'Student Problems'. It is quite useless to dwell on the latter theoretical irregularity, the deviant theory whose outcome is a 'totally aberrant slogan' (this, of course, concerns the theoretically unwarranted substitution of a situation of formal equality for a situation of substantial inequality: 'a slogan which proclaims "The Sorbonne for the students" should be examined under this precise relationship').[97]

However, it is necessary to take a brief detour regarding the former theoretical irregularity – the demand for a student salary – which will prove to have some truly surprising theoretical developments. We have just seen that a student salary is an ideological goal: the reason, for Althusser, is simple: *student labour is not immediately part of the process of capital valorisation*. And yet it is doubtlessly student labour: within the technical division of academic production, in fact, the categories of labour in general are preserved. The political vector of the union might be criticised, but not its existence. That is obvious: for if it is true that student labour is a labour-power that does not produce exchange value, it nonetheless finds its product in the '*assimilation* of an existing *knowledge*'.[98] Labour produces assimilation: we work to assimilate because labour, in the university, is synonymous with consumption (of knowledge). This is a form of consumption whose *value* is the preservation of the knowledge that is consumed (i.e., worked) according to specific abilities, determined by acquired knowledge. Academic labour, alongside learning, produces *self-valorisation* to the extent that the labour power acquires value through the assimilation of knowledge.

Does this mean that in academic production – and here we encounter a crucial theoretical implication, as we will see later – *the relation with the commodity is reversed?* In this context, labour does not produce an object to be exchanged, a commodity – i.e., knowledge – but, placed next to consumption, *already presupposes its exchange*.[99] In other words, *the structure of this mode*

---

97   Althusser 2011, p. 14.
98   Althusser 2011, p. 15.
99   Ibid.

of academic production can only be determined by presupposing the technical specificity of the pedagogical function. Indeed, it is only when starting with the formal assumption of the transmission (or exchange) of a generality (or a commodity) that it will be possible to establish an equivalence between labour and consumption (that is, one consummates an accumulation that finds in those *who* know the subjective element that, so to speak, 'doses' certain generalities with respect to accumulated knowledge). However, and this is the crucial point, it seems possible to integrate this technical specificity alongside production itself: that formal assumption is, in turn, qualified by the terms of labour, so that *the vertical pedagogical relationship between knowledge and not-yet-knowing is, ultimately, a relationship of consumption that finds its own product in the assimilation of the transmitted object, and its form of valorisation in the capacities that are engendered by its acquisition.* As a prerequisite for student assimilation and valorisation, *knowledge is a commodity.* To be precise, in the act of transmission the transmitted content (on the side of the transmitting person) is a commodity *without immediate value,* that is, its value is produced at the moment of its determined preservation (on the side of the receiver). *The valorisation of the object that presupposes the exchange occurs through its consumption and preservation.*

It is for this reason that the hypothesis of a remuneration for the student *qua* student is utterly devoid of any theoretical justification:

> In Marxist theory it is impossible to confuse the activity of assimilation and 'consumption' of knowledge, which keeps this very knowledge in the forms of skills (themselves undergoing gradual transformation to the extent that studies are continued), with social work. The concept of a 'student wage' [*salaire étudiant*] is thus without theoretical basis from a Marxist economic point of view. The student claim for remuneration must therefore be made from a completely different ground, taking into account the fact that student labour is not a social value directly producing exchange value.[100]

Of course, the knowledge acquired by the student can be exchanged within the circle of wage labour, 'for example, giving one-on-one tutorials in parallel with their studies, passing handouts, substituting for a doctor, or accepting different forms of moonlighting'. And yet, as a student, he or she is not a worker engaged in social production (i.e., he or she is not *immediately* part of the pro-

---

100   Althusser 1964, p. 105.

cess of valorisation of capital). And, as a wage worker, he or she is not a worker placed in the process of consumption of knowledge (i.e., he or she is not directly inserted in the process of valorisation of consumed knowledge): 'If he continues his studies, he performs two distinct jobs at once: a social kind of work, which produces exchange value (paid one-to-one lessons), and his work as a student, an activity of assimilation of knowledge.'[101] In short, 'the students' union (the UNEF) has a special feature dictated by the fact that students are not engaged in the direct process of production'.[102] Students are only *mediately* (or *indirectly*) engaged in the *mediated* or *indirect* process of social production, by means of those capacities they have *already* (*directly*) acquired through consumption and assimilation.

All of this is clear, except that the union could fall into a 'temptation' dictated by its particular status. Such a temptation is ultimately caused by the non-immediacy of the process of social production. This temptation pertains to a certain kind of investment: an *intellectual investment*. The capitalist regime, as if to superimpose the *mediated* nature of assimilated capacities and the *immediacy* of its social valorisation, has to conceive the assimilation of knowledge as *already* remunerable, 'having to ensure the high qualification of the labour power of future cadres in the social process of production'.[103] Academic consumption is already remunerable because, in the process of social production, the skills that are preserved are precisely those of the socialised labour power. In other words, the union has a temptation to view academic labour as remunerable because it is *socialisable* (*although not already socialised*), since any kind of socialised labour presupposes the academic labour of preservation of qualified skills. The union has 'therefore considered claiming student remuneration that would be included in the investment, or that would be based on the spread of the global wage, which is currently received *only over the course of a productive lifetime*'.[104]

This theory would be correct if it did not abstract from two fundamental (and co-dependent) conditions. The first pertains to the inability (or rather, disinterest) of capitalism in planning the recruitment of labour power (thus breaking the connection between the assimilation of knowledge and its investment in the forms of its valorisation). The second condition, quite simply, is that 'the capitalist regime, in the current state of university organisation ...

101 Ibid.
102 Althusser 1964, p. 104.
103 Althusser 1964, p. 105.
104 Ibid.

shows no need for this measure at all'.[105] This is linked to the students' social origin: only those with enough economic resources can gain access to the status quo of the university (and, according to Bourdieu, those who do gain this access lack the syntactic resources to continue their studies in the field of cultural reproduction). This is an 'economic situation in which family resources, personal expedients (moonlighting) and a few dozen thousand grants, roughly ensure the subsistence of students in the course of their studies'.[106] Capitalism welcomes this mode of (class) recruitment: 'the students' class origins and the current economic capitalist policy meet in this economically satisfactory *status quo* for the current capitalist regime of unremunerated student activity'.[107]

We already noted that for Althusser the political orientation of the union can be criticised, but not its existence. If these factual conditions make the issue of remuneration redundant, it is then necessary to modify the union's strategy, or in other words to intervene into the material process of class recruitment, rather than for the remuneration of those who have already been recruited due to their social origin: 'The students' union will then come to the conclusion that their demands must especially take into account ... the class conditions of the current recruitment of students at the University';[108] or again, 'the basic economic demand of the students ... must take the form of a demand for a school allowance distributed according to family income'.[109] Given capitalism's complacency towards the current state of (bourgeois) university organisation, remuneration is taken away (because it is ineffective on the basis of a *de facto* state of things) and an incentive is introduced to compensate for social inequality (as if this could change the relations of production within capital).

This is where the detour I have undertaken requires further analysis. A short 1965 essay by André Gorz (considered by many as the main ideologue of the UNEF), significantly titled 'Students and Workers' and later published in the collection of essays *Socialism and Revolution* [1967] (1973), provides us with an extremely valuable theoretical reference point.

Gorz's thesis is the absolute antithesis of Althusser's, and it can be stated by starting from an empirical premise, which is presented as axiomatic:

> During the past twenty years the development of the forces of production in the advanced capitalist economies has led to an accelerating qualitat-

---

105   Althusser 1964, pp. 105–6.
106   Althusser 1964, p. 106.
107   Ibid.
108   Ibid.
109   Althusser 1964, p. 107.

ive change in the nature of the labour power which is required by the social process of production.[110]

Althusser had already seen this. To talk about the skilled labour of future cadres in the social process of production suggests that, when labour power undergoes a qualitative change, assimilated knowledge enters into the process of production. From Gorz's standpoint what makes this thesis lacking is its insufficient radicality: the metamorphosis of productive forces (in particular, of the composition of the social base) produces contradictions that capitalism has to neutralise. Knowledge – far from being merely abstract – breaks and bursts into the mode of production, *this being the privileged object of its decomposition*; contained in the development of productive forces and determining their qualitative change, it represents – at least potentially – the factor that defuses social division. Indeed, in the metamorphosis of capitalist economies, knowledge is drawn into the process of production like the insect that falls into a spider's web. But doesn't such a metamorphosis of capital represent, at least potentially, its own folding? Does it not announce, at least as a dormant possibility, its own decay? There is an interesting contradiction here: knowledge is what makes capital productive, while also being what determines its internal gap (like the proletariat, because scientific and technical workers are nothing but the contemporary 'version' of a proletariat). It represents, so to speak, the negative of social totality, the object that 'chokes' – at least potentially and as long as there are no favourable moments of crisis – its substantial continuity.

Let us explore some further contradictions:

1. The first is related to the cost of the production of labour power and the tendency, by and within the capitalist regime, to prevent society from having to shoulder it. Such a contradiction necessarily leads to the overcoming of the bourgeoisie educational system. The need for an enlargement of the social base of academic recruitment (in terms of both *quantity* and *quality* of the labour power) means that a system in which the cost of education falls squarely on the families would fail. On the one hand, we have the necessity of widening the social base and, on the other, the intellectual qualification of the labour power. Thus, capital should replace unproductive labour with an already productive labour, although, *formally*, it would still be the same (student) labour: learning and assimilating determined skills. What changes is, so to speak, its *substantiality*: the determination of its function and its location in the field of labour power

---

110   Gorz 1973, p. 111.

recruitment in relation to the qualitative change of the process of production. The crisis of that educational system, then, makes it possible to claim certain rights, in particular, that of *an allowance for all students* qua *students, as remuneration for the social and socially productive character of academic labour.* It is here that the economic-political line of the union comes into play (the activity of the UNEF 'is thus a considered response to the crisis in bourgeois education and the partial reforms proposed by the capitalist state').[111] A social wage for all students would not only bring out the contradiction but, and this is the core point, it would cause it *to deflagrate in its anti-capitalist function*: 'Advantage must be taken of the need for a broadening of the social basis of university education to pursue the anti-capitalist implications of this necessity to the limit'.[112] A *socially based* welfare system for bourgeois education would only have the effect of 'accentuate the dependence of students either on their parents, in the case of those receiving no grant, or on the state or private bodies in the case of those receiving a grant'.[113] This would be a dependence that, in the case of working-class scholarship holders would produce a 'unassailable conformism' and a tendency to choose pragmatic study programmes; and in the case of those students with no bursary coming from bourgeois classes, this would increase their dependence 'on the goodwill of their parents [...] even after they have legally come of age'.[114] Only a social salary given to *all* students, justified by the socially productive character of academic labour as such, would 'set the students free from bourgeois educational, cultural, careerist and "elitist" standards, from capitalist standards of utility and profitability, and from the pressures exerted upon them by parents, the state, industry and their own lack of time and resources'.[115] Here, then, the contradiction unfolds: on the one hand, there is the necessity of widening the social base for the recruitment of skilled labour power; on the other, capitalism's willingness to economically support bourgeois education (even going so far as to 'choke' its monopolistic expansion, as demonstrated by the impossibility of reducing the weekly working hours due to a shortage of skilled labour), *in order to preserve the relations of social division.* This division would be produced by means of that which derives from the extension of a social wage to all students (as

---

111   Gorz 1973, pp. 118–19.
112   Gorz 1973, p. 116.
113   Gorz 1973, p. 117.
114   Gorz 1973, p. 118.
115   Gorz 1973, p. 119.

intellectual labour power), and from the alliance with the labour movement in its anti-corporatist function: 'to put it another way, the struggle
of the student unions for emancipation and valorization of the student
labor power is the equivalent, in the educational and cultural field, of the
workers' struggle in the field of industry'.[116] Ultimately, then, Althusser's
argument in favour of (what amounts to) a 'democratisation' of higher
education would be only a partial corrective (and, one might add, rather
ineffectual with respect to the modification of the relations of production). It should be emphasised that Althusser too believes the problem
to be inherent to the system of recruitment that underlies the bourgeois
educational system (a student salary, paid according to family income
would go in this direction, since it would still refer to the class conditions
of student recruitment). What differentiates Gorz and the union's stance
from Althusser's, then, is the position taken towards recruitment as a state
of affairs. For Althusser the goal is to *circumvent* it (as a state of affairs).
For Gorz and the union, the goal is to *obstruct* it (since it represents the
empty shell of an outdated *status quo*).

2. The second important contradiction pertains to the university education
necessary for the development of labour power and the tendency, of and
within capitalism, to preserve hierarchical relations of production. Such
a contradiction – if we keep in mind everything that we have said about
Althusser – necessarily leads to the suppression 'of the methods and content of traditional higher education, which has hitherto been regarded as
a school for the elite of the bourgeois society'.[117] This is particularly a suppression of the methods and the content of teaching: the need to increase
the general level of knowledge of the (university-level) social base creates
a crisis of the culture disseminated by traditional methods of transmission. On the one hand, there is a need for a form of teaching that would
conform to the current level of technical development; on the other, there
a need internal to capitalism itself to preserve classical methods of transmission so that such an increase of knowledge would not disrupt the
distribution of social tasks. There is thus a tension between contrasting
needs *located within the production process itself*: 'on the one hand, the
need created by the modern process of production for a higher development of human capabilities, and on the other hand, the political need
to prevent this development from leading to an increased autonomy of

---

116   Gorz 1973, p. 119.
117   Gorz 1973, p. 120.

the individual which would threaten the existing division of social functions and distribution of power'.[118] The danger entailed by the first contradiction, as we have seen, is the transformation, i.e., the enlargement,
of the social base (prevented by preserving school subsistence methods,
even at the cost of 'choking' the expansion of monopolies, and stimulated
by the tendential implications of the socially based wage). In this case,
the danger is the emancipation of the academic labour power, as a consequence of the increase in its cultural level and self-management abilities. Such emancipation is stifled by means of the *specialisation* of education, although this clashes with the evolution of technology ('it is not true
that modern technology demands specialists. What it needs is polyvalent
basic education concerned not with fragmented, predigested and specialized knowledge, but with initiation ... into methods of research and
technological invention').[119] In other words, in order to preserve the hierarchical structure of the relations of production, knowledge should be
specialised knowledge, and students should be 'specialists, incapable of
relating their particular knowledge to the general movement of science,
or their particular activities to the overall process of social praxis'.[120] Here
too, then, the objective is to let the contradiction unfold, and to give it an
anti-capitalist resolution (i.e., developing the anti-capitalist tendencies
that lurk within capitalism itself): 'what technological progress calls for
is not only a solid polyvalent education encompassing methodology and
theory, but also training in self-education, which presupposes a drastic
recasting of present teaching methods and curricula'.[121]

3.   The last contradiction pertains on the one hand to the ever-increasing
autonomy of productive labour and on the other to the condition that a
capitalist society actually assigns to skilled labour power. This necessarily leads to the suppression of relations of production. If, in the Taylorist
mode of production, labour power is represented by 'a pure quantity of
physical energy',[122] such that one worker is essentially interchangeable
with any other, then the introduction of knowledge into the production
process ensures that *a new type of worker is born*, who 'is often required
to have greater skills, and above all a higher level of general education,

---

118   Gorz 1973, p. 121.
119   Gorz 1973, p. 123.
120   Gorz 1973, p. 122.
121   Gorz 1973, p. 124.
122   Gorz 1973, p. 126.

than his immediate job calls for'.[123] If, for the first type of worker (who, so to speak, *works without thinking*) the relationship with the industrial process of production is only external (i.e., a worker one the one hand, and an object produced by means of a certain quantity of raw physical energy on the other), for the second (who, so to speak, *thinks while working*) the same relationship, due to the transversal nature of its qualification across different segments of the production process, is reciprocally combined with the activities of the skilled workers who make up that production process (establishing a 'co-operation among teams within which the traditional barrier between workmen, technicians and engineers fade away').[124] On the one hand, we have the growing autonomy of labour, granted by the cultural extension of the training process, to which capitalist process of production itself leads; on the other hand, there is the need to curb and repress it in order to preserve its social division. Here, then, the danger for capitalism is identified: *the acquisition of knowledge, with the breakdown of the natural basis of industrial hierarchy, and the possible appearance of forms of self-management.* This is a danger that capitalism prevents by preserving the social division and by perpetuating the 'old centralized hierarchic order, the arbitrary limitation of responsibilities and duties even where this has become unnecessary and a positive hindrance to productivity'.[125] Previously, the project of an alliance between the union and the party was functional to the assumption of an anti-corporatist position. Here, in a generalised movement that does *not* consider the explosion of the objective contradiction between capitalist relations of production and the nature of labour power to be inevitable, such an alliance is meant to actualise this merely latent possibility, turning it into a concrete power: 'hence the necessity of political and cultural work on the part of the working-class movement to make the contradiction clearly understood and to weld together the scientific and technical neo-proletariat, students and teachers, and traditional proletariat, by demonstrating the character and prospects of solutions to their own specific problems while taking full account of these problems' specificity and relative independence'.[126]

---

123 Gorz 1973, p. 127. For interesting articulations of Gorz's thesis that look at the transformation of the university during the last decade (and beyond), see Maltese 2014 and Roggero 2009.

124 Gorz 1973, pp. 128–9.

125 Gorz 1973, p. 130.

126 Ibid.

5   Knowledge as a Commodity: J-P. Milbergue on the Internal
       Contradictions of the (Capitalist) University

Based on what we have examined, Gorz's relationship with Althusser seems to
be merely an exterior, alternative theoretical stance. And yet, Gorz presupposes
Althusser's position, albeit critically, more than might initially appear to be the
case.

Indeed, the historically crucial point lies in a reference to the second contradiction (the conflict between the necessity of university education and the
preservation of hierarchical relations of production) and to the union's proposal to revise training methods (aiming towards an anti-capitalist overcoming
of that contradiction). Gorz refers (although only in a footnote)[127] to a paper
by Jean-Pierre Milbergue, 'La signification politique des rapports pédagogiques
dans l'Université française', which appeared in *Les Temps Modernes* in April
1965, about a year and a half after 'Student Problems'. This text is a revision
(or at least an alternative version) of the 'Réponse à la lettre adressée récem-
ment par Althusser à Queysanne' from December 1963, which Milbergue wrote
as a critical response to Althusser's open letter (and to which, in turn, Althusser
never responded).

Gorz is correct: Milbergue formulated the most theoretically solid critique,
certainly in the context of the student body, of Althusser's pedagogical framework.

∴

In his 1963 text Milbergue immediately hones in on the core issue: should we
evaluate the validity of Althusser's argument – according to which pedagogical
practice is defined by an objective distance between knowledge and not-yet-
knowledge – on the basis of the preliminary definition of 'knowing' as such or,
on the contrary, on the basis of a preliminary understanding of the theoretical
(in this case, according to Milbergue, it would be appropriate to say ideological) presuppositions which underlie that argument? Milbergue writes: 'one
can wonder about the validity of such a reasoning; it would indeed be necessary
to proceed to a Marxist criticism of the "knowledge" of which Althusser speaks,
to be able to then affirm that the objective distance that there is between knowledge and non-knowledge translates into an objective distance between the
professor and the student'.[128]

---

127   Cf. Gorz 1973, p. 69.
128   ALT2. A40-04.03 (D), p. 1.

This argument will be repeated in his 1965 text: *the pedagogical practice that Althusser speaks of cannot but represent the privileged corollary of bourgeois ideology.* This is already emphasised in § 4: for Althusser, to say that academic work does not produce a commodity that can be exchanged (producing instead the consumption and assimilation of a knowledge that is functional to its acquisition, that is, to its valorisation) does not imply a denial, but rather presupposes, that the pedagogical function of substantial inequality involves what was defined above as a kind of reversal of the relationship with the commodity (labour does not produce a commodity but rather it presupposes it as an exchanged object). It is here that Milbergue, although referring to Althusser's open letter, seems to anticipate the question that will later be implicit in 'Student Problems'. We have already outlined Althusser's ideological presuppositions: since bourgeois ideology is defined 'as the body constituted by moral, religious, political, cultural, etc. ideas, concepts, and models of thought', it follows that it can only be transmitted by means of a 'thing-like [*chosist*] conception of knowledge',[129] i.e., a conception that makes knowledge an object of exchange defined within the 'university commercial circle [*circuit commercial universitaire*]'.[130] In addition to making the disparity entailed by the objective distance that this practice implies functional to the integration into the circuits of production, this *makes pedagogical practice the only practice that is wholly suited to the transmission of the objects of bourgeois ideology.* This point should be stressed: pedagogical practice represents the *specific* form of the transmission of already-defined ideological objects, since these can only be transmitted through a formal relationship, grounded on an exchange of objects. A relationship whose vertical component – its objective distance – reflects, in the last instance, a relation that immediately implicates the *possession* of the object of knowledge (so that the relation of pedagogical practice can be understood not only as a relation of consumption and valorisation, but, more generally, as a relation of *appropriation* of the things it transmits). For Milbergue, to call it a pedagogical relationship *already* entails placing an object of ideological knowledge within this relationship. And when asking how this object can be transmitted (a problem for the state), one cannot but refer to the method of transmission proper to pedagogical practice, which is based on an objective distance, i.e., on a thing-like conception of knowledge.

---

129   Milbergue 1965, p. 1849.
130   ALT2. A40-04.03 (D), p. 2; Milbergue 1965, p. 1850.

Bourgeois ideology has developed a thing-like [*chosist*] conception of the knowledge. Knowledge has become a kind of merchandise, a stable, defined, and fixed object, without evolution, without immediate relation with a practice in movement [*pratique en mouvement*] and therefore taking its place within a new kind of commercial circuit, the academic commercial circuit.[131]

Again, the pedagogical relation, if based on this mode of transmission, is an ideological relation, being a thing-like relation – a relation that presupposes an exchange of objects that is functional to the transmission of ideological things (it could be said that, although it is not the case that every exchange in this relation is necessarily ideological, every ideological exchange necessarily takes place within this relation). Once again, starting from this redefinition of 'knowledge', this relation can be reformulated: 'a dialectical, scientific conception of knowledge allows [one] to demonstrate the relativity of the operational concept of "knowledge"'.[132] It is not an exaggeration to claim that, from this moment onwards, one cannot but admire Milbergue's theoretical gesture which, far from rejecting the Althusserian epistemological framework, *seems simply to take it literally*.

As such, there is a relationship between knowledge and not-yet-knowledge. What else can we say? Far from qualifying the specificity of the pedagogical function as a vertical function between two subjects however, this – *exclusively* – defines the scientific practice of a subject that is located at the level of existing theory (that is: at the level of a Generality II) and an object that is not yet theoretically practiced (i.e., of a Generality I). In other words, Althusser is well aware that scientific practice is defined by a creative function ('its function is to create')[133] of scientific generalities (Generalities III). It could be said, then,

---

131   ALT2. A40-04.03 (D), p. 2.
132   Ibid.
133   Ibid. Creation, that is, production, that is, labour. For a theoretical analysis of scientific practice, I recommend this passage by Althusser, from his 'On Materialist Dialectics' (Althusser 2005, pp. 188–9): 'But in the dialectic of practice, the abstract generality at the beginning (Generality I), that is, the generality worked on, is not the same as the generality that does the work (Generality II) and even less is it the specific generality (Generality III) produced by this labour: a knowledge (the "concrete-theoretical"). Generality II (which works) is not at all the simple development of Generality I, its passage (however complex) from the in-itself to the for-itself; for Generality II is the "theory" of the science under consideration, and as such it is the result of a whole process (the history of the science from its foundation), which is a process of real transformations in the strongest sense of the word, that is, a process whose form is not the form of a simple development (according to the Hegelian model – the development of the in-itself into the for-itself), but of mutations and

that the relation between knowledge and not-yet-knowledge does not define a relation of intersubjective inequality, but rather the subjective practice of the scientist, insofar as that relation necessarily reflects, as its criterion of theoretical validation, a relationship between knowledge (of the scientist) and not-yet-*known* (of the scientific generality, because one still knows an ideological generality). The point needs to be made explicit: if, for Milbergue, not-knowledge pertains exclusively to the unknown *object* (the un-practised nature), then on the other hand it is necessarily reflected in the *subject* who still does not know (i.e., the object is not known by a subject who does not know). But this subject – and this is crucial – is in a condition of not-knowing only in relation to the object that is not-yet-known (and not in relation to another more knowledgeable subject). This is as if to say that, in the relation between knowing and not-knowing, the side of the (unknown) object, far from being equivalent to that of the (unknowing) subject, conditions, as dominant side, its possibility as a side that only reflects its condition. This clarification, which is not present in Milbergue's analysis, serves to prevent a critique that would focus precisely on the explication of the subjective side of that relation. Indeed, we could ask: if not-knowledge also determines the condition of someone who does not know, why not inscribe this unknowing subject in a relationship (of substantial inequality) with another, knowledgeable subject? For Milbergue, this cannot be the case, since such a relation would simply be a scientific one, i.e., *simply an objective relation*. And if it was subjective, besides relating to one and the same subject (the scientist engaged in their theoretical practice) it would be exclusively the reflection of that objective situation (a situation in which the scientist has to deal with a Generality I not yet worked by a Generality II). Ultimately, then, it could be said that if knowledge is a science, non-knowledge is a non-science. On the side of the object (which is the dominant side), non-knowledge is un-known (rather than being the condition of another subject that still-doesn't-know) and, on the side of the subject – the only subject of theoretical practice (the reflected side) – it is the condition of the scientist before the creation of a generality.

---

reconstructions that induce real qualitative discontinuities. So when Generality II works on Generality I it is never working on itself, neither at the moment of the science's foundation nor later in its history. That is why Generality I always emerges from this labour really transformed. It may retain the general "form" of generality, but this form tells us nothing about it, for it has become a quite different generality – it is no longer an ideological generality, nor one belonging to an earlier phase of the science, but in every case a qualitatively new specified scientific generality'.

It is at this level, that of the scientist's theoretical practice (Althusser's Generalities III[)], that the objective distance between science and non-science really emerges. Non-science does not indicate the state of those who have not yet learned. It indicates the relationship between scientists and nature. Non-science is non-practiced nature, not science unknown by some.[134]

In this sense, Althusser's theoretical error would lie in an unwarranted substitution: 'to return to the functional distinction between scholar and teacher, we can say that the function of the teacher will not be the transmission of knowledge understood as developing in theoretical practice (science)'.[135] *The scientist is not a teacher and the teacher is not a scientist.* The scientist deals with a non-knowledge that is an unknown (a 'non-practiced nature'); the function of the teacher, on the other hand, far from being reduced to the mere transmission of 'theories that are fixed and appreciated because of their 'truth', or because of their definitive coherence',[136] is one of nurturing *a scientific aptitude to produce those generalities* 'and thus of facilitating the adoption of this attitude by those who have not yet been made aware of this mode of relationship with the object-knowledge'.[137] From this point of view, the pedagogical relation to which Althusser refers would represent nothing other than *a scientific relation displaced onto the pedagogical field, and therefore a humanised relation* – a relation shifted towards a context where *the unknown object would be replaced by an unknowing subject.* This would be a relation that, therefore, *removes the differential between the scientist and the professor, replacing it with a synonymity between roles and functions*: 'It may be necessary for pedagogical practice that the teacher is also a researcher, or even a scholar, but it is certainly not necessary that there be a confusion of roles or functions. Althusser does not avoid this trap'.[138]

This confusion, Althusser's intention notwithstanding (according to Milbergue, Althusser is stuck in a contradiction 'between his function as a theoretical Marxist practitioner and his status as a professor at the bourgeois university'), is wholly functional to the bourgeois system of teaching:[139]

---

134   ALT2. A40-04.03 (D), p. 2.
135   ALT2. A40-04.03 (D), p. 3.
136   Ibid.
137   Ibid.
138   ALT2. A40-04.03 (D), p. 4.
139   Ibid.

It is no accident that the confusion between scholar and professor was developed and maintained within the bourgeois University. Every professor, holder of a chair, wants to be a scholar, and he also wants to show it in the exercise of his function as a professor. But bourgeois society expects him to conform to academic consensus and administrative complicity, and to be object of public (for ex. by giving public lectures) or journalistic (see Aron) admiration. He's therefore expected to neglect his non-prestigious function of technician-educator in favour of his magical function of scientific innovator.[140]

The existence of this confusion, says Milbergue, is no coincidence. Because if it is true on the one hand that the corollary of bourgeois ideology can only be represented through a thing-like conception of knowledge (every ideological exchange necessarily takes place within a relationship determined by an objective distance, although the opposite is not true), then on the other hand this conception *cannot but presuppose that substitution* – i.e., it cannot but depend on the existence of an elective subject that is functional to the transmission of an ideological object: *the teacher is the exchange agent*. Surreptitiously defined as a scientist, she or he is its intermediary, because she or he is surreptitiously placed in the field of a qualitative discrepancy that makes knowledge and not-knowledge the specific (and humanised) qualifications of subjects: 'this method is essentially characterised by a relationship of exchange (in the commercial sense) between the custodian of the knowledge-commodity and the student requesting to receive it'.[141]

Milbergue's argument should not be underestimated. The fact that the function of the teacher differs from the scientist does not mean that scientific aptitudes, although they do not correspond to already-defined objects of knowledge, should not be transmitted. In other words, the denial of the method of ideological (or deceptively scientific) transmission does not mean that – assuming the determinacy of the professorial function – we should still speak of an *authentically* pedagogical method of transmission (i.e., referring to an 'institutional pedagogy where the role of the student body in the process of acquiring knowledge will be more and more preponderant').[142] On the contrary, it is precisely because the professor's function cannot be reduced to that of the scientist (who is creative of generalities that are defined on the basis of theoretical work on ideological generalities) that it is necessary to reformulate

---

140   Ibid.
141   ALT2. A40-04.03 (D), p. 5.
142   ALT2. A40-04.03 (D), p. 9.

a pedagogical practice that would represent an alternative to the ideological one. The relevant point, then, is that the negation of vertical practice – operated through the identification of a substitution of functions – paves the way for the theorisation of alternative methods of transmission. Only by rejecting the specific method of the bourgeois university (a method that works by substitution) is it possible to justify and theoretically legitimise the introduction of a new type of transmission. If we can talk about transmission at all (and we must do so because of the specificity of the professorial function), this cannot be reduced to the closing of an alleged objective distance that would determine a situation of substantial inequality. In other words, *this negation opens a space*, one which Milbergue (as it happens in his 1965 text) does not fill (and cannot fill: and this is the really programmatic, profoundly anti-Althusserian, point in his 1963 text, as will be seen later) if not for a brief reference to the *Groupe de Travail Universitaire* ('a kind of working collective is emerging from the current experience of systematic organization of the GTU. This movement has its own dynamics and can lead teachers to a different kind of teaching practice, with a different political meaning').[143]

The space which is opened, although still unfilled, *nevertheless finds in the student body the subject of its filling* (both politically and theoretically): 'the student is indeed in a field of dialectical contradictions which favour his political awareness'[144] He is certainly an *écolier prolongé:* 'the whole French educational system has led him to accept this status',[145] facilitated, in this voluntary submission (since, 'his future must appear promising, he must have a favourable social and professional status, the prospect of a happy future helps him to undergo certain initiatory tests')[146] by a dependence on his family 'both economic (a dependence on money) and psychological (an emotional dependence linked to an immaturity originated within and by the teaching situation)'.[147]

Yet, the students' social base is undergoing a metamorphosis that is essentially caused by exogenous factors which therefore function as *objective conditions* for the affirmation of an alternative status to that of the 'lifelong learner': that of the 'working student' (wage earner). These exogenous factors are represented by the qualitative 'democratisation' of university recruitment (of proletarian students whose demands for family autonomy and the completion of studies are different from those of bourgeois students); by the diffusion of new

---

143   ALT2. A40-04.03 (D), p. 10.
144   ALT2. A40-04.03 (D), p. 7.
145   ALT2. A40-04.03 (D), p. 6.
146   Ibid.
147   Ibid.

cultural models (like the lowering of the socially productive age: it is at this stage that 'one more often encounters problems of "human" responsibility'); and by the maturation of a political consciousness dictated by specific historical events (such as the Algerian war in 1954).[148] On the one hand, then, there is an objective (i.e., factual) but formal status, its formality determined by the non-correspondence with the metamorphosis of the social base; on the other, within the same educational system, a potential but achievable status (that of the student as intellectual worker), the feasibility of which is determined by exogenous factors of political awareness. By objectively conditioning the social base, these exogenous factors condition and awaken transformational movements within the university.

It is on the edge of this contradiction, then, that the student body becomes a subject ('the student is plunged directly into a propulsive contradiction [*contradiction motrice*]').[149] It is precisely *this* contradiction (in his 1963 text) that makes the student body the subject of transformation. Indeed, *this* subject needs to dissolve *the formal conditions for the preservation of the bourgeois educational system, because of the objective reality of a new social base.* That is, it needs to take a form without content (that of the *statut d'écolier prolongé*) and replace it with another that has an already given content (that of the *statut de travailleur intellectuel*). It is necessary for the student body to transform the ideological relations of education:

> Thus, the objective conditions for a profound transformation of the University are created. If the students still objectively have the status of *écolier prolongé* they nonetheless explicitly demand another status, that of intellectual workers in a democratically renovated University. Their objective status doesn't have the prevailing force of one of their professors: they are not within an organic link with the university structure, like the professors are, paid by the University and permanent in the University. They are in a transitory situation, they come to the University but they are not the University.[150]

There is a void or space, and the subject of its theoretical and political filling is known. To be sure, it is a subject, but *what* transformation can it bring about? We have said it above and will repeat it again later. The GTU, although indicating a political position (for 'the organisation of the GTU' represents a 'pre-

148   ALT2. A40-04.03 (D), p. 8.
149   ALT2. A40-04.03 (D), p. 6.
150   ALT2. A40-04.03 (D), p. 8.

paration for this qualitative revolution in the University'), does not constitute the completed form – provided that we can speak here of completion – of a new method of transmission, albeit laying the ground for it.[151] According to Althusser, the main question regarding the objective analysis of a specific object pertains to the legitimacy or illegitimacy of the identification between practices (of their confusion): theoretical *mediation* implies badmouthing (in an epistemological sense) the university as an object of an *immediately* political (that is, *ideological*) practice. It is here that for Milbergue a further breaking point arises, in addition to that relative to the replacement of functions (a real 'logical error').[152] Indeed, although political practice presupposes theoretical practice, they both require division. It is worth repeating: theoretical practice – the scientific analysis of the situation – is not a political practice which, generated by the former, 'merely' represents the (Marxist) specificity of a 'scientific technique'. Political practice is a scientific *technique* precisely because it is not a theoretical practice (as its adherent, it decrees its separation from it): 'One cannot in any way confuse the theoretical practice of a science with the practice of the scientific technique resulting from that very science'.[153]

But here is the crucial point: does Milbergue's critique of the functioning of bourgeois pedagogical practice not already indicate that Althusser's theoretical stance betrays nothing more than an analytical posture? Or better: is this systematisation of practices not exactly what drove Althusser into the 'trap' of substituting functions (which serve bourgeois ideology)? In short: doesn't this systematisation presuppose, once again, a thing-like conception of knowledge according to which scientific analysis – its theoretical products – far from merely producing instruments, produces 'things'? And aren't these 'things' separated from a political practice that *for this very reason* appears to be disjointed and separate from them ('historical materialism and Marxist political action cannot in any way be confused in terms of their specific practices')?[154] To be fair, Milbergue does not tell us much: how can we think of an alternative relationship between practices, if not through their dialectical circularity ('the relationship between theory and practice has long been analysed and it has been made clear that this relationship is dialectical'),[155] through the fact that a determining practice is in turn determined (in the very act of its active determination, as is the case of scientific practice), and that a determined prac-

---

151   ALT2. A40-04.03 (D), p. 7.

152   ALT2. A40-04.03 (D), p. 8.

153   872ALT/142/6, p. 7.

154   Ibid.

155   ALT2. A40-04.03 (D), p. 12.

tice is in turn determined (in the very act of its passive determination, as is the case of political practice)? In other words, how can we think of an alternative relationship if not through a co-determination that is a co-determinacy? Milbergue explains:

> It seems that we are dealing with the same error as the one analysed in our initial development on the pedagogical relationship. This error consists in considering operational concepts as things, in treating them as such, as realities, whereas they are only instruments. It consists in adopting a bourgeois ideological attitude towards the problem posed by theoretical practice. It consists in accepting the thing-like [*chosiste*] conception of 'knowledge' as the foundation of any process of scientific evolution. The science of which Althusser speaks is ultimately bourgeois science, it is an arrested science [*science arrêté*], that isn't confronted with the practice of the scientific techniques that it makes possible, that isn't put in relation with the practice of these techniques, and that isn't co-determined by the technical practice that it engenders.[156]

We know that there is a void and we know the subject of its filling – a theoretical and political filling that is played on a relationship of mutual determination. Theorising a method of transmission able to modify the thing-like paradigm (objective but only formal) means practicing it politically in order to practice it theoretically, and practicing it theoretically is possible because it is practiced politically – that is, every practice, far from being an analytical relationship (through simple adaptation), is dialectically practiced (through co-determination).

However, in Milbergue's eyes, Althusser's critique of Queysanne or better, the meaning of this critique, is entirely correct. In fact, it was formulated 'precisely because there is a gap between Marxist theoretical practice in the UEC, and more generally in the Communist Party, and the UEC's Marxist political practice in the university'.[157] It will therefore be necessary to produce a theory that begins from an effective politics, 'not for Althusser, not for a theoretical critique, but for the very evolution of the situation of students in the University'.[158]

This is Milbergue's genuinely programmatic thesis. The aim is to retrieve an *immediate* (theoretical) relationship that would be a 'theoretical expression of

---

156   Ibid.
157   ALT2. A40-04.03 (D), p. 13.
158   Ibid.

the political problem'[159] for a subject that, *produced* by a contradiction because dependent on objective conditions, is perched on the edge of a theoretical void opened by the critique of the substitution of the scientific function with the professorial one: 'The number one question, the real number one question for all communist students is that of identifying a Marxist theoretical practice with an immediate connection to the Marxist political practice in the University'.[160]

⁚

For my purpose here – to clarify Milbergue's relationship with Althusser – 'La signification politique des rapports pédagogiques dans l'Université française' can be seen as strengthening the argument regarding the thing-like conception of knowledge. Milbergue's thesis is actually quite simple. We have already seen that contradiction is a specific contradiction linked to the student body (which therefore becomes the subject of transformation). Here, in his 1965 text, this contradiction also affects the academic faculty. On the teachers' side, this contradiction lies in the content of the pedagogical practice while on the students' side, it lies in its method.

We are already familiar with Milbergue's argument. When it is taken back up here, Althusser's name is replaced by what Milbergue refers to as a 'common conception' (and it cannot be otherwise if it is true that, as we have already seen, beyond his theoretical intention Althusser does nothing but formulate the bourgeois pedagogical practice, as commonly understood): pedagogical practice is defined by the reduction of an alleged objective distance between the teacher and the student – an objective distance that is determined by the knowledge relationship between the subjects involved in that practice.

> A commonly invoked conception of pedagogical practice can be schematically formulated thus: there is a real distance between knowledge and not-yet-knowledge; the teacher holds knowledge, the student doesn't: he is in a state of not-yet-knowing.[161]

It is not necessary to repeat how this thing-like conception of knowledge is a specific corollary of bourgeois ideology. It is however useful to emphasise that the theoretically relevant point is the emergence of a contradiction within

---

159   Ibid.
160   ALT2. A40-04.03 (D), p. 14.
161   Milbergue 1965, p. 1849.

this relationship, for reasons that are related to the 'ideological rupture' produced by the modification of the relationship between the professorial body and knowledge.

Indeed, if it is true that pedagogical practice is formally functional to the transmission of ideological objects, then the desire to transmit a non-ideological knowledge – i.e., scientific knowledge (in the 1963 text this is referred to as an attitude capable of producing scientific generalities) – necessitates the revision of a practice with an alienated pedagogical function (and the 'excommunication' of the 'teacher' as operator of that domain) and the convocation of a new practice with a scientific pedagogical function (the introduction of the 'professor-pedagogue'). The requalification of the content of university teaching follows, by structural necessity, the position of a pedagogical practice that rejects the thing-like conception of knowledge, so that transmitting scientific knowledge *already* means getting rid of a bourgeois pedagogical practice based on objective distance.

It is clear, then, how the contradiction arises from the rift that opens between form (the teaching method) and content (the quality of the object transmitted). If we want to transmit an object of ideological knowledge, then there is full concordance between form and content (Milbergue calls it an 'organic bond'); if we want to convey scientific knowledge, then a contradiction emerges between form and the new content. This is a contradiction whose main aspect resides, for teachers, on the side of the object (that is, the desire to transmit non-ideological knowledge) while for students it resides on the side of method (since they 'live in constant reference to the social model of dependence').[162]

We should stress here, however, that Milbergue does not intend to formulate a new pedagogical practice (it would be completely useless to look for it in the text, and his brief references to a political model of self-management, to a non-directive model, as well as to the *Groupe de Travail Universitaire* do not constitute evidence of any attempt to do so). Milbergue simply points out the possible conditions for a reformulation of the pedagogical relationship, based on the redefinition of the object of knowledge.

Starting from an analysis of the same problem, the differences between Milbergue's and Althusser's theoretical framework (in 'Student Problems') are already evident. Although not explicitly referring to Althusser's writing, Milbergue also raises the question of how scientific knowledge can be articulated within a social domain in which the state, and therefore its ideological conditioning, is present.

---

162   Milbergue 1965, p. 1877.

The really surprising point is that if it is true that Milbergue may seem to simply defend an alternative thesis to Althusser's, it is equally true that he actually makes explicit reference to the 'Generalities' that Althusser introduced in his 'On the Materialist Dialectic'. Milbergue writes:

> On the one hand, the alienated pedagogical function proceeds directly from a teaching whose purpose is the transmission of Generality I. Method and content are then organically linked and inseparable, thus giving rise to bourgeois ideological teaching in all fields of knowledge. On the other hand, the contradiction between the desire to transmit Generalities III and the – sometimes unavoidable – need to alienate one's pedagogical function (material and institutional conditions of professional practice), or between the desire and the possibility of exercising a scientific pedagogical function and its necessary application to Generality I (programs, exams) – all these conflicts have made teachers more sensitive to the contradiction between content and methods. ... It is at this level of 'method-content' relations that the main contradiction of pedagogical practice currently lies.[163]

This is a truly extraordinary passage since, in addition to posing the same problem as Althusser, as we have already noted, Milbergue also mobilises the same categories that we have seen used in 'Student Problems': form (method), content (transmitted object), ideological object, scientific generality.[164] If for one of them the question is how to identify a new pedagogical practice that (as a form) would correspond to the transmission of a scientific generality (as its object); for the other, the question is how to guarantee the vertical pedagogical function since (as a form) it corresponds to the same generality (in a relationship that, as we have seen several times, is *conditioned*, on the side of the technical form, by the priority of the scientific qualification of the object of knowledge, while also being *necessary* for its validation).

The short circuit identified by Milbergue is therefore inherent in *the use of Althusser's system for an anti-Althusserian purpose*, since, starting from its theoretical vantage point:

1. Althusser would be squarely located in an ideological position because the objective distance of the pedagogical relationship can only be functional to the transmission of ideological generalities. This means that it

---

163   Milbergue 1965, pp. 1871–2.
164   Cf. above, §1.

can only presuppose a thing-like conception of knowledge. It follows that if, for Althusser, the correspondence between form and content responds to an authentic technical need that underlies the vertical pedagogical function, for Milbergue it always gives rise to bourgeois ideological teaching (and so Althusser would be an ideologue, a false scientist, emergent in relation to the replacement of functions).

2.   This is true because a scientific generality *literally* breaks the pedagogical relationship since, due to its being *qualitatively* different from an ideological generality, it engenders a contradiction (I refer, of course, to a central thesis of 'On the Materialist Dialectic' according to which among these generalities 'there is never identity of essence ... but always a real transformation').[165] It is as if, for Milbergue, this contradiction, far from being reconciled, would be the cause of a rupture. It is as if, for Milbergue, the denial of inequality and the introduction of contradiction translated the epistemological rupture from the sphere of science (a scientific generality has nothing to do with any realisation, both empirical and idealistic, of an ideological generality), to the domain of the relations of transmission of knowledge – thus reaping its metamorphic benefits. It is as if to say that these outcomes, far from defining a space of substantial inequality that would serve as the custodian of a scientific generality, rather aim at redefining the very outlines, functions, operational lines, class relations, and institutional outlines of the discourse around the university.

These outcomes in Althusser's work – at least when compared to Milbergue's theoretical model – will take a much more radical shape five years later, with the introduction of the *ideological state apparatuses*.

---

165   Althusser 2005, p. 185.

The School Does Not Exist: Scholastic Mythology and Ideological Reproduction in Pierre Macherey

Introduction

Throughout 1969, Althusser wrote two versions of the manuscript of *On the Reproduction of Capitalism: Ideology and Ideological State Apparatuses*. These manuscripts are the basis for the publication of 'Ideology and Ideological State Apparatuses (Notes Towards an Investigation)', which appeared the following year in issue 151 of *La Pensée*.[1] It is immediately worth noting that Althusser chose to develop his theses on the school in the text on the Apparatuses, a theoretical context that pertains to the reproduction of labour power and more generally to the reproduction of relations of production (corresponding, as I will show shortly, to Chapter III and Chapter IX of the second draft of the manuscript). To be sure, this is an ideal theoretical context – at least if we exclude everything that concerns 'Student Problems' and gloss over an unpublished text, 'Les Grandes illusions de l'École',[2] which is particularly interesting both due to the theses it expounds and because of the period in which it was written: shortly before, if not simultaneously with *On the Reproduction*, in 1968, probably between autumn and winter.

This is particularly relevant, moreover, if we take into account the fact that *On the Reproduction*, in addition to alluding several times to 'Schools' [*Écoles*] – an unfinished research project dedicated to an analysis of the school system that began around 1968 and involved Étienne Balibar, Pierre Macherey, Roger Establet, and Michel Tort (and, at least partially, Renée Balibar, as demonstrated by a short file of eleven type sheets, *additifs* to a chapter that has not reached us,[3] to which Althusser also attests in the unpublished text I just mentioned) – constitutes a 'theorisation' of that research project 'at its heart', according to Jacques Bidet's editorial note to the French edition.[4]

'Schools' was never completed due to political tensions among the participants, although the texts that remain available today testify to a certain theor-

---

1 Included in Althusser 2002.
2 Cf. ALT2. A14-01.08. For an analysis of this text, see *infra*, Chap. 3, Introduction.
3 Cf. ALT2. A14-01.02.
4 Althusser 2014, p. 31.

etical and terminological concordance among them. To demonstrate its intentions, the brief programmatic note contained in a leaflet on *Capital* and Lenin, written by Althusser (probably in 1969), reads as follows: 'Therefore, we are not going to talk about the reproduction of the relations of production, a question which is at the heart of *Capital* (mostly book III, but also book I), and of Lenin's work. We will have the opportunity to talk about it very soon, in two books that will shortly be available to readers'.[5] These are indicated in a footnote: the first is 'Qu'est-ce que la philosophie marxiste léniniste'; the second is, precisely, 'Schools', the collective work that should have been published, like the other, 'as part of the *Théorie* collection, published by Maspero, Paris'.[6]

Indeed, confirming Bidet's note, Althusser refers to 'Schools' four times in *On the Reproduction*. The first is found within a theoretical framework that is by now familiar and that, in the current context, needs to be further examined: that pertaining to the *modal* distinction between the technical and social division of labour. We are in Section IV ('The social division is the reality behind the "technical" division of labour: production, exploitation, and the class struggle in production') of Chapter II ('What is a Mode of Production?'). The technical division of labour, far from being defined according to the degree of development of a given society, *already* depends on its social purpose (hence, the 'ideological imposture' that underlies every attempt to think of the distinction as a real distinction, including that guiding 'Student Problems', whose flaws of 'technicalism' and 'theoreticism' Althusser denounces precisely in this section).

More precisely, the class distinction between intellectual and manual labour is analysed here as a specific distinction of the technical and social division, starting from a theoretical premise that we have already explored (if we think of Gorz): the qualification of labour and the issue of the distribution of jobs within the production process. The latter implies a limit on the number of available skilled jobs, defined by the technological unit of the means of production. The members of the working class occupy the posts of manual labour, while members of the other social classes ('engineers and technicians, as well as middle-level and upper-level supervisory personnel'),[7] have a partial control over the production process. Finally, the most important jobs are taken by the capitalists. Here is a first thesis: although all of these, from the worker to the middle and upper cadres, are wage earners, and although some workers actually manage to increase their rank in the technical division of the productive process ('a museum piece exhibited to encourage belief in the "possibility"

---

5   ALT2. A14-01.01.
6   ALT2. A14-01.01.
7   Althusser 2014, p. 37.

of the impossible'),[8] the distribution of jobs, dictated by their qualification, *is functional to class membership, which is what determines and conditions the distribution of jobs.* As we have noted several times: the technical division already implies the social division.

However, Althusser's brief clarifying footnote, whose scope will become immediately clear, must be emphasised here: distribution, being instrumental to class membership, is a function of the 'school system that "educates", more or less, different individuals … in ways that vary with the milieu from which they come'.[9] The technical division, in other words, *is justified by a line of demarcation* between 'a *monopoly* on certain contents and forms of knowledge, and thus on a form of "know-how"' (held by 'engineers, upper-level supervisors and technicians, factory directors and all their assistants') and those '*other* contents and forms of know-how' (proper of workers in general).[10] We know that the distribution of jobs is functional to class membership, whose presupposition is related to the monopolisation of certain forms of knowledge. This means that if knowledge establishes a prohibition (since its centralisation defines the social field of segregation within the production processes), then *it also defines the social character of each (alleged) technical division.* It could be said that the ideological imposture relating to the real distinction between the technical and social division is linked to a misunderstanding of the function of knowledge: not so much of knowledge as the content of every job in the productive hierarchy (the worker's knowledge, precisely due to his or her qualification, can be increased), but rather for the class division and its formal decomposition ('the idea that there are no social classes or that someone born a worker can "rise above his class"').[11] And, within this imposture of real separation, the existence of a self-regulated technical division is an illusion: the illusion of its distinct and effectively interspersed character, as if to alter the necessity of a hierarchy (i.e., of the technical division of production) would suffice to increase the contents of knowledge. Ultimately, no technical division can be separated from the social division because knowledge, in the circle of production, is functional to the modes of segregation (it could be said that any mode of segregation related to the modes of production, although enforced through repression, is fundamentally shaped by the formal decomposition of knowledge and its modes of appropriation). Althusser is clear about this: '*As far as the great mass of its* effects goes, however, the official monopoly on cer-

---

8   Ibid.
9   Althusser 2014, p. 38 n. 24.
10   Althusser 2014, p. 38.
11   Althusser 2014, p. 37.

tain kinds of knowledge and the practical prohibition that keeps workers from acquiring such "knowledge" maintain the omnipotence of the social division of the relations of production in the relations of a supposedly purely technical "division of labour".[12]

The hierarchisation that is essential for the direction of labour is a social hierarchy and therefore *defined by the position of knowledge and its monopoly*. The point here is that this monopolisation is determined by *the class distinction between intellectual and manual labour, a distinction that in turn is substantiated by different forms of schooling*. A longer or shorter period of schooling corresponds, as we have seen, to a (socially determined) distribution of jobs. This means that forms of schooling and (ab)uses of knowledge are arranged horizontally in determining the reproduction of modes of production. If production is a well-defined process – because the distribution of jobs is also well-defined – then different forms of schooling (i.e., the differential processes of intellectual and manual labour) produce and reproduce, in their very functioning, the same modes of production. Once again, this means that if knowledge defines the social character of the technical division, *the school is what underlies this social character*.

This explains why, for Althusser,

> the class distinction between 'manual labour and intellectual labour', to which Marx refers from *The German Ideology* on, is indeed a reality, despite the crude, crass nature of the formula. It is produced by all class societies. It is still produced, and increasingly produced, by modern capitalist class society, despite the 'spectacular progress of science and technology' and the growing numbers of 'intellectual workers' in new categories, such as 'researchers', whom we shall discuss when the time comes. That is why Marx was on the mark when he said that socialism should 'abolish the distinction between manual and intellectual labour'. That is why Lenin's desperate insistence on the need to establish a new, polytechnic school education (it unfortunately had small success), which would, moreover, combine manual labour in real production with intellectual labour, was – and is – so important.[13]

A footnote to this paragraph adds that: 'in *Schools* (forthcoming), we will publish a long text by Krupskaya on this question. The text leaves no room at all for

---

12   Althusser 2014, p. 39.
13   Althusser 2014, p. 40.

doubt: it evokes Lenin's almost desperate efforts and the failure of his educational policies'.[14] Intellectual and manual labour are direct expressions of the division of knowledge. The role of the school is crucial, since it represents – as demonstrated by all subsequent mentions found in *On the Reproduction* – the material (i.e., political and class) origin of social reproduction. Better still, the school is inextricably linked to the mode of production or, to anticipate one of Macherey's theses: every mode of education is determined by a certain mode of production.[15] And, if the productive chain indeed has a social character, it could not be otherwise (in fact, it is not a matter of skilled labour since, as we have seen, we are not referring to knowledge as a content that can be increased, but about the fact of its formal fractioning). It is as if to say that the introduction of knowledge in the field of production makes the school, just as necessarily, the determining factor of its hierarchy.

This leads back to 'Student Problems': social division 'comes *massively* into play, and in a "blinding" way (which doubtlessly explains why it is not always possible to "see" it), in the very *object* of intellectual work; *in the knowledge* the university is commissioned to distribute to the students'.[16] Of course, the non-separateness of *On the Reproduction*'s technical division pertains to the mode of production. And yet, the footnote about 'Student Problems', as well as Althusser's reference to 'Schools' and, of course, his thesis according to which the forms of schooling are essentially functional to the process of reproduction, clarify any misunderstanding (even partially normative ones, as the one suggested by 'Student Problems') concerning the possibility that the capitalist mode of production might correspond to a non-capitalist mode of education. Every form of schooling (whose defence from the interference of class domination was grounded, in 'Student Problems', on the real distinction between the technical and social division) is functional to the mode of production in which it is placed, according to a principle (even if a partially descriptive one, as the one suggested by *On the Reproduction* seems to be) that could be defined as *a principle of contemporaneity between mode of education and mode of production* (where the second term is the ultimately determining term of the relation of contemporaneity). Therefore, it could be said that, according to the same principle – and far from justifying modes of transmission of generalities that would be impervious to modes of conditioning of social division – *only a non-*

---

14   Althusser 2014, p. 40 n. 26.

15   Regarding the socialist mode of education, Macherey will say that it 'implies the laws of
      a different mode of production' from the capitalist one, with the result that it 'cannot be
      anticipated in the field of any other mode of production'. ALT2. A14-01.04 (B14-01), p. 8.

16   Althusser 2011, pp. 12–13.

capitalist mode of production can correspond to a non-capitalist mode of education, something to which Lenin seems to allude in his 'desperate attempts'.

Let us return Althusser's references to 'Schools'. The second one is contained in Section II ('Reproduction of labour-power') of Chapter III ('The Reproduction of the Conditions of Production'). This section can also be found in 'Ideology and Ideological State Apparatuses (Notes Towards an Investigation)'.[17] Its theoretical framework is clearly linked to that of the previous passage. Indeed, it evolves into a questioning of the ways in which, under a capitalist regime, the reproduction of the (diversified) qualification of labour power can be ensured. Althusser answers that

> It is ensured differently from social formations based on slavery or serfdom: the reproduction of the qualification of labour power no longer tends (it is a question of a tendential law) to be ensured 'on the job' (instruction during production itself) but, increasingly, outside production, by the capitalist school system and other instances and institutions that we shall discuss at greater length in a moment.[18]

This statement is substantially identical to the one contained in 'Ideology and Ideological State Apparatuses: (Notes Towards an Investigation)', but it is quite clear that in 1970, with the collective research project now aborted, the reference to 'Schools' that was present in the *On the Reproduction* manuscript ('Cf. *Schools*, forthcoming in autumn 1969')[19] was removed.

The third reference to 'Schools' is contained in Section V ('On Ideological State Apparatuses and the Ideological By-Products of Their Practices') of Chapter VI ('The State'). The correct understanding of the concept of ideological apparatus needs to acknowledge a paradoxical reversal, whose irony in addition to the fact that, perhaps due to an idealistic lapse, it had been identified by Stalin himself ('I am afraid that, on this point at least, I will have to show a little personal gratitude to Stalin for his hint')[20] – lies in putting the cart before the horse, so to speak ('a right thinking materialist should [have put] the horse before the cart').[21] Althusser writes that 'institutions do not "produce" the ideologies corresponding to them. Rather, *certain elements of an ideology (the State Ideology) "are realized in" or "exist in" the corresponding institutions and their*

---

17   In Althusser 2014.
18   Althusser 2014, p. 50.
19   Althusser 2014, p. 50 n. 5.
20   Althusser 2014, p. 82.
21   Althusser 2014, p. 81.

practices'.[22] For the moment it is not essential to dwell on this question, relative to the primary ideology (for which certain elements of the ideology of the state exist and are realised in a given apparatus and its practices), to the secondary ideology (for which it is the apparatus and its practices that produce the ideology) and to their relationship of non-exclusion (i.e., overdetermination). Institutions, in fact, keep producing, within their practices, forms of ideology that would otherwise be inexplicable. This is the case for religious practice, which produces 'inside the Church, certain forms of ideology: ecclesiastical ideology, for example'[23] (although others are realised in other practices); it is also the case of scholastic practice, which 'produces particular forms that may be termed *scholastic ideology'.*[24] And here, programmatically, Althusser indicates that other forms of this specific ideology will be discussed elsewhere: in a footnote, we find the same reference to 'Schools' that we noted above.

The fourth and final allusion to the 'Schools' project is contained in Section II ('There is One Dominant Ideological Apparatus – Today the School System') of Chapter IX ('The Reproduction of the Relations of Production'). Given this further reference to reproduction, it can be assumed that the argument of this section will be the closest to Althusser's intentions, as indicated in the brief programmatic note mentioned above. Here too, a substantially identical passage will be reproduced in 'Ideology and Ideological State Apparatuses (Notes Towards an Investigation)'. Althusser discusses a passage that, as we will see, was already a recurring element in both Macherey and Tort's texts, which were written in 1968 (March and July respectively), and in Baudelot and Macherey's historical surveys, which were written in October–November 1969, towards the end of the collective research project. The Church was the dominant ideological state apparatus of the pre-capitalist period ('the *absolutely dominant* position of the *religious* Ideological State Apparatus explains why all ideological struggle from the sixteenth to the eighteenth century ... was concentrated in anti-clerical, anti-religious struggle').[25] Since the French Revolution, in a complex process aiming at hegemonic affirmation, the goal was to overthrow it. If the Church was dominant for the feudal aristocracy, the school becomes dominant for the capitalist-commercial bourgeoisie (courtesy of the parliamentary-democratic ideological apparatus): 'We think that the Ideological State Apparatus that has been elevated to the dominant position in

---

22   Althusser 2014, p. 82.
23   Ibid.
24   Althusser 2014, p. 83.
25   Althusser 2014, p. 142.

mature capitalist formations ... is the scholastic ideological apparatus'.[26] And yet, although this Althusserian thesis is now famous, it is evident that its theoretical justification is completely unexpected: if it is true that we must speak of a substitution, it is in fact equally necessary to give a reason for *this* substitution, as well as its mechanism of operation.

In any case, it goes without saying that it is here that Althusser, in a footnote and using the same terms he had used in previous occasions, refers to 'Schools', a work which promises to answer all these questions. But there is an addition that is clearly missing in the 1970 text:

> Let us, however, here and now point out the very big difference between the capitalist school system and the feudal Church: the former, unlike the feudal Church, is not an 'economic power' and takes no part in capitalist exploitation. To be sure, we cannot say as much, even with all the required nuances, about certain domains of scientific research.[27]

Can we therefore claim that *On the Reproduction* is still an unfinished work? For the remainder of the chapter, we will focus on this collective project of 'Schools'.

1   The School and the Text: Representation and Synecdoche

Pierre Macherey's 'Les mythologies scolaires', dated 10 March 1968, is the first theoretically substantial text among those which have been preserved.

The preliminary theoretical framework that supports this essay seems to overlap with that presented in his *A Theory of Literary Production*, written two years earlier. The myth of the literary work is joined by the myth of the school, and the theoretician of aesthetics meets the theoretician of ideology, as if, after all, these two roles could really be separated. Indeed, what is at stake here – and Tolstoy's work, or rather Macherey's analysis of Lenin's aesthetic theses on Tolstoy's work[28] has a paradigmatic value in this sense – is the *multiplicity* of social determinations of historical formations (highly complex and overdetermined) and the need for the author 'because of his personal and ideological relation [to his age]',[29] to place himself in a *merely partial position* within the structure

---

26   Althusser 2014, p. 143.
27   Althusser 2014, p. 144 n. 3.
28   See chapter 19 in Macherey 1978.
29   Macherey 1978, p. 120.

(i.e., 'to participate at a single level, in ignorance of all the others').[30] This could summarised in a simple formula: the work is always *situated*, that is, it represents *a situation that defines and is defined by the totality of relations*.

Between a totality (of the structure) and an element that belongs to it (an element in the situation) there is no simple relation of exclusion (one would say of analytical exclusion: *either* the totality *or* an element of the totality), but rather a relation of otherness (one would say of dialectical otherness: an element of the totality *posits* the whole structure *through* its negation). The complexity of the structure means that the element, *qua element*, refers to the external conditioning of other elements ('its positive presence is less important than the fact that it is, as it were, inscribed from the outside [*creusé de l'extérieur*]').[31] But an element of the situation, precisely because it belongs to the situation, cannot grasp – like God's all-seeing eye – the whole of the structure (Schlegel certainly would not have accused Macherey of having 'lost himself, alone on false mystical paths').[32] The totality of the work is not visible to the eye. It does not consist in a relation of mechanical (i.e., expressive) immediacy.

However, it remains true that the work of art, precisely by assuming a partial perspective (in other words, being that which denies the totality in favour of the part it occupies in the situation), does not posit (as its own presupposition) a structured totality (as a totality of relationships: Macherey is not a Kantian, since for Kant the set of conditions for a given conditioned, being unintentional, is not itself given). It is the singularity of the element, placed within the structure, that, because structured, reflects the entire set of structural relations (we will soon see how). But it follows that this set, reaching back to that partiality, is given as an absent totality, or as an absence of totality. If it is true that an element of the structure cannot be separated from the structure it belongs to (the partial position is in fact a structured position whose emergence is internally conditioned by the relation it holds with other singularities, which are *in turn* conditioned by that partial position: this is what 'being in a situation' means), then it is equally true that it is only by singling it out (which is inevitable since, being already separated, it occupies a single place of the structure) that it is possible to refer to the totality of relations. *For this very reason*, on the one hand, this totality necessarily posits itself as (its own) lack: 'the work exists above all by its determinate absences, by what it does not say, in its relation to

30   Macherey 1978, p. 121.
31   Ibid.
32   As he had done, targeting Moritz's *Über die bildende nachahmung*, in Schlegel 1963. For more on this topic, see Clemente 2016.

what it is not',[33] while on the other, as a complex totality, *it can only be given when it is (negatively) posited by that partiality*: 'In defining the necessity of the work we are not trying to demonstrate that all the components of its writing and reading are previously and extrinsically *given*'.[34] *If the totality is given as an absent totality, this absence determines the presence of the work, being its (lack of) foundation*: 'to explain the work is to show that contrary to appearances, it is not independent, but bears in its material substance the imprint of a determinate absence which is also the principle of its identity'.[35]

The task of (scientific) critique is that of de-centring what lies at the work's heart – revealing that it is inhabited by a radical exteriority that determines its infringement, and which prohibits any attempt to retrieve its alleged completeness: 'we must not falter at the prospect of revealing formlessness and imperfection in the work'.[36] The work is a not-all: its identity is essentially dual and intrinsically altered or, even better, differential and interspersed. In other words, it is dependent on what it reflects but does not reveal. Therefore, it is autonomous because it rests on an exteriority about which it is silent, and yet which represents its negative foundation.[37] Here, then, the category of *production* (the fact that the work establishes an overdetermined relationship with its own conditions of existence: 'if the work is a mirror it is certainly not by virtue of any manifest relation with the period "reflected"'),[38] replaces the category of *creation* ('the proposition that the writer or artist is a creator belongs to a humanist ideology').[39] This is because creation necessarily refers to the *unity* of an intention – whether considered as objective, that is, responding to restrictive models placed outside of time (that which determines the illusory nature of normative criticism), or as subjective, that is, responding to an author's intentions (that which determines the illusory nature of empirical criticism).[40]

Differentiality, defectiveness, and 'uniduality' are all notions emerging from the rejection of the unity postulate. The work, precisely because essentially

---

33   Macherey 1978, p. 154.
34   Macherey 1978, p. 50.
35   Macherey 1978, pp. 79–80.
36   Macherey 1978, p. 79.
37   And this is why, for Macherey, every Marxist literary critique – or rather, every non-Althusserian Marxist literary critique that would simply aim at the clarification of the work's material presuppositions – would be, in this sense, nothing more than a mode of interpretative critique, consequently falling into the postulate of the depth of the work.
38   Macherey 1978, p. 121.
39   Macherey 1978, p. 66.
40   For a detailed historical reconstruction of the French debate on literary criticism in the 1960s see Benelli 1981.

altered, is necessarily traversed by a multiplicity: 'the postulated unity of the work which, more or less explicitly, has always haunted the enterprise of criticism, must now be denounced';[41] or again: 'the work does not derive from the unity of an intention which permeates it, nor from its conformity to an autonomous model'.[42]

Ultimately, critique strips away a work's determinate spatiality, its localised character, which on a metaphorical level indicates the work's supposed interiority. In order to understand its necessity, it is not enough to penetrate its depths; the cut which wounds it should be shown. The exchange produced by the reader thus has a revealing function for both the normative and empirical critic. In substituting one term for another, in the exchange of the work for another that is purified because it is sprouted on the manifestation of what was previously hidden (is this not the full gesture of every hermeneutic operation?) – 'in a single gesture two things are revealed – the *space* of the work and the content which fills this space'.[43] 'Space' and 'content' are notions presupposed by all critical illusions. The work *is* its unitary content and the unity of its content *is* the very space it fills. A localised content and a filled space: the work is the unity whose completeness already fills the abstract space with a *mythologised* representation, assuming we understand myth in a Romantic sense, as Macherey does, as the intransitive unity of signified and signifier.[44] For this reason, the work will be as ideological as that of the man-God who creates his own object, full of substance.

•••

This was a necessary excursus because Macherey seems to perform the same theoretical gesture: the myth of the work as a unitary space is juxtaposed to the myth of the school as a place that is a function of a fiction. Indeed, the school too is a *place*, established by its representation: it is 'the representation of a *place* [*lieu*], and ... this place appears as privileged through its representation'.[45] Once again, Macherey uses the term 'representation' with a reversal of the syntactic scheme of the statement: to say that the school is a place already means to

---

41   Macherey 1978, p. 78.
42   Macherey 1978, p. 40.
43   Macherey 1978, p. 75.
44   Moritz highlights precisely this point when he observes that: 'the concept "Jupiter" means in the domain of the imagination first of all himself, just as the concept "Caesar" in the order of real things means Caesar himself'. Moritz 1962, p. 192.
45   ALT2. A14-01.04 (A), p. 2.

represent it, just as to identify it with its representative content already means to place it. If, on the one hand, representation locates, on the other the place is always the *locus* of a representation, such that in Macherey's text the term 'place' always functions as a determinate qualification of the term 'representation'. The fact that the school corresponds to its own representational content means that it is the object that makes representation, so to speak, the transcendental principle determining its topology and the boundaries that define its consistency – the 'one-place' and the 'place-one' that it (representationally) fills. Macherey's argument is already outlined (and this defines, in this first part of his work, its essentially descriptive character): *for the ideological discourse, the school in itself is mediated by its representation, and the ideological transcendental principle that constitutes its symbolic status leaves no unrepresentable remainder.*

I refer to an ideological discourse because the school – its representation – has a distinguishing trait. It is the 'analogical place where political fiction is formulated, politics in the form of fiction'.[46] We will see later what it means to speak of an analogy. For now, it will suffice to say that the unity that is peculiar to any place, however privileged, is undermined precisely when its fictitious character is denounced, showing how ideological discourse is the discourse of an essential concealment. Fiction by definition always has a transitive character (a duplicity that establishes, as we will see, its analogical nature): how does the school pretend? What does the unity of its representation aim at? The fiction implied by that representation plays on the edge of an exteriority. As a representation, the school is internal, that is, undivided and separate; but, when considered in its fictitious function, it is *simultaneously* perched towards an exteriority. A unitary and unified representation (i.e., localised), it is also defined by a dissimulative function linked to an exteriority. But again, how does the school pretend? Macherey explains that:

> The school is the place *par excellence* where the contradictions proper to the capitalist regime are represented without the appearance of class struggle: it is the point on the ideological thread where class struggle disappears.[47]

This is its content: the representation represents a disguised reconciliation. The school, being a specific place, implies an essentially negative (because dis-

---

46   ALT2. A14-01.04 (A), p. 2.
47   ALT2. A14-01.04 (A), p. 2.

simulative) act, linked to a fictitious and programmed misrecognition. Hence its undeniable clarity: its *imago*, which ideology considers as the thing itself, dissolves class struggle. If politics is what addresses class struggle (the 'contradictions proper of the capitalist regime'), the school's fictional nature implies the *myth* (the representation) of a *community without conflict, because depoliticised*. Is it a coincidence that this myth was clearly formulated by literature (or at least a specific representation of it) starting in the fifteenth and sixteenth centuries, as testified to by a precise recurrence? We can see this in *Rabelais'* 'myth of Thélème'[48] which describes, for the first time, 'the fictitious aspect of the scholastic institution' showing how it is instrumental to representing society 'as a unified whole [*tout unifié*]':[49] 'Thelema is the prehistoric figure of the school as a place [*lieu*] of reconciliation'. We see it also in Rousseau, whose *Emile* – 'a child without school' just like Thélème's 'school without children' – 'plays the role of a place [*lieu*] of reconciliation'.[50] These are representations of a reconciliation designed on an (essentially ideological) imposture, a camouflage: it is always a place, a *lieu* – a *lieu-école* and a *lieu-enfant*.

Once again, a representation conceals and masks. We said that, in its fictitious character, it plays on the edge of an exteriority. Had Althusser not already shown that the differential process of the appropriation of intellectual and manual labour is what determines the school's reproductive and social character? Macherey seems to share this assumption. The exteriority of the modes of production and the essentially reproductive purpose of the school (its being 'real', so to speak, because defined by the technical division of knowledge, imparted 'in the flesh') represent the otherness that is concealed by its own representation (Bidet was therefore right to point out that *On the Reproduction* was 'at its heart' the theorisation of 'Schools'). While sharing Althusser's assumption, what is peculiar to Macherey's treatment is that already with the principle of representation he not only looks at the functioning of the mechanisms that generate the fiction, but also reveals how exteriority needs to be concealed (and perhaps we were right in emphasising how Althusser's analysis was permeated by issues that were not yet fully resolved).[51] The fictional nature

---

48   *Thélème* is the name of the abbey (or, rather, of the anti-abbey, for the common life lived within it is characterised by unconditional freedom – hence Macherey's indication) that Gargantua makes the monk with whom he shared part of the events that make up Rabelais's masterpiece build, at the end of his *The Very Horrific Life of Great Gargantua, Father of Pantagruel*.

49   ALT2. A14-01.04 (A), p. 3.

50   Ibid.

51   This also marks a tonal shift from *Pour une théorie de la production littéraire*. In that text, the aim was to show the (absent) exteriority of the artwork with respect to the illusory

of representation is established on this exteriority of the modes of production, because this fictionality, as a place of reconciliation, *is functional to the mechanisms of their reproduction.* Does this mean that behind (non-)political fiction there is a (class) politics of fiction?

It is here that Macherey's claim about literature could be reformulated: what must be denounced as false, for the critic of (scholastic) ideology, is the postulate of the unity of the scholastic apparatus. There is no inside (of the representation) and no outside (of production). Instead, inside and outside are given simultaneously in a relation of overdetermination:

> what distinguishes the school is therefore its being caught up in a relationship of over-determination: on the one hand, the school plays a 'real' role in the system of production, since it ensures the reproduction of the two forms of the division of labour; on the other hand, it plays an essential function in the ideological displacement, since it masks the real forms in which this division is realised, by forging the myth of a community without politics.[52]

In this passage, which merely outlines an argument, Macherey is saying that the school is part of a two-sided relationship that determines it as both inseparable and overdetermined.

Let us continue: 'the school plays a "real" role in the system of production, since it ensures the reproduction of the two forms of the division of labour'. I call *real* the level on which the school, while being *determined* by the mode of production, also *determines* its own reproduction (with what Macherey will later call the 'knowledge' 'in the flesh' imparted at school[53] and functional, through its supposed technical assurance, to the 'real' reproduction of the forms of the division of labour in general).

I call *imaginary* the level on which the school – as a *representation* whose content is *determined* by the modes of production of the 'real level' (in its ideological reversal of a community without politics, the representation of the school is not just any representation, but a specific representation of a specific mode of production, which shows that the depoliticisation of its representative

---

representations of bourgeois criticism. Here, on the contrary (even if it shares the same theoretical background), the aim is to see, by presupposing the exteriority of the modes of production, the reasons and mechanisms by which the ideological school representation functions.

52   ALT2. A14-01.04 (A), p. 2.

53   ALT2. A14-01.04 (B14-01), p. 1.

content leads to a politics of depoliticisation) – comes to have two functions. On the one hand, the representation conditions the functioning of the 'real level' (we will consider this later, for the moment all that is known is that masking is instrumental the reproduction through the covering of the class struggle: 'it is the point in the ideological thread where class struggle vanishes';[54] 'it masks the real forms in which this division is realised, by forging the myth of a community without politics').[55]

On the other hand, however, it also plays what could be defined a *synecdochal* function since, as an ideal representation, it replaces the 'true' social reality. A synecdochal function that, so to speak, produces a *doubling* of representations: *the representation of the school forged by (class-based) political society forges, in turn, the representation of a society without (class-based) politics.* Macherey seems to allude to this when he writes that 'society is like a school';[56] or when, again in reference to Rabelais' *Thélème*, he writes that 'the school is not only an instrument of representation of society, but it is the instrument of a certain representation: of a representation of politics that must necessarily pass through the fiction of the school, because it allows the representation of society as a *unified whole*'.[57]

The modes of production of the 'real level' determine the 'imaginary level' while the 'imaginary level' conditions the mechanism of operation of the 'real level'. On the one hand, determined by the modes of production, the school ensures 'the reproduction of the two forms of the division of labour'; on the other hand, because of those modes of production, it forges 'the myth of a community without politics' which, in addition to engendering (we can provisionally say: ideologically) their reproduction, takes the place of society through its own representation.

The implications of all the above can be reduced to three brief, interrelated observations:

1. *The Politics of Depoliticisation.* Dissimulation is determinate because the social agent of its production is determinate. It pertains to a specific instrumentality: the school conceals class struggle because it is the apparatus of the ruling class. Class struggle lies behind its own characteristic concealment, and concealment is what lies behind reproduction (as it ideologically conditions it). This thesis had already been anticipated by Althusser's hypothesis of a principle of contemporaneity between mode

---

54   ALT2. A14-01.04 (A), p. 2.
55   Ibid.
56   ALT2. A14-01.04 (A), p. 4.
57   ALT2. A14-01.04 (A), p. 3.

of education and mode of production, reducible to the notion of over-determination: '[the school's] representative (symbolic) status depends on the existence of a historically determined mode of production'[58] and 'the school as we know it can only be understood in terms of all the relations it has with the capitalist system'. Every mode of production lives in secret. This means that the principle of representation is indeed a transcendental principle (and therefore *a priori*: for the capitalist mode of production the school is what the theatre was for the ancient mode, and the church was for the feudal one – all representations that are functional to ideological reproduction). And yet it is an historicised transcendental principle ('this figure is not eternal') because the forms of production themselves are historicised ('compared to the ancient and feudal modes, the educational system occupied a completely different place'). This explains why Macherey quotes from Chairman Mao's letter to Cai Hesen: 'in today's world the schools and the press, which are the two most important instruments of education, are entirely under the control of the capitalists'.[59]

2.   *The Politics of Concealment.* Because of overdetermination, the class politics that determines the specificity of the mode of education is *a politics of equivocation: whenever it is said politically, it is said ideologically, that is, equivocally.* A further qualification of the representative content: if the school is the place of a fiction, it 'is the site of half-confessed political speculation'.[60] This is what was presupposed by the reference to the overdetermined contemporaneity of the notions of the interiority of the representative fiction and the exteriority of its disguising function. On this topic, this passage by Macherey should be quoted in full:

> [the school] is the place where a certain politics – determined by the interests of the bourgeoisie, and desperately supported by the petty bourgeoisie which is only really at home within the school – both appears (formulates itself, assumes a figure) and disappears. The image of the school is what obscures real political problems (those posed by class struggle): properly interpreted, it is the figure of avoidance.[61]

3.   *On reformism as referring to the synecdotal function of depoliticised representation.* Reformism is an essential specification: if at first we only knew about the existence of a synecdochal function, now we also understand

---

58   Ibid.
59   ALT2. A14-01.04 (A), p. 6.
60   Ibid.
61   ALT2. A14-01.04 (A), p. 6.

its effects: why does the school as representation takes the place of society, in a doubling of representations? Because, if society is like a school, 'then politics is like a reform'.[62] A reform 'replaces political action'. Within the real society, political action is replaced by a semblance of pedagogical action as what circumscribes the system of conflict resolution under spontaneous and disorganised forms: 'conflict can be resolved where it arises, the problem can be solved where it is posed: at school, pedagogy is nothing but the system of this ideal resolution'.[63] This is therefore one of the effects of the synecdochal function of school representation: if politics conceals (2.), *it also conceals the way out of this concealment.*

2   The Mechanisms of Fiction: Generation by Reduction and Pedagogical Separation

We have examined Macherey's analysis insofar as it is focused on the recognition of the 'fictitious character of the educational image'. What we will now attempt to do is identify 'which mechanism engenders this fiction'.[64]

The first generative mechanism is that of *reduction and pedagogical separation*. In order for the representation to fall within the boundaries of its ideological placement, it must be supported by mechanisms of material closure. A representation is not something that falls from above; it must be engendered through real practices of separation that support (in a specular manner) its ideal closure: 'this does not only belong to scholastic representation: it is a real closure [*fermeture*], which assigns to the institution its own place, essentially defined by the limits that protect it'.[65] A real limitation generates an ideal closure. The *fermeture* is a closure that arouses 'an attitude of respect' because it represents a 'sacred place, where a cult is performed'. It is not surprising that the school has stolen from the church – 'on which it was originally a dependent' – the sacred character of its symbolic space, after a 'schismatic' gesture of separation: 'both must occupy different places, which nevertheless have in common their being specific places'.

But in order to separate, an expert is necessary. This was the role of the Jesuits:

---

62   ALT2. A14-01.04 (A), p. 4.
63   Ibid.
64   ALT2. A14-01.04 (A), p. 8.
65   Ibid.

This separate place was invented, fabricated from scratch by specialists of separation, since they were ecclesiastics: precisely the Jesuits who opened the first colleges at the end of the sixteenth century, an institution that has been handed down to us practically unchanged.[66]

And its invention implies the formation of a social group, also invented and 'made from scratch' (this is the original meaning of the pedagogical action, if it is true that its action is formative): the student milieu is the social product of schooling since 'to educate means to break nature, and to substitute it with a created order': 'the school environment has been constituted as a separate, autonomous environment, subject to it its own rules'; or again: 'the school thus appears as the framework in which a particular 'social' group can function'.[67]

The Jesuits are the agents of separation, that is, the creation of an institution that represents the material framework for a new social group. These, in short, are the specific procedures through which it is possible to outline schooling practices.

1. *Moral formation procedure.* This is an unprecedented procedure, for two reasons. On the one hand, the moral formation of the individual is, for the first time, *openly assigned to an institution.* On the other hand, this entails that the very idea of education is completely displaced [*déplacée*] with respect to its traditional function (the transmission and reception of knowledge, starting from a position of preliminary deprivation). In this sense, regardless of its contents, education assumes a moral character (and therefore can be qualified, as the Bourdieu of the first half of the 1960s knew, according to the notions of sin and guilt, talent and grace.[68] All the ideological language relating to the qualification of mater-

---

66   ALT2. A14-01.04 (A), p. 9.
67   ALT2. A14-01.04 (A), p. 10.
68   I offer two exemplary quotations to substantiate this point. The first is from Bourdieu and Darbel 1991, p. 87: 'a church where certain chosen individuals come to nurture a virtuoso faith while conformists and hypocrites come to hurry through a class ritual, the museum can suddenly become a place of pilgrimage crowded with the close-knit ranks of the faithful, who, in New York, Washington, Tokyo, or Paris, wait patiently in long lines to have a brief glimpse of a masterpiece designated for collective adulation'. The second is from Bourdieu and Passeron 1979, pp. 69–70: 'what might be called the charisma ideology (because it valorizes "grace" or the "gift") supplies the privileged classes with a legitimation of their cultural privileges, which are thereby transmuted from a social heritage into individual grace or personal merit. Behind this mask, "class racism" can be flaunted without ever being seen for what it is'.

ially determined abilities – consider the 'artisanal technique of language' mentioned by Balibar when commenting on Bourdieu and Passeron – originates from this first separation procedure). Education 'is now determined from this original formation, which is realised by the school institution'.[69]

2. *Disciplinary procedure*. Discipline is the instrument of education. Morality is a thing (which has been formed and therefore produced), and it must be supervised. Ariès, who Macherey quotes, writes that 'the definitive establishment of a disciplinary code completes the evolution from the medieval school, a simple classroom, to the modern college, a complex institution, not only for teaching but for supervising and guiding the youth'. Life becomes political, not because it was not already so (that is, it was already regulated by particular forms of what some would call 'practices of subjectivation'), but because the process of separation causes it to replace, as a (disciplined) form of life, a (yet) un-formed form of life: 'this regulation accompanies the student in all the details of his behaviour: it replaces the constraints of "life", from which he is relieved, which now assume a rectified form'.[70] This has two implications: first, if life is a 'form of life' that replaces a life that is 'not yet formed', then separation establishes a regime of equivalence between the world of the school and the real world (in the sense that they both respond to their own rules): 'if it is separate, it is also an equivalent world, which, with the proper means, can take the place of the real world'. Second, it seems necessary to recall the transmission factor of scientific generalities – as defined by a relationship of substantial inequality (i.e., technically determined) – that precisely functions as the correlate of the educational process, accomplished through discipline (morality is constituted by hierarchisation and by verticality): 'the appearance of the function of the teacher (as educator) and of the pupil (as the real support of the educational enterprise)'.[71] This is as if to say that the Althusserian principle of substantial inequality is formally structured by the disciplinary procedure, working as a separating factor.

3. *Emulation procedure*. Although the school submits the students to a common form of life, this submission – inserted in a system of emulative competition – tends to 'encourage the development of individual originality, as long as it is affirmed within the framework of an essential conformity'.

---

69   ALT2. A14-01.04 (A), p. 10.

70   ALT2. A14-01.04 (A), p. 11.

71   ALT2. A14-01.04 (A), p. 11.

More precisely, the horizontality of the disciplinary form does not imply the verticality of individualities, as if the latter were a random effect of the former. On the contrary, 'it appears that one of the aims of the institution, under the disguise of educating, is that of selecting individuals: it is the idea of success that gives shape to the process of schooling, much more than that of learning'.[72]

4. *Written tasks procedure.* Linked to the emulation procedure, this is another unprecedented procedure, since previously 'only oral exercises were known'. It is functional to the implementation of the emulation procedure: 'these are the forms in which the principle of competition is realised'. Written tasks allow for the understanding of one student to be evaluated with respect to another and exams sanction the progression through educational stages. But, as seen in 3., learning is only the apparent role of education. This means that the evaluation of a student's understanding and the sanctioning of his or her degree of education essentially refer to '*success*' as the institution's specific purpose (the exercises 'are defined essentially by the fact that they are fictitious exercises')[73] and go to reinforce 'the separation that is constitutive of the scholastic universe'.

5. *Gradual teaching procedure.* Separation implies a separate temporality. Stepping into the classroom entails a 'farewell to the 'other world', the one that remains outside the school institution; when its doors close establishing a time that is unlike others'.[74] The gradualness of the teaching establishes 'a differentiated scholastic time' because teaching is hierarchical – it distributes the students 'in distinct classes' and the passage from one class time to another is sanctioned by a (written) selection procedure, instrumental for the emergence of individualities (by emulation).[75] Graduality is, so to speak, the archetypal procedure of all other separation procedures: writing and emulation, moral education and discipline are not, in other words, scattered elements 'but rather are part a systematic package'.[76]

6. *Procedure of the teaching of Letters.* For the time being – we will return to this topic later – it will suffice to quote Macherey:

> literary teaching has, from the very start, a general vocation: it is, as we will see, supportive of the idea of a total formation of the individual;

---

72   Ibid.
73   ALT2. A14-01.04 (A), p. 12.
74   ALT2. A14-01.04 (A), p. 9.
75   ALT2. A14-01.04 (A), p. 12.
76   Ibid.

more than a subject of teaching, it is a discipline, the 'speculative' support of the moral discipline imposed elsewhere.[77]

The separation of the scholastic world is the effect of these real procedures, and it is on the basis of this separation that the form of representation is generated. The real school is a complete and self-regulating artificial space ('invented, completely fabricated') 'which has substituted its own rules of operation for the laws of the real world'.[78] And yet, once again, we should not lose sight of the separation function. It is worth reiterating that the school is part of a real relation ('the relation between school and society is real'): on the 'real level', it is instrumental for the reproduction of the relations of production within a relation of overdetermination (relative to the technical forms of labour in general).[79] *At the same time*, the school is situated in an imaginary relation ('scholastic separation gives to this relationship the fantastic form of an ideal reconstitution'): here the function of the real separation is to support an ideal closure. Here we find again the *leitmotiv* of myth, place, and depoliticisation: 'the closed place of the school encloses within its limits a new and better society'. The school has a real function insofar as it occupies a real function; it has an imaginary function insofar as, as a determinate and determining representation, that real function also assumes an imaginary function.

A small step (it is an 'already mentioned topic'), but a step forward nonetheless: indeed, we already knew that the school is a representation; we now know one of the mechanisms responsible for its generation.

3 The Mechanisms of Fiction: Functioning by Pedagogical Analogy as an Act of Ideological Belief

With the second generative factor of fiction, that of pedagogical analogy, we reach a truly crucial passage in Macherey's text.

Let's return for a moment to the practice of scholastic exercises and tests which, for other practices such as moral education or the contents of teaching itself (in particular, the Letters), has a real paradigmatic value. The scholastic exercise, as we have seen, 'is difficult, and its result is sanctioned by a report: success or failure'.[80] But what is most important is that taking these tests *resembles* having a job ('it has all the appearance of a job'), albeit lacking

---

77   Ibid.
78   Ibid.
79   ALT2. A14-01.04 (A), p. 13.
80   ALT2. A14-01.04 (A), p. 15.

its essential character 'which is to be productive'. *In school, the student works unproductively.* In other words, and this is the point, the student works in a fictitious way (it is 'an artificial labour, because it is unproductive'). 'The school universe is a separate one, where a fiction is played, because it is a world where nothing is produced'.[81]

Of course, the scholastic exercise *is* a real practice (as well as the education and the contents that are taught: it is no coincidence that these are three of the separation mechanism's procedures, and the latter, as we have seen, is a real mechanism generating an ideal closure). The point, however, is that it triggers a mechanism placed in the order of fiction, even if peculiarly established: if scholastic work resembles real work, then it is *as if* it were real work. The result is that *pedagogical practice is an analogical* practice ('all activity is analogical, and it is carried out in the mode of the as if').[82] Thus, moral education, whose character is relative to the obligations, is also analogical: 'they are not speculative necessities of knowledge, which imply the submission to the order of the truth, but social obligations, which are first formulated in the artificial framework of the school'.[83] Even contents that are taught (again, those of the Letters) are analogical: 'literary teaching is the means by which this effect is generated: it is the epitome of a teaching that is not worthwhile for its own sake (it generates useless knowledge), but for something else, about which it says nothing'.[84] Society is already there, in a presence-absence: 'the discipline and the content of the teaching tend to realise this analogical displacement: for the child, the school takes the place of society; following this example, he learns what a real society is'.[85]

The pedagogical analogy is the second generative factor of representation. Why should it generate the content of the school as a representation? Once again: 'the school universe is a separate one, where the mechanism of a fiction is played out, because it is a world where nothing is produced'.[86] Macherey's statement must be taken quite seriously, since here the analogical mechanism (which stems from the fact that at school nothing is produced, but students work as if that was a real job) has an explicit causal link to the fiction of representation. It is a world in which nothing is produced, so the school permits the functioning of the mechanism of fiction. The analogy generates the fiction,

81   Ibid.
82   ALT2. A14-01.04 (A), p. 13.
83   ALT2. A14-01.04 (A), p. 15.
84   ALT2. A14-01.04 (A), p. 14.
85   ALT2. A14-01.04 (A), p. 16.
86   ALT2. A14-01.04 (A), p. 15.

and it cannot be otherwise: because if it is true that the school operates as if it was a productive place, *it is able trigger an analogical mechanism only on the assumption of a fundamental dissimulation*. If school operates *as if* it were society, then it is not society. The '*as if*', while referring to an exteriority, must by definition have a simple imitative relation with that which merely resembles: to imitate something does not mean becoming the thing that is imitated. In other words, an imitation performs a dissimulative function with regards to that which it imitates. Just as it recalls the imitated thing, it necessarily conceals it as something that is merely an object of mimicry. This explains how the fictitious dissimulation of representation is the necessary product of the analogical mechanism – it is only with the introduction of a fundamental dissimulation that it is possible to establish an imitative relationship. There is no analogy without dissimulation and there is no dissimulation without analogy.

This brings us to an important first clarification. We have said (§1) that the modes of production placed in the 'real level' *determine* the representative content of the school in the 'imaginary level' (according to the 'principle of contemporaneity' for which the representation of the school is not just any representation, but a specific representation of a mode of production). This is a correct but still inaccurate thesis (to use Kantian terminology: what is the schema that makes the modes of production 'fall into' the representation, so to speak?). The analogical mechanism is responsible for this determination. Indeed, representation can be nothing more than *the negation of the externality that is analogically recalled*: if society is divided into classes, and the school is *as if* it were that society, then the school, as a representation produced by the analogical mechanism, must conceal that division: in other words, 'it hides the real forms in which this division is realised by forging the myth of a community without politics'.[87] In short, *the myth of a classless community is engendered by the analogical mechanism, precisely because it turns the school into the analogue of the class society.*

Secondly, the analogical mechanism, besides being what generates the representation, *is also the mechanism that specifies its function* – something that allows it to occupy a privileged place compared to the simple but necessary one of separation. The reason is clear enough: if it is true that the school is *as if* it were society, not only it is *not* society (see the generative mechanism of fiction that we have just explored), but it has a specific imitative relation with society ('the school imitates the real'):[88] being its imitation, the school *conceals* society as much as it conceals *society*. If the analogy, by definition,

---

87   ALT2. A14-01.04 (A), p. 2.
88   ALT2. A14-01.04 (A), p. 13.

denies the external object of which the other is the analogue (society is *not* the school), it also necessarily presupposes it, being an analogue of *that* external object (the school is the analogue of society and nothing else). Insofar as it is based on a fundamental concealment, the analogy causes the representation to refer to that exteriority. This means that the school, as an analogue of society, *assumes its real content in order to disguise it as a reduced content* (*the analogy makes society present in school even in its absence*): 'the scholastic universe is a reduced universe, which reproduces in its own way, in its own dimension, society itself'.[89]

The school is a 'universe in miniature, which reproduces itself in its own way'. The school reproduces. But this is not a technically supposed reproduction (that of the school that imparts a knowledge that is mean to be functional to the technical division of labour in general), but a reproduction that is representatively performed. This means that the fundamental outcome of the analogical mechanism is that the school *qua* representation – its fictitious content being analogous to society – *prepares the students for society's modes of production* (here's a reference to the already-operational mechanism of fiction). We could therefore say that *the pedagogical analogy is functional to ideological reproduction*: 'the scholastic world … is essentially subject to the mechanism of ideological reproduction'.[90] Macherey articulates this point in a crucial passage:

> The school system *does not give the individual a place in society*: this place is already determined. It gives him his *relation* to this place: it adds a feeling of obligation to this real constraint. What the child learns at school is nothing but society itself: what he reads is the place that inscribes him within the social order.[91]

It is not the individual's place in society, but the relation that the individual will have with this place. Although not explicitly, this passage clearly refers to Althusser's claim in 'Marxism and Humanism' that

> ideology is a matter of the *lived* relation between men and their world. … In ideology men do indeed express, not the relation between them and their conditions of existence, but *the way* they live the relation between

---

89   Ibid.
90   ALT2. A14-01.04 (A), p. 15.
91   ALT2. A14-01.04 (A), p. 16. My emphasis.

them and their conditions of existence: this presupposes both a real relation and an *'imaginary'*, *'lived'* relation.[92]

Ultimately, Macherey's originality consists in taking this Althusserian passage
as the basic framework for his own argument. The fiction of scholastic representation does not concern a real relation with the modes of production: it is not
an expression of the 'real relation' of which Althusser speaks, since the place it
occupies in the division of labour in general is already determined by the scholastic mechanism of technical reproduction of the modes of production (what
was said in §1 concerning the articulation of the 'real level'). The fiction of
representation, on the other hand, serves to define the '*"imaginary"*, *"lived"* relation', that is, to produce 'a feeling of obligation' towards one's own conditions of
existence: *one must believe in reality. The school sanctions the fundamental act
of belief towards the modes of production – or, precisely, it imaginatively establishes* 'the place that inscribes him within the social order' (such that 'the school
environment is an artificial institution that symbolically represents the social
order').[93]

This is why the representation has been defined as 'ideological'. Indeed, not
only is its content ideological (since the community without politics is the negation of the externality that is recalled by analogy), but its function is too. It
predisposes the individual, through a feeling of obligation, to fit into the modes
of production. *The school system is a system of ideological reproduction: if, for
Althusser, ideology is related to the way in which the conditions of existence are
lived, for Macherey this depends on an analogical relationship. If – still in agree-
ment with Althusser – this is an 'imaginary', 'lived relation', for Macherey that
lived and imaginary relation presupposes the school as a representation.*

This brings us to a second, important clarification. I said above (§1) that
the 'imaginary level' conditions the very mechanism of operation of the 'real
level'. This is correct, but still somewhat inaccurate. This conditioning is possible thanks to the analogical mechanism. *Ideological reproduction determines
real reproduction as an effect of the analogical function.* We enter into the reality
of social division (which implies a 'real relation' with the 'conditions of existence') because, thanks to the school, we already believe in it (which implies a
lived and *imaginary* relation with those conditions of existence).

To produce a belief in reality: ultimately this is the function of the school as
fiction: 'in the conditions which are fixed to it, it essentially would have to gen-

---

92   Althusser 2005, p. 133.
93   ALT2. A14-01.04 (A), p. 16.

erate a fictional image of itself, supporting a diversion, whose direction, as we have seen, is not pedagogical, but political'.[94]

4   Five Hypotheses about School Apparatuses

The fact that, so far, Macherey's analysis has focused on the question of representation clearly leaves unanswered a rather elementary question: after all, aren't we are taught something in school? But that's not all. On closer inspection, it is precisely the *content* of this teaching that technically defines the *place* that will later be occupied within the social division of labour:

> Indeed, at school, the individual does not only learn an ideology that displaces in advance his relation to the place he will occupy in the system of production: he also acquires the 'knowledge' (whatever the degree of their rationalisation) that will allow him 'technically' to occupy this place.[95]

That is why, the 'real' school should be placed on what has been called the 'real level' – thus referring to the technical division of knowledge that is transmitted therein: indeed, it is this knowledge that, so to speak, 'really' reproduces the modes of production – if by this we mean, as we should, the *actual* contents of knowledge, instrumental to the distribution of jobs in the field of production. To think of schoolwork as an unproductive work that generates the representative fiction is, in this sense, still insufficient and analytically incomplete. This incompleteness could be addressed by asking: is this unproductiveness, if functional to the feeling of obligation, the same for everyone, since the modes of production imply a fundamental division, i.e., a class division?

And yet, it is precisely the generative analogical mechanism of the representation of the school as a unitary whole that ideologically reproduces those modes of production. On the one hand, we speak of 'real' reproduction; on the other, of ideological reproduction. The point, then, is to show how these do not refer to separate processes but rather should be seen as a single process of reproduction. *No knowledge is fully impervious to belief (in reality). All knowledge, even when true (as for its content), is false (by vocation). At every level it is subsumed by ideological reproduction.* In school there is no know-

---

94   ALT2. A14-01.04 (B14-01), p. 1.
95   Ibid.

ledge that either could or could not enter the circle of production. To over-turn Macherey's statement quoted above, we could say that the knowledge that will allow the individual to 'technically' take a place in the distribution of jobs is learned through the mediation of an ideology that anticipates its relationship with the place that the individual will occupy in the system of production. In a nutshell: *the technical division is always-already a social division*.

But if the school reproduces *class division*, then the knowledge that is trans-mitted therein must be characterised by a *fundamental division* (to anticipate: that between intellectual and manual labour). *The school does not exist:* it is a set of heterogeneous elements (and Macherey's hypothesis about Bourdieu and Passeron, we will see shortly, is paradigmatic) that are ideological by voca-tion because functional to reproduction. Therefore, it could be said that the representation, representing a unified whole, is also instrumental – in addition to the concealment of class division – *for the concealment of its own funda-mental division* (which, ultimately, is linked to the first concealment): it hides its inclusion of a technical division functional to social reproduction. This is why the school *presents* itself as a place of reconciliation: precisely because it is not internally unified, but rather divided and heterogeneous. *We go to school believing that everything is the same for everyone: the ideological mechanism has already begun to spin.*

Ultimately: it is not enough to speak of representation (as Macherey has done so far), because it then would be impossible to fully understand the schools' procedure of ideological reproduction (the unproductiveness of schol-astic work that triggers the analogy, although essential, is still analytically insuf-ficient). On the other hand, it is not enough to speak of technical modalities for the transmission of knowledge because, without referring to representation and to its function, it would be impossible to understand that such a technical division is already a social division.

Here Macherey introduces five hypotheses, which I will now briefly analyse.

4.1   First Hypothesis

Since the mechanism of ideological reproduction conditions what has been called 'real reproduction', then *the technical division is already a social divi-sion*. If the modes of production are technically reproduced, the technique of this reproduction is already socially mediated. Macherey sees no real divi-sion between technical and social division: ideological reproduction, although determined by the modes of production, reproduces them through an already socialised technical division. If the modes of production placed in the 'real level' determine the modes of education, the latter condition the technical reproduction in the 'real level', to the extent that the technical division is already a social division. Macherey's articulation of this point deserves to be quoted in full:

> Indeed, at school, the individual does not simply learn an ideology that displaces in advance his relation to the place he will occupy in the system of production: he also acquires the 'knowledge' (whatever the degree of their rationalisation) that will 'technically' allow him to occupy this place. I propose, as a working hypothesis, that in the school as we know it the mechanism of ideological reproduction occupies a dominant position, and it is always in relation to this mechanism that the heterogeneous elements of school learning are determined in the last resort. That is to say that, on the one hand, the school does not transmit the 'technical' elements of a real learning which would be, on the other, reinscribed in a fantastic configuration: school learning, whatever its content, takes place in the forms fixed by the mechanism of the ideological reproduction.[96]

We should not avoid Charybdis only to fall prey to Scylla: while we should not believe in a real pedagogical process – that is, one that would be technically detached from the influence of social reproduction ('this hypothesis is itself an effect of the ideological process, which tends to assimilate social process of formation and technical acquisition') – this does not mean that our analysis can terminate with the representation of the school as a unified whole. In other words, it is necessary to identify what both precedes and conditions 'the functioning of this mechanism': *the process of social selection*. Clearly, this process is not technically produced, as if the social distribution of the school population could find its *ratio essendi* in natural attitudes ('the famous aptitudes [*aptitudes*] are the pedagogical reverse side of the real inequalities, that is to say that they are socially determined'). This means that the school, although 'it represents itself as an unified whole' is actually constituted by the juxtaposition 'of different appearances, which transmit heterogeneous contents to different audiences'.[97] In fact, how would it be possible to reproduce the modes of production – that is, to look at class division – if not by transmitting heterogeneous contents by means of heterogeneous apparatuses (essentially represented by the three cycles of teaching), through a technical division that is already ideologically conditioned? 'Very different things are "conceived" under the notion

---

96   Ibid.
97   ALT2. A14-01.04 (B14-01), p. 2.

of school, whose natures are in fact conflicting: at the same time, the notion of education does not have any meaning in itself, since it represents the combination of heterogeneous formations.'[98]

4.2   Second Hypothesis

Given that the school, as a unified representation, is actually the place of a heterogeneous superposition of apparatuses (again, represented by the three cycles of teaching), we can advance this hypothesis: for each determinate historical condition, there is a determinate system that assigns a specific *place* to a specific apparatus, thus generating a specific configuration (heterogeneous and not unified). This means to deepen the principle of contemporaneity between mode of education and mode of production alongside the apparatuses that are behind representation: if the (historically determinate) mode of production determines the mode of education, then 'to each type of social formation, there corresponds a determinate mode of education'. There are four of them: the ancient, the medieval, the capitalist, and the socialist. If the system (in Macherey's sense, a heterogeneous system) is not (its) representation (the latter unifies, the former is not unified: it is a 'system of heterogeneous places'), it is however a *dominant system*: the heterogeneity of the apparatuses is what constitutes the determinateness of the system in which they are placed, starting from the dominant place occupied by one of them (the specificity of every form of education thus resides in the fact that, determined by specific social forms, it has a dominant place occupied by a specific dominant apparatus). Thus, for the capitalist mode of education, 'the dominant place is occupied by higher education (directly meant for the training of the bourgeoisie)', so that the other elements of the system 'are determined in relation to it'.[99] It follows that the specific ideology of every mode of education is determined by this relationship of domination (a particular mode of education ensures 'the dominance of one apparatus over the others, and determines the ideology of the whole through this relationship of domination').

4.3   Third Hypothesis

The third hypothesis concerns the capitalist mode of education and, more precisely, it is related to the principle of its constitution (of heterogeneous apparatuses), or rather, to the positioning and connotation of this principle. Here, Macherey uses the example of Bourdieu and Passeron. What's so interesting

---

98   Ibid.
99   Ibid.

about them? The fact that, starting from a hypothesis concerning the functioning of the educational institution as a *unified system* (the claim that 'the school
institution, at all its levels, functions as a system'),[100] they adopt a method that
merely describes that institution (this hypothesis 'bends in advance this project [the school] to the form of a particular method which is the description').
From the very beginning this approach is invalidated by a *systematic ideology*
(for they take the school to be 'a self-sufficient whole; if the school is a system,
it is self-sufficient'). Although Bourdieu and Passeron's theoretical presupposition is ideological ('an earlier and implicit judgment controls the method'),
it nonetheless offers an insight on the real functioning of the capitalist mode
of education ('the ideological thesis ... can become a theoretical thesis': i.e., a
descriptive analysis can lead to a theoretical analysis). In fact, Bourdieu and
Passeron's perspectival error can only be caused *by the particular nature of the
object analysed*: they were able to apply a preliminary form of representation
(complete and sufficient to itself) to the school *because this representation is
generated by the school as an object. The school presents itself as a unified system.*
This leads Macherey to formulate the hypothesis according to which scholastic
ideology – its self (re)presentation as a unified whole, functional to ideological
reproduction – is *adequate* to the functioning of the apparatuses that constitute it: 'it is the ideology of the school system that generates the different apparatuses of schooling, and not the other way around'.[101] In other words, Bourdieu
and Passeron *said the right thing but they are wrong in saying it* (or, in other
words, by developing an ideological analysis 'they unknowingly developed a
theoretical hypothesis'): the descriptive stance they assume is ideological (it
produces an 'ideological thesis') but, *for this very reason*, it shows that the constitution of the capitalist mode of education is itself constituted on the grounds
of its own representation. It is precisely because the constitution of the capitalist mode of education is (according to a theoretical analysis) determined
at the level of its ideology that Bourdieu and Passeron could incur this perspectival mistake (a skewed perspective that generated an ideological analysis).
It is as if the description of all levels of the system as a unified whole, although
ideological (because it presupposes the unity of the system), shows that the
heterogeneity of the apparatuses of the system present themselves as a unified system. In short, Bourdieu and Passeron's analysis and Macherey's have
the same content, but Bourdieu and Passeron are wrong:

---

100   ALT2. A14-01.04 (B14-01), p. 3.
101   Ibid.

By reproducing the ideology of the CME, we immediately attain something of its real constitution. This is only possible because the constitution of the CME is determined at the level of its ideology: it is the ideological configuration which regulates the functioning of scholastic institutions, and even the division of the apparatuses which is proper to the CME ... Here, it appears that the theoretical analysis can give us more than a description: it allows us to find – at the level of the ideological arrangement, and as a principle of the CME – a form of division which effectively *places* the one in relation to the other, without unifying them in any way other than at the level of representation, the heterogeneous elements, which are given as the elements of the system, and which are effects of the functioning of the school ideology. In brief, what constitutes the CME as such and gives it its cohesion, if not its unity, is first determined at the level of school ideology.[102]

4.4   Fourth Hypothesis

Since the structure of bourgeois education is determined at the level of its ideology, the latter *articulates that structure by means of a series of exclusions*. The ideology of the capitalist mode of education 'has the particularity of formulating itself through a series of oppositions: training/instruction, literary studies/scientific studies, culture/professional training, moral education/physical education'.[103] Scholastic ideology, being instrumental to ideological reproduction, once again arranges the composition of the educational apparatuses. But to speak of composition means referring to a heterogeneous dominant system (Second Hypothesis), and a dominant place being occupied by an element of the dominant opposition (the exclusion ensures 'the division between two places, one of which is dominant').[104] In other words, it means referring to a hierarchy which, meant to achieve the reproduction of the modes of production, is ideologically connoted:

> the CME is realised by means of such a hierarchical structuring. This is not surprising, considering that its *primary* function is to ensure ideological reproduction. It is in relation to this reproduction that all the elements of the educational process take their place.[105]

---

102   ALT2. A14-01.04 (B14-01), p. 4.
103   ALT2. A14-01.04 (B14-01), p. 5.
104   ALT2. A14-01.04 (B14-01), p. 6.
105   Ibid.

But this hierarchical structuring necessarily produces a *devaluation* of one of the terms of the opposition (which is part of the very term of exclusion). This means that if every mode of production belongs to a ruling class, then its ideological reproduction is ensured by the element which occupies the dominant position, precisely because every element of the opposition is ideologically arranged. One of Macherey's examples helps to demonstrate the characteristic exclusion operated by the capitalist mode of education. In the opposition between general education (formation) and particular education (instruction) the ideological mechanism consists in presenting the process of formation – which is really a particular education ('general education is a particular education [for example the study of Letters]')[106] – as a general education that, as such, ensures the ideological reproduction of the forms of the division of labour ('general education is the "cement" of social life'). The generalisation of partial knowledge, besides being ideological because instrumental to the process of reproduction, implies the devaluation of true knowledge: 'in such a way that what is ideological has the appearance of a more complete knowledge, and conversely, that what is truly knowledge takes on the appearance of an incomplete knowledge'.[107]

4.5   *Fifth Hypothesis*

Given that the technical makeup of the system of bourgeois education must be formulated through an ideological process of exclusive (and devaluing) hierarchical structuring of opposing terms, it is possible to identify, within this 'series of oppositions', a *fundamental exclusion*. In the introduction to this chapter, we noted how for Althusser, intellectual and manual labour are direct expressions of the division of knowledge, so that the technical division is defined as an *already*-social division. Macherey writes: 'all of these exclusions which ensure, each in their own way, a dominant position to the ideological reproduction, are in turn determined by a fundamental exclusion [*exclusion fondamentale*], which commands the whole series. This exclusion is: intellectual labour / manual labour'.[108] This is the fundamental, ideological exclusion that determines the functioning of the capitalist mode of education. Each binary opposition of that mode of education (formation/instruction, literary studies/scientific studies, etc.) is determined once and for all by a more fundamental exclusion: all oppositions 'function on the model of this division, and within the hierarchical relationship generated by it'. The point must be stressed:

---

106   ALT2. A14-01.04 (B14-01), p. 5.
107   ALT2. A14-01.04 (B14-01), p. 5.
108   ALT2. A14-01.04 (B14-01), p. 7.

the fundamental exclusion that supports a devaluation is the only stable element in any class society ('as Althusser pointed out in our discussion, it belongs to any class society, and not only to the capitalist mode of production'), and *not* the terms of the binary oppositions ('the terms that are represented are not fixed once and for all by their belonging to a rigid and completely predetermined framework'). In other words, although the terms (formation/instruction, literary studies/scientific studies, etc.) are the *specific* terms of the capitalist mode of education, the fundamental exclusion (intellectual labour/manual labour) that determines them is reproducible in social conditions other than capitalist ones: '*what remains is the form of the relation* ... In other words, any variation made in the form of the initial exclusion can be reproduced at different levels'.[109] Two observations should be made here: like binary oppositions, the fundamental exclusion is ideologically determinate: 'that is what guarantees, in a general way, the reproduction, in all its forms, of the social division of labour'. Thus, the relation between intellectual and manual labour, as well as the specific binary oppositions it determines, represent the law of constitution of the capitalist mode of education as a mode of ideological reproduction: 'the CME is the set of effects produced by this determination'. Secondly, if the unproductiveness of school work triggers the analogical mechanism (§ 3), then the analogical mechanism is generated by the fundamental division insofar this determines school work: 'it appears that, determined from this law of exclusion, school work will necessarily be unproductive work'.[110] *If at school the student works as if he or she were really working, then – being defined by intellectual and manual labour – the analogy is the analogy of the fundamental exclusion:*

> The sidelining [*la mise à l'écart*] of production, which constitutes the scholastic world as an artificial world, generated from its own limits, is expressed in a series of exclusions, and generates the forms in which the process of schooling is realised. The pedagogical analogy is thus a characteristic feature of the MEC: it is the inescapable figure of the separation which constitutes the bourgeois school as such.[111]

---

109   Ibid.
110   ALT2. A14-01.04 (B14-01), p. 8.
111   Ibid.

5   Culture and Ideology: Roger Establet

Towards the end of his essay, Macherey identifies the pedagogical outcomes of schooling (which can 'produce specific effects that derive their reality from the system that generates them').[112] More precisely, the school system implies a causal reversal: its effects are themselves taken for causes and presupposed upon entry into the system that generates them. *Enfant* and *culture* – these are its specific effects ('the child and culture ... are products of the capitalist school system: *pedagogical effects*, not natural realities given outside the system').[113] If there were a grammar of scholastic ideology, the reversal of causes would be a noun (the child and culture as external and presupposed natural realities), while the critical identification of that mechanism would be a transitive verb (the child and culture as realities generated by and functional to the process of bourgeois schooling): *the infant presupposes infantilisation and culture presupposes acculturation.*

By now, the adage is familiar: the student works, but unproductively. It seems clear, therefore, that the analogical mechanism which is instrumental for ideological reproduction is also what concerns the agents of reproduction. Or better, it is what composes them beyond any preliminary identification (what makes them 'from scratch'): 'in the definition of the child we find something that we have already used to define the schooling process: the child is an unproductive being'.[114] The child is unproductive but his or her unproductiveness is analogical (the essence of the child and its representation is therefore ideological): it takes on the aspect of immaturity which defines the irreducibility of class-time as a factor of separation (school-time prepares for the time of production and, one might say, immaturity is the name which presupposes assimilation and feelings of obligation). It is the separation that, truly limiting the space of schooling practices, defines the child's immaturity as unproductiveness. The analogy requires a separation if unproductivity is indeed not production: this means that the child does not exist. It is not a given but a created product (who is unproductive because school work is unproductive, and vice versa): 'this separation is not the index of an independent (naturally separate) existence, but the means by which a constraint is indirectly exercised that will eventually insert it into the process of production (starting from the mechanism of ideological reproduction).'[115] To say 'child' is to say 'subject' – understood

---

112   ALT2. A14-01.04 (B14-01), p. 11.
113   Ibid.
114   Ibid.
115   Ibid.

as a subject of interpellation: it is a created support that was never previously individualised: 'to protect childhood is to guarantee the success of the regulated process that ensures the domination of one class over the others'. Things start to get more interesting when Macherey moves on to the idea of 'culture':

> On this point, there is not much to add to Establet's article. A few remarks, however. It is necessary to show how 'culture' is nothing more than what is determined by the work of the dominant ideology. However, it is also important not to confuse this ideology with the culture that *results from it* (which was somewhat the case in E.'s article). Culture is also a product of the school system: it is what the dominant ideology becomes when it has passed through the complex functioning of its mechanism. This is what allows us to understand that there can be one dominant ideology, but several cultures.[116]

Here Macherey is referring to Establet's essay 'Culture et idéologie', which appeared in the July–August 1966 issue of the *Cahiers marxistes-léninistes* (the same issue which included Balibar's text on Bourdieu and Passeron's *The Inheritors*), which was titled *Art, langue et lutte des classes*. In the same issue, together with Establet's short text, there are two other essays by Macherey ('À propos de "L'amour de l'art" (Bourdieu et Darbel)' and 'Les Paysans de Balzac: un texte disparate'); one by Balibar ('Marxisme et linguistique'); Badiou's first philosophical essay, written after his first two 'novels' ('L'autonomie du processus esthétique'); and finally some documents that were meant to constitute the theoretical backbone of the issue as a whole: one text by Stalin ('À propos du marxisme en linguistique', which supports the text of Balibar), one by Lenin ('Tolstoï, miroir de la Révolution russse', the essay on the basis of which Macherey will start his reasearch on literary production), and one by Mao veneries ('Interventions aux causeries sur la littérature et l'art à Yenan'), which supports Badiou's essay.

Althusser refers to Establet's 'Culture et idéologie' only twice. The first occurrence can be found in a letter (the last one) dated 31 July 1966 and addressed to Bourdieu – a rather significant context since, as we will see, Establet engages with Bourdieu and Darbel's *L'amour de l'art*, written in 1966. The set-up is by now familiar: with this letter Althusser seals the relationship of substantial theoretical affinity between his group and Bourdieu's theses. What is interesting for our purposes is the following:

---

116   ALT2. A14-01.04 (B14-01), p. 12.

when reading your work, I learn a lot of things, things that are indispens-able to me; and more than 'things' I also learn concepts, the ones you use to think the realities (the 'things') you deal with. These concepts interest me very much, as you can imagine, and you will not be surprised if, on sev-eral occasions, in what I am going to write, I find myself in the position of quoting them, and, with your permission, of borrowing them from you. You have seen what Establet did to some of your concepts in his very brief paper on 'culture' in *Démocratie nouvelle*. I hope that he has not distorted your thought too much, I will do my best not to betray it. But you should already know that what you have written (and what you will write, consid-ering what you have already written) is for me, for all of us, of the greatest theoretical importance.[117]

Althusser's rather cautious tone might suggest that Establet's theses not only do not fully align with Bourdieu's, but also depart from Althusser's own position ('I hope that he has not distorted your thought too much, I will do my best not to betray it' ...). The irony is that here Althusser seems to put a good face on it. Every misunderstanding about the recognition of Establet's spell is in fact clari-fied the second time that Althusser refers to 'Cultures et idéologie'. This can be found in 'Cremonini, Painter of the Abstract', an essay dated August 1966 and published in the magazine *Démocratie Nouvelle* in November of the same year. Here Althusser writes:

> Every work of art is born of a project both aesthetic and ideological. When it exists as a work of art it produces as *a work of art* (by the type of critique and knowledge it inaugurates with respect to the ideology it makes us see) an *ideological* effect. If, as Establet has correctly, but too briefly, noted in a recent article, 'culture' is the ordinary name for the Marxist concept of the *ideological*, then the work of art, as an *aesthetic object*, is no more part of 'culture' than instruments of production (a locomotive) or scientific knowledges are part of 'culture'.[118]

The juxtaposition of these two passages is interesting: later, I will explore in greater depth the reason why, but I would like to anticipate it here. What is worth highlighting are the implications (which are not merely historiograph-ical) of combining the concept of culture with that of a work of art. This move

---

117   ALT2. C1-05 (B), p. 2.
118   Althusser 1971, p. 241.

is wholly legitimate theoretical considering that Establet's use of the concept of culture (to which Althusser refers in both passages), differs from that of the Bourdieu of *The Inheritors*, while it follows the one articulated in *The Love of Art*, also written in 1966. Therefore, and this is the core issue, it can be hypothesised that 1966 – while still sealing a relationship of continuity with Bourdieu (as testified by the letter Althusser wrote to him) – is *also* the year in which, beginning with Macherey's theses regarding the utterly peculiar relationship that the object of art entertains with ideology (in particular: 'Lénine critique de Tolstoï' written in 1965, to which Althusser refers in a 1966 text, linked to that on Cremonini: 'Lettre sur la connaissance de l'art (réponse à André Daspre)'), Althusser seems to take distance from the positions expressed in his own letter. If the ideology mentioned by Establet can be traced back to the 'culture' (of art) to which Bourdieu refers, then the work of art – *as an aesthetic object* – does not belong to the domain of sciences, *but neither does it belong to that of culture* (as Bourdieu argues).

Let us now examine Establet's text, starting with a preliminary question: how should we define 'culture', and the conditions under which it can become an object of study for historical materialism? The assumption is that, as an object of study, it responds to its function as a concept (an epistemological assumption: 'the word "culture" must be interrogated according to the status that is assigned to it by actual scientific practices').[119] In other words, it requires a clear definition, produced by a well-defined theoretical structure that leaves out the ambiguous connotations given to it by ordinary language ('we will therefore leave aside the ill-determined meanings of the word'), by a rigorous protocol of observation, and by a limited field of application.

The most interesting point lies in the definition of culture that Establet derives from ethnography: 'a set of actualised [*actualisés*] patterns of behaviour in a given [*definie*] society'.[120] If the cultural is the set of all the models of behaviour that are part of a social structure, the structure is, culturally, a structure of heterogeneous models that refer to relations of force implied by the social form, since the latter can be defined as 'a set of objective structures that distribute the means of production and power between individuals and social groups, and that determine social, economic, and political practices'.

The cultural refers to and expresses the social form or, alternatively, the models of behaviour refer to and express the objective structures of the social form. But *to refer to something does not mean to assimilate it* (or, as Establet says, to

119   Establet 1966, p. 15.
120   Establet 1966, p. 16.

homologate), as if, for example, the model of bourgeois behaviour were the container of natural gifts that disregard, precisely, their being *expressive* of a (bourgeois) structure, as that which refers to the set of objective structures. We must not fall into the idealistic (i.e., ideological) trap that considers the terms 'culture' and 'social formation' to be synonymous: 'far from designating the whole of a social formation in an idealistic language, the concept of culture defines a clearly distinct field: culture is therefore opposed to society.' Establet's point, then, is to show how – assuming this expressive separation – in the context of the 'social' the 'cultural' represents something residual, something that, while belonging to that domain, cannot be reduced to it. The example of consumption (broadly conceived, to include the consumption of cultural objects) in the capitalist regime is paradigmatic: consuming 'is not only actualising an economic practice' (a practice that is determined by the means of production distributed by the objective structures of the social form); to consume is also to flaunt ('expressing membership in a privileged group. ... The model of behaviour imposes itself as a norm').[121] This means that *the cultural is a normative field* that dictates the guidelines of what should be done or, better yet, of *how* it should be done. And if one consumes by actualising an economic practice (defined by the place it occupies within the set of objective structures of the social form), then the models of behaviour, being normative (that is, expressing a belonging to a specific social group), are systematically arranged: 'this norm works in a system: consuming properly means not consuming improperly, that is, as others consume. The models therefore function as norms, and the system of norms, essentially differential, constitutes a structure'.[122]

Here, then, the connection to Bourdieu becomes clearer. This is because *if the social structure is a structure of relations of force, then the normative structure of actualised behaviour is what qualifies those relations of force as relations of meaning.* It is as if to say that culture indicates a stance that gives an imaginary meaning to the brute fact of social positioning (naturalising it or, rather, pretending to naturalise it): 'it is this reflection of relations of force as relations of meaning at the level of practices themselves ... that defines the "cultural"'.[123] A reflection, of course, but what kind of reflection is it (or what kind of expressiveness)?

On this point, let us consider in full three important clarifications made by Establet:

---

121   Ibid.
122   Establet 1966, p. 17.
123   Establet 1966, p. 17.

a) Reflection does not mean homology, the adequate expression of one system by the other. If culture expresses the social, it is by masking it. Therefore, the methods of the consumption of artworks reject their objective determinations and, for this very reason, contribute to maintaining their effectiveness. The relation between the elect and the work of election, which guides the conduct, permits the constitution of a closed universe of imaginary barriers (predestination) that masks, by legitimising and perpetuating them, the real barriers (level of education).

b) It goes without saying that the 'social' takes precedence over the 'cultural'. Unless one wants to conceive a signifying system that wants to signify itself!

c) These two observations do not exclude, but indeed explain, the relative autonomy of the cultural with respect to the social. The modes of realisation of the practices are significant only when forming a system. For example, taken in its own right, photographic practice can mean both cultural distinction and vulgarity. The sign is justified only within the integral system that gives it its place. There is therefore no one-to-one correspondence from a 'cultural' element to a 'social' one, but rather a relation between two systems.[124]

For the moment, we need to briefly examine the first of these points. Culture has a *non-transparent relation* with society ('the modalities of the consumption of works of art', which refers to cultural behavioural norms, 'reject their objective determinations', which refer, for those norms, to their social position). As for this first point, therefore, what was anticipated above remains valid. The Bourdieu that is functional to the explanation of the cultural mechanism is the Bourdieu of *The Love of Art*. All references to the work of art and to education should therefore be taken seriously. The first, in fact, leads us to acknowledge – at least in a hypothetical way, if we pay proper attention to Bourdieu's arguments – that *the paradigm of functioning of cultural practices in general is defined precisely by the cultural practice of consumption of objects of knowledge (specifically: objects of art).*[125] Every social practice, whether it be an economic practice, a political practice, or a social practice, is a cultural practice, and every cultural practice – hypothetically, one might say – *is a practice that is grounded on the consumption of artworks.* On the other hand, the

---

124   Ibid.
125   It is hardly a coincidence that Althusser cites Establet in a text related to art.

reference to instruction or education, which for Establet represent the real barriers, derives its importance from the fact that it creates an explicit circularity (and Macherey himself will acknowledge this in his review of Bourdieu's text) between *The Inheritors* (according to which bourgeois origin allows one to place oneself within the framework of a 'cultural privilege' that underlies scholastic success) and *The Love of Art* (according to which it is only through scholastic education that one can assimilate the codes of use of objects of knowledge).[126]

Here is an exemplary passage from the latter work:

> Not being able to invoke rights of birth (which his or her class historically denied the aristocracy) or the rights of nature, a weapon in the past levelled against nobiliary distinctions which would run the risk of backfiring against bourgeois 'distinction', or the ascetic virtues which allowed the first generation of entrepreneurs to justify their success by their merit, can call on cultivated nature and naturalised culture, on what is sometimes called 'class', by a sort of Freudian slip, on 'education', in the sense of a product of education which seems to owe nothing to education, on *'distinction'* a grace which is merit and a merit which is grace, an unacquired merit which justifies unmerited attainments, namely heritage. In order for culture to fulfil its function of legitimating inherited privileges, it is necessary and sufficient that the link between culture and education, at once obvious and hidden, should be *forgotten* or *denied*.[127]

It is now possible for Establet to formulate his hypothesis: 'the ideological is the place where historical materialism can rightfully appropriate the concept of "culture"'.[128] If the cultural mechanism derives its normative efficacy from the essentially negative gesture of its objective determinations, might it not be joined to the ideological mechanism, since the ideological – as Althusser notes in 'Marxism and Humanism', which Establet references here – expresses the way that individuals relate to their own conditions of existence? More precisely, could we not conclude that the cultural must be integrated into the ideological, so that the denial of the link with one's social position can be removed from the ideological recovery to the conditions of existence?

---

126   *L'Amour de l'Art* [The Love of Art] cannot really be understood except in relation to other books dealing with scholastic inequality: its reading presupposes, in particular, that of *Héritiers* [*The Inheritors*] (Bourdieu-Passeron)'. Macherey 1966, p. 9.
127   Bourdieu and Darbel 1991, pp. 166–7.
128   Establet 1966, p. 18.

It is clear that when couched in these terms, Establet's argument is rather problematic (Althusser described it to Bourdieu as 'a very short paper on "culture"' and, in his article on Cremonini, he wrote: 'as Establet has correctly, but too briefly, noted in a recent article ...'[129]). Establet himself often repeats how his work has only a hypothetical and provisional status, consisting of 'approximate and certainly questionable'[130] observations; or again he explains that 'it is necessary to specify it: we have been able to highlight only some conditions of this work. They seem necessary to us, but they were always bound to be schematic and brief'.[131] It is thus a rather problematic theoretical stance: if there is indeed a link between culture and ideology, what kind of link is it? Perhaps a relation of *identification* (as Macherey alludes to when he writes that 'it is also important not to confuse this ideology with the culture that *results from it* (which was somewhat the case in E.'s article)', or as Althusser himself argues when he writes that '"culture" is the common noun [*nom commun*] of the Marxist concept of the ideological')? Or maybe a relation of *articulation*, as Establet himself suggests – although he elsewhere uses expressions such as 'to translate [*traduire*] "cultural" as "ideological"' – when he writes that 'a silent discourse "spoken" at the same level as practices (the "cultural" as we have defined it) has its necessary place alongside the explicit discourses that take centre stage'?[132] And if we speak about a relationship of articulation, how can the discourse of cultural practices be articulated with that of the ideological imaginary?

Finally, after the passage we examined above, Macherey writes that

> culture is also a product of the school system: it is what the dominant ideology becomes when it has passed through the complex functioning of its mechanism. This is what allows us to understand that there can be one dominant ideology, but several cultures.[133]

---

129 Althusser 1971, p. 241.
130 Establet 1966, p. 15.
131 Establet 1966, p. 18.
132 Ibid. Establet goes on to explain that: 'When we are able to construct the concepts of a precise articulation, to replace this descriptive "aside", then the theory of ideology will have made serious progress'. As I noted, Establet's essay appeared in July–August of 1966. Here, we can see him use terms like *articulation* [*articulation*] and *discourse* [*discours*]. It is impossible not to think of Althusser's 'Three Notes on the Theory of Discourses', where the notion of articulation is literally central. This text was written in the same year (in the context of a research group that included Badiou, Balibar, Duroux, and Macherey, but not Establet). Has there been some kind of influence? See Althusser, 'Three Notes on the Theory of Discourses', in Althusser 2003.
133 ALT2. A14-01.04 (B14-01), p. 12.

Culture, the product of the school system, becomes dominant ideology when it passes through its own mechanism of functioning. If scholastic culture is functional to ideological reproduction, then it is the culture of the ruling class. If the technically imparted teachings are ideologically defined (because they are functional to the reproduction of the modes of production), then school culture, produced by the school system, is an ideological culture. Culture, in school, is a dominant ideology; it is not just any culture, but a culture functional to ideological reproduction.

But then, what is the relationship between the one (of the dominant ideology) and the multiplicity (of excluded cultures)? In the third point (c) we looked at, Establet writes that 'the sign is justified only within the integral system that gives it its place. There is therefore no one-to-one correspondence from a "cultural" element to a "social" one, but rather a relation between two systems'.[134] If, on the assumption that the 'social' takes precedence over the 'cultural' (b), the relation between the former and the latter is a relation between two systems (with a relative autonomy, (c): this makes it possible for bourgeois culture, proper to the bourgeoisie, to be adopted by proletarians and to replace their sub-culture, and *vice versa*), how can the sign be assigned a meaning only within the system that gives it a place? This is clearly where the differential system comes into play ('the system of norms, essentially differential, constitutes a structure';[135] 'culture is a system of differences').[136] We must imagine the cultural field as a horizontal plane, composed of specific cultures; they have a certain placement, *not because of their specific content, but because of the relations they have within the structure*. Consider the example of photographic practice used in point (c): it can mean 'both cultural distinction and vulgarity', but whatever its meaning, the content of one's practice remains unchanged. Indeed, both its placement and its significance are differentially (by its structural and formal placement) rather than essentially (due to their specific and material content) determined.

And yet, the elements that make up the cultural plane are not connected by a relation of equivalence. For if, as Macherey put it, there is a dominant ideology – that of the ruling class – then the dominant culture also belongs to the ruling class. *This means that the ruling class regulates the regime of cultural distinctions and is the agent that positions the components of the horizontal plane.* This thesis must be emphasised: it is precisely because the cultural field is composed by multiple components that the dominant culture does not aim at a

---

134   Establet 1966, p. 17.
135   Ibid.
136   Ibid.

horizontal diffusion, as if to eliminate multiplicity in order to establish unity. The opposite is true: the function of the dominant culture is to maintain the differential placement of the multiplicity of sub-cultures, *precisely in order to define their inadequacy and to exclude their conformity to the dominant cultural component*. Establet writes that:

> We therefore understand the precise meaning of 'dominant culture': culture of the ruling class. It is not a matter of the universal diffusion of the models of behaviour of the educated class. On the contrary, the goal is the positioning of these models as exclusive referents, in relation to which all other models must necessarily define themselves and in relation to which they define themselves as inadequate.[137]

A dominant culture, by defining the placement of cultural components, excludes them. It is no coincidence that Establet alludes again here to Bourdieu's text: 'It is in reference to their lack of bourgeois culture ... that the proletarians lost in a museum define their relationship with works of art'. It is a thesis that leads to a very radical conclusion (which is in fact Bourdieu's own, which is precisely why Establet shares in it). Take the example of the enjoyment of a painting by Renoir: to say that proletarian culture is defined by its inadequacy with respect to bourgeois culture *means that the work of art refers to the codes of its enjoyment as codes that are determined – time after time – by the conformation of the horizontal plane and by the social agent that guides its composition.* The being of the work, to use the famous formula, depends on its being perceived (the ultimate reason why the object of art is defined as a 'symbolic good'). Like a linguistic code, its being wholly depends on the social processes that regulate its decoding (that is, scholastic education teaches that *the work of art does not exist*). Bourdieu writes that 'as a system of principles whereby the universe of representations supplied to a given society at a given moment in time can be classified into complementary categories, the artistic mode is like a social institution'.[138] And if 'this set of instruments of perception which makes up the means of appropriation of artistic goods (and of cultural goods in general)' is given to 'a given society at a given moment in time',[139] *then under certain historical conditions it is possible to produce proletarian codes of enjoyment, assuming the existence of a proletarian political practice.* Establet explains that:

---

137   Ibid.
138   Bourdieu and Darbel 1991, p. 41.
139   Ibid.

it must undoubtedly be admitted that, under historically specific conditions, in terms of political practice the regime of cultural distinctions can
be overthrown: in a revolutionary period proletarian political culture can
become dominant. But let us leave aside this extremely important point,
since it cannot be properly examined in just a few lines.[140]

Proletariat and revolution, of course ... But is this the last word of the artwork?
And can it only be an ideological word?

$$\bullet\bullet$$

Macherey's reference to Establet's text is important not only because of the
content of 'Culture et idéologie' and the relationship that it has with 'Les mythologies scolaires'. Indeed, another of Establet's essay played a formative role for
the collective work 'Schools', particularly in reference to the notion of culture.
I am referring to 'Sur l'école bourgeoise, la culture bourgeoise', dated 3 March
1968, two years after 'Culture et idéologie', and one week before 'Les mythologies scolaires'. It is now necessary to take a deeper look at this essay – starting
from the points of convergence it has with the two texts I just mentioned, which
we will explore below – not only, so to speak, for documentary purposes, but
also, and above all, in order to complicate the very notion of culture.
   Stylistically 'Sur l'école bourgeoise, la culture bourgeoise' is divided into two
parts: the first is titled 'Culture Générale'; the second, split into three numbered
sections, seems to consist in a deeper analysis of 'point two' of the first part. If
we exclude section one and section three of the second part, the remainder of
the essay is composed of fragmentary material, almost like research notes written in a quasi-axiomatic form, which were probably meant for further elaboration. This is why it is necessary to quote the first part of the text in its entirety:

> relation of the bourgeoisie and the intellectual layers of the petty bour-
> geoisie to the dominant ideology is inculcated in a massively dominant
> way in the scholastic apparatuses, either by decisive mechanisms of rein-
> forcement, for the heirs [*pour les héritiers*], or, for the others, by primary
> inculcation.
>
> objective basis of ideological unity (its unity is not mythical, but in and
> by the ideology of the present school apparatuses)

---

140   Establet 1966, p. 18.

∴

Thanks to RB [perhaps Renée Balibar] the means of inculcation are known. I propose that we reflect on the following hypothesis concerning the main material of inculcation:

1st   there is a spontaneous aesthetic ideology (SAI) that defines the relationship between an art practitioner and his practice.

2nd   the SAI is overdetermined: it is not only the effect of the mode of aesthetic production [*mode de production esthétique*] but also, and perhaps above all, of the mode of economic production which supports the former, and consequently of the specific combination of the mode(s) of production of art(s) and the dominant mode of production.

3rd   it seems to me that general culture is nothing other than the scholastic inculcation of the SAI which characterises artists who produce in a capitalist social formation.

4th   the SAI always combines very easily with bourgeois MC [perhaps mass culture [*culture de masse*]] (for reasons to be studied, although some are already known: see Sartre's insightful work on Flaubert's ideology; and R. Moulin's work on the relationship of painters to the painting market).

5th   the process of scholastic inculcation, which tends to put into communication cultivated man [*homme cultivé*] and the artist, must be understood as the means of inculcating the SAI, and metonymically-metaphorically the associated MC, in a certain number of vectors.

6th   the SAI is the famous code of which Bourdieu has correctly identified the existence and the effects of 'culture', but which he mistakenly takes to be the code of art itself.

7th   the decisive place of scholastic inculcation in this matter is due not only to its mass character, but above all to the necessity of three elements of the SAI.

8th   this selection of the most idealistic and bourgeois elements of the SAI is what Bourdieu has identified as the function of consecration of the school. This function seems to me to be exercised less on the artworks than on the 'pieces' chosen so as to enable the SAI to be found through commentary. See, for example, the consecration of surrealism, with Alquié's book – surrealism is a humanism. [XXX] To be put to the test.

        NB: the materialist principle (Vladimir, Tse, R.B., Pierre, Alain) according to which one should not take artists at their ideological word is in a completely different sense an academic watchword; in this case, it is a question of restoring the right to retain only the idealistic elements of the SAI. Cf. the way in which Malraux cites painters, sometimes to confirm his commentary, sometimes to enrich the anthology of errors about art.

9th   the dominant SAI seems to me to be already fixed in Hegel's description of Romantic art, and which is really aimed at the SAI, not and for good reason a mode of aesthetic production. The sartreries, malrauteries, vangogheries, aragoneries, including in some of their components the surrealist manifestos, are nothing but a refinement of the Hegelian description (cf. also Ph. È, *le règne animal de l'esprit*):
- art is a substitute for religion
- the dominant 'category' of art is subjectivity
- the object of art, the thing itself, is the manifestation of subjectivity
- art is above, outside, below, beyond the world, history, classes; the term engaged art [*art engagé*] should not mislead: art gets involved [l'art s'engage], like the civilians in the Legion (still foreign, see Mallarmé); like the bourgeoisie, art ignores classes, especially the bourgeoisie, which does not know them.
- art is creation
- art is freedom

10th   it seems clear to me that there are affinities between this SAI and the bourgeois MC, and that the occultation of the affinity allows the inculcation of the MC by the SAI. Also, it seems clear that general culture is only the inculcation of this SAI. It remains to be seen how the spirit, the SAI, comes to artists.[141]

I want to focus on a few notable elements of this passage. As we can see, Establet suggests the existence of a triangular relation between the dominant ideology (he speaks of the bourgeoisie's and the petty bourgeoisie's relation with 'the inculcated dominant ideology'), the spontaneous aesthetic ideology (which is general culture itself), and the scholastic apparatus (the dominant ideology is 'inculcated in a massively dominant way in the school apparatus'). The scholastic apparatus is where the inculcation of the dominant ideology takes place, through a general culture that is nothing other than the spontaneous aesthetic ideology (see the 3rd point above). Therefore, it could be said that the theoretical assumption underlying the inculcation of the dominant ideology and the inculcation of spontaneous aesthetic ideology – two distinct but related processes – is that aesthetic ideology is *not* equivalent to the dominant ideology: it represents only the *part* that is functional to its inculcation.

---

141   ALT2. A14-01.03 (A), pp. 1–2.

In school, in short, we learn the dominant ideology because we are taught a general culture that is an aesthetic *ideology* precisely because its function, to inculcate the dominant ideology, is ideological. However, we should acknowledge that if it is true that insofar as it is an effect of the combination of aesthetic modes of production with the dominated mode of production, 'the SAI is overdetermined' (the 2nd point above), the question of how aesthetic ideology, as it is inculcated, is instrumental for the inculcation of the dominant ideology – and therefore, for the reproduction of the modes of production (at least for now, because the question will be explored in greater depth, starting with Macherey's theses on the teaching of the Letters, in the second part) – still remains open.

Another observation here is that above, with regard to 'Culture et idéologie', we assumed that by 'culture' Establet meant the cultural practice of consuming objects of art as a (aesthetic) paradigm for the functioning of cultural practices in general (economic, social, political). The convergence of points 3, 4, 5, and 10 seems to confirm this hypothesis. With point 3 above the hypothesis is indeed verified, since general culture, if it is already an aesthetic ideology, is therefore an aesthetic culture that represents the modes of decoding of which Bourdieu speaks (but – we should note – still imprecisely: see point 6 above). And there is more: if we assume that the CDM to which Establet refers (without, however, offering any definition of it) in the fourth, fifth, and tenth points represents the whole of the cultural practices of the ruling class, then general culture as an aesthetic culture (as per his 1966 article) is what inculcates mass culture ('metonimically-metaphorically' [point 5]; 'affinities between the SAI and the bourgeoise CDM' [point 10], 'the SAI always combines very easily with the CDM' [point 4]. Thus, it could be said that the generality of general culture, as an aesthetic ideology, is nothing but the generality of cultural practices in general).

The idea that general culture, as a spontaneous aesthetic ideology, represents the *part* of the dominant ideology that is functional to its own inculcation is the underlying thesis of point three of the second part (I am starting here for the sake of exposition). Let us briefly examine it: 'in French, the word "culture" is ambiguous: it refers simultaneously to two traditions'.[142] The first is ethnological: it should be remembered that, in 'Culture at Idéologie', Establet defined culture, precisely on the basis of its ethnological value, as 'a set of actualised [*actualisés*] patterns of behaviour in a given [*definie*] society'. It is not surprising, then, that in line with the ethnological tradition adopted in 'Sur

---

142   ALT2. A14-01.03 (B3), p. 1.

l'école bourgeoise', Establet aims, presupposing a relationship of identification between culture and ideology, precisely at the definition of culture he formulated in 1966:

> culture-Kultur (German), culture (English) = sum of the works of a society + sum of the behavioural patterns of the social subjects of that society = sum of the products + normed relations to these products = dominant ideology = ideology of the dominant class (cf. Establet, 'Culture et idéologie', CML, 12–13).[143]

The second tradition to which Establet refers is more closely linked to the French use of the word: 'the second [tradition] is humanistic and more specifically French: = cultivation (English), *bildung* (German); cf. the expressions: cultivated man, highly cultured individual, uncultured, general culture'.[144] In sum, the culture Establet writes about in 1966 is represented here as what establishes an identity relationship with ideology (in the first sense), while general culture – the spontaneous aesthetic ideology he writes about in 1968, in the first part of 'Sur l'école bourgeoise' – is a humanist ideology, as it is presented in the second part of that text.

Therefore, being ambiguous, the term 'culture' is equivocal (we should 'ban the word "culture" from our lexicon'). An unequivocal substitution is necessary: *ideology* should be used for the first meaning of 'culture', and *bourgeois humanism* for the second. Indeed, it is important not to confuse the two meanings of the word (that is, not to fall into the paralogism of mistaking 'a part for the whole', making bourgeois humanism the universal form of ideology in general). Because if it is true that, starting from the first part of 'Sur l'école bourgeoise' the partial status of general culture with respect to the dominant ideology could only be deduced (from the triangular relation between dominant ideology, general culture, and the scholastic apparatus), here it is on the basis of this fundamental division that the mechanism for the inculcation of the dominant ideology is explicitly triggered. Bourgeois humanism, is nothing but 'a fragment' of the dominant ideology:

> It is essential not to confuse these two meanings and to understand that meaning II (general culture) is only a fragment of meaning I. The humanist ideology of general culture, which selects and valorises certain intellec-

---

143   Ibid.
144   Ibid.

tual products in a given field (art, literature) and which imposes normed relations to these products (the normed relation defining the content), is only a particular aspect of the ideology of the dominant class. It concerns only a fraction of the ideological field (art and literature) and affects only the bourgeoisie and petty bourgeoisie. For the bourgeois class and for certain elements of the petty bourgeoisie, it is possible (to be demonstrated) that humanist ideology is the dominant aspect under which the process of inculcation of ideology takes place.[145]

For the bourgeois class, then, humanist ideology would be 'the dominant aspect under which the process of the inculcation of ideology takes place'. This means that 'general culture' is the name of a relation – it is the 'the particular relation that the bourgeoisie has with its ideology'.[146] Bourgeois humanism is the part of the dominant ideology that is instrumental to its learning. In other words, humanism is bourgeois because the agent of its enjoyment is bourgeois (this explains how the content of general culture is determined by the subjective relationship with this content).

Here the scholastic institution comes into play, according to a trajectory that has already been observed in the first part of Establet's text (the school is the place of inculcation of a spontaneous aesthetic ideology). There is nothing new here: the bourgeois family ('father's library, reading suggestions, the family record collection', etc.) and the classic secondary education (high school), together with higher education, which goes to bolster the former, are the answers to the question 'what are the places where this general culture is inculcated'? And there is more: here, we encounter two other theses that will also appear, a little later, in Macherey's text. First, we have already seen how the opposition between education and training represents the characteristic exclusion (Hypothesis Four) of the capitalist mode of education, as determined by the fundamental division between intellectual and manual labour (Hypothesis Five). This means that humanist ideology, as an aesthetic ideology, is the content of the knowledge that is transmitted to the bourgeois and the petty bourgeois class: it is clearly located on the side of intellectual labour: 'for the proletariat, the notion of general culture does not exist'.[147] Second thesis: we have seen that, in the first part of 'Sur l'école bourgeoise', the question of how (by which means of inculcation) aesthetic ideology – i.e., bourgeois humanism – was functional to the inculcation of the dominant ideology, as overde-

145   Ibid.
146   ALT2. A14-01.03 (B3), p. 2.
147   Ibid.

termined by the modes of production, was left open. Here, this question is answered by the thesis pertaining to the teaching of the Letters, which will later be expounded by Macherey ('Literary education ... is the epitome of an education that is not worthwhile for its own sake (it generates useless knowledge), but for something else, about which it says nothing';[148] 'from the very outset, literary education has a general vocation: it is, as we shall see, integral to the ideation of a totality of the individual'.)[149] If general culture is the relation between the bourgeoise and its own ideology, 'the means of inculcating this specific ideology are located in the techniques of literary teaching' (such as, for example, the commentary and the dissertation).[150] Through the technical teaching of the Letters the individual learns about the bourgeois man:

> Through literature, the student learns about the universal man. Pascal, Montaigne, and Racine painted men as they are: in each of them, in each of their writings, the human condition speaks; in describing themselves, they described all men ... There is a human essence, an eternal man with no relation to economic and social structures. The bourgeois individual is hidden behind the mask of the eternal man: indeed, they taught about the *bourgeois man* under the guise of a universal human condition.[151]

Point two concerns the placement of the educational apparatus within the social division of labour, and within the system of ideological inculcation. Here too Establet proceeds by means of programmatic notes, and it is better to quote this section in its entirety.

1) the problem must be dealt with in a capitalist social formation, which can only be done differentially [*différentiellement*].

2) the current division of the object is not self-evident: the "school" only has an ideological unity; the different school apparatuses each simultaneously and unequally fulfill distinct functions (reproduction of the social division of labour; ideological inculcation, training in science); the importance of this or that function varies according to the class(es) enrolled in school; crucial point: NONE of the functions performed by the different school apparatuses is performed exclusively by them. It follows that the subsequent provisional topology [*topologie provisoire*] is a cross topology [*topologie croisée*].

---

148   ALT2. A14-01.04 (A), p. 14.
149   ALT2. A14-01.04 (A), p. 12.
150   ALT2. A14-01.03 (B3), p. 3.
151   ALT2. A14-01.03 (B3), p. 4.

I   – the school apparatuses also have other functions besides ideological inculcation:
     – reproduction of the social division of labour through specialised, exclusive and segregative technical training.
     – teaching of science, in order to increase the productive forces. Note: the teaching of science, always saturated with ideology, is exclusively outsourced to the petty and bourgeois schooling apparatus.
II – the school apparatuses do not have the monopoly of the reproduction of the social division of labour.
     this is an obvious theoretical point, but I underline it in order to dissipate the petty bourgeois illusion of 'meritocracy'.
III – the function of the educational apparatus is to inculcate ALL aspects of the dominant ideology.
     note: the school does not limit itself to inculcating the cultural ideology; cf. point three.
Inculcation is always done on two levels:
     practical subjection
     ideological-theoretical subjection
(the sign of the cross, prayer versus the catechism)
and it always concerns the relation to the three instances.[152]

We are by now completely familiar with the theoretical progression we find in this passage, and indeed we could claim that Macherey's text is nothing more than a lengthy commentary on it. Therefore, I will simply point out the points of convergence between the two authors. This text mentions ideological unity ('the school has only an ideological unity') – which will be the unity of the representation, functional to the dissimulation of both class division and the heterogeneity of its fundamental division. Indeed, distinct functions of the 'different apparatuses' are mentioned (because the social classes involved in the process of reproduction are distinct: Macherey, as we have seen, will argue that the school is constituted by the juxtaposition of different devices delivering 'heterogeneous contents to different audiences'.[153] This explains why Establet claims that 'the school does not limit itself to inculcating the cultural ideology': precisely because the cultural ideology – bourgeois humanism – is the partial ideological mediator that inculcates the dominant ideology in the ruling class, i.e., it defines the relationship of the ruling class with *its own* ideology, as the dominant form of ideology). More precisely, Establet

152   ALT2. A14-01.03 (B2).
153   ALT2. A14-01.04 (B14-01), p. 2.

claims here that the apparatuses are functional to the 'reproduction of the social division of labour' and that their function is 'to inculcate ALL aspects of the dominant ideology' – not only by inculcating 'the cultural ideology' (as we have seen in point 3), but also by operating at the level of both practical and ideological-theoretical subjection. More unusual is the brief appearance of what can be defined as the argument for the non-exclusivity function of the school system ('NONE of the functions performed by the different school apparatuses is performed exclusively by them'; 'the school apparatuses do not have the monopoly of the reproduction of the of the social division of labour').

We should remember that these words were written in March 1968, and the social climate, in the streets of Paris, was extremely volatile. It is therefore obvious that, starting from the (theoretical) presupposition of the imposition of systems of teaching, the lines of political practice need to be correctly defined: we can hear echoes of the question that was first posed by Chernyshevsky, and then by Lenin: 'what is to be done in the school, of the school, for the school, against the school?'[154] First of all, we should not fall into the linguistic trap of speaking of a 'crisis' (turning the university and the educational institution into something that goes beyond their actual realities). This concern will resurface in Macherey, who considers reformism to be a mere placeholder (synecdochal and depoliticised) for organised political action (§1). He claims that 'the "crisis of education" is thus an ideological theme, which is necessary in a capitalist regime for the functioning of the idea of the school and what it stands in for'.[155] Establet writes that 'the so-called crisis of the university is only perceived by the bourgeoisie and by the intellectual layers of the petty bourgeoisie'.[156] There is also another pitfall to avoid, relative to the idea of a strategic program: the bourgeoisie and the petty bourgeoisie, in order to defend their respective positioning, can count on a support base *whose power does not derive from number, but from hegemony and ideological domination* ('these are masses which, according to Gramsci, can be counted in the thousands, not in the millions').[157] This is as if to say that what must be overthrown is, first of all, the *symbolic status* (the representative content of the institution):

> To aim at designing, at all costs, a strategy for proletarian university amounts to making the university for the proletariat without the pro-

---

154 ALT2. A14-01.03 (B1), p. 1.
155 ALT2. A14-01.04 (A), p. 2.
156 ALT2. A14-01.03 (B1), p. 1.
157 ALT2. A14-01.03 (B1), p. 2.

letariat: in short, to choose, in the name of the proletariat, between the existing possible strategies, thus between bourgeois and petty bourgeois class positions.[158]

So, what is to be done? Neither programs nor reforms but – again, programmatically – it is necessary to define the operational lines of theoretical practice. Ultimately, this tenet characterises the analysis of all members of Althusser's group, and in particular Establet, functioning for them as a guide to political practice.

> To locate the exact placement of the problem of the school among other political problems.
>   To denounce, in a well-founded and detailed way, the scholastic apparatus as a state apparatus in the service of the ruling class.
>   To make it easier for others to detect and denounce these effects.
>   To break the link between certain 'schoolchildren' – university students – and the school apparatus, even in the struggles they are waging against it today, in order to involve them in decisive struggles.[159]

6   On the Ownership of the Means of Expression (and the Genesis of the Class-Based School): Michel Tort

'Pratiques littéraires et pratiques scolaires' is the title of a short, undated essay written by Michel Tort as a commentary on Macherey's 'Les mythologies scolaires'. Here too, the context is that of bourgeois cultural practices: 'P. Macherey's text, "Mythologies Scolaires" is fundamental for the analysis of all bourgeois cultural manifestations, which are: the production of objects deemed to be "works of art" on the one hand, and their consumption on the other'.[160] Of course, production is different from consumption. And yet, Tort suggests a relation of double implication: if, on the one hand – to use Establet's words[161] – general culture, as an aesthetic ideology, is defined by its relationship with the artwork (on the side of consumption), then on the other hand, in the capitalist mode of production, the artwork (on the side of production) is defined

---

158   Ibid.
159   ALT2. A14-01.03 (B1), p. 3.
160   ALT2. A14-01.05, p. 1.
161   Whose influence seems to surface from the link between the 'bourgeois cultural events' and the 'universe of literature'.

by its relationship with general culture. In short: *both the production and the consumption of the object respond to the same principles (which are social and class-based).* Tort clearly states that: 'the material transformed by production is determined by the same causes, and governed by the same social antagonisms as the mode of consumption'.[162] If the consumption of the artwork, in school, is the consumption of the ruling class (for it to be inculcated its own ideology, as Establet puts it, on the basis of a fundamental division between intellectual and manual labour, to continue with Macherey), the production of the consumed object responds, in school, to the (ideological) needs of the ruling class. Consequently, if the educational institution is home to general culture *qua* aesthetic ideology, then the analysis of that institution (like that performed by Macherey) can represent, at the same time, the analysis of a 'particular sector of education (i.e., that of 'literary training')' that is, 'of what is consumed at various levels'. In summary: production refers to consumption (and *vice versa*), and consumption refers to the institution: to understand the institution ultimately means to understand production as defined by the consumption of the object it produces.

Starting from this presupposition, we could summarise one of Tort's basic arguments as follows: *the self-representation of the school as a unitary whole defines the representation of the literary universe as a unitary whole:* 'we can understand that, in our bourgeois culture, "the universe of Literature" is described as "the scholastic universe" in which it appeared'.[163] The school is the place where the mode of consumption of the literary object is defined, and its ideological unity also defines the literary object as a unitary whole: a product delivered within the school as the proper place of its consumption. If production and consumption are the fundamental (and mutually determined) demands of bourgeois cultural practices, the object produced is imparted in a space without residue that ideologically defines it as a whole without residue ('as a self-sufficient whole, supposedly independent of other political and economic "systems"').[164] In short: (scholastic) representation, functional to ideological reproduction (by cultural inculcation), generates the representation of a (literary) object which is adequate to the function of scholastic representation (ideological reproduction). At this level we are clearly still on the surface of mythological unity (that is, still within *the context of the One*) – and therefore of (disguised) class struggle, which also concerns, we will soon see, the artwork and its modes of expression, and its (dissimulated) fundamental division,

---

162   ALT2. A14-01.05, p. 1.
163   Ibid.
164   ALT2. A14-01.05, p. 2.

which, as we have seen, concerns the school apparatus. The representation of consumption (or better: the representation of the place [*le lieu*] in which consumption happens), defines the representation of production (or better: the representation of the object inculcated in the space in which consumption takes place). Tort writes that 'literary production is thus linked to teaching and criticism, which try to make consumers imagine, in an interesting self-interested way, that a literary work is a beautiful Whole closed on its Secret';[165] and that 'in fact, the Teaching of Literature as it is taught in classrooms, and the preaching of Literary Criticism, supposedly free of all conformism and servitudes, enters into a determinate relationship with the texts that are produced because of a historical conjuncture'.[166]

Here, then, Tort introduces a quite ingenious hypothesis: what if the modes of aesthetic production, as structured by the capitalist strategy of reproduction, were only an application of the modes of production in general? Clearly this is not a simple analogy. Why? Once again: if general culture *qua* aesthetic ideology is for the ruling class, and if the production of the artwork is linked to its consumption, then all of this can only lead to one conclusion: *the production of the artwork is based on the ownership of the means of expression of the ruling class*. Tort writes:

> It is in the interest of the bourgeoisie to control the literary market, to reserve for itself the profits of production and to organise consumption democratically. Democratically: that is to say, unequally, so that the ownership of the means of expression does not leave the class of those who already possess it, either as writers or as readers, while the labour of a class without the right of ownership gives an essential contribution to the production of this literary fiction.[167]

In short, the language of artwork is not just any language. In the capitalist system of production, *the literary text is the index of an exclusive and programmed selection – it is the index of a region of language that is defined by a (class) decision, that is, of a struggle for the appropriation of the means of expression*.[168] The mode of literary expression is a private mode of expression, both in its act of appropriation (for one class) and deprivation (for the other classes). One could also say that, for Macherey, the work performed in the school is

---

165   ALT2. A14-01.05, p. 4.
166   ALT2. A14-01.05, p. 3.
167   ALT2. A14-01.05, p. 5.
168   A similar thesis can be found in R. Balibar 1974. See also below, note 179.

the (analogical) work that makes us bend our knees (that is, that makes us believe in reality). More specifically, intellectual work makes the ruling class bend its knees; intellectual work – for Macherey, but even more consistently for Establet – consists in literary learning (for the former, literature is 'in solidarity with the idea of a total formation of the individual' and is 'the speculative support of the imposed moral discipline';[169] for the latter, it inculcates the idea of a universal man). Here, then, we understand Tort's insistence: to do this, to know how to bend one's knees, *one must know how to speak the language that produces the belief in reality* (in the passage I quoted he writes that: 'the ownership of the means of expression does not leave the class of those who already possess it').[170]

Language is a transversal surface, cutting across all speaking beings. But consumption implies, as we have seen, knowing how to talk or, which is the same, it requires for everyone – according to social class – to say things in his or her own way. The proletariat, then, is excluded from the enjoyment of the artwork seen a function of reproduction (the artwork is for the ruling class, and consumption is linked to production).[171] Tort distances himself from the hypothesis that language would be something natural, as if it were an original endowment of any speaking being. Because if language is a surface that cuts through all social classes, then the artwork that splits this surface with a gesture of appropriation (the artwork that makes a selection) *reflects the antagonisms of those social classes*. At the end of the passage quoted above it was said that 'the labour of a class without the right of ownership gives an essential contribution to the production of this literary fiction': does this not mean that class struggle within the modes of production is reflected in a class struggle within the modes of appropriation of the means of expression? 'Yet linguistic and cultural inequality is both the displaced image of economic inequality, and a further means of confirming economic inequality, to exploit its advantages'.[172] The literary text,

---

169 ALT2. A14-01.04 (A), p. 12.

170 That is why I hypothesise that behind both Tort and Macherey's theses, we should detect the influence of Balibar's review of Bourdieu.

171 Roland Barthes famously argued – in his *Writing Degree Zero* (Barthes 1977) – that literature is inherently modern. Regarding the statement, 'the artwork is for the ruling class, and its consumption is linked to production', I refer to Jean-Claude Milner's brief commentary on Barthes' thesis: 'this modernity begins, roughly, with the advent of the bourgeoisie as an economically and politically dominant class. At least in France. We could easily conclude from this that French literature provides us with the very model for Literature, just as the English Industrial Revolution, according to some, provides us with the very model for capitalist industry'. Milner 2021, p. 46.

172 ALT2. A14-01.05, p. 7.

an *uncreated* object (it refers to an Author external to any linguistic conflict of appropriation), *is the object produced by an original gesture of accumulation and, therefore, of exclusion.* In short, if at school the literary work is the framework of a bourgeois linguistic selection (or production) aimed at consumption for the bourgeois class, on the other hand, it is also produced *by excluding a voice.* At the base of literary production there is only one determining factor: *class antagonism, as what refers to the subtraction of a language functional to its own* (*the ruling class's*) *reproduction* (indeed, the artwork is 'yet another way to confirm economic inequality'). The language of the bourgeoisie (and the bourgeois artwork) exists only on the basis of class struggle in the field of language in general. Behind language there is an essential linguistic inequality, determined by the appropriation of the means of expression: 'the existence of a non-owning productive proletariat, with the linguistic antagonisms that stem from this fact: this is the basis of literary production'.[173]

We can thus understand that, to the extent that an artwork is the result of a (class) gigantomachy, *it has no author* or, better, *it reduces the work's authorship to the private index of the social group that leads the struggle of appropriation*:

> Although the *apparent worker* responsible for the apparent 'work of art' is the author indicated by a signature, a member of the Société des Gens de Lettres, possibly in possession of the work's copyright – 'Racine', 'Balzac', 'Robbe-Grille' (names which, by the way, mean quite different things from what 'Sophocles' or 'Cicero' meant for a Roman, or 'Racine' for Madame de Sévigné) – *the real literary producer* is by no means this private owner. The real producer is the part of the social classes within which the text is desirable; in other words, the real producer is *the coalition of class interests for which such fiction is a weapon of combat.*[174]

Let us consider the example of Balzac: his modes of expression are those of the bourgeoisie (and they are for the bourgeoisie). This, however, could be said to be Balzac's 'real position'. Indeed, he is the one who actually wrote, say, *Eugénie Grandet*: and yet, as we have seen, the simple gesture of writing is not enough to indicate him as the author ('the real literary producer is by no means this private owner'), as if his own inner intentionality were to really speak through his writing. And yet, have we not said that the artwork's function is ideological ('the right to economic property is in fact accompanied, under specific

173   ALT2. A14-01.05, p. 6.
174   Ibid.

conditions, by a right to the ownership of linguistic and aesthetic means')?[175] The scare quotes that Tort applies around the authors' names should be taken seriously. If Balzac's modes of expression are those of the bourgeoisie (which indicates the position that he really occupies within the struggle for the appropriation of the means of expression), then it is true that, ideologically, the work bears the Name of 'Balzac', as if he were the Author, external to any linguistic class struggle (as if the artwork, as Macherey puts it, were not produced from an overdetermined linguistic material, but was simply created). In sum, on the one hand there is Balzac; on the other, his Name. Doesn't this mean that it is precisely at the level of the Name that the school, as a unitary representation, consumes the work as a unitary whole? Doesn't the Name, precisely insofar as it hides the singular index of a generalised struggle (the material author in his real position), also hide the fundamental class division responsible for its production? Ultimately, isn't the function of the Name that of permitting a fundamental concealment? Doesn't the Name serve to hide the fact behind its production? Here we could reintroduce the notions of 'real level' and 'imaginary level', allowing us to formulate the following theses:

1. The literary work simultaneously occupies a place on the 'real level' – if by this we indicate the real factors of its class production – and on the 'imaginary level', if we define its function as essentially reproducing the modes of production of the ruling class (inculcating a universality starting from a speech act, – that of the work, and a knowing-how to speak, that of the bourgeoisie, at school).

2. If, as Macherey suggests, the representative content of the school is located in a space 'where the contradictions specific to the capitalist regime are represented without the appearance of the class struggle',[176] in the same way the Name imprinted on the work is instrumental for the concealment of the social fact responsible for its production ('the [author's] signature is only a legal cover for the aesthetic operation ... Rather, the refraction of the linguistic conflict into an image of private life makes it beautiful for a bourgeois imagination').[177]

3. We have already seen how Tort believed that 'literary production is thus linked to teaching and criticism, which try to make consumers imagine, in an interesting self-interested way, that a literary work is a beautiful Whole closed on its Secret'.[178] We are now in a better position to make sense of

---

175   ALT2. A14-01.05, pp. 5–6.
176   ALT2. A14-01.04 (A), p. 2.
177   ALT2. A14-01.05, p. 6.
178   ALT2. A14-01.05, p. 4.

this: if in school the aim of the work is to inculcate the dominant ideology, on the operative assumption of a unitary representation motivated by a dissimulation, (2.), then *it is the school that defines the work as a unitary whole, an authorial object.*

4. Balzac, occupying a real place within the linguistic field (a field of conflict on the 'real level'), did not write in order to be read at school. Rather, it is the school that makes a selection based on the work's modes of expression. Only the struggle for the appropriation of the means of expression in the field of language in general is truly structural and on the 'real level'. The school intervenes *at a later stage* – that is, it selects works according to a linguistic mechanism that is functional to the '*coalition of class interests for which such a fiction is a "weapon for combat"*'. On the other hand, however, the Name, like the work (on the 'imaginary level'), is generated from an imaginary necessity ('the world of education is trying to make consumers imagine') that is functional to the ideological mechanism of reproduction. In other words, if Balzac, on the 'real level', writes free from the constraints of scholastic consumption (that only *later* will eventually select his work), then on the other hand, it this consumption – functional to the ideological reproduction of the modes of production – that *produces the Name and the Work, after the fact.*[179]

---

179   To underscore this complete theoretical affinity, I will quote in full a passage by Renée Balibar, which is taken from an unpublished dossier composed of eleven untitled and undated typewritten sheets. Balibar sent this text (on a Sunday) to Althusser, with this introductory note: 'Dear Louis, I am sending you some insertions that Pierre had asked me for; I told him to do whatever he wants with them'. It is difficult to say where these additional notes, requested by Macherey, should have been placed in the context of 'Schools'. Considering their topic – which, roughly, pertains to the relation between the reproduction of the production relationships and the content of school textbooks – it can be assumed that they were meant to be placed within the section on culture. Regardless, it is precisely because of Tort's question of the Name that I am interested in quoting Balibar's notes. The most important element that qualifies scholastic practice is the constitution of what Renée Balibar calls a *Corpus d'Auteurs* or *Grands Auteurs*. These 'great authors', for the use that is made of them in school, are functional to the mechanism of ideological reproduction of the ruling class insofar as they define the very being of its social composition. As if to say that two ingredients are necessary to make the bourgeoisie: the ownership of the means of production and ... Racine! 'When a pupil talks about "his books", he mentions his *Morceaux Choisis* (in the form of a literary history, yesterday Lanson and Chavaillier-Audiat, today Lagarde and Michard), or the novels, poems, and literary commentaries that have lulled him to sleep on the fringes of school hours (Balzac and Stendhal, Baudelaire and Rimbaud, Paul Eluard, Sartre, etc.). The individual variations of this choice may be considerable, but the structure of the collectively accepted set is rigid. The repertoire of

5. Therefore, the argument that was proposed in the first section of this chapter – aimed at bringing together Macherey's texts on the school and on literary production, and at highlighting a common argument, adequate to shed light on the same myth – proves to be anything but idle. Indeed, Tort writes that:

These brief insights, for which we will provide some evidence, are already confirmed not only by the analyses of 'Mythologie Scolaires' but also by P. Macherey's *Pour une Théorie de la Production Littéraire*. Macherey has clearly denounced:

– the metaphysical confusion between 'Reading' and 'Writing' that afflicts the current state of our culture
– the continued avoidance of a theory of real production, permitted by the preservation of ideals of 'artistic creation'
– the reduction, convenient for the reigning culture, of the meaning of a text to a timeless theme
– the organised disregard of the real disparities that can be found in literary fiction

These conclusions lead us to question what common interests are involved in the production of fiction and in the formulation of the standard guidelines for its interpretation.[180]

: :

---

the Great Authors, the relationships between them, including the role attributed to the recognised non conformists, are determinate and constitute the student's primary knowledge. ... The bourgeoisie has a cult of art, which it has turned into the privileged vehicle of religion and morality. ... It imagines Literature as a world of individual genius styles making a career in a history of Genres and Schools. The composition of the bourgeois world of the Great Authors varies in name and justification according to the actual political and social situation. The historical glories of Racine, Homer, Mallarmé, Nerval, are neither immutable nor arbitrary, but conceal their remote economic causes under interpretative "meanings". The permanent fact is the possession of a well-defined linguistic heritage thanks to which the cultivated elite elaborates an allusive mode of expression, based on allegories, morphological and syntactic undertones, and the whole arsenal of figures of speech, for which rudiments of Latin and foreign languages are required. From its esotericism, it does not only derive a superficial and conspicuous benefit. The class consciousness of the dominant bourgeoisie actually needs this literary corpus in order to represent itself to itself and to others. The being of the bourgeoisie goes through Racine and Mallarmé, just as the money of the bourgeoisie goes through Balzac'. ALT2. A14-01.02, pp. 7–8.

180   ALT2. A14-01.05, p. 8.

'Pratiques littéraires et pratiques scolaires' allows us to make a detour towards another one of Tort's texts, clearly linked to 'Schools'. Written on 23 July 1968, after the commentary on Macherey's essay, and titled: 'Sur le procès historique de formation de l'École de Classe – Scolarisation des formations, scolarisation obligatoire, "démocratisation"'.[181] Considering how close in time this essay and one we have just examined are, it seems appropriate to take a closer look at it.

Macherey's only historical coordinate, as we have seen, pertains to the mechanism of real separation of the school space that was enforced by the Jesuits (the creation of colleges at the end of the sixteenth century). Tort argues that, precisely due to the historical stance that underlies his July 1968 text, things are necessarily more complicated. Therefore 'Sur le procès historique de formation' can be taken, at least for the moment, as the historical basis of the theoretical considerations that appear in 'Schools' (including those of Macherey, whose origin can easily be traced back to Tort's considerations).[182]

We can introduce three theses at the core of Tort's essay. We are already familiar with the first one: every educational apparatus is determined by a mode of production, based on what we have called the 'principle of contemporaneity between determinate modes of education and determinate modes of production'. And if, in general, each social formation is ultimately defined by a specific division of labour, then each educational apparatus has the function of placing each individual within the respective social formation. Tort writes:

> every social formation comprises, in extremely diverse forms, an apparatus or a set of *educational apparatuses*, distinct or not from other institutions (family, state), responsible for making individuals from each generation physically, technically, and ideologically fit to function in specific positions of the division of labour. The development of the productive forces and the modification of the relations of production regulate the transformation of the educational apparatuses, their internal devices, the positions they fill, the classes they form and reproduce according to the relevant aspects.[183]

Second thesis: scholastic education is a specific form of education. Although it first emerged under non-capitalist conditions, it is only with the capital-

---

181   ALT2. A14-01.06.
182   Cf. below, Chapter 4.
183   ALT2. A14-01.06, p. 1.

ist mode of production that the educational apparatuses come to play a fundamental role. Not, and this is crucial, because of the *content* they transmit (its specific function), but rather because of *the modalities* of this transmission.

> The term *scholastic education* can be used to designate a type of education which appeared under modes of production that predate capitalism – although, for reasons to be specified later, in the capitalist mode of production it eventually comes to play an essential and dominant role in relation to other types of education. *Scholastic education* is not distinguished from other types of education because of its *content*: thus, it cannot be opposed to military training, apprenticeship, initiation, etc., since military instruction, or the skills of a trade, can be dispensed in 'military', or 'professional' schools. *Scholastic education* seems to be able to incorporate any content: its originality lies in the way it delivers this content, namely through a suspension of actual practice.[184]

Third thesis. To use Macherey's formula, the school not only does not exist because there are apparatuses positioned, behind the representative content of its myth, by a fundamental division that the representation itself takes care to conceal. The school does not exist because, precisely at the level of these apparatuses, *their situation changes according to the development of the specific (capitalist) mode of production.* Assuming that, as a mode of education, it is as determinate as the mode of production under which it is placed, the scholastic institution – and not its representation – is an institution that undergoes transformation in lockstep with the mode of production which determines it. In short: the stages of the development of capitalism as a mode of production function as the laws of transformation of the scholastic institution as a mode of education. Tort indeed highlights

> the constant *transformation* of this education, i.e., of the various apparatuses of instruction and education, according to the development of capitalism, which defines the law of this transformation. It is therefore necessary to always carefully specify to which state of development of capitalism this or that apparatus corresponds to, as well as the relationship between apparatuses, which it would be erroneous and anachron-

---

184   Ibid.

istic to project into the past (cf. below: the 'School') as belonging to a given stage of the development of capitalism.[185]

Final thesis: 'the essential character of formations, from the beginning and up to the present capitalist mode of education, is that of being *class formations*'.[186]

Starting from these premises, we can roughly outline the following historical survey of the formation of the class-based school.

A First stage (*from caste school to class-based schools*). This corresponds to a period that goes from the late Middle Ages to the beginning of the nineteenth century. Class separation is permeated by the separation between castes ('if the class separations from the end of the Middle Ages to the beginning of the nineteenth century borrow from the castes their clearcut character, they remain *class separations*').[187] The stage of development of capitalism is that of a market economy ('an essentially market phase'), and if this stage of development defines the law of determination of the mode of education (as per the third thesis above), the essential characteristics of this mode of scholastic education can be summarised as follows:

   – scholastic education occupies a subordinate placement compared to other types of education ('it is far from dominant compared to the other formations') and its function can be reduced to a preparation for university entry tests. The subjects that partake to the process of scholastic education are, essentially, the nobility and the upper bourgeoisie.
   – in terms of the state, scholastic education is disorganised – in other words, it is left in the hands of private initiatives, assuming a substantial indifference vis-à-vis its public utility: 'the way that schooling is provided is a matter for wealthy families to decide, as is the organisation of studies, but perhaps above all this means that the education of the population as a whole is not a problem, or at most just a private matter'.[188]

   Religious (ecclesiastical) ideology is the dominant ideological formation of this stage of the development of capitalism.

B Second phase (*of the class-based schools*). This corresponds to the first three quarters of the nineteenth century, and it is engendered by the growing demands of the world of industry. The bourgeoisie is thus in

---

185 Ibid.
186 Ibid.
187 ALT2. A14-01.06, p. 2.
188 Ibid.

charge of introducing innovative educational systems, since the development of the productive forces requires the training of skilled workers ('technicians, competent civilians, or military officials' hailing from the lower and medium bourgeoisie, as well as proletarians) who can be distributed across the various levels of the division of labour in general.[189]
These innovations concern:

- the creation of primary education [*enseignement primaire ou élémentaire*], meant for the poorer classes (Tort, on this point, quotes a prefectural report of 1864 which states that: 'they will not be suspected of empty theories and pipe dreams. If they wanted to spread education among the workers, it was because the interests of industry, as well as of the working classes, demanded the dissemination of the sciences that would help it to progress').[190]
- the introduction of vocational education [*enseignement professionnel*]. Tort, here quoting from a document of the English Department of Science and Art: 'everyone knows that it is through the sketching of a blueprint that the apprentice gets on with the worker, the worker with the foreman, the foreman with the engineer, the builder, the architect, etc. Drawing is truly the language of industry'.[191]
- the modification of the traditional apparatuses [*appareils*] of so-called secondary [*secondaires*] education, with the introduction of areas of modern scientific education.

The class-based school system, on the other hand, is characterised as follows:

- the mode of scholastic education – which, in the previous period, was subject to other modes of education – acquires considerable prestige, mainly because of the weight of primary education [*enseignement primaire*]. A significant fact is that state institutions begin to introduce examination procedures for allowing entry into the public service.
- scholastic formations have the essential characteristic of corresponding to class formations (which is particularly evident for the bourgeoisie of the time). More precisely, secondary education [*enseignement 'secondaire', ou 'des classes supérieures'*] corresponds to the classical and modern education of the *lycée* and it is intended for the large bourgeoisie and the aristocracy, as well as for the middle bourgeoisie. Technical education [*enseignement technique*] is intended for

---

189   Ibid.
190   ALT2. A14-01.06, p. 3.
191   Ibid.

the middle bourgeoisie and for a part of the petty bourgeoisie. Finally, primary [*primaire*] education – with its professional [*professionnel*], industrial [*industriel*] and intermediate [*intermédiaire*] extensions – is intended for the proletariat and for the lower strata of the petty bourgeoisie and the higher stratum of the working class. The point is both that technical and primary education are explicitly conceived and developed by the industrial bourgeoisie as education 'for the "poor" and the "average" social classes'. This is a variation on the theme of the appropriation of the means of expression, at the level of the forms of education: 'this class character is slightly disguised in the dominant terminology in France ("primary", "secondary") because the democrat-ising ideology wants to avoid the direct enunciation of class differ-ences, something that, conversely, the English aristocracy has no issue at spelling out'.[192]

– the scholastic system is composed of heterogeneous apparatuses which do not constitute a unit ('although the apparatus of the present scholastic system is already constituted in its essential lines, a very important feature of the system in this form is its lack of unity'). There is no single school because different schools are meant for different classes:

> in other words, there is a set of apparatuses 1) primary-elementary,
> 2) upper primary or further education (vocational, industrial etc …)
> 3) classical or academic etc … which prepare for universities. But
> those that come before are *not articulated* as to lead to the others.

This is because the apparatuses are not like the parts of an organism (like 'merely scattered members of a single body') that makes them work in tandem. Rather, they are separate systems because they are 'three unequal and mutually exclusive complete systems', which mirror the exclusionary nature of class separation ('whose laws of exclusion are the laws of class'). The school system is an open and heterogeneous system of closed (because complete) and exclusive (because unequal) systems. This is what ultimately leads to the removal, from the field of education, of the notion of 'democratisation', since this – if not *de re*, at least *de jure* – should imply the participation to every scholastic apparatus: how could a system that – not just *de re*, but also *de jure* – explicitly assigns its different apparatuses to different social classes be called 'democratic'? Here, if we speak of democratisation, we once

---

192   Ibid.

again use an ideological language: 'the ideology of democratisation is one of the justifying ideologies of openness with which the bourgeoisie covers up the self-interested increase of the theoretical level of the working classes'.[193]

- the transformation of the traditional educational system 'was only made possible by a particularly spectacular state intervention'. It is the state, the 'bourgeoisie's instrument of domination', which takes care of the school and its configuration. Its task, therefore, is to present the educational processes, at every level, as subject to a universal (and therefore ideological, guided by the 'progress of enlightenment and education') necessity, and to instil 'the needs of the bourgeoisie' in the mental habits of the popular classes.[194] However, until the last quarter of the nineteenth century the state had not yet decided on the compulsory nature of education.

- moral (state) ideology comes to be the dominant ideological formation after a struggle against religious (ecclesiastical) ideology. Far from being an afterthought, moral ideology represents an essential presupposition for the harmonious functioning of the economy. This is why Tort writes that, 'in school, the children of workers do not only learn a minimum of scientific knowledge, but also political *economy*. Moralisation is part of the economic and political rationality of capitalism'.[195]

C   Third stage (*of the class-based school*). It corresponds to the period that goes from the end of the nineteenth to the beginning of the twentieth century. In this period, the state's innovations to the educational system were still insufficient to raise the level of theoretical education of the (popular) masses, which was a minimum requirement to respond to the needs of industrial capitalism. More precisely, this was due to the outflow of large portions of the working classes and the petty bourgeoisie from the process of schooling. Therefore 'the bourgeoisie organises ... the *Class-based School* [*École de Classes*] system, whose essential characteristics are as follows':[196]

- unlike the phase of the class-based schools, the school system of the class-based school is a system of heterogeneous apparatuses that constitute a unit (a 'unified system [*système unique*]') that goes from

---

193   ALT2. A14-01.06, p. 4.
194   Ibid.
195   ALT2. A14-01.06, p. 5.
196   Ibid.

kindergarten to university. If class separation, in the phase of class-based schools, was ensured by the exclusive and unequal heterogeneity of school apparatuses *qua* class apparatuses (class law is the law of separation of apparatuses so that this separation mirrors class separation), class separation in the phase of class-based school is ensured by scientific mechanisms of orientation whose function is 'to scientifically ascertain the class abilities of individuals'. Starting with the pseudo-scientific methodology of the selection mechanisms (the parameters used for intelligence tests, for example, make the proletarian child idiotic and retarded),[197] we witness a democratisation of the education system – *de jure* but not *de re*, since behind the faux-egalitarianism promoted by the recruitment procedures for access into the school system, at all levels, we ultimately find 'the identical operation of all three apparatuses'[198] (primary, technical, classical) as class apparatuses.

– if in the previous phase scholastic education was the primary form of education, it now becomes mandatory. It is clear, however, as Tort notes, that the obligatory nature of education does not rhyme, so to speak, with its democratisation (as a certain 'cretinism of democratisation' would have it): indeed, 'if compulsory schooling had really been justified by the "democratisation" of education, it is not clear why it would have stopped at primary level'.[199] Once again, compulsory education is a coercive bourgeois instrument that is functional to the formation of proletarian and petty bourgeois skilled labour:

> primary education becomes an obligation only because of the industrial bourgeoisie's need to ensure that no one in the working

---

197 I borrow this example from Tort 1974, in which Tort further develops arguments elaborated in the 'Schools' project. Indeed, Tort already writes that: 'A) Intelligence tests make the children of the popular classes appear "less intelligent" than others. This conclusion must be carefully examined because, if accepted as valid, it would have the consequence of a) justifying school segregation and the division of labour on the basis of "scientific" criteria; b) denying that the working class, which in this case consists of less intelligent individuals than others, is today the class that bears a historical future. B) It can be doubted, looking at the facts, that intelligence tests actually measure what they claim to measure: individual aptitude. Indeed, IQ can considerably vary in the same subject. With these two elements (A and B) at hand, we justifiably conclude that these tests are not neutral instruments of a neutral psychology, but rather ideological devices intended to reinforce and justify the rule of the bourgeoisie over the people'.

198 ALT2. A14-01.06, p. 5.

199 Ibid.

classes and petty bourgeoisie escapes the obligation to go to school and receive an education that will enable them to more effectively serve industry in the long term.[200]

- more so than in the previous period, the state – which is in the phase of imperialism and monopoly capitalism – intervenes exclusively to rigidly define the organisational parameters of education and the educational institution, a single system of distinct apparatuses (whose placement, Macherey would say, is determined by the analogical fundamental division between intellectual and manual labour). Thus, Tort briefly mentions that 'the introduction of compulsory elementary schooling can be compared to the introduction of compulsory national military service, taking place, around the same time, in many capitalist countries'.[201]

D   Fourth and final stage (*still on class-based school*). It begins immediately after the World War I and represents a further transformation of the class-based school (third phase). Its peculiarity lies in a shift of attention towards secondary [*secondaire*] and higher [*supérieur*] education, it being understood that even the proper functioning of the primary training apparatus [*apparareil primaire*] is not sufficient to satisfy the demand for an even more qualified workforce. These are its essential characteristics:

- the shift towards secondary education is reflected in an extension of compulsory education: it no longer covers only primary education [*primaire élémentaire*], but also vocational education [*enseignement professionnel*].
- the transformation of the class-based school takes the form of a generalised 'secondarisation', 'which, in the long run, is oriented towards the problem of admission to university, which is a key issue'.[202]
- the push towards a generalised schooling introduces 'a new relationship between training and production'.
- a correct analysis of the question of democratisation needs to steer clear of two opposite misconceptions. On the one hand, the democratisation (in terms of recruitment) that is *de facto* guided by the development of the capitalist school should not be underestimated, as certain 'petty bourgeois jeremiads' do. On the other, the process of democratisation should not be described in idealistic terms – as it was during

---

200   Ibid.
201   ALT2. A14-01.06, p. 6.
202   Ibid.

the third phase – referring to 'the need for education, for the progress of enlightenment' since, once again, it is guided by the law of the development of capital.

- the dominant ideology, although still a bourgeois ideology, begins here to change its meaning. We should not be surprised, since all of Establet's texts which I have analysed so far rest on this fundamental argument. The moral ideology that was a prerequisite for the harmonious functioning of the economy ('based on the values of work, the economy, and long since grounded on a problematic or antagonistic relationship with religious ideology'), is replaced by *the bourgeois ideology of culture* articulated through completely new vocabulary ('at no time in the 19th century were school subjects considered as elements of "general culture"').[203] It is self-evident that this cultural ideological formation reflects the increasingly decisive role assigned to the secondary [*secondaire*] level of education 'whose culture is the native ideology'.

- generalised schooling has the effect of introducing 'private pressure groups, traditionally characteristic of class-based schools, in the form of "Associations of students' parents"'[204] into the very framework of educational processes. For Tort, these associations are clearly class associations functional to give control, in the class-based school, to the ruling classes and to the offspring of the ruling classes.

---

203   ALT2. A14-01.06, p. 7.
204   Ibid.

'Schools'

Introduction

In the introduction to Chapter 2, we focused on identifying the textual references to 'Schools' in Althusser's *On the Reproduction of Capitalism: Ideology and Ideological State Apparatuses*. The chapter focused on Macherey's 'Les Mythologies Scolaires' (the earliest essay-length document, among those currently available in the archives, pertaining to that collective project) and, in particular – to adopt the language of the note that was attached to the first chapter of 'Schools' – its 'appreciation, critique, and rectification', especially in Establet and Tort's work in its wake.

In this chapter we will deal directly with the three chapters that comprise 'Schools'. As a way of introducing this task, I will offer a brief analysis of an unpublished text by Althusser, which can be found among the drafting materials of the collective work. Written at least five months before 'Schools', this text examines some of its most important theoretical questions.

The essay is composed of twenty-two typewritten pages, written between the autumn and the winter of 1968 and dedicated to what are called the 'Grandes Illusions de l'École'. Althusser writes that 'the first of these illusions may be called a Philosophical Illusion, because it concerns knowledge of the school'.[1] A philosophical illusion is one of knowledge. Far from being simple, this is an illusion whose statute informs the illusory nature of other illusions (as we shall see): the illusory nature of every illusion, then, is located in the domain of a philosophical illusion. Here we encounter merely an apparent paradox: the philosophical illusion is engendered by a *proximity*, that is, by a certain kind of *immediacy*: 'we all know the school *from experience*, since we all spend several years of our lives there'. Immediacy is proximity to experience. The illusion of knowledge, then, is an empirical illusion. Thus, if the philosophical illusion defines the illusory nature of other illusions, then concerning the school, every illusion is an empirical illusion. We have not really taken any distance from the representational status of the school in Macherey (and it is no coincidence, as we shall see later, that the illusions Althusser analyses concern precisely the school's unity, as well as its very existence). Indeed, according to

---

1 ALT2. A14-01.08, p. 1.

Macherey the unitary representation (or the myth that runs through it) was inherent in what the school presents of itself (the representation was a determined and predetermined presentation: for the concealment of class struggle, i.e., for the concealment of the fundamental division between intellectual and manual labour). Here, in Althusser's text, this thesis is completely turned on its head: the school's representation, the fact that it (re)presents itself in a certain way, is the representation *of* a determined subject: a philosophical illusion, proximity, and immediacy.

School is an articulate object. It is irreducible to the experience of the pupil or the teacher (its subjects), as well as to the administrators. Its knowledge, one might say, springs from the synthesis of all their experiences: 'if we collect the experience of the teachers and professors, as well as the administrators, we will have knowledge of the school'.[2] It seems clear that the epistemological presupposition that underlies this kind of argument is that, in the context of a subject-object relationship, an object can only truly be known if it is brought into being by a subject, who therefore has the prerequisites to be able to grasp it theoretically. So, if we aim to obtain knowledge about the school, it will be necessary to consider the *élèves* and *maîtres* as the only actors who, from their vantage points, are able to outline its contours: they are the ones who make the school and who can know it and, eventually, also make it known to those who have little familiarity with it. It is as easy as that: just add their experiences together. Proximity and immediacy: 'it is not surprising, then, that practical experience of the school is knowledge of the school'.[3]

For the sake of brevity, *I will refer to a true-factual proposition as any empirical proposition 'x' (here: the student) whose correctness is determined by the preliminary production of the known object, and that is able to produce a general thesis about the known object if compounded with empirical proposition 'y' (here: the teacher).* This kind of generality of the theoretical thesis, which I call *extensive theoretical generality*, is determined by nothing more than the summation of true-factual propositions. Incidentally, it is interesting to note that Althusser identifies an 'inventor' of this kind of proposition:

> the first to formulate it was the Italian philosopher Vico. He said: 'Truth is what we have made' (*verum factum*). He said: men did not make Nature, that is why it is mysterious: but it is men who make history, and that is why they can understand and know it. Hence the formula quoted: men

---

2   Ibid.
3   ALT2. A14-01.08, p. 2.

can only reach the *truth* when they seek to know the things they have *made*, not the others.[4]

It is precisely this kind of proposition that Althusser, *as a Marxist*, wants to reject ('this obviousness of the school is the first Great Illusion that must be dispelled').[5] Consider an example that is *not only* an example: the practical experience of economic life. Regardless of their position in society, everyone buys or sells something. 'What could be more transparent than an exchange?': in the cycle of production the capitalists buy machines and raw materials just as they buy the labour power of those who are responsible, through the use of those machines, for the transformation of materials into finished products. Meanwhile, the workers sell their labour power for money, which is useful for the purchase of other products.[6] The capitalist exchanges money for labour; the worker exchanges labour for money: 'Buying, selling: it's all about exchanging'. Buying and selling are placed in a transparent relationship of symmetry that – considering how this exchange presents itself – seems to put the two commodities on a plane of absolute equivalence of value. And if this exchange is the basis of economic life, then both the capitalist and the worker, starting from the specificity of the mutual position, are the theoretical actors of a specific kind of true-factual propositions, instrumental to the production of a general theory: 'it would suffice to add together all the experiences of buying and selling, even the most complex ones, to obtain a picture of economic life'.[7]

As we have seen, Althusser, as a Marxist, rejects the validity of true-factual propositions. Indeed, for Althusser Marx allows us to see that the reality of economic experience is not equivalent to the truth of its knowledge: 'But we know, since Marx, that this is a Great Illusion. The simple experience of economic practice, and even all the experiences put together, do not give us the knowledge of economic life'.[8] Transparency is an appearance: the symmetry of the relationship lies on the representational plane. The fact that the exchange is anything but free and equal (since 'the worker is *obliged* to sell the use of his labour power to the boss in order to live')[9] and, above all, the fact that the wage received by worker is not at all equivalent to the value of the product of his labour (but only to what is necessary for his reproduction), introduces

---

4 ALT2. A14-01.08, pp. 2–3.
5 ALT2. A14-01.08, p. 1.
6 ALT2. A14-01.08, p. 3.
7 Ibid.
8 ALT2. A14-01.08, pp. 3–4.
9 ALT2. A14-01.08, p. 4.

'something obscure, which is not directly visible' *at the heart of the gapless total-ity that is defined by the equivalence relation.*

The smooth surface of the representation is disturbed by ripples, created by an anomaly, by something opaque that prohibits its closure so to speak, and that the dominant ideology (particularly the legal one that states that 'men are free and equal by nature') needs to conceal, something that in this case, needless to say, is represented by surplus value, 'which is not directly visible, and which must therefore be drawn from the shadow'. This is to say that *the (scientific) logic of valorisation transgresses the (true-factual) ontology of representation*, if by the latter we mean that which makes the market the set of equivalent values designating the relationships between commodities, that is, the field in which the exchange commodity appears as homogeneous and structured by stable and predictable relationships.

Hence, there are 'two conclusions that are crucial to our study', as well as a methodological premise.[10] The first conclusion is that if the sum of the empirical propositions is completely irrelevant towards the production of a generality which would grant the theoretical grasp of an object – just as irrelevant, for this generality, as the production of an object that will eventually be theoretically grasped by the one who produces it – then the use of true-factual propositions cannot lead to the theoretical grasp of social reality because the real structure is not given through experience. Surplus value, Althusser writes, 'eludes human consciousness'.[11] This is an absolute distinction, with no possibility of synthesis: empirical propositions, however complex, merely circulate on the representative plane of what is intentionally presented; scientific propositions belong instead to the technically *unrepresentable* (i.e., unintentional because extra-conscious) residue that lies at the centre of real valorisation (the extortion of surplus labour). In short: '*Vico is wrong*'.

Let us therefore go back to the beginning: Althusser's work focuses on the school, just as in economic practice it is necessary to distinguish between what is presented and what is, so to speak, real:

> the school is not transparent, what happens in the school cannot be reduced to what happens between the teacher and the students. In order to understand what happens in the school, it is necessary to shed light on the system of obscure relationships that determine what happens therein.[12]

---

10   ALT2. A14-01.08, p. 5.
11   ALT2. A14-01.08, p. 4.
12   ALT2. A14-01.08, p. 5.

Let us proceed to the second conclusion. To say that, in economic terms, the system of obscure relations (the relations of production) is *real* (it produces surplus value) while its representation is *illusory* (representing the market as a field structured by equivalences) is, all in all, still an imprecise statement. In fact, between the level of representation (let us finally call it by its proper name: *ideology*)[13] and the level of surplus value as a factor of valorisation, there is an absolute distinction but no relationship of exclusion. Here we have an exquisitely Althusserian thesis: ideology is instrumental for real functioning ('in social matters, nothing obscure happens without this obscurity being covered by the illusion of transparency') and every social sector operates through ideology ('everything that functions in society does so "on ideology" – on an ideological illusion').[14] Like legal illusions, which are instrumental to a straightforward representation of exchange, they are also instrumental to the production of surplus value: 'the Great Illusions of the school, which give the school its transparency, are also essential to the functioning of the school as we know it'. In other words, it is *an illusion that is anything but illusory*: far from defining itself through self-predication, it has a tangible grip on real social functioning. For Althusser, then, the goal is to identify the scholastic illusions (and to find out what their function is).

We noted above that the philosophical illusion has a privileged character, being an illusion of transparency and immediacy. It is an illusion among illusions, whose illusory nature informs all the others. And, on closer inspection, it cannot be otherwise: how could other representations be identified if not from experiential content? It is here that we encounter the methodological premise we mentioned above: 'how do we go about identifying and discovering them [the school's other illusions]? We propose a simple method. It consists in taking at face value the *content* of the practical experience that we have of the school'.[15]

And what do we see in the school? The answer is particularly interesting, especially since it seems to express the distance that Althusser now takes from the theses expressed in 'Student Problems'. Indeed, in addition to discerning

---

13   Cf. Althusser 2005, p. 231: 'It will suffice to know very schematically that an ideology is a system (with its own logic and rigour) of representations (images, myths, ideas or concepts, depending on the case) endowed with a historical existence and role within a given society'. In this sense, every true-factual proposition, although it may not be ideological for theoretical purposes, is necessarily ideological by vocation.

14   ALT2. A14-01.08, p. 6.

15   ALT2. A14-01.08, p. 6.

the school's existence as a unity (we will return to this below), we see once again what was already highlighted in that essay:

> we see that, in its functioning, the school brings into play several types of characters: the pupils, students, on the one hand, and the teachers and professors on the other. The teachers and professors *teach*, that is to say, communicate to children, adolescents, and young men (schoolchildren, pupils, students) increasingly extensive elements of Knowledge … On the one hand, there are those who possess Knowledge (teachers and professors) and on the other hand those who start from non-Knowledge (children) to progressively acquire, in the course of their studies, rudiments, then elements, then organic parts of Knowledge and culture.[16]

It is therefore a question of examining, in a preliminary manner, what Althusser calls the *Great Obviousnesses* [*grandes Evidences*]. At the end of this short preamble, Althusser mentions these:

1.   the unity of the school
2.   the child
3.   the child's psychology
4.   pedagogy
5.   the teachers
6.   knowledge and culture
7.   *laïcité*
8.   democracy and democratisation
9.   the existence of the school

∴

The first illusion is that of unity. This is not surprising, considering how we have already seen that Macherey dedicates the entire second part of his 'Les Mythologies Scolaires' to unity: 'when we look at our idea of the school, we think of it as an institution with a profound *unity* in essence'.[17] Moreover, and this was Macherey's thesis as well, reformism is precisely a politics of reduction to the One.[18] Once again: 'the school is essentially one'.

---

16   ALT2. A14-01.08, p. 7.
17   ALT2. A14-01.08, p. 9.
18   Macherey writes that reformism, linked to the question of the crisis of the school, 'is therefore an ideological theme, necessary for the functioning of the school idea, and of what

The representation of unity refers to two spontaneous *images* that, as we will see, play a central role in the first chapter of 'Schools':[19] the line and the pyramid. The line represents the course of studies 'as one speaks of the course of a river', and it is the image of a vertical gradation in which the relationship of substantial inequality between students and teachers is considered functional to the progressive acquisition of attitudes and knowledge. The difference between teaching cycles (primary, secondary, higher) is one of degrees placed on the same line, ascending by means of accumulation and progressive assimilation.

However, the image of the line remains insufficient, because 'this "course" of study, this line which leads through the grades of childhood education all the way to adulthood, is not traversed in its entirety by all children'.[20] The image of the pyramid thus comes into play. The phenomenon of the school dropout is in fact relatively contingent with respect to the need for unity: 'this image has the advantage of being able to represent not only the unity of the school, but the place that the school masses occupy within that unit'.[21] It is quite clear what the pyramid is supposed to represent. As opposed to the line, it measures an inversely proportional dimension: as the gradation increases something else decreases (so that the base of the pyramid coincides with primary education, 'compulsory education until the age of sixteen', or to a state of non-knowledge, while the tip corresponds to the upper, third degree of education 'already reduced', i.e., to a state of acquired knowledge that technically removes the difference between the agents that are part of the relationship). In short, 'the unity of the school remains intact: it is always the unity of a continuity' and it is 'always based on two conditions: age and degrees towards the acquisition of knowledge'.[22]

The image of unity must be taken seriously because it implies that the process of schooling is like a *finite* line that stretches between non-knowledge and knowledge (that is, the finiteness of the line is determined by the determination of its ends). This means, then, that if continuity is made possible by the existence of knowledge, acquired knowledge is made possible by continuity: without knowledge the very condition of continuity would be lacking, but without continuity the condition of its condition of possibility would be lack-

---

it stands in for, in the capitalist regime: in this sense it is a positive representation, which serves the smooth running of a mechanism'. ALT2. A14-01.04 (A), p. 2.

19   This suggests that Althusser's text was only preparatory material for the chapters of 'Schools' that we can read today, particularly the first and third.

20   ALT2. A14-01.08, p. 10.

21   ALT2. A14-01.08, p. 11.

22   Ibid.

ing. On the one hand, the line leads somewhere (starting from a determinateness that is an absence); on the other, it is defined by its own goal (it is its reason for existence). It follows, then 'that the *raison d'être* of the school is its End. From the beginning the school process is haunted by the End, which is its end and also its objective: knowledge and culture'.[23] The End is the condition of the One, that is, it is the condition of intelligibility of the intermediate gradations and of the significance of their incompleteness: 'if the school is One, this does not mean that the rudiments of knowledge taught in primary school, the elements of knowledge and culture taught in secondary education, and the science and culture dispensed in higher education are only intelligible in terms of this knowledge and this culture'.[24] In short, the unity of the steps (gradations of a knowledge that is imparted by means of a vertical pedagogical relationship) is determined by the complete unity of assimilated knowledge (as the end of the process of transmission, therefore introducing a horizontal relationship). This could be enunciated through a simple true-factual proposition: *the One of the school is the One of knowledge.*[25]

---

23   ALT2. A14-01.08, p. 12.

24   Ibid.

25   It is on the basis of this true-factual proposition that I believe we must begin to seriously reconsider the *entire* theoretical production of German classical philosophy (Kant, Fichte, Schelling, Hegel, Humboldt, and Schleiermacher, but also the lesser-known Henrik Steffens with his 1809 *Lectures on the Idea of University*) concerning the question of the university. The fundamental concept that ties together the work of these thinkers, especially Fichte, Schelling, and Hegel, is 'the unity of knowledge, whose presupposition is the Absolute: the indispensable *prius* of non-empirical knowledge, whatever the irrelevant controversies that divided the three in the definition of this Absolute may be. The school and, especially, the university, understood as the 'school of the art of the scientific use of the intellect' – according to Fichte's definition – must be forms that embody the realm of ideas, organs responsible for the formation of the educated man, who is 'he who knows how to impose on all his actions the mould of universality, and who has renounced his particularity and acts according to universal principles', as Hegel famously put it'. Tessitore 1995, p. 621. Armando Rigobello, in a volume dedicated to the question of the university in nineteenth-century philosophy, writes that, in general, 'the discovery of a unifying principle gives rise to an organic conception of knowledge and consequently to a unitary interpretation of the world and human events. Already in the first centuries of Western philosophical speculation, in Greece and Sicily, we witness the formation of philosophical communities that, in those conceptions and interpretations, captured an ethical-religious message meant to be translated into an ideal of life, such as to constitute the criterion of an experience of a common life, dedicated to the search and the contemplation of truth. So great is the power of a unified and organic vision!' In short, here too the question is that of the 'unity of knowledge in the nineteenth century and the related question of the university in some significant thinkers of that century; a correlate that becomes a privileged point of observation to grasp the nature of the central theme as a whole. In fact, the aim

It follows that a real understanding of unity takes place when the End is reached, i.e., 'from the perspective of higher education'.[26] *It is only from the tip of the pyramid that unity can be discerned:* 'in fact, there is a scholastic unity *only* for those who have achieved culture (which is provided by the superior stage [*le Supérieur*])'. It follows that all those who remain outside ('for all those who dropped out after the primary stage [*le Primaire*]'), *there is no unity, but only a plurality of distinct schools with no relationship between them.*

This is a crucial point. It is precisely from the acknowledgment of this fact that, for Althusser, it is possible to identify 'something obscure' that can be the object of a real theoretical hold (or, conversely, that it is possible to identify the ideological function of the unitary representation that is the object of a true-factual proposition such as 'the One of the school is the One of knowledge'). Although the fact of the lack of unity can also be identified in the context of the spontaneous representation of the school (consider the function of support of the pyramid), for Althusser it has quite another meaning.[27] Thus, if it is true that the paths of those who drop out are 'interrupted paths from the point of view the myth of the unity and continuity of the school', *this continuity is not interrupted* 'from the point of view of production'.[28] In other words, production gets rid of the myth of experiential unity: the school is a set of discrete and discontinuous units, instrumental for the formation of a specialised worker (that is, as we will see below,[29] of *its value*): 'there are not degrees (and therefore continuity), but *radical discontinuities*, and there are not schools, but distinct school apparatuses, which are practically *without communication between them*'.[30] There is no dissipation with respect to unity. Everything, in school (better: in schools), happens as it should. The multiplicity of continuous gradations, ascending by accumulation – i.e., its transparency, its experiential immediacy – hides the plurality of formations through a representation: finite,

---

is to address the subject from the point of view of a broad methodological question (the method of academic teaching) and of a singular community experience (the community of teachers and learners in academic life)'. Rigobello 1977, pp. 7, 8–9. The best collections of German writings on the question of the university are Anrich 1964 and Ferry, Pesron, and Renaut 1979.

26   ALT2. A14-01.08, p. 13.

27   This is a representation by virtue of which it is sufficient, for Althusser, to introduce reforms (which are therefore ideological): 'with a better pedagogy we could undoubtedly overcome the shortcomings of aptitudes; with a true democratisation of education (study allowance for the children of working-class families) we could overcome the inequality of family resources'. ALT2. A14-01.08, p. 11.

28   ALT2. A14-01.08, p. 13.

29   Cf. *infra*, § 3, § 4.

30   ALT2. A14-01.08, p. 13.

concluded, and incoherent because of their lack of communication. It is therefore clear that, if it is true that production removes the myth of continuity, *it also removes the End/Aim of knowledge*. An end that, ultimately, is a condition for the existence of the representation itself. At school, there is no knowledge (as a projected End), but only production, which makes knowledge acquired at the level of every interruption something already accomplished. Ultimately, this is what motivates the illusory nature of the illusion of unity:

> We are therefore victims of a terrible illusion, of whom all those we thought were 'abandoning the course'/the royal road of the school are the crying witnesses. This illusion consists in believing that the End of the school is to lead children towards the heights of (superior) culture: this is false. When we see how the school system actually works, and where it leads, we are forced to conclude that we are daydreaming.[31]

Production and knowledge are two sides of the same domain (ideology is in fact instrumental to real functioning), a clash of giants, relative to the illusion of unity. Macherey spoke of a myth, just as Althusser does: 'the beautiful continuity of the "line", an uninterrupted path from primary to higher education, is nothing but a myth'.[32]

Things become even more interesting with regard to the second illusion that Althusser relays, that of existence, 'which is probably the most surprising, and the most persistent one'.[33] In short, we are in the realm of the theory of value ('we will once again take a diversion through Marx').[34] More precisely, we are in the context of the distinction between *value* (that is, the value that belongs to the commodity, as it represents a certain amount of socially necessary labour) and the *value-form* (that is, the *exchange value* that expresses and makes value visible in the form of a certain amount of money). Consider once again the act of exchange as a factor in economic practice, *as it presents itself*: 'for us, it is *obvious* that a commodity has an *exchange value*'[35] (as, one might say, was clearly seen by 'the great Englishmen: Smith and Ricardo').[36] I walk into a *boutique* and I want to buy a suit (Althusser's own example): 'we ask: *how much?*' The clerk sells the suit, and the customer buys it for what it is worth (after asking

---

31   ALT2. A14-01.08, p. 14.
32   ALT2. A14-01.08, p. 13.
33   ALT2. A14-01.08, p. 16.
34   ALT2. A14-01.08, p. 17.
35   ALT2. A14-01.08, p. 18.
36   ALT2. A14-01.08, p. 17.

how much it costs!). This experiential presupposition can be expressed through the following true-factual proposition: *'The value of each commodity can be defined as a certain exchange value, that is, a certain amount of money'*: 'a suit is worth 100,000 old francs, a pair of shoes 10,000 francs, a loaf of bread 80 francs, a return trip by plane 90,000 francs etc.'[37] The exchange is immediate, and immediately evident: it is transparent. But, Althusser comments, 'this is precisely where Marx comes in. Marx says: things are neither natural nor obvious'. Indeed, *in this example there is a confusion between value and the form of value.*

In order for a commodity to have a certain value (a certain value-form or a certain exchange value) it must be able to be placed in an equal relationship with another commodity in general (i.e., 'it must first be *worth* something in general'), a relationship such as that according to which '1 suit = 10 pairs of shoes = 100,000 francs'. What is obscure within the structure of this exchange is precisely this equivalence, or this comparison: 'How can I put the sign "=" between 1 suit and 10 pairs of shoes? Because the same "socially necessary amount of labour" is represented by 1 suit and 10 pairs of shoes'.[38] The amount of socially necessary labour is the foundation of value [*fondement de la valeur*], that is, of the fact that one suit and ten shoes, commodities made of different materials, are equivalent in terms of time of production. And it is precisely such a foundation that disappears [*disparaît*] in the commodity market: 'no one sees it, and there is no one to keep track of the amounts of socially necessary labour represented in each commodity, and thus to put them in an equal relation'.[39]

But there is more ('if we stay here, we are not at the end of the path'). The question of the *social meaning* of value ('what are we talking about when we talk about this *proportion of socially necessary labour?*') is inherent to what Marx calls the law of value. Althusser refers to the famous letter that Marx sent to Kugelmann on 11 June 1868, which he prefers to redefine as the '*law of distribution of the available social labour in a given society in a determined proportion*'. Marx writes:

> Every child knows that a nation which ceased to work, I will not say for a year, but even for a few weeks, would perish. Every child knows, too, that the masses of products corresponding to the different needs required different and quantitatively determined masses of the total labour of

---

37   ALT2. A14-01.08, p. 18.
38   Ibid.
39   ALT2. A14-01.08, p. 19.

society. That this *necessity* of the *distribution* of social labour in definite proportions cannot possibly be done away with by a particular *form*
of social production but can only change the *mode* of its *appearance*, is
self-evident. No natural laws can be done away with. What can change in
historically different circumstances is only the *form* in which these laws
assert themselves. And the form in which this proportional distribution
of labour asserts itself, in the state of society where the interconnection
of social labour is manifested in the *private exchange* of the individual
products of labour, is precisely the *exchange value* of these products.[40]

This passage from Marx is important for Althusser because it leads to the
insight that if a commodity has a value, without the distribution of available
labour power, that commodity would exist because there would be no production. It is precisely the fact that the commodity represents a given quantity
of labour power that leads to this distinction. On the one hand there are the
demands of distribution, which are valid *for every society* (Marx says that natural laws cannot, by definition, be suppressed). On the other, there is the form
taken by the law *with respect to* the type of society (Marx says that, under
determinate historical conditions, the form under which natural law presents
itself can be transformed).

  This means, then, that if the form of value called 'exchange value' can represent the specific form of a certain type of society (a capitalist one), it is equally
true that, as the law of value or distribution of available social labour persists,
that form, in another type of society, can be modified – such as it would be in a
socialist society for example, where the law of value would not be accompanied by the means of competition but rather 'by the conscious anticipation of
planning'.[41] All of this has fundamental consequences for Althusser:

> this is the significance of Marx's distinction between value (i.e., the law
> of value: the law of distribution of the proportions of socially available
> labour power) and the value-form. It questions the *existence* of the value-
> form ... It undermines its existence: this means that it makes its *contin-
> gency* visible, and behind this contingency the necessity of other forms of
> existence, when a new form of society is realised.[42]

---

40 Marx and Engels 1965. Translation available at: https://www.marxists.org/archive/marx/
    works/1868/letters/68_07_11-abs.htm.
41 ALT2. A14-01.08, p. 21. On the question of planning Althusser could be referring to Bettel-
    heim 1966.
42 ALT2. A14-01.08, p. 21.

The distinction calls into question the existence of the value-form insofar as *non-existence is on the side of contingency* (i.e., the distinction calls into question the former, thus making the latter emerge). The contingency of a form, that is, causes the necessity of its substitution. It is not that the non-existence of the form of value belongs, so to speak, to the illusory nature of its position (i.e., to the fact of its absence while existing); rather, the form *is* but could also *not* be (thus contravening the evidence of the representation that explicates the *necessity* of the equivalence of the commodity-money exchange). The form of existence, as a specific manifestation of a specific social conformation, is, but could as well not be: it did *not* exist before it was, and it will *not* exist afterwards.[43]

It is precisely at this point that Althusser's theoretical gesture pertaining to the illusion of the school's existence is made explicit: 'the same applies to the permanent necessity of the school, that is to say, of its *existence*, as given to us in the great obviousness that we have mentioned: as an indispensable acquisition *for any society*'.[44] The *non-existence of the school is the non-existence of the school-form*, as a specific (contingent) form of a specific (capitalist) social system, which takes as its reason for existence the (*indispensable*) *process of formation of the labour power, as a natural law*. What persists in any type of social formation is the educational process (just as what persists, as a natural law, in the succession of every social formation is the distribution of socially available labour). What is contingent – i.e., not necessarily permanent – is the form that from time to time, as its manifestation, ensures the necessity of education (just as exchange value is what makes the law of value manifest in a determinate way and in a given historical period). Thus, the illusion of the school's existence pertains to the illusion of its *permanence*: the school is a form, that is, a specific form – nothing more (at least at the moment), and nothing less. This could be stated by means of a simple scientific proposition: '*the school is a school-form*'. Althusser writes:

> we would say: schooling is the school-form of a process that is indispensable to any society. Marx argued that it is a natural law that the total amount of labour power available in any society must be distributed in a proportional manner in order for production and reproduction to take place, and therefore for society to exist. We would also say: it is a natural law that what is guaranteed in our society in the school-form should

---

43   On the very central question of contingency see, among others: Pippa 2019 and Morfino 2002.

44   ALT2. A14-01.08, p. 20. The concluding italics are mine.

be guaranteed in every society. But what is thus assured, in the school-form, which could be assured otherwise in other forms once the structure of society is changed? It is *the reproduction of the qualification of labour power*. This reproduction is indispensable for the existence of any society. But it is an illusion to confuse the necessity of this reproduction with the form in which it is assured in our society: the school-form, as we know it.[45]

Althusser here echoes Marx: value is to the form of value what the educational process is to schooling. Could Althusser's position be Marxian only from a formal point of view? This is a crucial question, and after this lengthy preamble, it can only be answered through a detailed examination of 'Schools'.

1   *Schools 1*: The Ideological Representations of the School and their Theoretical Identification

The first chapter of the work is signed by Étienne Balibar. Dated 28 April 1969, it is a typewritten file consisting of 48 pages with the title 'Some bourgeois ideological representations of the school'. There are a few hand-made corrections to the text, but very few additions – if we exclude those still to be included ('without prejudice to other modifications, the text I sent presupposes two types of complements, without which it is unusable: 1°/ statistical complements ... 2°/ notes').[46] Still, as it stands, the text had to be substantially ready for printing. This is what the accompanying note says:

> this first mailing represents the drafting of Chapter 1, which is already being submitted for appraisal, criticism, and correction, not only in view of its final form, but also in view of the drafting of what is to follow. The six existing copies, in addition to the one I am keeping, are sent to: Althusser, Macherey, Tort, Baudelot, R. Balibar.[47]

The chapter starts from an Althusserian methodological premise (which we analysed above): scientific knowledge of the school presupposes the identification of the set of its representations, first of all the juridical-descriptive ones

---

45   ALT2. A14-01.08, p. 21.
46   ALT2. A14-02.03, p. 1.
47   Ibid.

('enshrined in institutions and in administrative acts') and the properly operational ones ('of its functioning, and of the activity of those who attend it, 'teachers' and 'pupils'').[48] These are representations that – and here we encounter a variant of Macherey's thesis on reformism as a synecdotal function of depoliticisation – not only stand behind those 'who want to *reform* it or to transform it', but also those who, 'no longer talk about transforming it, but want to destroy it' (keeping in mind that this was written only a year after the events of May–June 1968).[49] We will take a closer look at this below. For the moment it suffices to say that any spontaneous representation of the school, however critical, remains, as a representation, *fundamentally* entangled in the mechanisms of its functioning: spontaneous representation is an ideological representation and thus it refers to bourgeois ideology as 'realised in the functioning of school institutions'.[50] This is nothing new, for it is another way to express, in Althusserian parlance, the ideological nature of experiences.

It is therefore a question of getting out, to *'get out of school, get out of the ideology of the school, and get out of the dominant bourgeois ideology'*, that is to say, to move towards a real and theoretical, rather than ideological, domain: class struggle (whose non-obviousness causes it to be re-imported into the school, since it determines all the modes of existence), and Marxist theory (whose production of knowledge of the capitalist mode of production must be imported[51] in the school as we will see later on, since it represents 'a largely unexplored object').[52]

. .
.

Balibar's analysis in this opening chapter does not add anything substantially new with respect to what the Macherey of 'Les mythologies scolaires' and the Althusser of 'Les Grandes Illusions de l'École' have already taught us. Therefore, to avoid any kind of redundancy I will limit myself to recalling the theoretical pivots of its argument, referring from time to time to the place of their original formulation.

---

48   Ibid. From here on I will refer to the page number reported in the file rather than the one used by the archive (which starts from the two unnumbered pages of the accompanying notes).

49   Cf. above, Chapter 2, §1.

50   ALT2. A14-02.03, p. 2.

51   Cf. *infra*, from §3 to §6.

52   ALT2. A14-02.03, p. 3.

Every representation of the school presupposes a certain way of representing its function: a 'what is done', which in turn refers to a 'who does it' (teachers
and students) and a 'why it is done' (teaching and learning functioning as evidence which 'do not appear to be open to discussion') of its own existence (as
an institution), that is, of its unity and autonomy ('distinct from other social
institutions such as the Church, the Army or the Administration').[53]

Teaching and learning as specific functions of the schooling process present
themselves as operational factors within *every* social type. But when the specificity of the process' (scholastic) conformation is removed from this process,
those functions present themselves as *natural necessities* ('since this necessity
is common to all human societies, it is apparently a *natural* necessity').[54] In
every society someone teaches and someone learns, hence the naturalness,
matched by the spontaneity of what is presented therein – everything else
is but a variation. In *every* society, therefore, the naturalness of teaching and
learning presupposes the naturalness of two determinations, instrumental to
the process of education: 'these two "realities" are the *child* on the one hand,
and *culture* or *knowledge* on the other'. It is obvious: how would an educational
relationship be possible without something to transmit and without a subject
responsible for its assimilation? 'The child appears clearly this time, as a natural, biologically defined reality; as the first stage of development or growth
of man in general'.[55] Childhood is the *conditio* of growth that starts from zero
and ends with 'adults with a defined place in society'.[56] The child is a 'half-man'
because it does not correspond to what man is in general (as a social being). A
horizontal line can thus be drawn: at one end there is what is (and what must
be, in order to enter the process of schooling), at another there is what it must
become: in the middle, the process of education as a cultural process.

The zero point from which the child begins, in fact, is the zero degree of
knowledge – the child's being is entirely defined as *a being that lacks something*:
'what children lack at the outset therefore also has, within the limits of the spe-
cies or human essence, a necessary and natural reality. This is what we will call
culture or *knowledge*'. The lack of knowledge defines what the child lacks, and
if this is a fact of nature, the knowledge and the culture that it must assimilate are also facts of nature: 'necessary and natural realities', 'given', 'points of
departure'.

---

53   ALT2. A14-02.03, p. 5.
54   ALT2. A14-02.03, p. 6.
55   Ibid.
56   ALT2. A14-02.03, p. 7.

Childhood is a *thing*, just as culture and knowledge are *things*. It is interesting to note how Balibar relates them: if, in fact, it is true that the child defines his or her lack as a lack of knowledge, then the essence of man in general *necessarily* refers to the vertical mode of transmission. Childhood is a thing that welcomes an absence, just as knowledge is a thing that, in the act of its transmission, produces a presence (that is, the fact itself that acculturation makes man in general: 'it therefore comes to fill a *void*, it settles in the place of *nothingness* (ignorance, lack of culture)').[57] Culture and childhood, then, are natural data, but they cannot be easily decoupled. Knowledge (or its transmission) and childhood are in a relationship of horizontal implication: it is impossible to think of childhood without culture (indeed, the infant is defined by this natural deprivation); it is impossible to think of culture without transmission (that is, without considering that the adult becomes itself thanks to the assimilation of culture). This refers, then, to the impossibility of thinking of 'man in general' without the process of schooling as a natural datum.

> It is then clear how, in this ideological representation, which nevertheless has all the appearance of absolute necessity and obviousness, the place of teaching and the school is inevitably left out. Since the *child* on the one hand, and *culture* and *knowledge* on the other, exist and cannot be ignored, and since they must be brought into contact with each other, teaching is nothing other than the necessary form of this contact. *A passage from ignorance to knowledge, from lack of culture to culture.*[58]

But let us go a step further: 'Every society is based on the performance of a number of different functions by its members, which must be fulfilled in one way or another'.[59] Society organises production, organises defence, and organises organisation itself. Society, at the level of its representation, is a generalised organisation of determined roles, that is, determined by specific and *technically defined* functions: by organising distinct and separate functions, the division of labour in general refers to the technique of their position. It is an obvious representation: 'in civilised societies, this diversity of functions determines a more or less complex division of labour'. In other words, technically speaking, 'doing' is a know-how that refers to the fact that one *must* possess a know-

---

57   ALT2. A14-02.03, p. 8.
58   Ibid.
59   ALT2. A14-02.03, p. 9.

how, therefore presupposing that the specificity of each function is a fact of nature. In the context of representation, the social totality consists of invariants that, their position being permanent, need only be occupied: there are those who produce, those who defend, those who organise – only specialisations are needed to occupy those positions. The division of labour is a technical division of labour.

In the same way, in school we teach and learn so that the school reproduces that kind of division: 'it is a technical necessity to entrust to a specialised, autonomous institution this well-defined function, distinct from the others: teaching, training, and education'.[60] This is a division technically qualified by a spontaneous representation. The specificity of teaching has, for Balibar, a 'capital importance', for it reduces the whole problem of schooling to the technical terms of its function. This is precisely the role of pedagogy, whose technicality defines that of the educational process: 'pedagogy as a technique of teaching requires the idea that teaching is a branch of a technical division of labour in society'.[61] And, if it is true that what is seen in the first instance is 'something done' that refers to 'someone who does it', then pedagogy will pertain, with regards to the object, to the knowledge that is transmitted ('there will be a "pedagogy of history", a "pedagogy of literature", a "pedagogy of mathematics", etc.'); and, with regards to the natural user of the transmission, to the subject of assimilation ('pedagogy cannot be scientifically rationalised without a scientific knowledge of *the adult* and *the child* to whom it is addressed', like a 'sociology of education' and a 'psychology of the child').

Here we are presented with a real *theoretical link* with Macherey's argument (and with what Althusser will later argue in *On the Reproduction*) concerning the always-already social qualification of the technical division.[62] The idea that the division of labour is a technical division has a noble origin: 'we already encounter it in antiquity, for example in Plato',[63] and it is also formulated in the first period of general development of the capitalist mode of production, 'notably by Adam Smith and the "classical economists"'.[64] But, and this is Balibar's point, this is an ideological representation ('the fact that the ideological representation of the school also presupposes a certain idea of the "division of labour"

---

60   ALT2. A14-02.03, p. 10.
61   ALT2. A14-02.03, p. 11.
62   For Macherey see above, Chapter 2, § 4; for Althusser see above Chapter 1, § 1, and Chapter 2, Introduction.
63   ALT2. A14-02.03, p. 12.
64   ALT2. A14-02.03, p. 13.

leads us to a first critique').[65] Indeed, to refer to the capitalist mode of production 'of which Marx gave us a detailed theory' implies that 'one social class
exploits another' whenever it organises material production and the extortion
of surplus labour.[66] The mode of production, that is, has what might be called
an effect of *technical defactualisation* of the demands of the totality of society,
insofar as it defines them as unnatural variants (and, as Althusser would have
it, *contingent*, precisely because they only belong to that mode of production),
instrumental for the maintenance of the division between the capitalist bourgeoisie and the working class proletariat. Balibar writes that they 'are justified
only by the need to maintain the existing social order, ultimately based on class
exploitation'.[67] In short, the organisation of society 'is not simply a matter of
specialisation, of distribution and combination of useful tasks between individuals'.[68] Or better: the division of labour is not simply a technical division,
provided that the technicality of the positions is preserved due to necessity of
the functions ('this division therefore unquestionably has *a technical aspect*').[69]
In other words, the division does not imply that know-how should presuppose
the specificity of the function as a natural given (to be occupied). On the contrary, *the technical division of labour is entirely informed by its social division*.
This implies that

> the social division of labour, which commands all 'technical' divisions, is
> thus always partly determined by the existence of the bourgeoisie and
> the proletariat, and by their antagonism. Any definition of society which
> leaves this reality 'aside' is an abstract, metaphysical definition, an idealist
> definition.[70]

Or even that

> the social division of labour, i.e., in the final analysis, the division of antag-
> onistic social classes, directly controls the processes of purely 'technical'
> appearance, and their historical evolution, at the level of material produc-
> tion itself.[71]

---

65   ALT2. A14-02.03, p. 12.
66   ALT2. A14-02.03, p. 13.
67   ALT2. A14-02.03, p. 14.
68   ALT2. A14-02.03, p. 13.
69   ALT2. A14-02.03, p. 4.
70   Ibid.
71   ALT2. A14-02.03, p. 15.

A 'metaphysical' definition of labour is thus replaced by a materialist definition which, however, remains hidden and voiceless in the context of representation. Balibar says that the technical evidence '*always* [has] the function of masking the reality of the social division of labour and the division of division of social classes, [confining] them to a more or less secondary region of society'.[72]

In short, 'we will see that the function of the school is not to transmit knowledge or culture, abstractly defined, but to reproduce, according to its own means, an existing division and antagonism of classes'.[73] This leads to two conclusions.

First, the removal of the technicality of its determination *leads the process of schooling to occupy heterogeneous positions, varying according to the change of the modes of production.* The (ideologically functional) permanence of its position still makes room for a relative continuity. This is *another theoretical link*, for this thesis refers to what has already been defined as the 'principle of contemporaneity between modes of education and modes of production', a thesis that is therefore easily integrated with Tort's historical reconstruction of the process of the formation of the class-based school.[74] The exclusivity of the technical division places the schooling process on a level of functional *equivalence* with other social bodies. We defend, produce, and educate because one must defend, produce, and educate: their operational necessity – synonymous with their eternity (and vice versa) – makes it so that the (functional) concealment of their sociality pertains to the relative (functional) heterogeneity of their functions on the plane of a coexistence. Indeed, as we will see when we turn to the second chapter of 'Schools', by presupposing the necessity of the reproduction of the individual qualities, conducive to productive labour (what in Althusser would correspond, for now only from a formal point of view, to the notion of value), the school represents the specific – and therefore dominant – form of that necessity in the capitalist mode of production (a specificity which, therefore, is contingent: it has the status of the notion of value-form). We will see later the nature of this domination and of this specificity.[75] For now it will suffice to say that the 'principle of contemporaneity' expresses the fact that, in the ancient or feudal mode of production, the school (or better, its 'antediluvian' form, as Balibar defines it in the second chapter of 'Schools'), besides being 'always subjected to and incorporated into other institutions'[76]

---

72   ALT2. A14-02.03, p. 16.
73   ALT2. A14-02.03, p. 17.
74   Cf. Chapter 2, Introduction and §1, §3, §4 and §6.
75   Cf. *infra*, §6.
76   ALT2. A14-02.03, p. 18.

(the Faculties and the Medieval Schools were assemblages of the ecclesiastical apparatus), was not determined by the fulfilment of that necessity: 'ancient or medieval societies, for example, dominated by modes of production based on slavery or serfdom, gave school and school education a completely different, much more limited place'.[77]

Secondly, the removal of technicality from the notion of the school *leads to the removal of the fundamental metaphysical presuppositions of its representation, being presupposed to be natural data.* The removal of technicality causes the denaturalisation of culture, knowledge, and childhood as 'universal, objective "realities" necessary for the functioning of all societies'. Here we have a *third theoretical link*, of Macherey's conclusions on culture and childhood in 'Les mythologies scolaires', as well as of the debate that was provoked by that text, in particular Establet's ideas about culture.[78] In 'Les mythologies scolaires' childhood and culture 'are products of the capitalist school system, pedagogical effects, not natural realities, given outside the system, and serving as its support'.[79] In what amounts to the same theoretical gesture, Balibar writes that:

> It is not *culture that precedes the school*, as a given object that would have to be disseminated and transmitted; on the contrary, it is the existence of the school and school education ... that gives the *specific form of 'culture'* to the production of scientific work, aesthetic activity, and a whole part of ideology. Therefore, it is actually *the school that produces culture*, despite its apparent autonomy.[80]

Similarly, childhood as a natural representation must be critically examined. I quote the entire passage in Balibar on this point:

> The 'child' and 'childhood' are ideological notions produced and inculcated in all of us by the functioning of particular historical institutions within the capitalist mode of production. Our idea of childhood, which shapes our practical attitude towards children, is essentially produced by the functioning of the *family* and the *school*, as capitalism constitutes them. The child is not, therefore, an already given biological reality that would enter the school as it is, to *encounter* school activity, to become a 'schoolchild', a 'schoolboy'. Actually, *it is the school system* which, to an

---

77   Ibid.
78   Cf. above Chapter 2, § 5.
79   ALT2. A14-01.04 (B), p. 11.
80   ALT2. A14-02.03, p. 18.

essential extent, *makes the child 'in its image'*. It is not the child who, by his or her independent existence, gives rise to the school that receives him. It is not true that there is a school, or schools, because there are school-age children: on the contrary, there are school-age children because there is a school system. The notion of childhood is socially determined.[81]

Let us return for a moment to the exclusivity of the technical division: it leads to representing the school as a unit. Indeed, if there is a single technical function for disseminating knowledge (the natural thing to fill a lack), then there must be a single apparatus deputised to it, that is concatenation of representations: the representation of the technicality of the division of labour supports that of its function (and of its natural presuppositions) and, with it, that of its very consistency. As they appear, in fact, the real formations (elementary, middle, and high school) are in a relationship of complementarity. The specialisation that determines their multiplicity lies in their reduction, or rather, the specificity of each formation is given because the multiplicity as a whole is given ('the school is organised according to a single overall plan').[82] A diversity is what composes a totality: 'all these formations form a whole' because they stand in a relationship of complementarity, of cooperation – 'they always presuppose a "common background" (or even a "common core") of *"general* culture"' (education)'. Primary education lays the foundations thanks to which middle education will later impart a 'general culture' that, in turn, precedes and makes possible further scientific and literary specialisation (culminating at the university level). Far from being separated, the various stages of education stand in a relation of transmission, or it is the very separation between certain singularities that presupposes their communication which is effectively the same. They are differences that stand in a relation of correspondence, which means, precisely, a relation between the elements of a multiplicity. If the school, then, is *an* organism, it is an organism *in ascension*: the determinacy of an element refers, in a relationship of unity, to the influence of the determination that precedes it ('it is a continuous movement from one class to another, from one "level" of teaching to another').[83]

The notion of continuity is joined to that of the One. It is here that, in what amounts to a *fourth theoretical link*, Balibar employs Althusser's images, from a year earlier: 'that of the segmented line and that of the school pyramid', in

---

81   ALT2. A14-02.03, p. 19.
82   ALT2. A14-02.03, p. 24.
83   ALT2. A14-02.03, p. 25.

fact, are the expressive images of the ideal that the school needs to embody.[84] The former, at least in appearance, takes into account the degrees of age and the complexity of knowledge in a movement which, in addition to being progressive ('the movement of all those who go through it from bottom to top, just as they go through the degrees of their own individual perfection from bottom to top')[85] is also progressist ('because the progression it institutes is the progression of knowledge, which is proclaimed by bourgeois and petty-bourgeois ideology as a good in itself'). The second takes into account the empirical fact of the dropout rate: regardless of the inequality of attitudes (which can be overcome through the improvement of transmission techniques) or of the material conditions of access (which can be remedied through social measures of democratisation), the principles of operation of the schooling process remain intact ('they depend on ... causes *external to the school*').[86] And this is precisely what the image of the pyramid expresses: 'the pyramid simply shows us that a selection is made: some children drop out along the way. But, in the necessary logic of any representation that sees the school as a unit, these dropouts are immediately explained, if not justified'.[87]

Having reached this point, two brief clarifications are necessary. The first could be articulated in a true-factual proposition such as: 'the unity of the school refers to its uniqueness'. The schooling process is an organic one, i.e., it systematically encompasses a sequence of ascending levels. Now, this means that its rationality *categorically excludes* the possibility that anything else might overlap with its function: born from a tough struggle ('the One School historically stems from the One Church, before opposing it'),[88] it maintains its position ('on the secular mode' of its 'principles of operation'). Nothing escapes the grasp of its 'social and civilising mission'. In short, if the unity of the school explains, so to speak, its *intensive* dimension (it expresses its consistency and *internal* cohesion), its uniqueness, contained in but not reducible to unity, explains its *extensive* dimension (it expresses its domination by means of its function, and its exclusivity in relation to *other* sectors), then 'the school is one, therefore there can only be one school (for all)'.[89]

The second clarification could be formulated thus: 'if it has any function, the school's effect is necessarily a unifying one'. The ideological representation

---

84   ALT2. A14-02.03, p. 26.
85   ALT2. A14-02.03, p. 27.
86   ALT2. A14-02.03, p. 29.
87   Ibid.
88   ALT2. A14-02.03, p. 30.
89   Ibid.

presents the school as a privileged place where the objectivity of knowledge, as well as the procedures through which it is dispensed, *erase the differences* between the subjects of assimilation. Subjective differences disappear because the lack of being (of what one must become) cuts through, in a regime of absolute equivalence, the entire spectrum of the recipients of the transmission: in school there are no separate subjects and classes, but only gaps to be filled ('*differences* due to family and professional origin, and therefore to class origin, disappear or should disappear').[90]

Here, we encounter a *fifth theoretical link*. We have seen how, referring to the vertex from which the One posits itself, Althusser wrote 'that the *raison d'être* of the school is its End. From the beginning the school process is haunted by the End, which is its end and also its objective: knowledge and culture'.[91] Similarly, Balibar writes that 'we can only speak of the unity of the school from a certain point of view, which our previous description denounces: to do so, we must take the point of view of the school's end. The end it has set itself: "ever higher towards culture and knowledge"'.[92] This leads him to write, quoting Althusser verbatim, that 'indeed, there is unity of the school for those who have reached culture (provided by the superior level) *and only for them*';[93] or that, in short, 'the school is continuous and unified only for those who go through it in its entirety: a determined *fraction* of the population, mainly originating from the bourgeoisie and the intellectual layers of the petty bourgeoisie'.[94]

As a representation, the school is placed in the order of the purely *imaginary*. Here we can see how the dropout rates, expressed by the image of the pyramid, have a truly revealing meaning: in school, *for* the school, they represent nothing more than a *de facto* imperfection that (momentarily) contradicts its rightful role (the pyramid expresses precisely this fact, as a support for the straight line of its continuity). To push Balibar's thesis even further, we could say that if representation is an immediate presentation, *it presents its (ideal) form as its (real) content*: the school does not correspond exactly to what it is but, in fact, to what it must become – the contradiction of the school dropout is, with respect to the One it *now* claims to be, an ineffective residue to be eliminated (and, for this very reason, reformism is functional to dissimulate social division). The multiplicity of scholastic compartments (as intransitive elements of education) is removed because what is posited is a unity, declared

---

90   ALT2. A14-02.03, p. 31.
91   ALT2. A14-01.08, p. 12.
92   ALT2. A14-02.03, p. 35.
93   Ibid.; in ALT2. A14-01.08, p. 13.
94   ALT2. A14-02.03, p. 36.

as a parameter of its function. In this sense, then, in order not to fall into the trap of representation it is necessary to turn what is real about it into its *already* actualised content, and to turn its actual content into what is *already* realised: *its reality is its content and its content is its reality*: 'to put an end to the ideology of the school therefore means ceasing to examine the contradictory, and sometimes sordid, realities of the school in the light of what they should be in order to realise its ideal'.[95]

It is in this sense that Balibar here carries out a (*sixth*) *theoretical link* with Althusser's thesis on the specific meaning of school dropout: for those who 'abandon' after primary school there is no unity, but rather '*there are distinct schools, with no connection between them*. There are neither "degrees" (hence continuity), but rather *radical discontinuities*, nor are there schools, but *distinct schooling processes*,[96] *without any real communication between them*'.[97] This leads to the thesis (again taken *verbatim* from Althusser) according to which those who drop out of school walk 'interrupted paths from the point of view of the myth of the unity and continuity of the school. *But they are not at all interrupted from the point of view of production and of the labour market*'.[98]

In short, the truth of the schooling process is not a truth of knowledge, but of labour;[99] it does not belong to the technical division (wherein knowledge is a transversal object to be consumed); rather it belongs to the social division (wherein assimilated knowledge, as we will see,[100] is already instrumental for the valorisation of wage labour). It is not something internal (like the End), but something that lies outside it (like production). So, Balibar observes that,

> the school should not be seen from the point of view of its ideal end, which is *internal* to it, but from the point of view of its various real terms, which are *external* to it, and yet command its functioning from the start.[101]

Those who 'drop out' *do not actually drop out of anything*, because the knowledge they have *already* assimilated, along the lines of a distinct and contradictory scholastic process (which exists only in function of its irreconcilable difference with other ones), *is already functional to the distribution of jobs in*

---

95   ALT2. A14-02.03, p. 34.
96   In the same passage, instead of '*separate schooling processes*', Althusser writes '*separate scholastic apparatuses*'.
97   ALT2. A14-02.03, p. 36; in ALT2. A14-01.08, p. 13.
98   ALT2. A14-02.03, p. 38; in ALT2. A14-01.08, p. 13.
99   Willis 1977 is a precious resource on this point.
100   Cf. *infra*, §3, §4.
101   ALT2. A14-02.03, p. 38.

the field of production. This is the *real*, and indeed demystifying, point of view. Indeed, the truth of social division (or of knowledge as a factor in its reproduction) includes class struggle as that which informs the educational processes (the imaginary absence of social division, Balibar writes, constitutes 'a permanent and effective weapon for the bourgeoisie to use in class struggle').[102] The exclusivity of the technical division (and the representations it supports) is ideological because the disguise of social division is ideological and functional.

Here, then, we encounter a *final theoretical link*, this time with Macherey's thesis on the functionality of representation, which, through a series of implications relating to the technical division, showed how behind political fiction there was a (class) politics of fiction, capable of hiding both class struggle, and the fundamental division between intellectual and manual labour.[103] Performing the same theoretical gesture, Balibar writes that bourgeois ideology 'turns the school into a place where class struggle and its irreconcilable contradictions are miraculously cancelled out',[104] and that (Macherey's text is quoted *verbatim*) 'school is the place *par excellence* where the contradictions specific to capitalism find expression without the appearance of class struggle'.[105] Of course, the school is not the only state apparatus dedicated to the displacement of contradictions, but rather is a place ideologically occupied by beautiful souls and plays, in relation to that displacement, a dominant role 'due to the power of the images it spontaneously creates'.[106] Compared to the other apparatuses, and precisely by virtue of the images it produces, the school is much more: *it is the symbol of the nation itself* (which through bourgeois law responds to the same logic of a false declaration: 'bourgeois law is not the exact representation of the realities it covers [i.e., the class antagonism inherent to the monopoly of the means of production and the expropriation of free labour]'):[107] 'both the *school* and the *nation* are ideological fantasies, necessary for the functioning of a society dominated by the capitalist mode of production'.[108]

In conclusion, it could be said that *labour represents the anti-dialectical factor*[109] *of the school's idea(l)*. It does not have knowledge as a unifying factor. The university, the supreme phase of education, has the function of a first

---

102   ALT2. A14-02.03, p. 44.
103   Cf. above, Chapter 2, §1 and §4.
104   ALT2. A14-02.03, p. 44.
105   ALT2. A14-02.03, p. 47, in ALT2. A14-01.04 (A), p. 2.
106   ALT2. A14-02.03, p. 46.
107   ALT2. A14-02.03, p. 34.
108   ALT2. A14-02.03, p. 47.
109   In the Kantian sense of a critique of the unconditional totality – here, the school as a unitary whole – for a given condition – here, the real processes of schooling.

unmoved mover in the context of the metaphysical cosmology that is the school.[110] It 'is the centre from which ideological representations of the school proceed'[111] – what remains is the distinction: of the processes of formation and of the social classes responsible for their attendance. *Ultimately, the proletarians do not have (the) school* (which does not mean that they should have it ...).

2   *Schools II*: The Characteristics of the School-Form as a Social Form

We can now turn to the second chapter of 'Schools'. Composed of only twenty-four pages and titled 'Capitalist Mode of Production and Schooling', it is part of a typewritten file signed by Balibar which also includes the third chapter. Like the first chapter, the following two had to be substantially ready for publication: they were composed 'from a first draft, taking into account the opinions of Macherey, Tort, Baudelot'. There are no handmade corrections, and the same warning contained in the first submission also appears here: the text 'should be supplemented on certain points by the addition of some statistical justifications and a number of quotations illustrating the positions that are only outlined in passing (in notes)'. The comment on what the definitive form of the Table of Contents should have looked like is more useful:[112] the first three

---

110   On this topic, see Bonvecchio 2012.
111   ALT2. A14-02.03, p. 42.
112   A first version of the final plan is dated 9 September 1968 and signed by Balibar. I quote from ALT2. A14-01.07, p. 2:
      PLAN DEFINITIF proposé:
      INTRODUCTION
      Ière PARTIE (l'Ecole n'existe pas)
      chap. I: Une ou plusieurs écoles?
      chap. II: les appareils scolaires et les deux formes de la division du travail
      IIère PARTIE: Mode de production capitaliste et mode d'éducation capitaliste.
      chap. III: de la production capitaliste à la scolarisation
      chap. IV: les appareils scolaires et l'appareil d'Etat
      chap. V: à quoi sert le système scolaire?
      IIIe PARTIE: (structure et contradiction du système scolaire)
      chap. VI: démocratisation de l'enseignement ou école bourgeoise?
      chap. VII: le problème de la 'formation professionnelle'
      chap. VIII: le problème de l'enseignement technologique
      chap. IX: le problème de la 'culture'
      conclusion: la contradiction du M.E.C.
      IVe PARTIE:
      chap. X: que fait l'écolier? qui fait l'écolier?
      ABREGE

chapters were to be followed by three more chapters. Although the project was ultimately aborted, the titles of those chapters that were never written tell us something that, in one way or another, we already knew. The fourth chapter was to be titled 'Intellectual and Manual Labour' [*Travail manuel et travail intellectuel*]; the fifth 'Schooling and the Reproduction of the Dominant Bourgeois Ideology' [*La scolarisation et la reproduction de l'idéologie bourgeoise dominant*]; the sixth: 'The school as an ideological state apparatus and its place in the overall process of the reproduction of capitalist production relations' [*L'École, appareil idéologique d'Etat, et sa place dans le procès d'ensemble de la reproduction des rapports de production capitaliste*]. Moreover, if we take into account the fact that in the opening page of the second chapter, there are two handwritten additions – '*1 Partie*' and, just before the title and in brackets, '*Introduction*' – it seems likely that the analysis of bourgeois ideological representations, precisely by virtue of its content, was meant to be a simple premise of the work as a whole.

∴

With 'Schools 1' we have the unmasking of a fiction. Once the domain of the school, as an imaginary object, is excluded by identifying the primacy of social division (a vantage point from which 'the school does not exist', because what is excluded is the technical unity of its function) we are left with a discrete plurality of schooling processes ('antagonistic schooling processes whose unity is fictitious').[113] Once knowledge has been taken out of the picture ('we have said that schooling is not simply about moving from ignorance to knowledge'), what remains is labour. Once the interiority of the teleological principle of unification (the One of the school is the One of knowing, that is, the End) is shown to be missing, what remains is the exteriority of the real terms towards which the students are directed ('these terms, or outcomes, which must absolutely be mentioned in the *plural*, since they are different and even antagonistic, are necessarily *external* to the school itself'). The plurality of social positions defines a plurality of schooling processes. Truth is not something internal to the school, guiding its consistency, its internal or external unity, and its unification. Rather it is placed within the framework of its exterior function: 'this is what Marx defined as the mechanism of the reproduction of social relations, or more precisely the mechanism of the reproduction of the dominant social relations

---

CONCLUSION: (les appareils scolaires, la lutte des classes et la révolution prolétarienne)
GLOSSAIRE, DEFINITIONS, INDEX

113   ALT2. A14-02.04, p. 50.

of production in a given historical society'.[114] It is now necessary to clarify the meaning of this statement, and it is precisely here that the first steps towards the definition of the school as a social form (for reproduction) are taken. The text continues as follows:

> we will say, for the time being, that schooling has, as its social content, *an aspect*, a part of the process in which the reproduction of the relations of production is realised. The relations of production cannot be reproduced in their characteristic social form (for example, the *capitalist* form) without the *individuals* who are subject to them, and who belong to distinct social classes, being reproduced in a particular way, with certain 'qualities' and in certain quantities ...
>
> But the school-form concerns only one aspect of this reproduction: that which is commonly referred to, in a very imprecise way, as the technical, scientific, ideological, 'training' of individuals.
>
> Actually, this content is transformed in its very nature, along with each new historical mode of production, which gives it a definite social form. The important thing is to understand that this form is not eternal.[115]

We can easily break down this passage into three core theses:

1. The process of schooling is only a part of the general process of reproduction or, more precisely, it is only an aspect (albeit the dominant one) of the general mechanism of the *qualitative* reproduction of labour power ('"qualities" and in certain "quantities"') functional to a specific (capitalist) social form. On the assumption that the capitalist *form* has a *content*, defined by specific relations of production [*les rapports de production*], we must imagine the apparatus as a whole as placed in a horizontal plane whose pieces are overdetermined: determined by the capitalist form (which, as we will see in thesis 3, defines their specific form), they (that is, their content: 'schooling has a social content ...') determine the specific content of that social form (of expropriation of surplus labour: 'relations of production cannot be reproduced ...').

2. The content [*ce contenu*] of the schooling process is the 'technical, scientific, ideological, "cultural" "education" of individuals' – common and 'very imprecise' designations, Balibar notes, because they risk being formulated only from the standpoint of their technical function. Let us

---

114   ALT2. A14-02.04, p. 51.
115   ALT2. A14-02.04, p. 54.

repeat: if the process of schooling is a part of the process of reproduction, then we are entitled to speak of education only on the assumption of its social function, that is to say, that every educational process is a technical one (that is, the knowledge transmitted is certainly a know-how), but its technicality is, in all respects, subject to its social function (know-how as such is placed in the context of the social distribution of jobs).

3. The content of the schooling process is a form or, more precisely, is the specific content of the schooling process (thesis 2); it is the specific form of a mode of education in general because it is determined by a specific social form (i.e., capitalism: thesis 1). As a content that is a form, a form that is a content, the school is, in fact, a 'scholastic form'. It seems evident that behind this idea there is the Althusserian notion of a 'school-form [*forme-École*]' which, as we have seen in the introduction to this chapter, refers to the impermanence of its specific content, presupposing the necessity (or the permanence) of the process of formation of the labour power in general. Therefore, to say that the various processes of schooling are the configuration of a mode of education in general, not only implies that every mode of production in general must have a corresponding mode of education, but also that a mode of education in general represents, so to speak, the substrate of all of its formal realisations. Thus, the contingency of the scholastic form ('this form is not eternal') presupposes the necessity of the permanence of a mode of education in general, provided, however, that this necessity is reduced to that of the exclusive position of *one* of its formal realisations. In other words, there is no mode of education in general (just as there is no mode of production in general), *except as a heuristic notion* instrumental to the explanation of the non-permanence (i.e., contingency) of each of its specific conformations (such as the plural processes of schooling). Ultimately, the school is not eternal because it is a formal realisation of the mode of education in general, just as the social (capitalist) form responsible for its determination is also not eternal.

It is no coincidence that, when approaching the contingency of the scholastic form, Balibar makes use of the 'principle of contemporaneity between modes of education and modes of production'. He writes that: 'each mode of production that becomes historically dominant develops a training regime, a *mode of education* of its own, which in turn becomes a powerful instrument of its extension and historical domination'.[116] This stance suggests that *the 'principle*

---

116   ALT2. A14-02.04, p. 55.

of contemporaneity' excludes archaeological investigation, which is functional to the production of a theoretical thesis. In fact, precisely on the assumption that the school is a school-form (that is, on the assumption that each form implies the irreducibility of its own content with respect to other forms of explanation of a generality, such as that of the mode of education), those that Balibar defines '"antediluvian forms" of schooling' – although they may historically clarify some aspect of the school-form ('this or that "piece" of schooling, or aspect of the various current school systems') – still 'cannot by themselves give an understanding of the *form* itself', just as, we could say, it would be completely useless to refer to an antediluvian form of modern capital, such as usury, in order to define it.[117]

With these three theses in place, we can now proceed towards the domain of the school-form as a social form (that is, a specific form that is instrumental for the reproduction of the relations of production) in order to identify its essential characteristics. First, in Chapter 2 we saw how Macherey reduced the process of separation (generated by specific operators, i.e., the Jesuits) to the set of all real practices (moral formation, discipline, emulation, etc.) that are materially functional to support the ideal closure of the school as a representation.[118] Here, too, separation is presented as 'the first and most important feature of the school-form'.[119] However, its direction is inverted. For Balibar, in fact, separation refers to the possibility of implementing the educational processes in the field of production: if, on the one hand, this requires a certain type of knowledge (defining the simply technical aspect of social division where everyone, regardless of the position he or she occupies, must possess a minimum level of education), on the other hand it *presupposes* (here, the separation of the school-form) those plural processes themselves, insofar as they produce finished products (that is, knowledgeable subjects) to be distributed according to the place they are to occupy in the field of social division (this is what defines the pre-eminence of the social division over the technical division: anyone with a minimal level of education must occupy a certain position).

> The consequence of the separation of schooling is that all social activity, and in particular the work of material production, appears as the implementation of what has been previously elaborated, 'formed'. Conversely,

---

117   For a more detailed analysis of the issue see the discussion in Chapter 4, § 3.
118   Cf. above, Chapter 2, § 2.
119   ALT2. A14-02.04, p. 56.

schooling appears as the training or the preparation of what is indispensable for any socially 'useful' activity, and which we will designate as capacities, strengths, or human aptitudes.[120]

If separation encompasses a problem of adaptation ('the results of school education must coincide with the "requirements", the "needs", the factors materially required by the various socially "useful" practices'), it is equally true that this adaptation encompasses the fact that capitalist production *demands* the schooling of its subjects.[121] This means *that in order to be productive it is necessary to be schooled subjects.* In the two-way relationship between school and capital, both the position of capital and that of the school, their respective positions are decisive (insofar as the form of capital as seen in thesis 3, determines that of the school, and the content of the school, as seen in thesis 1, conditions that of capital). It is precisely because the scholastic form concerns the preliminary, and therefore separate, education of the agents of production that it performs the reproduction of the relations of production.[122] Balibar is clear about this: 'the development of capitalist production and the functioning of capitalist relations of production require and historically impose the *schooling* of all its agents'.[123] In short: the school *always already* entails an adaptation to the process of production, just as capital *always already* entails the generalised imposition of the plural processes of schooling.

The second characteristic of the school as a social form is presented as an effect of the first and pertains to 'the legal nature of the outcome of schooling'.[124] This is an important point, which I would formulate in these terms: assuming that all operations relating to the circulation of commodity are legally mediated (i.e., they are codified by bourgeois law through the forms of property, contract, and juridical personality), the problem of the adaptation of the scholastic form to socially useful activities, both raised and resolved within the labour market (i.e., again, in the sphere of the circulation of a particular commodity such as the knowledge that is functional to production), necessarily leads to the question of the juridical nature of knowledge. The legality of the circulation of knowledge, as a product of the processes of schooling, is posited as the legality of the circulation of commodity. Therefore, 'the res-

---

120   ALT2. A14-02.04, p. 57.
121   ALT2. A14-02.04, p. 58.
122   Or that, conversely, in non-capitalist societies the antediluvian forms of the scholastic form play no role in this reproduction.
123   ALT2. A14-02.04, p. 59.
124   ALT2. A14-02.04, p. 61.

ult of schooling must be sanctioned by a *certificate of schooling*, by a *certificate of aptitude*, by a *diploma* (which implies an examination) or by a *title* (which implies a competition)'.[125] Of course, these are different qualifications. However, they are completely equivalent with respect to the following characteristics.

1. If we posit separation, the legal sanctioning of qualifications represents, to use a Kantian terminology, the schema that *guarantees* the transition from the space of education to that of its social function ('it is the condition for the *passage* of individuals from the schooling process into the production process').[126] If separation raises the problem of adaptation (as it does, since the school-form is, precisely, separate from the production process) that problem is solved by the sanctioning of qualifications. And since schooling is *already given* in the form of a qualification, the types of knowledge it distributes are already *instrumental to their own circulation*. This can be reversed by saying that if it is true that sanctioned qualifications guarantee a passage, and if it is true that only scholastic knowledge can lead to such qualifications, then all non-scholastic knowledge appears, in the eyes of capital, to be useless because it is unsanctioned. This is anything but an idle fact, and we will explore this theme in detail when examining the third (and fundamental) chapter of 'Schools'. Suffice it to say that the absolute uselessness of *non*-scholastic knowledge is related to the value of schooling and the utility of the knowledge imparted therein, which entirely depends on its being sanctioned. This means that uselessness is not placed in the order of the content of knowledge (clearly, a self-taught person can have the same knowledge-content of a schooled individual) but in that of the *form* of that content, which is, precisely, that of a sanction that defines *the use and value* of knowledge (*of labour power*). Moreover, it seems clear that the system of sanctions must be distributed, not only within the scope of the schooling processes themselves, but by operators with the proper authority: 'grades, rankings, diplomas, etc. cannot be awarded by just anyone: they must be awarded by authorities who are *entitled* to do so by virtue of their own titles, diplomas, and appointments'.[127]

2. Given the legal nature of the sanctioning of qualifications, each of them is necessarily an individual one. Here it suffices to quote Balibar's words:

---

125 ALT2. A14-02.04, p. 62.
126 Ibid.
127 ALT2. A14-02.04, p. 63.

'one cannot, within the framework of bourgeois law, institute a collective sanction, one can only sanction a "collective work" or a "collective formation" by transforming it again into juxtaposed formations of *individuals*, i.e., by individually attributing (possibly the same) grades, diplomas, and certificates'.[128]

3.   Since assimilated knowledge is both usable and used knowledge (1), the scholastic subject, as an individual subject (2), *is an owning subject, whose object is owned precisely because it was individually sanctioned*: 'the outcome of schooling is akin to a "property" right'.[129] A title, a diploma, or a certificate are legal documents that sanction the ownership of knowledge (they make it publicly recognised): the subject is the owner of *his* education and *his* knowledge. A certain paradox emerges: 'since it concerns the individual himself, "owner" of his training, his knowledge, his culture etc.', the sanction ratifies things after the fact (of assimilation). This paradox could be formulated thus: whose training is it if not of those who have already been trained? We are still close to the aforementioned theory of value and of the sale of labour power (1) which we will further examine during the analysis of the third chapter of 'Schools'. For now, it suffices to say that if the legal sanctioning guarantees the transition from the field of training to that of production (in the sense that it is only school-imparted knowledge, the only sanctioned form of knowledge, that is functional to its own circulation), then the introduction of labour into the circuit takes place *in two separate stages that act retroactively* (as a sort of *après-coup*). From the point of view of capital, *for* capital, the training (which as it is of *someone*, is already *of* someone) does not precede the sanctioning; on the contrary, the *sanctioning 'makes' education* in the sense that, on the assumption that it must be an outcome of the processes of schooling, it is found to be (legally) realised (i.e., useful) only through what it posits: a title, a diploma, a certificate: a sanctioned qualification. This could be summarised in the slogan: '*You own your knowledge because it is yours!*' The same goes for point 1: property is not placed in the order of the content of knowledge (to stay with the example of a self-taught individual: it is quite clear that their *education* belongs to *them*) but, once again, it pertains to the *form* of the sanction that defines the acquisition of scholastic knowledge: 'what counts in the juridical form of the school sanction is not the paradoxical or uncertain appearance of the thing possessed, because

---

128   ALT2. A14-02.04, pp. 63–4.
129   ALT2. A14-02.04, p. 64.

it is enough to consider ... that a diploma is simply the title of ownership of a diploma, and this is how it works in practice'.[130]

Along with sanctioning, school separation also has another effect: 'as a result of school separation, the school does not present itself as a workplace but – a new paradox – as the place of a certain, quite singular labour, "schoolwork"'.[131]

The school is where a singular kind of labour takes place, it is where students have a job that is not a job. Balibar offers the same reason as that found Althusser's 'Student Problems', where the union's idea to remunerate university work had been criticised.[132] Assimilating knowledge cannot be reduced to social labour, producing exchange value: 'the student's demand for remuneration must therefore be based on a completely different basis, taking into account the fact that the work of the students is not a social value directly producing exchange value'.[133] Similarly, Balibar writes that 'the schooled individual, as long as he remains caught up in the course of schooling, does not create "values", nor does he render a "service" to "society"'.[134]

The 'labour' that takes place in school is distinguished from labour itself: 'schoolwork is therefore labour only *by analogy*'.[135] In a way we are once again rehearsing one of Macherey's arguments, provided we keep in mind that the target here is the mechanism of social reproduction through scholastic formation, rather than that of ideological reproduction.[136] In fact, although the pupil's schoolwork certainly presupposes that of the teacher (without this presupposition the process of schooling itself would be impossible), the position that the former occupies in the relation of transmission is not merely passive. The process of formation is a vertical process that does not, however, allow the pupil to be a passive object ('the pupil is therefore not a simple subject, a simple "object" that the teacher or professor would work on, form'),[137] but, on the contrary, it envisions him as the agent that makes the work of the professor effective: 'it is the child who essentially "forms" himself through his own labour and will: if he cannot or will not "work", the result of schooling is not achieved.'[138]

---

130 Ibid.
131 ALT2. A14-02.04, p. 65.
132 Cf. above, Chapter 1, § 4.
133 Althusser 1965, p. 105.
134 ALT2. A14-02.04, p. 65.
135 ALT2. A14-02.04, p. 68.
136 Cf. above, Chapter 2, § 3.
137 ALT2. A14-02.04, p. 66.
138 ALT2. A14-02.04, p. 66.

The educational process, therefore, refers to an act of education on the part of those who must be educated. This means that, while presupposing the preservation of the notions of subject and object (of labour in general), the educational process (as 'analogical' labour) blurs their distinction. It is precisely here that schoolwork appears to be only 'analogically' labour, since 'what characterises socially "useful" labour is that its result is detached from the worker, whether it is a "service" or an independent object that others can appropriate or consume'.[139] In short: the student is both subject and object of his own action. In the educational process there is no fixed and static individuality (that of the student): if to educate (oneself) means to labour, then (for the student) to say 'I' *already* means to labour. Students are indeed students to the extent that they are being educated (although it is clear that at this level, we should also include those who get their education outside the schooling processes), and their education is what determines what they are. The student's identity is not a firm identity that can or cannot be formed: as a student, the student's identity is an identity that is *essentially* in formation – it is, in fact, both the subject and product of their own action. Their individuality is the product of their labour and, conversely, the product of their labour is their individuality:

> this is the fundamental social character of 'schoolwork': the fact that it has the individual himself, as its 'object', that it is a work of transformation, or rather: a metamorphosis of the self that is carried out, as it were, on site. There is no *material* distinction between the author (or subject) of this 'labour' and its result, only a juridical one.[140]

Here we should highlight how Balibar claims that, in the educational process, there is no material distinction between subject and object. This thesis must be taken seriously: it explains how the singular nature of schoolwork seems to refer to the paradoxical nature of sanctions in general ('it is the labour proper of the pupil that is individually sanctioned'), in addition to the paradoxical nature of the legal sanctioning of a property. Above, in thesis 3, we (rhetorically) asked: who should own the education received by the students? The answer is obvious: no one but those who are educated – provided that this education (*qua* final result) corresponds to the agent of the education (*qua* subject who labours). The apparatus of sanctions can therefore be explained as follows:

139   Ibid.
140   Ibid.

on the material assumption that the educational process in general (both in school and out of the school) blurs the distinction between the subject and the object of labour, the sanction intervenes in the (exclusively scholastic) order of a legal separation between subject (consider the sanction of individuality) and object of education (as its property: consider the sanction of appropriation) in order to guarantee the transfer of knowledge towards the domain of its social function (consider the first sanction). In other words, the school assumes that each of its sanctions refers to the legal functioning of the subject-object distinction at work in the educational process (in general): the legal distinction, instrumental for the circulation of knowledge (in the process of schooling 'the qualities that he must possess in order to enter a socially "useful" practice are reproduced from generation to generation'),[141] intervenes in the order of material indistinction insofar as it inscribes knowledge within the framework of the bourgeois law of exchange and of property:

> in the functioning of the school-form, it is the result – i.e., the legally sanctioned and recognised appropriation of a knowledge, a culture, or a qualification – which dominates the social form of the training process and imposes its characteristics on it. Since this result is a legal sanction, school 'labour' is individual labour; and since this sanction confers property on the individual, the individual appears to 'produce' his own property in schoolwork.[142]

However, there is one last characteristic of the school as a social form: 'compulsory education'.[143] This is another feature with which we are familiar: recall what Tort wrote in 'Sur le procès historique de formation de l'École de Classe – Scolarisation des formations, scolarisation obligatoire, "démocratisation"':[144] here the compulsory nature of education, in the third phase of its historical evolution (that of the class-based school), was required to counteract the dropping out of the working class. Similarly, Balibar writes here that 'the constraint was direct when, during the 19th century, the aim was to impose schooling on the working classes',[145] as well as 'schooling for children in the countryside'.[146] Indeed, the 'family allowances' are a form (not immediately evident) of the

---

141 ALT2. A14-02.04, p. 67.
142 ALT2. A14-02.04, pp. 68–9.
143 ALT2. A14-02.04, p. 69.
144 Cf. above, Chapter 2, §6.
145 ALT2. A14-02.04, p. 69.
146 Ibid.

same constraint because they 'are only paid if the children are in school'. The following are, in short, the characteristics of compulsory education.

1. Tort already highlighted the decisive intervention of the state, an apparatus dedicated to the regulation of the organisational parameters of education, including its compulsory nature as one of the fundamental characteristics of the class-based school: 'compulsory schooling requires massive state intervention in the organisation of education and the institution of a more or less close dependence of the school on the state as an instrument of the big bourgeoisie'.[147] Along the same lines, Balibar writes here that 'compulsory education manifests the necessary link between the development of the school-form and the capitalist state, in particular the "democratic" capitalist state, whose apparatus imposes, organises, regulates and controls compulsory education'.[148] The consequence can therefore be formulated as follows: since the scholastic form as such is compulsory, and since this imposition (entailed by bourgeois law) can only be governed by the capitalist state as a specific and separate apparatus, then, although the scholastic form is distinct (in content)[149] from other specific forms of the capitalist mode of production, *it is not independent*.[150] If there is no school without obligation, then there can be no school without the state (on the assumption that without the state there can be no obligations): 'the school-form is therefore not independent of the other elements of the system of capitalist social relations. Its simple description shows us that it is interwoven with both bourgeois law and the capitalist state, which dominate its realisation'.

2. The obligation to attend school seems to entail, with regard to the general principles of the individual freedom of bourgeois law, a certain paradox that makes the school similar, in its juridical status, to the family institution: *the law both proclaims freedom and imposes constraints* (in the family context, 'bourgeois law limits the right of the individual through family law, by establishing "paternal power"'). In both cases, however, this paradox is only apparent. If 'freedom' and 'constraint' are the aspects of this paradox, then, by a sort of synthesis that is already operative in the bourgeois juridical order, it can be seen how constraints engender freedom. If the *puissance paternelle* limits the individual freedom of the child, because they are considered 'a "minor" by law', the compulsory nature of

---

147   ALT2. A14-01.06, p. 6.
148   ALT2. A14-02.04, p. 71.
149   Cf. thesis 2 above, at the beginning of the section.
150   ALT2. A14-02.04, p. 72.

the schooling process acts precisely against this first constraint, 'as a limit-ation of family law: it asserts the right of the child against the "unlimited" character of paternal power'.[151] Although it is not examined further, this second characteristic, the compulsory nature of schooling. must be taken seriously: it suggests that in the capitalist mode of production the man-agement of the legal status of 'minors' – in relation to social reproduction and precisely to the extent that it is related to it – *belongs to the school, not to the family*. This presupposes the mechanism of spontaneous ideo-logical representations with which we are well acquainted (the child as a 'missing being') that is, 'the ideological recognition of a "natural" need for education, culture, etc., in "the child"'.

3. Above I said that constraints engender freedom. Considering that we are in the context of social reproduction, to speak of 'engendering' means nothing more than stressing how 'in the capitalist mode of production, universal compulsory education goes hand in hand with the universal freedom of labour'.[152] Here we identify the relationship between socially useful labour and (analogical) schoolwork. Although real labour is sub-ject to well-defined *material* constraints ('anyone who does not possess the means of production or interest-bearing property titles is forced to work for a living, in the form of a recognised activity of social utility'), it is legally free: labour posits material constraints, but it is free. On the other hand, to assume that schoolwork is ideologically based on a natural *need* rather than on a *desire* ('if not in the virtuous individual who makes his duty or his objective needs his desire: the "good student"') means that – once again, in the register of ideology – the compulsory nature of educa-tion is the prelude to the juridical freedom of real labour. The compulsory nature of analogical schoolwork precedes the formal 'freedom' of real labour.

4. There is one final characteristic of compulsory education: it not an extrin-sic qualification of the schooling processes, as if schooling could just as well be voluntary: 'it is in fact necessarily present in schoolwork itself, on a daily basis. That's because it is not an extrinsic feature of the school-form'.[153] Schoolwork is in fact characterised 'from start to finish' by its compulsory nature. This is another familiar stance: think of what Macherey considered to be the specific procedures that characterise the

151   Ibid.
152   Cf. above, Chapter 2, § 2.
153   ALT2. A14-02.04, p. 73.

practices of schooling – particularly the procedure of written homework and of moral education.[154] Here too, schoolwork represents '*duties*, in the legal and moral sense of the term: imposed tasks that create personal responsibility for the individual'. And, just as schoolwork is a duty, the disciplinary organisation of the school itself refers to a duty (once again, consider Macherey's disciplinary procedure): 'schooling is itself organised according to a *discipline* to be respected. In school everything is compulsory (or possibly forbidden). It is a world of rights and duties'.[155] The so-called *nouvelle pédagogie* (which tends to do away with traditional scholastic duties and discipline through the suppression of the pedagogical relationship) is no exception, since here too 'the form of obligation does not disappear at all: it is immediately found in the equally legal and moral, equally bourgeois, form of the "contract" concluded between teachers and taught, teachers and pupils, and its own obligations'.[156] In short, 'the compulsory nature of schoolwork could not disappear without a profound transformation of the school-form itself'. It is here that the second chapter of 'Schools' comes to an end, and this is the important scientific proposition that spells out what, at least for the moment, has been ascertained:

---

154   Ibid.

155   For an extended critique of the *nouvelle pédagogie*, which I will not explore in my analysis of the text, see Macherey in ALT2. A14-01.04 (A), pp. 16–23. I quote here a paradigmatic passage: 'the school thus retains its function of subjecting the child to an order that it wishes to ignore: in the new school, the function of concealment is only redoubled, since this submission, well camouflaged, has become tolerable; the school anguish is thus suppressed, which was the obligatory correlate of the old method ... We would say that the blindness has been displaced and reinforced. At school, the child learns to spontaneously bend to the demands of an order which never appears directly in the pedagogical act: this does not mean that it is absent. Thus, to be "free" (responsible ...) is to be forced without knowing it ... Two remarks: 1/ the order remains, but its presentation is implicit, 2/ the requirements of the division of labour are formulated exclusively as those of a technical division (everyone must have a place: the whole ambiguity concerns the notion of place)'. It follows that one of the effects of the *pédagogie nouvelle*, is 'a move towards the irrational. An obscure freedom has replaced a legible constraint. But the content of this "liberation" remains identical to that of the old submission: what is no longer admitted as a constraint becomes incomprehensible spontaneity. This is the magic of the group, which mixes the cards and erases all traces of class struggle'. Ibid., 19–20. The privileged target of the *Écoles* group's attacks against the *nouvelle pédagogie* was Célestine Freinet. See especially Freinet 1968–1969 and Freinet 1969. See also E. Freinet 1969.

156   ALT2. A14-02.04, p. 73.

the school-form is the form of an analogical, compulsory labour which is materially separate from productive labour, giving the individual legal 'ownership' of his own education.[157]

3   *Schools III*: Schooling and Wage Labour

We step into the third chapter of 'Schools' (the final one that is available to us) in *medias res* with this passage from Marx's *Capital*:

The value of labour-power is determined, as in the case of every other commodity, by the labour-time necessary for the production, and consequently also the reproduction, of this specific article. Insofar as it has value, it represents no more than a definite quantity of the average social labour objectified [with]in it. Labour-power exists only as a capacity of the living individual. Its production consequently presupposes his existence. Given the existence of the individual, the production of labour-power consists in his reproduction of himself or his maintenance. For his maintenance he requires a certain quantity of the means of subsistence. Therefore the labour-time necessary for the production of labour-power is the same as that necessary for the production of those means of subsistence; in other words, the value of labour-power is the value of the means of subsistence necessary for the maintenance of its owner. ...

His natural needs, such as food, clothing, fuel and housing vary according to the climatic and other physical peculiarities of his country. On the other hand, the number and extent of his so-called necessary requirements, as also the manner in which they are satisfied, are themselves products of history, and depend therefore to a great extent on the level of civilization attained by a country; in particular they depend on the conditions in which, and consequently on, the habits and expectations with which the class of free workers has been formed. In contrast, therefore, with the case of other commodities, the determination of the value of labour-power contains a historical and moral element. Nevertheless, in a given country at a given period, the average amount of the means of subsistence necessary for the worker is a known *datum*.

The owner of labour-power is mortal. If then his appearance in the market is to be continuous; and the continuous transformation of money

157   ALT2. A14-02.04, p. 74.

into capital assumes this, the seller of labour owner must perpetuate himself 'in the way that every living individual perpetuates himself, by procreation'. The labour-power withdrawn from the market by wear and tear, and by death, must be continually replaced by, at the very least, an equal amount of fresh labour-power. Hence the sum of the means of subsistence necessary for the production of labour-power must include the means necessary for the worker's replacements, i.e., his children, in order that this race of peculiar commodity-owners may perpetuate its presence on the market.

In order to modify the general nature of the human organism, in such a way that it acquires skill and dexterity in a given branch of industry, and becomes labour-power of a developed and specific kind, special education or training is needed, and this in turn costs an equivalent in commodities of a greater or lesser amount. The costs of education vary according to the degree of complexity of the labour-power required. These expenses (exceedingly small in the case of ordinary labour-power) form a part of the total value spent in producing it.[158]

With the third chapter of 'Schools', titled 'Scolarisation et travail salarié', we reach the fundamental theoretical moment in Balibar's analysis. It is necessary to temporarily bracket what we have learned so far: if the first two chapters dealt with the ideological representations that support the school, and the essential characteristics that constitute it as a social form, we now approach the mechanism of functioning of capital itself.

In Balibar's analysis, Marx's passage refers to the general framework of the theory of wage labour and, more precisely, to the analysis of the means of production and labour power, the two factors whose combination is functional to the production of value.

At first, the development of Balibar's arguments is rather didactic. By the term means of production, 'I mean the raw materials, work instruments (manual tools, simple or complex machines, motors and energy generators, automation) and, secondarily, the fixed installations (buildings, etc.) of production'.[159] These intervene in production by taking two *inseparable* aspects: as elements of the labour process (i.e., as elements of the productive forces whose use value refers to their material quality and quantity) and as commodities representing a certain *value* (which corresponds to the quantity of labour that is socially necessary for their reproduction).

---

158   Marx 1992, pp. 274–6.
159   ALT2. A14-02.04, p. 80.

The term labour power 'should be understood [as] the workers themselves'. Labour power also plays a role in production with two distinct but inseparable aspects: workers are the agents of the labour process (as elements of the productive forces, for the quality and quantity of work supplied) but they are also commodities that represent a certain value (which corresponds to the amount of labour socially necessary for their reproduction). Marx wrote that 'the capitalist epoch is therefore characterised by the fact that labour power, in the eyes of the worker himself, takes on the form of a commodity which is his property; his labour consequently takes on the form of wage labour'.[160] This claim needs to be clarified: in the capitalist mode of production, workers are conceived by means of two categories. The first is legal: workers are 'free', or at least formally so ('free to move and transact as they please').[161] The other is economic: the worker is, in fact, a unit of labour power. It is clear that in the 'capitalist epoch' the two categories are materially indistinguishable: to say, as Marx does, that the labour power takes the form of a commodity that belongs to the worker is equivalent to saying that in the production process, labour power is a commodity which is only formally free to be exchanged (and thus to be waged), unlike, for example, the 'mode of production based on slavery', in which the worker is indeed a commodity, but a commodity without freedom (not even a formal one: 'the use of labour power is incompatible with its freedom'; or, conversely, only he who is outside production is free).

Just as the means of production cannot materially enter into the process of production, except as value (i.e., as a commodity that is sold and purchased), so labour power can enter into that process 'only on the condition of entering it as *value*, thus [*donc*] in the form of commodity, in the form of wage labour'. *Donc* – a conjunction that suggests an immediate implication between value and wage labour: labour power, presupposing the legal freedom of the worker, is exchanged as a commodity with a definite value (determined by what is spent for its reproduction) and therefore is waged labour power: 'we can say that labour power only appears as a value with waged labour'; or, again, labour power 'is only effectively valued if it is exchanged (for a sum of money which, on average, corresponds to its value)'.[162]

Let us keep our focus on labour power as an element of productive forces. To say 'the value of labour power' means, as we just noted, to refer to the mechanism of its reproduction: the value of wages is determined by the value of the commodities which the worker consumes in the reproduction of their labour

---

160 Marx 1992, p. 274 n. 4.
161 ALT2. A14-02.04, p. 81.
162 ALT2. A14-02.04, p. 83.

power. Of course, 'these commodities are of a very diverse material nature and are consumed under very different social conditions'.[163] And yet, in spite of their diversity, they contribute to creating the value of labour power in proportion to their value, that is, in proportion to the quantity of labour that is socially necessary for their production. Once again: the value of labour power is determined by the value of the commodities functional to its reproduction.

This is the meaning of Marx's passage, quoted above, where he 'analyses the different "items" or "factors" of the worker's consumption, which contribute to the reproduction of his labour power, and thus to the formation of his value'.[164] From the point of view of reproduction, individual consumption can be articulated into three socially organised processes ('particularly in the forms of family and schooling'): natural needs 'such as food, clothing, fuel, and housing' (including a historical element which, dictated by 'the level of civilisation attained by a country', and by 'the habits and expectations with which, the class of free workers has been formed', is included in the determination of value itself); the means of subsistence of the 'fresh labour power' (presupposing the necessary continuity between the worker's presence on the market and his mortality); and finally training and education (on the assumption that labour power, at every level, has specific 'skill and dexterity' as required by a given occupation).[165]

In the capitalist mode of production, if labour power has a value, then it should be remunerated with a wage, and its wage-earning capacity implies its being exchanged. The 'free' worker exchanges his labour power which therefore, as Marx says, takes the form of a commodity which he owns, and the value of which refers to the value of the commodities consumed by the worker for their reproduction. Labour power, then, receives a determinate value only if it is reproduced as a commodity – a commodity, Balibar stresses, that is *relatively independent*. Indeed, Marx's own passage refers to the 'labour-time requisite for the production of labour-power'. How can we refer to the necessity of labour time if not by presupposing a specific and historically separate social process, distinct from the production of other commodities (precisely, the process of consumption, instrumental to reproduction)? Given the necessity of reproduction, it is necessary to distinguish it from production otherwise 'this expression would be an abstraction, with no correspondence to any social form realised in society'.[166]

---

163   ALT2. A14-02.04, p. 82.
164   Ibid.
165   ALT2. A14-02.04, p. 83.
166   ALT2. A14-02.04, p. 84.

Given the necessity of the distinction, the question then becomes: 'how can this condition be realised?' We are given the answer:

> in the capitalist mode of production, and only there, by the existence of *an autonomous sector of social consumption*, devoted to the reproduction of labour power. Hence, correlatively, the existence of *a sector of production of the means of consumption, as commodities*.[167]

Here, for Balibar, it is crucial to highlight this relative autonomy, this relative separation of individual consumption from the sphere of production: the units of capitalist production are *separate* from the units of individual consumption in which the products that are necessary for the material life of the workers are placed, that is, 'the maintenance of their labour power, the reproduction and the breeding of their offspring'.[168] This goes beyond the acknowledgment that the means of consumption are something other than the sphere of production: indeed, it is evident that consumer products, being necessary for reproduction, are, in fact, *produced* as *products*. What is stressed here, rather, is that it is precisely the process of consumption, or, better still, the distribution and division of the means of consumption, that is *separated* from the process of production: the means of consumption, 'products in the production sphere', must be consumed 'in distinct consumption units, must take place through a circulation of products, outside the sphere of capitalist production'.

The separateness and the distinction between the process of production on the one hand and the process of consumption on the other, however, are *not* absolute. The sphere of individual consumption is irreducible to the sphere of production, although, as the sphere of the reproduction *of* labour power, it assumes *an organisational form* typical of the capitalist mode of production: *the three factors of individual consumption are the three factors of consumption of the wage worker alone*. In short, the consumption process is indeed an *autonomous* process, but only a *relatively* autonomous one. *It is social*:

> this relative autonomy of individual consumption, of the sphere of individual consumption and of the consumption units which constitute it, is therefore by no means a *natural* phenomenon. It is a social phenomenon,

---

167   Ibid.
168   ALT2. A14-02.04, p. 85.

the very condition of the existence of labour power as a commodity, and thus of the wage-labour/capital relation, and which the functioning of capital reproduces ceaselessly.[169]

4 Schooling and the Reproduction of Labour Power

Let us summarise the argument of the previous section with a theoretical proposition: *wage labour takes place in the context of the exchange of labour power as a commodity, whose value is determined by the value of a relatively autonomous consumption process that is functional to its reproduction.* But let us now take a step further. Balibar wants to emphasise three consequences of the fact that, as Marx says, educational expenses are one of the factors contributing to the value of labour power. First: *schooling is included in the sphere of consumption and is external to the sphere of production.* He writes:

> schooling, as a material process, is first of all a part of the process of reproduction of the value of labour power, subject to the general conditions of the reproduction of the value of labour power in the capitalist mode of production.[170]

Labour power, as Marx had noted, must acquire 'skill and dexterity in a given branch of industry, and becomes labour-power of a developed and specific kind'. The process of schooling as a (third) factor of consumption is a relatively autonomous process. If education is the material cause of the attainment of skill and handiness ('a certain preparation or education is necessary'), then it is also the material cause of a *qualitative modification* of 'general nature of the human organism' (Balibar writes that 'schooling is a particular form of constitution of the material *quality* of labour power') – a modification which is, *essentially*, instrumental to the adaptation to the means of production, seen as further elements of the productive forces: workers cannot enter into the process of production if not equipped with 'the specific qualities that allow them to be combined with the means of production'.[171] In the first place, then, education is subject to the degree of technical – both technological and scientific – development corresponding to the degree of development of the labour process of specific sectors of production ('chemistry, metallurgy, agriculture, etc.').

---

169   Ibid.
170   ALT2. A14-02.04, p. 87.
171   ALT2. A14-02.04, p. 86.

Secondly, education itself is subject to the social form of the process of production, that is, to its being a process of valorisation of capital ('under the domination and effective direction of capital'). Therefore, it could also be said that the social form of the capitalist mode of production and the degree of development of the means of production are elements that determine both the placement of education within the process of reproduction (the capitalist form determines, on the formal level, the school as a social form), and the degree of development of the qualification (which, on the level of content, is the outcome of education) functional to the combination with the means of production.

We have already discussed the indivisibility of relativity and autonomy. It is now clear why: to speak of relativity (determined by a double submission: both to the capitalist form and to the degree of development of the means of production) means that the *quality* of labour power must be, as such, *already* at work in the production process. In other words, if it is true that the process of education is subject to the treatment of the modes of production (its relativity, or double submission), the opposite (its autonomy) is equally valid: in order to function, the mode of production presupposes an educational process that must have *already* taken place. The worker is always a trained worker, and to say that this training has *already* taken place means that the process of material consumption is (relatively) distinct and separate from that of production (which, therefore, is active insofar as it determines its form and content and, at the same time, it is passive because it is conditioned by it). Balibar thus writes:

> schooling, being supported by material "consumption", entering into the constitution of the value of labour power, is tendentially inscribed in the sphere of social consumption, and therefore outside the sphere of capitalist production, into which labour power enters as already constituted value, to be spent on its various productive uses.[172]

The process of schooling, therefore, belongs to the sphere of the worker's material consumption. That is how it can be said to represent (as we have done in §3) a (third) factor in the valorisation of labour power: in addition to the value of the means of subsistence necessary for the sustenance of the workers, the value of labour power corresponds to that of the means of their education. 'The value of material instruments (and "services" consumed) in

---

172 ALT2. A14-02.04, p. 88.

schooling enters into the reproduction of the value of labour power.'[173] This thesis is entirely consistent with Marxian logic, but Balibar insists that

> it should not be forgotten that schooling uses – directly or indirectly, in greater or lesser quantities – material instruments which are products of human labour (and therefore commodities) and consumes the 'services' of teachers, administrators, etc., who must themselves consume commodities.[174]

This warning ('it should not be forgotten ...') leads to a positive thesis: 'the most important theoretical and practical point is that schooling is not and cannot be free'.[175] The value of schooling (the value of its services and of its material instruments) plays the same role as the means of consumption of the individual (the first factor identified by Marx) and the family (the second factor). Consequently, the monetary equivalent of this value must be considered as a *part of the variable capital* (which, to put it briefly, is represented by the 'real' wage – later we will appreciate the meaning of this specification) *rather than of surplus value* (or profit), which should be invested 'according to the official technocratic terminology, "in" the training of the youth, and in projects of "general interest"'.[176]

In fact, Balibar's claim is crucial because, in addition to opening a path for the analysis of the modes of concealment of distribution relations in a capitalist system, it allows us to clarify, by means of a question that is also an objection, a node that is placed outside of the sphere of production. Since the formation of labour power must already be at work in the sphere of production (the adaptation to the degree of development of the means of production presupposes an *already* mastered skill), how can the wage correspond, together with that of the first two factors of reproduction, to the value of the (scholastic) commodities necessarily consumed *before* entering into the production process? In other words: what makes it possible for the wage (of labour power) to include expenses for education (for those who do *not* yet belong to labour power, because they are still engaged in the educational process)?

If the value of education is defined by the value of the material tools necessary for the educational process and, moreover, it is evidently impossible for

---

173   Ibid.
174   ALT2. A14-02.04, p. 87.
175   ALT2. A14-02.04, p. 88.
176   Ibid.

such expenses to be borne by the students, then for Balibar the aim is to demonstrate that those expenses *are already borne by the waged workers*. In other words, for Balibar it is a question of understanding, for *each* wage earner, how a part of each worker's salary serves (directly, for those who have children; indirectly, for all other workers, through taxes) the educational expenses of future labour power – on the assumption that, once again, those who are educated cannot bear the costs of their own education. This is how we should understand the observation that *a part* of the value of the means of schooling 'is well and truly spent directly by the workers (school supplies, travel, tuition fees, boarding fees, etc.)' – and that, consequently, it is part of the *individual wage*[177] – while another part is a 'community "state" expenditure' (which leads to the problem of the social nature of taxes). Here too, however, public expenditure only *seems* not to be shouldered by the individual worker. Indeed, the mechanism of taxation results in a redistribution of educational expenses placed 'on the shoulders of all workers', so that a part (or better: *most*) of them indirectly bear the cost of an education that a part (or better: *most*) of the future labour power will never receive (higher education), not to mention 'the children of the bourgeoisie' whose family income does *not* derive from a wage 'but actually from *profits*', that is, by what is *already* a part 'of the surplus value extracted from the workers'. In short, although the costs of education do not refer to the wage of the user of the educational process (i.e., the student, because schoolwork is an analogical form of labour that does not create value), they still refer to the wage of that part of the labour power that is already part of the production process. Therefore, a part of the wage of the current labour power is destined to go towards the education of the (still unrealised) future labour power. Workers shoulder the cost of all educational expenses alone. They directly pay for the education of future labour powers which, so to speak, depend on them (as part of their wage: from this point of view, this makes educational expenses similar to those meant for family sustenance). Moreover, they indirectly pay for the education of those who do not depend on them (through taxes, redistributed by the state): the workers pay for the education of the labour power emerging from their own social class but, above all, for that of the bourgeoisie. In short, 'everyone seems to spend what in fact only some have actually produced, provided that all seem to have "equal opportunities" to benefit from: this is what the bourgeoisie calls democracy'.[178]

---

177 This wage, moreover, considerably increases the importance of family consumption: this corresponds to the second factor of valorisation identified by Marx.

178 ALT2. A14-02.04, p. 90.

We come now to the second of the three consequences Balibar highlights. *Schooling constitutes the individual formation of the labour power which is regarded as the private 'property' of the worker*. The character of schooling 'in the whole process of reproduction of labour power' refers to its specific effect on that labour power: 'the "training" of the technical and ideological qualities necessary for its *use*'.[179]

To talk about a 'use' implies that technical and ideological training is a commodity that can be sold and purchased, and it therefore presupposes that the economic and legal forms of the exchange of commodities in general ('value, price, supply, and demand, etc. on the one hand; property, contract, freedom, and individual personality on the other') apply to it 'and to the worker, as a seller of labour power'.

At the same time, the producer has a 'very peculiar' relationship with the worker's training. Indeed, to the extent that this education has a use (which is a function of its material qualities) and a value (expressible in the value form of money) in occupying a socially defined place on the labour market, in order to be object of *a relationship of contractual exchange* (with the capitalist) it must be *a legal property* (of the worker). It could be said that education – as a product of schooling, as an exchange commodity – is always accompanied by *a void of property to be occupied*: it is occupied by the capitalist during the productive use of labour power ('the production time, provided for in the contract'),[180] and it is preliminarily occupied by the worker himself, who therefore appears 'as the owner of "his" *individual* labour power'.

Balibar's thesis is both a reactivation and an expansion of the analysis of the sanctioning of the ownership of one's received education, as conducted in the second chapter of 'Schools'.[181] There, after all, a certain paradox appeared: who should own education if not those who take part in the educational process? And does not the very notion of labour power entail that the factors of reproduction are inseparable from the (body of the) worker? We now know that, in the order of the reproduction of labour power, *appropriation is the necessary prerequisite for the exchange of one's education* (individual qualities of labour power are 'legally sanctioned as individual qualities, so that they can be considered as private "property" of the worker').[182]

But that is not all. Through the notion of property, the *formal* necessity of the scholastic separation, in the capitalist mode of production, becomes

---

179   Ibid.
180   ALT2. A14-02.04, p. 91.
181   Cf. above, § 2.
182   ALT2. A14-02.04, p. 91.

clear because it is linked to the individual ownership of education. Not only, as we have seen in the first consequence (schooling is included in the sphere of consumption, and is external to the sphere of production), must the process of school reproduction be subjected, in the order of its contents, to a separation by *adaptation* (the education of labour power must already be operative in the sphere of production, and this precedence defines its autonomy). The process of reproduction itself must also necessarily be subjected, in the formal exchange of education, to a separation that entails the *precedence* of the worker's ownership of their education because it is the legal and the formal (contractual) condition of its exchange in the labour market. In short: adaptation to the means of production involves handiness and skill (i.e., training), and in turn, this presupposes that these abilities are formally *owned by* the worker, so that they can be exchanged, that is, treated as commodities:

> The reproduction of the qualities of labour power is ordered in its content, in the final analysis, by the process of production, to which they must be 'adequate'. But it is at the same time necessarily external to this process of production, because it must take place as a process of individual formation of labour power, under the individual responsibility of the worker, who appears here as the owner of his labour power, and the qualities which it must materially possess in order to be materially negotiated on the labour market.[183]

We come now to the last consequence. *Schooling contributes to the extension of the exchange of wage labour power outside the sphere of production.* If schooling is only a form of reproduction of the qualities of labour power, it follows that it 'historically assumes the waged form of work: its capitalist form'. The thesis leads to a simple but fundamental theoretical proposition: *the school is an effect of wage labour which, as a specific form of labour in general, is the cause of the schooling process.* To some extent, we are already familiar with this thesis, thanks to Balibar's claim that 'the development of capitalist production and the functioning of capitalist relations of production require and historically impose the *schooling* of all its agents':[184] capitalism requires that labour power should possess 'a minimum "intellectual" quality, within the simple "manual" work itself'.[185]

---

183   Ibid.
184   ALT2. A14-02.04, p. 59.
185   ALT2. A14-02.04, p. 92.

The extension of the scholastic form is not only expressed in productive labour (in the capitalist sense, i.e., productive of value and surplus value). It is also visible in 'other spheres of social activity, just as the domination of capital extends to these sectors themselves'. The domination of capital entails the extension of wage labour and, therefore, to the social conditions of reproduction.

The point, however, is *not to trace an order of mechanical succession* between the extension of capitalist rule and the extension of the forms of reproduction. Balibar thus writes:

> in the history of capitalist societies, the extension of the capitalist mode of *reproduction* of labour power can precede the penetration of capital into certain spheres of crafts, trade, and agriculture in small family farms. The labour power of family farms is unsalaried labour power: it is therefore not a commodity; it has no value as such. However, just as the means of production they use are all commodities in today's capitalist society (the purchase of which subjects them to the domination of the industrial market), so is the reproduction of labour power capitalist in form: the means of consumption are no longer, with a few exceptions, products of the farm itself, but commodities on the capitalist market of means of consumption. And, in the same way, the technical and ideological training of the peasant workers is transferred to compulsory schooling, at least that of the 'elementary' level.[186]

Between the first thesis (the school as a factor of reproduction is an *effect* of wage labour) and the second (the school as a factor of reproduction *precedes* wage labour) there is *no* contradiction, since the second is placed in the order of the extension of the domination of capital (which refers to the first position):

> thus the formation of the necessary elements for the capitalist *labour market* accompanies or even precedes the development of the capitalist relations of production and the extension of capital, with the support of the state, *and on the basis of the general dominion of capital within society*.[187]

---

186   ALT2. A14-02.04, pp. 92–3.
187   ALT2. A14-02.04, p. 93. The concluding italics are mine.

5   Once again on wage theory: the wage-form and the notions of
       'Labour' and 'Qualification'

We can now supplement the theoretical proposition stated at the beginning of
the previous section with the following: *schooling, as a factor in the reproduction of labour power, is placed in the order of consumption external to the sphere
of production which is sanctioned through the legal ownership of education (as its
outcome), and which contributes to the expansion of wage labour power outside
the scope of production (in the proper sense).* We have thus reached the crucial
part of Balibar's analysis:

> we must now take a further step, which is clarified by the development of
> wage theory. For although the social reality of wage labour consists in the
> sale and purchase of human labour-power on a social scale, and therefore
> in the existence of a 'labour market' which is in fact *a market for labour
> power*, this does not manifest itself directly in practice. And, in the same
> way, schooling does not manifest itself directly in practice as a process of
> reproduction of human labour power contributing in some proportion to
> the formation of its value.[188]

To talk of wage labour is to talk about the sale and purchase of labour power
[*la vente et l'achat de la force de travail*]. Indeed, the worker is *forced* to sell his
labour power ('anyone without the means of production or interest-bearing
property titles is forced to work for a living') as a commodity whose value is
determined by the value of the means of its reproduction, and the capitalist buys it for a sum of money (wages) which corresponds, on average, to its
value.[189] Thus the labour market is, *in fact*, the labour power market ('the existence of a "labour market" which is in fact a market for labour power'). But there
is more: from this logic what follows is the valorisation of capital. Labour power,
insofar as it is placed in the sphere of the production process, is placed in the
order of a quantitative increase of labour time that gives rise to surplus value,
which is part of the commodity that is produced (that is: the labour necessary
for the reintegration of the value of labour power takes up only part of the
entire working day).[190] In other words, the logic of wage labour is necessarily

---

188   ALT2. A14-02.04, p. 94.
189   ALT2. A14-02.04, p. 72.
190   '[T]he labour-process may continue beyond the time necessary to reproduce and incor-
      porate in the product a mere equivalent for the value of the labour-power. For this, six
      hours alone would be sufficient: but the process lasts longer, say for twelve hours. The

one of exploitation, since it refers to an extortion: it implies, within the process of labour itself, a distinction between necessary labour (for the reproduction of labour power) and surplus labour (non-waged and not reciprocated by the capitalist).

And yet, Balibar claims that *as they present themselves in economic practice*, things are different.[191] This is an absolutely crucial point. Everything here pivots on this *presentation* (just as everything, as we already know, pivots on the presentation of the school, on its spontaneous representation, guaranteeing the functioning of the plural processes of schooling).

To understand this, we should take a step back. We have seen how Althusser, in 'Les Grandes Illusions de l'École' and with regard to the illusion of existence, placed his argument in the context of the theory of value: exchange value finds its real foundation in the quantity of labour power that is socially necessary for the production of the object exchanged (and which makes a suit, on the one hand, and ten pairs of shoes, on the other, equivalent in terms of production time, even if manufactured with different materials). And yet, *as it presents itself*, exchange value forces every commodity to find value in an absolute equivalence with a certain amount of money. However, the difference between wage labour and the quantity of labour employed in the production of the commodity that is exchanged *does not appear* (this is the point) *in the act of exchange*. As it presents itself, the value is wholly inherent to the commodity itself, and what disappears [*disparaît*] in the commodity market is precisely the logic of the extortion of surplus labour, extra labour giving rise to a surplus

---

activity of labour-power, therefore, not only reproduces its own value, but produces value over and above this. This surplus-value is the difference between the value of the product and the value of the elements consumed in the formation of the product, in other words the means of production and the labour-power'. Marx 1992, p. 317.

191   'Suppose the working day consists of 6 hours of necessary labour and 6 hours of surplus labour. Then the free worker gives the capitalist 6×6 or 36 hours of surplus labour every week. It is the same as if he worked 3 days in the week for himself and 3 days gratis in the week for the capitalist. But this fact is not directly visible. Surplus labour and necessary labour are mingled together. I can therefore express the same relation by saying for instance, that in every minute the worker works 30 seconds for himself and 30 seconds for the capitalist, etc. It is otherwise with the *corvee*. The necessary labour which the Wallachian peasant performs for his own maintenance is distinctly marked off from his surplus labour on behalf of the *boyar: one* he does on his own field, the other on the seignorial estate. Both parts of the labour-time thus exist independently, side by side with each other. In the *corvee* the surplus labour is accurately marked off from the necessary labour. However, this clearly alters nothing in the quantitative relation of surplus labour to necessary labour. Three days' surplus labour in the week remain three days that yield no equivalence to the worker himself, whether the surplus labour is called *corvee* or wage-labour'. Marx 1992, pp. 345–6.

value (appropriated by the capitalist) which then becomes part of the commodity produced (and which, if sold, produces value).

In that context, I suggested that we would later be in a position to answer a question that was defined as crucial, pertaining to the theoretical status of the Althusserian use of the theory of value: does it play a merely formal role? We can now offer an answer. The theory of value, as we know, is valid from the formal point of view (the law of value is to the form of value as the process of qualification is to the form of schooling) *but also from that of content*: indeed, if for Althusser exchange value, *as it is presents itself*, is grounded on the absolute symmetry of purchase and sale (in order to conceal the exploitation of labour power that was necessary for the production of the exchanged object) here, in the same way, the exchange of the education of labour power (what, we will see, will be defined as 'qualification') presents itself 'in practice' as *an exchange of equivalent commodities of equivalent value:*

> the sale and purchase of labour power presents itself, in practice, in a different *form*, which is the wage-form proper, expressed in the legal categories necessary for the functioning of capitalist relations of production. In order not to contradict these legal categories, the whole 'exchange' between 'owners' – one brings his commodity to the market while the other brings his money – must be presented as an exchange between *equivalent* commodities, representing *equal* quantities of value, or an exchange in which the price (which is the universal social form of value) corresponds exactly to the value of the commodity. This explains why the sale and purchase of labour power is presented in a new form: as the sale and purchase *of labour.*[192]

Until now we have referred to wages and labour power. In this passage, as we can observe, two new related notions are introduced: economic practice (the presentation of exchange, or the exchange as it presents itself) produces a series of theoretical distinctions placed in what can be designated as *the order of the epistemology of wage labour* (and the theoretical propositions that can be formulated from the analysis carried out so far) and *the order of the imaginary representation of wage labour* (and the true-factual propositions that can be formulated from the analysis that follows) as distinct yet inseparable orders, since the latter is the condition for the functioning of the former. (In this regard, we should remember how Althusser claimed that 'in social matters, nothing obscure happens without this obscurity being covered by the illusion of transparency'.)[193] In other words – to avoid generating any misunderstanding – between the order of epistemology and representation, there is no relationship of exclusion, as if the latter were replacing and erasing the former. The illusion, as Althusser says, is more of a covering (an act of occultation) than a replacing (an act of elimination). Here the discourse pertains to a certain effectiveness of this illusion. It is as if one said: 'Marx showed how things are, and things – at least until 'Schools' was written! – should keep going the way they are supposed to go. But for that to happen, they must give the impression of going otherwise'. In short: Balibar's category of 'form' (*forme différente, forme nouvelle*, and *forme-salaire* itself) indicates that the *content* of the process of real capital valorisation (through the extortion of surplus labour) persists precisely because it seems to take, *en pratique*, another direction.

In the passage quoted above, the first two distinctions are easily identifiable. The (theoretical) notion of the wage does *not* correspond to the wage-form (a notion referring to the change of form of the notion of wage) because the (theoretical) notion of labour power does *not* correspond to 'labour' (a notion referring to the change of form of the notion of labour power). In economic practice – the sale and purchase of labour power as they present themselves – we have to deal literally with the *metamorphosis* of those notions (we shall see shortly what this 'new' or 'different' form serves): what is exchanged is not labour power, whose value exhausts only a part of the labour process, but the 'labour' whose 'value', as it presents itself, is exactly equivalent to the wage-form paid out by the capitalist (and not to the part relative to its reproduction). Let us consider Marx's example (see footnote 190 above): the daily labour process is twelve hours long; six hours are the labour time necessary for the reproduction of labour power, while the remaining six amount to surplus labour (which, therefore, underlies the process of capital valorisation, provided that the commodity incorporating them is actually sold). The value of labour power expressed through wages is the value of six hours of necessary labour (since the value of labour power is the value of the means of its reproduction, including the schooling process). However, as it presents itself, value is placed in a relation of absolute equivalence with the entire labour process, so that surplus labour and, therefore, the real factor of valorisation, disappears from the notion of 'labour': 'labour', as an experiential representative of labour power, *becomes part of the exchange value* – that is, labour is *the de-socialised simulacrum of labour power*.

---

193   ALT2. A14-01.08, p. 6.

We can thus understand why Balibar claims that the wage of the worker does *not* correspond, in the order of representation, to the value of his reproduction but rather 'it is deemed to be the "price of labour", and is determined in practice in relation to the "value of labour"' (note the scare quotes).[194] In the same way we understand how the capitalist '"pays the labour" of the worker, and to the worker, for whom his wage is the price conceded by capital in proportion to "his labour"'. Once again: although it is *actually* an unequal exchange (what for the capitalist is the valorisation of capital, for the worker is surplus expenditure of labour power), it *appears* as an exchange of equivalent commodities, an appearance of absolute equality that conceals the substantial inequality between necessary labour and surplus labour where 'labour' corresponds, *sic et simpliciter*, to the 'price of labour'.

In short, if, as Althusser claimed in 'Les Grandes *Illusions de l'École*', Marx had questioned what was self-evident for 'the Great Englishmen: Smith and Ricardo'[195] (that a commodity corresponds to its exchange value), for Balibar – now and on the basis of the permanence of the validity of that theoretical gesture – the aim is to *recover that evidence* in order to show its 'immense practical importance'.[196] The order of the epistemology of wage labour is indeed, as stated above, distinct from that of its representation, but it is also inseparable from it: in economic practice one enters the workplace as one enters the shop of which Althusser spoke – if there is a fetishism of commodities, there is also a fetishism of labour power (that is, of 'labour') as an equivalent commodity. This is precisely what makes the relations of production work.

A final distinction should be highlighted. We have seen that labour power is not 'labour' and wages are not the wage-form; but if the educational process is one of the commodities consumed by labour power, it follows that a 'change in the form of wage' imposes 'on schooling a corresponding change of form, which alone constitutes the developed "school-form" proper, and which is of immense practical importance'.[197] This, then, is the last distinction: as it presents itself, 'schooling *appears* practically as *the process of constituting an individual "qualification" of work* (and of the worker)'.[198] The education of labour power, as the outcome of school consumption (which is separate, and *one* of the factors that compose its value) does *not* correspond to a 'qualification' (which, we shall see, represents the *only* imaginary criterion of valorisation of 'labour' and, there-

---

194 ALT2. A14-01.08, p. 6.
195 ALT2. A14-01.08, p. 17.
196 ALT2. A14-02.04, p. 95.
197 Ibid.
198 Ibid.

fore, the only criterion to determine the wage-form). Once again: these are different orders, distinct and inseparable.

Before proceeding, it is possible to further clarify Balibar's arguments concerning the legal sanctions of individuality and appropriation. In this regard, let us recall the opening of the passage quoted above: 'the sale and purchase of labour power presents itself in practice in a different form, which is the wage-form itself, and which is expressed in the legal categories necessary for the functioning of capitalist production relations'.[199] Of course, we are not surprised to see bourgeois legal categories described as sanctions. At first,[200] in fact, they functioned as a 'schema' for the transition from the space of education to that of its social function (knowledge is already functional to its circulation), and, above all, we saw how they sanction the *individual ownership* of education (in a more or less paradoxical way since learning is in fact inseparable from the user who learns: the student is both subject and object of his or her work which, for this very reason, is work only by analogy). After that,[201] we saw that the appropriation sanction was the condition of possibility for the *exchange* of one's own education: if it is true that adaptation to the means of production, as Marx says, requires 'skill and handiness' (i.e., training), this presupposes that, in order for them to be treated as commodities, they must be, at least initially, considered as the worker's property. How can a commodity be sold unless we (legally, that is, ideologically) presuppose it to be owned by the seller (the worker), and to be freely exchanged with the capitalist? Or again: how can we conceive of the sale of a commodity like education if not by, (legally) *detaching it, so to speak*, from the workers and considering it to be their property? In short, we know that the bourgeois categories of individual freedom (presupposed by contractual exchange) and property (of one's education) are the conditions of possibility for the exchange of commodities. Now we know that these commodities, as they present themselves, are commodities of equivalent value. Legal sanction, in other words, accompanies (as a separate ideological instance) the metamorphosis of the notion of labour power (whose productive qualities are indeed inseparable from the worker). Furthermore, the notions of individuality and property *already* presuppose the change of form of this notion. *The legal ownership of education is already the legal ownership of a 'qualification'.* The sanction, as seen in § 2, intervening precisely in the order of the subject-objective indistinction of education (by *separating* the subject and the object of the assimilation of knowledge), *already* looks towards the change

---

199   ALT2. A14-02.04, p. 94.
200   Cf. above, § 2.
201   Cf. above, § 4.

of form of sale and purchase. Referring to the wage-form as expressive of the value of 'labour' (rather than labour power), this expresses itself, Balibar notes, 'in the legal categories necessary for the functioning of capitalist relations of production'.

This first step can thus be summarised as follows: the field of economic practice, if traced back to the order of representation, is distributed into three factors: 'qualification', 'labour', and 'wage-form' – the metamorphosis of the notions of education, labour power, and wage. I may then immediately anticipate Balibar's next theoretical step which is to show how the 'qualification', and therefore the scholastic form as its social presupposition, far from being one of the factors of the consumption of labour power (like the education of which it is a representation), and therefore one of the factors of its value, *is the dominant factor of economic practice itself, as it can be traced back to the order of representation.*[202]

∴

Let us take a closer look at the notion of 'qualification'. Balibar writes that 'the analysis of the notion of qualification must be linked to two immediately striking features in the history of "developed" capitalist societies: the extension of the wage-form, and the existence of an accentuated wage hierarchy'.[203] Let us begin with the hierarchisation of the wage-form.

Far from being a generic notion, 'labour' is always and necessarily given in a determinate form ('the "labour" that is thus paid in the form of wages is necessarily spent in a certain concrete form') and the determinate nature of 'labour' corresponds to its *specialisation* ('it is a certain *specialisation* of labour, more or less defined'). This is the first aspect of a 'qualification': 'the specialisation of the work that the wage is supposed to pay for, is the first component of its qualification'. As a specialisation (as a definite form) of 'labour' (as an equivalent commodity), a 'qualification' is an attribute that is inseparable from the notion of 'labour', for the latter always refers to a certain degree of 'qualification'.

It follows, then, that if the exchange, as it appears, takes place between equivalent commodities, *a greater degree of 'qualification' will correspond to a higher tier of wage-form*: 'the existence of a wage hierarchy always refers directly to a hierarchy of "qualification" of labour'.[204] 'Labour' is always qualified, and every qualification is quantified: the notion of 'unskilled labour', or work without any

---

202   Cf. *infra*, § 6.
203   ALT2. A14-02.04, p. 96.
204   Ibid.

degree of specialisation, does not exist: '"unskilled" labour is not an absolute concept; it is a category relative to "skilled" work'. In short, the 'qualification' of 'labour' is the basis of the wage-form (i.e., its 'value': 'the hierarchical scale of qualifications ... is linked to that of "value of work"');[205] *a given amount of 'qualifications' will correspond to an equivalent quantity of wage-form.* This implies that *the 'qualification' determines the 'value' of 'labour'*:

> there is, for both the worker and the capitalist, a certain *power* or *capacity* for labour which prefigures the labour itself, and which indicates in advance its 'value' with respect to a certain wage, which will be 'equivalent' (a monetary equivalence) to this value.[206]

If, as it presents itself, the value of labour power (as the value of the means of its reproduction) is equivalent to the degree of its 'qualification', then the criterion for the quantification of the wage-form (as the expressive form of the value of 'labour') is necessarily dependent upon a measurement of this 'qualification' (as an attribute that cannot be separated from the notion of 'labour'): 'as a *labour* qualification, it seems to be *measurable*, for example on the basis of an "analysis" of tasks and work stations'.[207] The measurement of this 'qualification' implies that the value of 'labour' can be '*objectively* measurable'.[208] In other words, 'its measure appears to be independent of the will of the worker as well as that of the individual capitalist', and it is therefore necessary 'that the 'qualification' of the worker be referred to an objective scale from the point of view of the individual worker and capitalist'.[209] Moreover, if the scale of this 'qualification' is nothing but a hierarchy of ascending degrees, covering the whole 'diversity of jobs' and the various 'specialisation of tasks',[210] then the employment contract should be stipulated between 'free' agents: 'this hierarchy itself appears as objective, independent of individuals and circumstances'. However, the hierarchy of qualifications is 'historically variable', if by this we understand both the (capitalist's) tendency to downgrade and, precisely, to de-qualify the worker, as well as the opposite: the workers tend to requalify their 'qualification', although 'in its broadest sense, for a given period, it should be considered fixed'.

---

205   ALT2. A14-02.04, pp. 107–8.

206   ALT2. A14-02.04, p. 99.

207   ALT2. A14-02.04, p. 98.

208   ALT2. A14-02.04, p. 99.

209   ALT2. A14-02.04, pp. 99–100.

210   ALT2. A14-02.04, p. 100.

We will see here what the criterion for the (allegedly) objective measurement of the 'qualification' is, and how it can perform this function. What is important here is to note that the scale of 'qualifications', the criterion to quantify the wage-form, is not related to a physical measure (as with labour power) such as labour time or performance (how well adjusted the worker is to the production process) but rather to a social process, a manifestation of a natural hierarchy (a hierarchy that would be 'objective, constant, precise ...'):

> this is the criterion to which capitalist workers and employers refer, confronted as individuals on the labour market: an objective social qualification, which the employer demands, the worker strives to obtain, and the employer in turn must recognise on an average scale [*reconnaître en moyenne*].[211]

In this sense, Balibar's follow-up claim is not surprising: the wage-form, in practice, appears to be *irrationnelle*. In the final section we will see how this irrationality is resolved. For the moment it suffices to say that if the wage of wage labour is, *in fact*, the wage paid to a labour power which is *already* at work in the sphere of production (it corresponds to the quantity of labour necessary for its reproduction), then, as it presents itself (i.e., as a wage-form), it expresses the value of a commodity (precisely, the 'qualification') which, sold 'freely' (and initially) by the worker, *necessarily anticipates its implementation in the process of production*. In this way, Balibar asks: what does it mean to talk of 'a work "qualification", as a basis for determining the wage, i.e., the "price of work"?'[212] It means that 'labour', to be sold as a commodity, must possess 'a material existence, whatever it may be, separate, independent of the worker's person, *and prior to the use of the commodity, i.e., to labour itself*'. This is why (as Balibar claimed above) the 'qualification' is 'a specific *power* or work *capacity*', and that, as an attribute of 'labour', it indicates its value 'in advance'. The value of 'qualification', in fact, far from being evaluated in terms of its efficacy within the labour process (as happens for labour power, whose quality, resulting from the processes of schooling, is realised in its adaptation to the means of production), must *anticipate* – as a power or a capacity – its own implementation in the production process: 'labour should in some way precede itself, which is an absurdity: the irrationality proper of the wage-form'.[213]

---

211   Ibid.
212   ALT2. A14-02.04, p. 98.
213   ALT2. A14-02.04, p. 98.

Let me repeat what was already stated in the first part of section 5: the epistemological order of wage labour is both distinct and inseparable from that of its representation. Economic practice produces a field of distinctions whose elements are placed in both the order of the epistemology of wage labour and that of its representation (which, changing the former's form but assuming the preservation of its *content*, is a condition for its functioning). Here, then, we encounter a crucial question because the social meaning of those distinctions is essential: if the elements placed in the first order (labour power, wages, the training of labour power as a result of consumption) refer to the logic of the extortion of surplus value, to what logical structure do those of the second order ('labour', wage-form, 'qualification' as the inseparable and hierarchical attribute of 'labour', giving it value) belong? The answer is as simple as it is crucial (and this is why, referring to the changing form of the schooling process, Balibar wrote that the notion of 'qualification' is 'of an immense practical importance'):[214] explaining the exchange of equivalent commodities, the elements that compose the field of representation are placed in the imaginary logic of self-valorisation of capital. If 'labour power' refers to the mechanism of extortion of surplus value, 'labour' refers to the imaginary logic of self-valorisation of capital. It cannot be otherwise: if an exchange presents itself as taking place between commodities of the same value (so that 'labour' is exchanged for 'wage-form'), then *what is hidden by this appearance is precisely the surplus of labour power, the real element of valorisation*. Balibar writes:

> one understands how the social form of qualification functions in practice despite, or rather because of, the 'irrationality' of the wage-form of which it is an aspect. *All labour* is supposed to be paid, and it is supposed to be paid *at its value*, i.e., according to its 'quality', which is a function of the 'qualification' of the worker. In this way the surplus-value contained in the value of the commodities produced by labour appears *as created by capital*, the 'other element' of production. All distinctions between the labour necessary for the reproduction of labour power (which is actually remunerated) and *surplus labour* (which is unpaid, and appropriated without counterpart by capital) thus disappear. Thus all trace of *the exploitation* of labour, which is ultimately based on this difference, disappears. *The 'qualification' of the worker is thus, like the whole wage-form, a mechanism allowing labour power to be exploited, while this exploitation is concealed and goes unrecognised.*[215]

---

214   ALT2. A14-02.04, p. 95.
215   ALT2. A14-02.04, pp. 100–1.

The 'qualification' is an attribute that cannot be separated from the notion of 'labour', representing its true value. Value does refer to the consumption of labour power, but in the order of representation it changes form: it is the natural and coextensive effect of 'qualification'. The *entire labour process* unfolds along a series of equivalences. The wage-form dispensed by the capitalist is worth the 'labour' of the worker; the 'labour' of the worker is worth the wage-form of the capitalist. There is nothing more transparent. The workers exchange their 'labour' for the capitalist's wage (form), paid according to its worth, that is, according to the degree of the 'qualification'. Therefore, the notion of 'qualification' conceals the distinction between the labour that is necessary for the reproduction of labour power ('which is actually remunerated') and surplus labour ('which is unpaid, and appropriated by capital with no compensation') as an explanatory distinction of the real valorisation of capital if it is true that, by determining the value of 'labour', 'qualification' determines the degree of the wage-form as an expression of that value. Surely, capital creates value: but in the *imaginary* logic that guides economic practice *as it presents itself, the value of capital is a self-valorisation*, because what that logic conceals and disregards is *the distinction* (between the labour that is necessary and surplus-labour) *that is at the root of surplus value*. This can be summed up with the following theoretical thesis: *'qualification' is an ideological notion*.

Let us now consider the second of the two features of the notion of 'qualification', as identified by Balibar: the 'extension of the wage-form'. This is inherent 'to the activity of the capitalist himself' and to all 'the functionaries of capital' in charge of 'ensuring that its authority and interests are respected in the production process'.[216] Here too the category of 'qualification' plays an essential role. Indeed, 'the growing concentration of capital' entails an increase of the complexity of tasks related to the management, supervision, direction, and organisation 'of capitalist exploitation'.[217] Balibar seems to refer to the chapter 'Interest and Profit of Enterprise' in the section 'The Division of Profit into Interest and Profit of Enterprise' of *Capital*. Here, Marx writes that 'the part of the profit that falls to the active capitalist, now as profit of enterprise, appears to derive exclusively from the operations or functions that he performs with the capital in the reproduction process'.[218] The functions of supervision and management *present themselves* as a different kind of labour in their function but equivalent in their position in the production process, 'so that the labour of

---

216   ALT2. A14-02.04, p. 102.
217   Ibid.
218   Marx 1992, p. 497.

exploiting and the exploited labour',[219] far from presenting themselves – as they really are – as having opposite functions (if the wage of the latter is placed in the process of exploitation, that of the former, as a surveillance wage, is already on the side of profit), 'both appear identical as labour. The labour of exploiting is just as much labour as exploited labour'. And if the 'labour' of the worker is always 'qualified' labour, the same appears to be true of the capitalist's 'labour'. Balibar is performing the same theoretical gesture found in the exposition of the first feature of the notion of 'qualification': there, considered as an attribute of 'labour', it was instrumental to the concealment of surplus labour; now, for the same reason, it is instrumental to the concealment of the specificity of the entrepreneur's work (as exploitative labour, whose supervisory wage, based on the capitalist mode of production, is a constitutive and integral part of profit). He explains:

> the category of qualification necessarily has the first role: it has the function of making the 'labour' of supervision and management appear as *a job like others* (therefore remunerated by a wage like the others) and at the same time *a job above the others* (therefore remunerated by a higher wage than the others). A job among others (therefore of comparable 'value'): i.e., a job with a specific qualification (any qualification implies specialisation). That is to say, a specific qualification of the 'job' in question (if we analyse this position we discover a considerable amount of *responsibility*, a burden that everyone knows is heavy to bear, exhausting for the human labour power). Let us understand a specific qualification of the 'worker' in question (let us analyse the *competence* he needs – it is a natural necessity! – we can see that he needs a particular highly specialised *training*). A job above others: since the competence and knowledge needed to *direct* the work of others necessarily requires a higher qualification.[220]

But that is not all, because the extension of the wage-form that accompanies that of 'qualification' does not pertain only to the 'labour' of surveillance of the capitalist: 'the trend in capitalist societies is that all socially recognised activities are thus "labour", to which specific "qualifications" correspond, justifying specific "wages"'.[221] The determinateness of 'qualification', insofar as it determines 'labour', also determines its wage-form. This is a formal procedure

---

219   Marx 1992, p. 453.
220   ALT2. A14-02.04, p. 104.
221   Ibid.

involving *all* social practices, even if 'if their contents are profoundly different and even antagonistic', as is the case with exploited labour or the labour
that exploits, that is a formal process of extension because the relations of production are extensive (at least in a tendential way) in every sector of social
reality ('of their complete domination'). The extension of capital immediately
implies the extension of the wage-form (at least tendentially: 'let's call this
trend *a "generalised wage trend"*') because what capital promotes is, alongside
that of 'labour', the extension of 'qualification'.[222] *The extension of the labour
power market outlines (at least tendentially) the boundaries of the social totality
through a generalised system of 'qualifications' which provides an objective scale
of measurement of the value of 'labour' – which in turn makes the generalisation
of the wage-form tendential:* 'society appears formally (i.e., legally) as a set of
variously and unequally "qualified" workers'.[223]

6 Schooling as a 'Technical' Criterion for Measuring 'Qualification' and as a Principle for Establishing Individual Attitudes

In the previous section, immediately before the analysis of the notion of 'qualification', I suggested that the school-form is the dominant factor of economic
practice, since it can be placed in the order of representation. Indeed, if 'labour'
is always qualified, and if this 'qualification' is what determines the objective
measure of the wage-form, *then the school-form, as it is presented, is what directs the exchange relationship, because it functions as the objective measurement
criterion of 'qualification'* (we will soon see why). Not only is the school-form,
as it is presented, the material condition of the constitution of 'qualification',
but, more radically, *it is also the condition of possibility of contractual exchange.*
If there is no 'labour' without 'qualification' then there can be no exchange
without the school-form: indeed, the removal of the latter – taking away not
only the material possibility of obtaining a 'qualification' (as its constitutive
instance) but, above all the (supposed) objective criterion of its measurement –
*would also take away the wage-form itself, being an effect the grade of the quali-
fication.* Balibar is clear about this:

> schooling, the existence of a social school system, is an instrument for the
> 'objective' definition of qualifications and for the distribution of individu-

---

222   ALT2. A14-02.04, p. 105.
223   Ibid.

als on the scale of qualifications, which is indispensable for the stipulation of employment contracts and the generalisation of waged labour.[224]

*The school-form, as a process of the formation of labour power, insofar as it
appears as a process of constitution and objective measurement of the individual
'qualification' of 'labour', is also the principle of economic practice because, as it
presents itself, the value of 'labour' is the value of its 'qualification'.*

Balibar, however, writes that the school-form 'is an instrument [*un instrument*] for the "objective" definition of qualifications' and not 'the instrument'
[*le instrument*]. In fact, this is made explicit: 'schooling is not the *only* system
that fulfils this function'.[225]

The criterion of 'qualification', in fact, can be guaranteed while the employment contract is stipulated, both as the result of 'a "test" which the capitalist
designs according to his particular interests and the internal standards of his
company'; and as the result of 'a "training" (learning) process within the company, conducted and assessed according to its particular standards'.[226] But that
is not all. The 'qualification' can also be determined 'with the help of psycho-
technical tests, incorporated into the institutions of "vocational guidance" and
"scientific organisation of work"' and placed at all levels of the scale of production: *tests* for skilled workers, *tests* for junior officials, and *tests* for managers,
used to identify their 'leadership skills, entrepreneurship, profit orientation,
etc.'.[227] These are measurement criteria that share both the function and the
'objective' trait of this function with the school-form ('they are valid for any
individual; they are "scientifically controlled", etc.').[228]

And yet, these measurement systems are only *partial* systems 'whose scope
is doubly limited': they are limited to a *specific* unit of production, enterprise
or administration (i.e., the space of that measurement is only the space of the
enterprise that adopts that measurement) and, precisely for this reason, they
are limited to *certain* levels of the scale of qualifications (i.e., the measurement
is conceived only as functional to those units of production).

On the contrary, the capitalist labour market – and this is Balibar's point –
requires a system that (at least tendentially) could be 'doubly general'. First,
this is because the 'free' workers, with a certain periodicity, are relocated to the
labour market. This means that they are periodically disconnected from the

224   ALT2. A14-02.04, p. 106.
225   Ibid.
226   Ibid.
227   ALT2. A14-02.04, p. 107.
228   Ibid.

individual unit of production (they are 'not attached to a particular company') and, consequently, are periodically forced to evaluate their 'qualification' on that market through a measurement criterion that is necessarily placed *above* the particular measuring methods of companies.[229]

Second, the measurement system must be general – i.e., it must extend to the *entire* hierarchical scale of 'qualifications' (and not only to certain levels of this scale, as is necessarily the case for the company that adopts its own measurement) – because it is only within this scale that a 'value' can be attributed to each 'qualification' (including that required by the company), which is therefore hierarchically determined by comparing the various 'qualifications', placed within a the general measurement system.

---

229   The reason for this continuous relocation of the worker in the labour market is linked, for Marx, to the continuous development of the technical and technological base of big industry. But 'Schools' and *Capital* put a different emphasis on the generality of the education system. For 'Schools', the *generality* of education *pertains to a criterion of measuring 'qualifications'*, which is necessarily placed above the individual units of production (the new employment of the worker cannot be contractualised and measured with the criteria of the productive unit that he has abandoned); for Marx, on the other hand, the *generality* of education refers to *the generality of the labour activities themselves* (i.e., their variations) made possible by education and that are brought about by large-scale industry (*contradictorily*): the generalisation of the possible labour activities of the individual worker, although representing 'a matter of life or death' for large-scale industry, tends in fact to the abolition of the old division of labour. Marx wrote that 'large-scale industry tore aside the veil that concealed from men their own social process of production and turned the various spontaneously divided branches of production into riddles, not only to outsiders but even to the initiated. Its principle, which is to view each process of production in and for itself, and to resolve it into its constituent elements without looking first at the ability of the human hand to perform the new processes, brought into existence the whole of the modern science of technology. The varied, apparently unconnected, and petrified forms of the social production process were now dissolved into conscious and planned applications of natural science, divided up systematically in accordance with the particular useful effect aimed at in each case ... Modern industry never views or treats the existing form of a production process as the definitive one. Its technical basis is therefore revolutionary, whereas all earlier modes of production were essentially conservative. By means of machinery, chemical processes and other methods, it is continually transforming not only the technical basis of production but also the functions of the worker and the social combinations of the labour process. At the same time, it thereby also revolutionizes the division of labour within society, and incessantly throws masses of capital and of workers from one branch of production to another. Thus largescale industry, by its very nature, necessitates variation of labour, fluidity of functions, and mobility of the worker in all directions. But on the other hand, in its capitalist form it reproduces the old division of labour with its ossified particularities ... large-scale industry, through its very catastrophes, makes the recognition of variation of labour and hence of the fitness of the worker for the maximum number of different kinds of labour into a question of life and death. This pos-

It is precisely the school-form that, with respect to partial measurement systems, represents this generality: 'this explains why the *fundamental* method for defining "qualifications" has historically been the school system, which has the advantage of this double generality over all others'.[230] The school's measurement system does not wholly replace those employed by businesses. Between the two there is not a relationship of exclusion but rather a foundational one (indeed, 'all partial systems actually work *on the basis* of the basic system, the school system') both from the point of view of the *results* of schooling ('hence the requirement to be able to read and write in order to enter the selection tests to the inclusion of school diplomas as "points" among others in the scale of tests for hiring "managers"'),[231] and from that of the implementation, by the partial systems, of '*practical notions* that are attached to schooling: notion of knowledge, individual performance, *ability*'.[232]

The school, therefore, is the fundamental factor for the measurement of 'qualification'. If, as seen in the previous section, the degree of 'qualifications' determines the tier of the wage-form (that is, its 'value'), then 'schooling is thus always organised in a "complete" system, parallel to the system of qualifications, which covers (at least potentially) the entire range of specialisations and the entire hierarchy of possible "training" during a given period'.[233] The school as an objective measure and material principle of 'qualification' organises itself as a complete system because the system of 'qualifications' is complete as a

---

sibility of varying labour must become a general law of social production, and the existing relations must be adapted to permit its realization in practice. That monstrosity, the disposable working population held in reserve, in misery, for the changing requirements of capitalist exploitation, must be replaced by the individual man who is absolutely available for the different kinds of labour required of him; the partially developed individual, who is merely the bearer of one specialized social function, must be replaced by the totally developed individual, for whom the different social functions are different modes of activity he takes up in turn. One aspect of this process of transformation, which has developed spontaneously from the foundation provided by largescale industry, is the establishment of technical and agricultural schools. Another is the foundation of *ecoles d'enseignement professionnel*, in which the children of the workers receive a certain amount of instruction in technology and in the practical handling of the various implements of labour'. Marx 1992, pp. 616–19. On the omnilateral development of the inclinations and aptitudes of the individual, cf. *infra*, note 243. On the historical placement of vocational schools in the context of class-based school education, cf. above, Chapter 2, §6. On the contradictory relationship between education and capital (a question closer to Gorz than to Balibar), cf. above, Chapter 1, §4.

230   ALT2. A14-02.04, p. 108.
231   Ibid.
232   ALT2. A14-02.04, pp. 108–9.
233   ALT2. A14-02.04, pp. 109–10.

hierarchical system which hierarchically determines the value of 'work'. Once again: 'through schooling, any specialisation appears within a hierarchy, any hierarchical superiority is justified as a specialisation'.[234]

And yet it is necessary to ask: if it is clear that the school is, as it presents itself, a dispenser of 'qualifications' (it is their material cause just as, in fact, it is the material cause of the formation of labour power), *why* should it also function as the criterion of measurement of those qualifications?

The answer is simple: just take a step back and consider the first bourgeois ideological representation of the school that Balibar had identified in the first chapter of 'Schools'.[235] There, it was said that 'it is a technical necessity to entrust to a specialised, autonomous institution this well-defined function, distinct from the others, which is teaching, training, education'.[236] So the school-form is the fundamental criterion of measurement because, as it presents itself, *what it dispenses is given technically (or so it claims): the distribution of 'qualifications' is a technical distribution that takes place within its unit.* The 'qualifications' should be considered as characterised by 'objective, codifiable differences of a "technical" nature to which schooling essentially gives the basis of differences in *"knowledge"*'.[237] And if a 'qualification' is a 'labour qualification', then 'schooling prefigures and prepares an organisation of labour in which all the posts appear as technical posts, "labour" posts distinguished by a certain complexity of knowledge' – a technically determinate knowledge – ('from its "minima" to its "maxima"') which, within the labour market, will thus determine the wage-form.[238] The technicality of its (alleged) division is the foundation of its objective measurement: every 'qualification' that is dispensed is already a 'qualification' placed on an (allegedly) objective measurement scale for the (alleged) technicality of its distribution. The school can both guarantee the 'qualifications' (as that which is materially responsible for their constitution) and be the objective (technical) criterion of their hierarchy because it is characterised by a technical division. It is the very fact of presenting itself as an instance of a technical nature that allows it to measure technically, in the act of constitutive distribution, the (alleged) objective complexity of distributed knowledge.

And if 'qualification' is, on the one hand, a merely technical 'qualification' and, on the other, an inseparable attribute of 'labour', then the process of

---

234   ALT2. A14-02.04, p. 110.
235   Cf. above, §1.
236   ALT2. A14-02.03, p. 10.
237   ALT2. A14-02.04, p. 110.
238   ALT2. A14-02.04, p. 107.

schooling, as an allegedly technical process, justifies (and conceals) the distribution of future workers 'in the social division of labour, which then never
appears in its true function'.[239] This is a distribution which, as an effect 'of
the development of capitalist relations of exploitation', still appears to be
'the product of an autonomous mechanism, apparently quite independent of
exploitation and even prior to its possibility'.

But let us look at it from the other side, namely those who receive an education. By entering school (as it presents itself), they join the process of technical
distribution of the 'qualification'. If, as we have just seen, next to the transmitted object, the scale of the 'qualifications' ('from its "minima" to its "maxima"')
is hierarchically structured because of the technical nature of the transmission, on the side of the subject the student assimilates a 'qualification' on the
basis of a natural aptitude and competence towards a job whose 'value' is variable because the technical complexity of the 'qualification' he must assimilate
is variable: 'this is precisely the outcome of schooling: to build up individual
"aptitudes" and to record them. To make the individual the *owner*, to officially
attribute them to him'.[240] The school (socially) constitutes aptitudes for labour,
and *it is only on the basis of this (social) constitution that an alleged technical
distribution of 'qualifications' is given.* The system of 'qualifications' mirrors the
system of individual aptitudes towards labour ('the school system is represented as adequately corresponding, (at least potentially), to an objective official
representation of job or worker categories').[241] But, one might object, if the
aptitude to work is the condition of possibility for the assimilation and the
technical transmission of 'qualifications', then it seems logical that it must be
something already constituted (as a natural fact). There is no contradiction:
the school can identify and discover work aptitudes because, in a circular process, it is that which (socially) constitutes them: 'the schooling process can
"detect" (or believe it detects) aptitudes, with the best of intentions, *because it
is responsible for their production – indeed it does not produce anything else'.*[242]
This is a way of saying that it is precisely the apparent identification of work
aptitudes (construed as natural facts) *that hides the sociality of their constitution:*[243]

---

239   ALT2. A14-02.04, p. 111. On the social division see above, §1.
240   ALT2. A14-02.04, p. 112.
241   ALT2. A14-02.04, p. 110.
242   ALT2. A14-02.04, p. 114.
243   The question of the link between 'natural' attitudes and education is by no means new.
      For example, in the twentieth section of *The Principles of Communism*, written in Novem-
      ber 1847 (two months before the Manifesto), Engels writes that the disappearance of the
      division of labour (or of society into classes) will necessarily lead to a labour that, undi-

it is clear here how the specifically bourgeois notion of 'human nature' is the product *par excellence* of a social process, of the functioning of a social form necessary for the existence of capitalist relations of production.[244]

The school constitutes and measures 'qualifications' and work aptitudes: it presents itself as that which discovers them, but is actually the foundation of their *distribution*. The system of 'qualifications' corresponds, for a genuine preestablished harmony, to the system of individual aptitudes; the constitution of the former corresponds to the *simultaneous* constitution of the latter.

We can break down Balibar's argument into a series of steps:

---

vided, will therefore be grounded on the omnilaterality of individual attitudes, since that division promotes precisely their unilateral character (it 'makes one a peasant, another a cobbler, a third a factory worker, a fourth a stock-market operator'). It is particularly interesting to note that, for Engels, the decisive role for the realisation of omnilaterality is played precisely by *an education combined with undivided productive work, that is, industrial education*: 'education will enable young people quickly to familiarize themselves with the whole system of production and to pass from one branch of production to another in response to the needs of society or their own inclinations. It will, therefore, free them from the one-sided character which the present day division of labour impresses upon every individual. Communist society will, in this way, make it possible for its members to put their comprehensively developed faculties to full use'. Engels 2020, pp. 35–6. On the pedagogical implications of this passage, consider Manacorda's comment: 'education, being "industrial" – that is, a union of education and productive labour or "Fabrikation", have as its method an internship carried out on the entire production system – will pursue the purpose of removing young people from all unilateralism and developing them omnilaterally, with the practical result of making them willing to alternate their activities, not only in accordance with the needs of society, but also with their personal inclinations. At the root of this pedagogical choice lies the historical hypothesis of the division of labour, and the consequent division not only of society into classes but also of man himself, closed as he is within his own unilaterality. It is also necessary to recover the unity of human society as a whole, and the omnilaterality of the individual man, through a perspective that unites, even if just by suggesting it, individual and social ends, man and society'. Manacorda 1966, p. 8. Clearly, the theoretical paradigm of 'Schools' rejects such a thesis, since, as in the case of Bourdieu and the notion of culture, Engels's theoretical gesture begins from the notion of aptitude (or inclination) which is, insofar as it is constituted socially, a purely ideological notion. In this sense, it would be interesting to bring together the thesis on the ideological character of the notion of aptitude to what Marx writes in one of the notes (published posthumously, in 1925) to *Wage Labour and Capital* (a text that is the result of a series of conferences held in December 1947, before the Union of German Workers in Brussels). For a detailed examination of the pedagogical question in Marx (not at all reducible to the note in Wage Labour and Capital, as can also be understood from footnote 229) and Marxism in general, see Manacorda 1971a and 1971b.

244 ALT2. A14-02.04, pp. 114–15.

First: an aptitude is presented as something discovered and verified but it is actually a constituted product and, above all, it is an aptitude *for* acquiring capacities and competencies (these terms, along with 'aptitude', had already been employed by Balibar in relation to work: 'a work *capacity*, a *"competence"* or an *"aptitude"* to work'):[245]

> schooling constantly *discovers and highlights* individual aptitudes, which it considers to be 'learning aptitudes', i.e., aptitudes for acquiring abilities or competence. The more schooling develops, the more obvious this emphasis becomes. Today's school systems represent an increasingly pure realisation of this trend.[246]

Second: On the basis of that discovery (i.e., of that production), the school directs users towards a corresponding training:

> according to this observation, it [the school] *selects* and *orients* individuals. Hence the essential functions of the mechanism of schooling: examinations, competitions, and tests, which appeared to us from the outset as a characteristic feature of the school-form.[247]

Third, according to the aptitudes that have been identified and to the orientation that follows, the school is then ready to distribute (so-called) knowledge which, at the time of entry into the labour market, will be represented by 'qualifications':

> at the same time, it provides individuals with the knowledge, skills, etc., according to which their abilities can be recognised: the element in which, by a preestablished harmony ... they manage *to reveal themselves*, like a chemical reagent suddenly reverses the presence of acid in its dosage. It sees its results in terms of its own pre-existing programmes.[248]

Finally, the knowledge distributed according to the aptitudes that have been identified (which is to say, constituted) is in itself an (explicitly constituted) aptitude that should be practiced and put to work in the 'labour' market (as 'qualifications'). More precisely, based on the second and third steps, it could

---

245   ALT2. A14-02.04, p. 112.
246   ALT2. A14-02.04, p. 113.
247   ALT2. A14-02.04, pp. 113–14.
248   ALT2. A14-02.04, p. 114.

be said that the schooling process tailors the individual skills, determined by the acquired knowledge, on the basis of an allegedly natural attitude that is simply identified but which is actually socially produced:

> finally, as school knowledge, whether 'general' or 'specialised', *is itself only an aptitude*, which precedes an eventual implementation 'in life', 'in practice', according to the effect of what we have called school separation, schooling produces 'aptitudes'.[249]

Let me briefly summarise:
1. The degree of a 'qualification' determines its 'value' ('the existence of a wage hierarchy always refers directly to a hierarchy of "qualification" of work').[250]

---

249   ALT2. A14-02.04, p. 114.
250   ALT2. A14-02.04, p. 96. Now that all the theoretical elements of the analysis have been presented, it is possible to shed further light on the causal relationship between the 'qualification' and its own 'value'. If wage labour is the specific form of the capitalist mode of production and if, as Balibar says, the capitalist mode of production as well as the proper functioning of its relations of production 'require and have historically imposed the *schooling* of all its agents', then it seems clear that the school, as a factor in the formation of labour power (note: *not* 'labour') and, therefore, its value (note: *not* 'value' in general), is an *effect* of modes of production, which, in turn, are the *cause* of its position. In other words: schooling is a necessary effect of wage labour, since it is one of the factors necessary for the reproduction of labour-power, which must adapt (through skill and handiness) to the means of production. But things, as they appear, seem to be reversed: in fact, *it is the school, as an instrument of objective definition of 'qualifications', that is the cause of the wage-form* – to the extent that, as seen when exploring the first feature of the 'qualification', the degree of the first varies in accordance with the second. Balibar states it explicitly, at the beginning of the third chapter of 'Schools': '*schooling is an effect of wage labour. Or, more precisely: the development of the school-form is an effect of the development of wage labour, and, in turn, a condition for the existence of the wage-form*'. Note the terms that are employed: first, when we talk about school as an effect, we talk about wage labour; later (but this 'later' is anything but chronological), when we speak of the school as a condition of existence, we speak of wage-form. It is clear that the simultaneity *en retour* of the different position of schooling does not entail any contradiction since it refers to the distinction between the order of the epistemology of wage labour and that of its representation: in the first order, schooling as a factor in the reproduction of labour power is an effect of wage labour; at the same time, in the second (the two orders, as we have seen several times, are distinct but inseparable) the school, as a criterion for the objectivity of 'qualification', becomes the cause of the wage-form. This thesis suggests an important conclusion: if it is true that, in fact, it is the capitalist who controls the relationship with the worker, *as the exchange presents itself it is instead the 'qualified' worker who, through their schooling, guides that relationship*.

2.   The measure of a 'qualification' occurs in the very act of its (alleged) tech-
     nical distribution (it directly refers to 'objective, codifiable differences of
     a "technical" nature to which schooling essentially gives the basis of dif-
     ferences in *"knowledge"*).[251]
3.   The distribution itself is grounded on the (allegedly) natural discovery of
     individual attitudes (which are actually socially constituted) leading to an
     (allegedly) technically divided labour, and to the bespoke production of
     individual skills, determined by the knowledge that was received on the
     basis of the discovery/constitution of aptitudes.
This leads to a simple conclusion:

> the social objectivity necessary to define the 'value' of work, to 'qualify'
> it, is based, first, on the 'natural aptitudes' that schooling discovers in the
> individual and, second, on the 'individual skills' that schooling produces
> and measures.[252]

The progression is: (alleged) discovery of individual aptitudes; (alleged) technical distribution of (alleged) knowledge, transmitted in the context of an
(allegedly) unified instance, based on that discovery; *ad hoc* production of
individual skills, i.e., 'qualifications' determined by the knowledge that was
acquired in the schooling process; exchange of 'qualifications' whose measurement criteria are established in the very act of their (alleged) technical
distribution; exchange of 'qualifications' whose 'value' is defined by the technical complexity of its composition. In short, as Balibar puts it: 'the social
objectivity necessary for the definition of the "value" of work and its "qualification" is always grounded on the "natural aptitudes" that schooling discovers in the individual'. Without natural aptitudes there would be no 'value'
since there would be no occasion to technically distribute 'qualifications' as
well as no criterion to measure value. The technicality of the distribution of
knowledge is a condition for its measurement and it serves as a response to
the natural aptitudes of the students. The aptitude is the foundation of the
objectivity of 'value' because, ultimately, it decrees the technical complexity
of the 'qualification' to be assimilated into the technical process of their assimilation.

   The aptitudes appear to be natural so that 'schooling appears to be what
gives content to individual equality and freedom'; or, to say it otherwise, 'all

---

251   ALT2. A14-02.04, p. 110.
252   ALT2. A14-02.04, p. 114.

class differences are obscured, and replaced by individual differences'.[253] The supposed naturalness of individual aptitudes conceals, within the educational process itself, the reality of the social composition of the students, or the fact that, ultimately, the measure of a 'qualification' responds to the existence of the relations of production: based on individual aptitudes, 'the notion of "qualific-ation", which thus makes it possible to translate into practice the domination of capital over labour-power, combines the idea of specialisation and that of hierarchy'.[254]

But there is more. We have already seen, in § 5, how the notion of 'qualific-ation' refers to the irrationality of the wage-form, by expressing the 'value' of a commodity (precisely, the 'qualification') which, sold 'freely' (and initially) by the worker, necessarily anticipates its 'implementation "in life", "in practice"', in the process of production: labour', to be sold as an equivalent commodity, and necessarily has 'a material existence, however separate, independent of the worker's person, and prior to the use of the commodity, i.e., to labour itself'.[255] Such 'labour', in other words, 'should precede itself in some way, which is a con-tradiction in terms', while the worker 'must appear, at the time of the contract, as the "owner of the work" he provides, when the work does not yet exist'.[256] In this sense, it was said that at the moment of the 'free' stipulation of the employ-ment contract (the worker is legally sanctioned as owning their 'qualification'), the worker appears as the owner of 'a determinate power [*puissance*] or capa-city [*capacité*] for work' which, precisely 'prefigures the work itself, and which indicates in advance its "value", in view of a determinate wage that will be "equi-valent" (in monetary terms) to this value'.[257]

This last point leads to the identification of a further imposition – in addi-tion to that of 'qualification' – which is linked to the schooling process. First of all, a *capacité* results from the scholastic process of constitutive identifica-tion of attitudes for work. Here, in the theoretical context of this individuation, Balibar uses the same terms he employed when discussing the irrationality of the wage-form: 'the worker appears as the owner of a capacity, and himself as a work capacity, a "skill" [*compétence*] or "aptitude" for labour (for labour of dif-ferent "value")'. In short, if until now we have been told that skills and aptitudes are only a mere foreshadowing of 'labour', *we now know that such notions are already a socially defined product.*

---

253 ALT2. A14-02.04, p. 110.
254 Ibid.
255 ALT2. A14-02.04, p. 98.
256 ALT2. A14-02.04, p. 111.
257 ALT2. A14-02.04, p. 99.

By way of conclusion, one further point should be stressed. Along with attitudes, the school produces 'the "duty" to materialise, and to spend itself little
by little in labour'.[258] The school produces the attitude and, simultaneously,
the sense of duty that leads to its implementation. If the attitude is something
natural, the imperative to realise it will be just as natural. To repeat a passage I quoted above: 'anyone who does not possess the means of production
or interest-bearing property titles is forced to work for a living, in the form of
a recognised activity of social utility'.[259] From this vantage point, the double
imposture of the schooling process is revealed: by concealing surplus-labour
through the notion of 'qualification' – and by means of the idea of a 'natural
aptitude' or, better, the imposition of a duty to realise it through labour – *it
obfuscates the material imperative to join the process of production* by offering
the ostensible reason that *they have to realise their own nature*. Balibar explains
that:

> we know that the worker is simply forced by material necessity to earn a
> living for himself and his family, and to sell his labour power on the cap
> italist labour market. So, we see that the system of previous economic,
> legal, and ideological forms – from the wage-form to the school-form –
> has a very remarkable mode of operation, essential to the reproduction of
> capitalist relations of production: it represents as a duty what is already a
> constraint.[260]

In short, if it is true that 'qualification' conceals the fundamental role played by
the distinction between necessary labour and surplus labour for the valorisation of capital, and if only the school-form can function as the technical unit
of measurement of 'qualifications' according to aptitudes, then, as it presents
itself, the school-form as a social form is the dominant apparatus. This is not
just because, as we have seen throughout the second chapter, it is the apparatus dedicated to the ideological reproduction of the relations of production,
but also because it intervenes directly in the logic of extortion (concealing,
through a commodity that is believed to be equivalent, the excess expenditure of labour power) and in that of constraint (concealing, through the duty
to materialise one's own attitude, the material need to enter the production
process). It directly intervenes in economic practice itself. *The school is the dominant apparatus for ideological reproduction, because it masks and conceals –*

258   ALT2. A14-02.04, p. 112.
259   ALT2. A14-02.04, p. 72.
260   ALT2. A14-02.04, p. 72.

both on the side of the object (by means of the idea of 'qualification', which 'des-
pite its immense practical importance, is in fact an illusory notion')[261] *and on the*
side of the subject (by means of the idea of 'individual aptitude', 'a specifically
bourgeois notion', which is the 'product of a social process') – the fundamental
character of wage labour: exploitation.[262]

Thus, at the same time as the exploitation of labour power represses the
very notion of labour power, the worker is identified with a profoundly
illusory object, with a fictitious 'personality' which has only an imaginary status, at the level of the ideological representations generated by
the objective mechanism of the wage-form; this object is an 'aptitude' or
'capacity' for labour. It is both a destination and, as necessity dictates (or
even virtue), a disposition to labour. Or it is labour itself in the form of a
capacity, an 'ability' to be realised.[263]

---

261   ALT2. A14-02.04, p. 117.
262   ALT2. A14-02.04, pp. 114–15.
263   ALT2. A14-02.04, p. 113.

Outlines of the History and Geography of Class-based School Education

Introduction

The final written product of 'Schools' is a set of fifty-three typewritten pages that comprise three notes on the geography and history of the class-based school. Baudelot and Macherey wrote these notes between 31 October and 3 November 1969, six months after the chapters Balibar authored.

The first note (dated 31 October) outlines the background presuppositions of the other two, which are dedicated to geography (dated 1 November) and history (dated 3 November) respectively. Before commenting briefly on the point that most concerns us here, we can examine the first note in its entirety:

A false concept: mode of education
A new concept: mode of ideologisation

In the work so far, we have used the term mode of education, which is an equivocal concept. There was implicitly a metaphorical relationship between mode of education and mode of production. However, the idea of education cannot be placed on the same level as production; in particular, it cannot serve to systematise the representation of a set of modes, since it is specific to a particular mode of production: the CMP [Capitalist Mode of Production]. Hence an implicit contradiction in our reasoning: we strive to destroy the eternal ideology of pedagogy but we find it again in the concept that was used to analyse and distinguish pedagogical ideologies. Therefore, we must remove this concept from all our demonstrations.

The concept must be removed, but the correct reasoning which it indicated must be retained: the place of the school apparatus in a capitalist social formation is determined, and this determination must have an equivalent in other modes of production. This determination consists, materially, in the articulation between the ideological state apparatuses. According to the modes of production, the nomenclature of these apparatuses varies (thus the school apparatus does not have to appear in the analysis of the AMP [Ancient Mode of Production] or even of the FMP [Feudal Mode of Production]). Above all, the relation (of domination) between the existing apparatuses is fundamentally different in the FMP, the Church apparatus dominates, relying on the Family apparatus (cf. forthcoming note): this domination excludes the constitution of an organised school apparatus, which is moreover in no way required. In the CMP, this relationship is completely transformed. The emergence and constitution of an organised school apparatus that tends to occupy a dominant position, i.e., to control the functioning of all other apparatuses: this is the fundamental meaning of the generalised schooling process.

It is therefore necessary to constitute a new concept which would help us to unify this reasoning. Within each mode of production (and under its determination), we shall thus speak of a specific mode of ideologisation, which consists of nothing other than the relationship between the ideological apparatuses.

NB. The fact that the concept of ideologisation is emphasised in this way does not present any of the disadvantages that arose in connection with the notion of education: from a materialist point of view, human beings are indeed 'ideological animals', but not animals that need to be educated (education [*éducation*] being the antithesis of training [*dressage*], a representation that is only valid within humanist ideology, and indeed founds it).

What does ideologisation consist of, or in other words, what is the content of each mode of ideologisation? These questions can only be answered in the case of class societies: the formation of the quality of labour power takes place within the framework of submission to the dominant ideology. It is the connection and the relationship of these two processes which constitutes ideologisation. This is a relation of domination: effect 1 is produced under effect 2. The content of a mode of ideologisation is thus the production of what we have so far called the double effect (the concept of double effect is thus deduced).

NB. Two consequences: 1. Ideologisation has, as its material support, the formation of the quality of labour power. The position of non-workers in relation to a mode of ideologisation can thus be derived: a mode of ideologisation functions first of all for the bearers of labour power. / This is absolutely true for the CMP, see Part I, Ch. 2. / The demonstration remains to be done for the other modes of production.

2. The junction between the two processes takes place at the level of language acquisition, which is the place of production of the double effect, the place of ideologisation. Hence the specific and primordial role of the question of literacy.[1]

This passage offers a rectification of what in several different ways has been called 'the principle of contemporaneity between modes of education and modes of production'. In the preceding analyses all of its special applications were measured against the general thesis that any change of the mode of production provokes a corresponding modification of the mode of education – which implies that a given mode of production always and necessarily refers to a certain mode of education. Once again,[2] its most straightforward formulation can be found in the second chapter of 'Schools': 'each mode of production that becomes historically dominant develops its own *mode of education*, which in turn becomes a powerful instrument of its extension and historical domination'.[3]

This is a formally imprecise principle. In the framework of a regime of practical-theoretical equivalence, it is impossible to draw a horizontal line between the two, as if the position of the first structurally referred to the position of the second and vice versa. The thesis is clear and does not leave room for alternative interpretations: 'the idea of education can never be equated with that of production'. It was perhaps operative in the analysis carried out in the 'work so far', just as – as we will see again later – it is operative for the historians of the scholastic institution: a misunderstanding ('the concept ... was equivocal') dictated by a (ideological) perspectival error that concerns what first Balibar[4] and then later Baudelot and Macherey[5] called *antediluvian forms of education*, as well as its *primitive and transitory forms*. We will examine both in more detail below.

It is certainly ironic that, after producing a concept of education, the authors of 'Schools' fell prey to its suggestion. Is there a better way to ascertain the theoretical correctness of such a concept, that is, to test its practical and ideological pervasiveness? Indeed, the idea of education engenders a misunderstanding, dictated by a perspectival error: the substitution of a simple *logic of backward causation* (the educational form of the past is only a projective

1   ALT2. A14-02.05 (A), pp. 1–2.
2   Cf. above, Chapter 3, § 2.
3   ALT2. A14-02.04, p. 55.
4   Cf. above, Chapter 3, § 2.
5   Cf. *infra*, § 3.

production of the present – the *only* moment when we can really speak of education) in favour of a logic of position (the form of the past, precisely because of that undetected backward causation, appears to be an eternal form of education – 'the eternal ideology of pedagogy'). This is what the authors of 'Schools' had identified: the contemporaneity of certain modes of education to certain modes of production – that is, the eternity of education in general (as a heuristic concept of its specific modes).[6]

Here, however, it is not a question of claiming that such non-equivalence of the relationship between the mode of production and the mode of education – the very impossibility of placing them 'on the same level' – would concern *the simultaneity of their determination*, as if mere traces of the ancient or feudal mode of education (specific modes of the ancient or feudal modes of production) lurk under the capitalist mode of production and education. In other words, when considering the 'principle of contemporaneity between modes of education and modes of production', *it is not the notion of 'contemporaneity' which needs to be rectified*, as if, again, some kind of asynchronous persistence of a form of education lurked in this principle which denies the possibility of the simultaneous relationship between certain modes (of production and education). In fact, it is quite the opposite. *It is precisely the idea of education* (as well as, *a fortiori*, that of schooling) *that has no value for the production of an argument on the modes of reproduction and education of labour power in general* (it is, from the theoretical vantage point of this generality, 'a false concept'). Or, more precisely, we should say that the expository value of that idea, *being a specific form of the mode of ideologisation in general* ('a new concept'), is limited to the capitalist mode of production. Again, there is no interpretive leeway: the idea of education 'is specific to a particular mode of production: the CMP'. Although every mode of production corresponds to a mode of education (of labour power), *education itself, within the framework of the ancient or feudal mode of production, does not exist* ('the school apparatus does not have to be part of the MPA's analysis or even the MPF's'). And if it seems to exist, it does so only retroactively (as an 'antediluvian form'), from the vantage point of the capitalist mode of production (in which, once again, education conveyed by the process of schooling is the real ideological factor: something which does not invalidate the analysis conducted so far).

It has been said that, of the 'principle of contemporaneity', only the notion of 'contemporaneity' remains. Every determinate mode of production is in fact a condition of its own 'nomenclature', and each nomenclature is composed of an

---

6   Cf. above, Chapter 3, § 2, point 3.

'articulation between the ideological apparatuses of the state' which are hetero-geneous yet unified by a dominant ideological apparatus – or, to turn it around, in general, in the tendential control of all other apparatuses the dominance of the dominant one flows horizontally from the whole of their articulations. This means that if any dominant ideological apparatus belongs to a determ-inate mode of production, any mode of production will have a determinate mode of ideologisation – since ideologisation in general (and this is a variation of an Althusserian thesis[7]) consists in the 'training of the quality of the labour power' in the framework of the submission to a general mode of ideologisation (a 'double effect concept').[8]

The principle of contemporaneity is therefore the 'principle of contempor-aneity between modes of ideologisation and modes of production' only insofar as a specific mode of production requires a specific kind of training of labour power (as stated in the first consequence: 'a mode of ideologisation works first for the bearers of labour power'): 'within each mode of production (and under its determination) we shall speak of a specific mode of ideologisation, which consists of nothing other than the relationship between the ideolo-gical apparatuses'. Education is the mode of ideologisation specific to the CMP, and the school is the ideological apparatus assigned to its function: the schol-astic apparatus occupies a certain dominant place in capitalist formation, and indeed it is *only* the scholastic apparatus that occupies such a dominant place.

---

7 Cf. above, Chapter 3, Introduction.
8 On the question of submission to the dominant ideology, I refer to this passage by Michel Tort, included in an unpublished text, included in *Écoles*. It is dated 16 March 1969 and titled 'Sur les effets de répression et d'idéologisation et leur rapport': 'what does it mean that ideologisa-tion is repression? It means that repression does not only manifest itself when ideologisation meets obstacles, but also in the subtle forms of non-repression declared in ideological dis-courses and practices. The problem, however, is how these conceal repression. I propose the use of a model: the lollipop model. It is clear that the practice of sucking corresponds to a social form of domination of cumbersome impulses by their circumscribed application on an autoerotically satisfying object. We observe that the recourse to this practice corresponds to the impossibility of violent repression given the age of the subject (he is not at the age of reason = the age of repression). We could then advance the hypothesis that ideology can function in a generalised way as a dummy (oral, visual, kinetic dummy, etc.), that is to say, as repression-satisfaction. It is clear that this does not only shed light on the school-forms of ideologisation, but on all the forms of ideological domination that tend to take the form of a lollipop: sports (autoplastic), television-broadcasting, advertising practices – whose import-ance for ideological domination is so considerable. It is towards this form of repression that the pedagogical-Faurian updating of the French system is directed, of which we have ana-lysed some manifestations in the primary school under the name of new pedagogy (interest in the child, spontaneity, etc.) and which must serve as an ideology for the reorganisation of the whole system'. ALT2. A14-02.01, pp. 1–2.

So, 'the relationship (of domination) between the existing apparatuses is fundamentally different in the FMP, since it is the Church apparatus that dominates'. The perspectival error, in this sense, consisted in considering the mode of education (a particular form of the mode of ideologisation in general) to be the general form of ideologisation (or of the education of labour power) of all modes of production ('from a materialist point of view, men are indeed "ideological animals", but they are certainly not animals that need to be educated'). In other modes of production there is no education and no school, just as the modes of ideologisation of the ancient or feudal modes of production do not exist in the capitalist mode. However, it is quite evident that ideological apparatuses do exist: the family (for the ancient one) and the Church (for the feudal one), *even if their existence is completely ineffective* ('this is the fundamental meaning of the process of generalised schooling').[9]

1   On the Historical-Geographical Differences in the Establishment of Schools in Three Capitalist Countries

The analysis of the geography of the class-based school of three capitalist countries – France, England, and the United States – and of the history of class-based school in general (which necessarily contains that geography), has the goal of highlighting:

1. a number of *convergences*, which can be explained by the fact that although appearing in a different order and with different forms, in all three cases the *single school* represents the highest stage of the class-based school (at least tendentially)

2. a number of *divergences* which refer to 'the specific forms taken by bourgeois democracy in these three countries, which are the effect of the specific conditions of the class struggle'.[10] The geographical diversity of the historical processes of democratisation refers to different educational processes of the class-based school. Still, the class-based school, representing the framework in which its stages of development take place, ensures that such divergences do not alter its definition but, rather, contribute to broaden it.

∴

9   On the notion, already mobilised by Balibar, of 'generalised process of scholarisation', cf. above, Chapter 3, § 5.

10   ALT2. A14-02.05 (B), p. 1.

The nature of Baudelot and Macherey's notes entails that their exposition rather than analysis can take a rather systematic form. I will therefore begin with the three forms of bourgeois democracy – assuming that in these case studies, it performs the function of politically and ideologically ensuring the hegemony of the ruling class – as well as the implications that these have on the educational process of the class-based school:

1) France. With regard to the process of democratisation, the French case is characterised by the alliance between the 'bourgeoisie and petty bourgeoisie against the privileged (aristocracy) and against the popular masses'.[11] Within the framework of this historical process, and in relation to the educational process of the class-based school, three fundamental characteristics can be identified:

   1. *the growing importance of the petty bourgeoisie* and, with it, the emergence of the scholastic question, which 'appears early on' and becomes a political stake in which the petty bourgeoisie 'is immediately involved'. With the scholastic question, the school therefore appears as a specific space with its own laws that, in its (ideological) representation, is 'where the petty bourgeoisie feels at home'.[12]

   2. the schooling process is immediately carried out under the *centralised control of the state* (I will return to the meaning of this centrality when examining the English case). Not only does the state have its 'legal monopoly' (which likely refers to the fact that the schooling process can only be sanctioned by the state and in the state) but it also exercises 'its control over the scholastic institutions' directly (likely a reference to the fact that only the state can determine the centralising forms of school reforms, in order to merge 'the scholastic institutions in a unified system');

   3. with regard to the relationship with other ideological apparatuses 'the school has simply replaced the church as the dominant ideological apparatus'.[13] *The relationship is therefore conflictual* ('from which a conflict is brought to the forefront'). The scholastic educational process is a progressive process of violent replacement of an already formed apparatus.

2) England. With regard to the process of democratisation, the English case is characterised by an alliance 'between the landed aristocracy and the

---

11   Ibid.
12   ALT2. A14-02.05 (B), p. 2.
13   Ibid.

industrial and commercial bourgeoisie'. Differently from the French case, the weight of the petty bourgeoisie in England is quite irrelevant (it has 'no role to play in the functioning of the ideological apparatus and the constitution of bourgeois democracy').[14] Within the framework of this historical process, and in relation to the educational process of the class-based school, three fundamental characteristics can be identified:

1. *the importance of the aristocracy and its ideology:* 'the school was made by and for the dominant class'. This means that if the school is an aristocratic institution, then it is *a caste school*. Although only a transitional form of the class-based school (the caste school, it will be seen later, is still a class-based school, although it is not reducible to its form realised as a single school), it 'tends to be preserved by the introduction of a number of devices of which the stock exchange system is the best example' (for this reason, 'the caste school-form represents an unparalleled obstacle to the achievement of the single school in England').[15]

2. the schooling process is realised through the state, *without being centralised*. The notion of 'centralised state', in fact, is not equivalent to that of 'state' and the fact that the former does not intervene in the educational process of the caste school does not necessarily entail the inactivity of the latter: 'one should not confuse state and centralised state'.[16] In every social formation (including the English and the American case), the school system was always 'placed under the domination and effective control of the state'. What varies, following the changing forms of the state, is only the specific form of this domination. In both England and France (and in the United States) it is the state that dominates. But in England, unlike France (though like the United States), the state does not exercise such dominion through forms of operational control, nor through legal monopoly (consider that the Ministry of National Education in England was established in 1944). Instead, it intervenes into the particular competences of 'private associations and regional authorities: both represent the power of the state'.[17] In this sense, any debate on the conflict between the public and the private 'is based on an

---

14 Ibid.
15 ALT2. A14-02.05 (B), p. 3.
16 ALT2. A14-02.05 (B), p. 2.
17 ALT2. A14-02.05 (B), p. 3.

ideological confusion (ideological and political): there is nothing in the state except the private interests of which it is the instrument'.[18]

3.   regarding its relation with other ideological apparatuses, 'the dominant position of the school apparatus is contested by the family (which imposes the school by order and controls it directly through its subsidies)'.[19]

3)   United States. With regard to the process of democratisation, the American case exhibits an 'extravagant character'. The bourgeois revolution, in fact, takes place in two moments that take 'the form of splits.' The first was the War of Independence (1775–83), when the rising bourgeoisie cuts ties with its English aristocratic origin. This is an interesting point: *the split is in fact a primarily geographical one* 'since the two classes are separated by an ocean; on this occasion, America ceases to be New England, and it becomes the New World'.[20] The second was the Civil War (1861–65). The split at that point is internal and concerns two factions: the industrial bourgeoisie of the north and the agrarian bourgeoisie of the south. Once again, this is first and foremost a geographical division. The defeat of the southern states leads to the emancipation of the blacks and, with it, to the 'constitution of a dominated class, without which the dominant class obviously cannot survive'. *In fact, they must be free in order to be exploited as labour power* (so 'black workers form the basic cell of the American working class'). In short: *after the War of Independence, the American aristocracy is pushed abroad; after the Civil War the proletariat is made foreign.* The hands of the bourgeoisie are 'free and white'. In contrast to the case of France (where the petty bourgeoisie, as the social body that poses the scholastic question, is *flanked* by the bourgeoisie as the ruling class), or the case of England (where the industrial bourgeoisie is *flanked* by the aristocracy as the social body that poses the scholastic question – as a caste school), *the American bourgeoisie is alone*: free from 'compromising and binding alliances'.[21] Hence 'the original features of American democracy':[22] to exercise its hegemony, the bourgeoisie 'does not need to make any external compromises' – which however does not mean being completely free from contradictions (which 'remain internal to the bourgeoisie, and expose its different layers'). Moreover, in addition

---

18   ALT2. A14-02.05 (B), p. 2.
19   ALT2. A14-02.05 (B), p. 3.
20   Ibid.
21   Ibid.
22   ALT2. A14-02.05 (B), p. 4.

to the 'importance of inter-individual competition (individuals compet-
ing for power and profit)', the peculiarity of the American situation gives
rise to 'particular forms of bourgeois ideology: the ideology of luck, of
the frontier, of freedom, of skills, of work, of *making money* ...'. To put
it briefly: against the myth of a state without history ('the facile image
of the New World'), American democracy should be understood as characterised by its own contradictions 'which are all symptoms of specific
forms of class struggle'.[23] As in the previous cases, within the framework
of this historical process, three fundamental characteristics pertaining to
the constitution of the school system can be identified:

1. the implementation of *a system of mass education*, necessary for the
    realisation of bourgeois hegemony. This was originally produced by
    means of supplementary measures for immigrants and, ideologic-
    ally, through the idea of an 'American nation, which can only be
    created through the school'.[24] The American school system, unlike
    the European ones (in which secondary education 'tends to preserve
    the form of a caste school'), presents itself as a single 'bloc' that, as
    far as at the end of the nineteenth century, is not split into primary
    and secondary levels. Subsequently, after World War I, 'under the
    influence of Dewey and his disciples', the apparatus takes on the
    ideological form of the *progressive school* (which along with the pre-
    paratory school, is one of the ideological forms of the class-based
    school, as we will see below).

2. the schooling process takes place through the intervention of the
    state which is, in its duties (essentially concerning control), subser-
    vient to the indications of the federal states: 'it is, as we have seen in
    relation to England, the original form of realisation of "state" power'.

3. some 'contradictions inherent in the operation of the single school'
    appear. The first relates to the scholastic practices whose conforma-
    tions correspond to the 'irregular' structure of the American state.
    The school apparatus is indeed a 'bloc', *but it does not respond to
    a geographically equivalent measure*. School practices are irredu-
    cible to each other – they welcome 'geographical disparities: by
    state; by neighbourhood; in the city and in the country ... Dispar-
    ities in the teaching of trades, in funding, in school populations'.[25]
    The second contradiction relates to the question of the performance

---

23 Ibid.
24 ALT2. A14-02.05 (B), p. 5.
25 ALT2. A14-02.05 (B), p. 5.

of the school system. Point 1 mentioned the ideological form of the progressive school, and it is precisely this kind of school that, since World War II, starts to be criticised ('by families, and leaders of the state apparatus, especially the military').[26] The complaints concern the formation of cadres of the ruling and military classes, on the assumption that '"progressive" education would lead to a waste of "talent", and to a (downward) levelling of educational standards'.[27]

2   The *école préparatoire* and the *école progressive* as Ideological Forms of the Class-Based School

The three case studies, referring to heterogeneous processes of democratisation, also refer to heterogeneous processes of formation of the class-based school, as a specific apparatus for promoting the ideology of the capitalist mode of production. And yet, the concept of a class-based school can only function as a theoretical indicator. It does not exist as such ('it is not a simple concept that refers to a single, harmonious content'),[28] or rather, it exists only in the distinct forms that actually realise it from time to time, provided that this is not understood as a simple succession of forms, as if the overcoming of one would entail the ultimate resolution of the other, in a clear horizontal progression: 'it can simply be said that at a given time and place, one of these forms is dominant; but this domination presupposes a dominated form which can always reappear, and pass from the status of an outdated form to that of the future of the school apparatus in which it continues to exist.'[29]

The class-based school is realised in two forms: the *caste school* as a transitional form (i.e., the school *of* the ruling class *for* the ruling class – consider the English example), and the *single school* as 'supreme form [*forme suprême*]' (i.e., the school *of* the ruling class *for everyone* – which, as a supreme form, is an attractor indicating the convergence of every heterogeneous educational process of the class-based school). Baudelot and Macherey's notes make extensive (and somewhat confusing) use of homonyms. For example, the caste school is a transitional form, but it is not placed into the transitional phase of the historical formation of the class-based school and is not assimilable, of this phase of transition, to its transitional forms. It is for clarity of exposition and brevity that

---

26   ALT2. A14-02.05 (B), p. 6.
27   Ibid.
28   ALT2. A14-02.05 (B), p. 7.
29   Ibid.

I therefore express the double realisation (through the transitory form of the caste school, CAS, and the supreme form of the single school, SS) of the class-based school (CBS) as a specific apparatus belonging to the capitalist mode of production (CMP) with the formula: CBS = CAS(tr.), SS(sup.) ∈ CMP. Later I will integrate this formula with other, more general ones.

As an ideological apparatus, the CBS is realised in the two forms of *preparatory school* (PRES) and *progressive school* (PROS: like the American one, at least in appearance). The notes suggest a certain symmetry between the forms: the PRES is the specific form of the CAS and the PROS is the specific form of SS. In this sense, it is possible to express this further, twofold realisation as follows: CBS = CAS tr. (PRES), SS sup. (PROS). Let us now examine the differences between these last two forms.

The idea of preparatory teaching develops around the sixteenth century, with the Jesuits (who, as Macherey argued in 'Les Mythologies Scolaires', were the professionals of separation) and is taken up, to a certain extent, in France after the Napoleonic reform (which explains why 'the French school system as a whole is itself marked by this preparatory aspect of its dominant schooling network').[30] It is a teaching for 'the ruling class as a caste' and its content focuses on 'cultural indoctrination (the Humanities)' and its institutional form is based on a 'tripartite education (cultural, technical, vocational)'. Its peculiarity (from which it derives its name) lies in the fact that it is oriented 'towards an exteriority': preparatory teaching prepares, precisely, for 'the actual exercise of hegemony by individuals belonging to the dominant class'. From this exteriority, we see 'a number of privileged themes: the cult of excellence, hierarchy, competition, creativity, distinction'. It follows that its specific effects are 'elimination and sectioning', and it promotes the 'cult of effort' and 'book worship'.[31]

Progressive teaching, on the other hand, was developed in Germany around the same time, at the urge of the Protestant tradition. If preparatory teaching promotes the ideology of culture, then progressive teaching promotes 'experience and practice'.[32] Far from being a caste-based teaching, it presents itself as a mass or 'popular teaching (*volkschule*)'. The institutional form is that of the single school (so that 'the tradition of Protestant education in Germany and the USA [through John Dewey] is part of this form'). As for the recruitment of students, progressive education – which unlike the selectiveness of

---

30   ALT2. A14-02.05 (B), p. 8.
31   Ibid.
32   ALT2. A14-02.05 (B), p. 9.

preparatory education is grounded on a formal democracy and on 'the equality of individual opportunities' – it is 'open, generous, non-selective, subject to the laws of harmonious development of abilities'. Its teachings are destined to all students because, being diversified, they are 'by definition adapted to every need'. And if preparatory teaching leaned towards the exteriority of its own end, progressive teaching 'has no other purpose than itself'. The school has nothing to prepare for, because the real world is already experienced in its current form. And yet, this only concerns its declaration: the world it claims to be is 'made from scratch' and its opening is only a particular form of separation. It is in this sense that in both preparatory and progressive schools, 'the child is waiting, but this wait takes different forms'.[33] The features of openness and non-selectivity make progressive teaching appear as an impoverished and mediocre school. It is a timeless school, in which everyone has their own time or, better still, a school in which a single time flows according to different rhythms ('progressive schooling is not equally valid for all'). It is clear, then, that the ruling class, having entered into the progressive system (and having manufactured it from its own peculiar situation) 'by democratic vocation', does not wonder how it would be possible to evade it, but is rather concerned about reforming it 'so as to recover gifts and talents, and make free competition more effective'. The answer is within reach: we said that the historical (and therefore ideological) forms of the class-based school should not be construed as phases along a progressive/horizontal line. Rather, they are best understood as positions that can be exchanged at certain times and in certain places. Obviously, then, the improvement of the progressive system can only take place 'by borrowing from the forms of preparatory education'.[34]

3   On the Historical Processes of Formation of the Class-Based School: The Antediluvian Forms

The fundamental characteristic of the class-based school is its historical status. It is not an institution that sprung into being in its final form, but it was rather constituted 'through a history whose moments must be carefully distinguished'.[35] This thesis is only apparently harmless. Indeed, on closer inspection it seems to contradict the rectification of the 'principle of contemporaneity' I

---

33   ALT2. A14-02.05 (B), pp. 9–10.
34   ALT2. A14-02.05 (B), p. 10.
35   ALT2. A14-02.05 (C), p. 5.

presented above. The question is simple: if we talk of contemporaneity, how could the school have a history? The scholastic ideological apparatus is the dominant ideological apparatus *of* the CMP, and *only* in the CMP. And yet, this is not *the result of a (subject-less) process of formation*: as such, the CBS, as a theoretical indicator of the forms that realise it (CAS and SS), exists only *in* capital and *for* capital (in this sense all the historical-geographical heterogeneities of the CBS are squarely located in the CMP and can only be there). As such, however, the process of 'its' formation is historically carried out 'within the history of two other ideological apparatuses (two, essentially): church, family'. The point should be stressed, and it is no coincidence that I have put 'its' formation in scare quotes. This is because if it is true that on the one hand, some of the elements that constitute it as a state apparatus are also present in *other* modes of production (Church and family refer, precisely, to their specific modes of ideologisation) and, on the other hand, that the school is the ideological apparatus of the CMP, and only within the CMP there can be a school, then some of the elements that constitute it are not *essentially* functional to its constitution (where they come from, the school does not exist). In other words, *they are constitutive elements that have no meaning other than what is given to them by the ideological apparatuses in which they are placed*. This is clearly stated: 'the first elements of what will constitute the school apparatus do not exist in their pure state, as already constitutive of this apparatus, but develop within other apparatuses'.[36] Some constituent elements of the CBS belong to the family, *and it is there that they have their specific meaning*, while others belong to the Church. Having an ideological meaning (they are determinate elements of determinate apparatuses of ideologisation), *they have no scholastic meaning except at the time of their constitution and, therefore, at the time of their specific re-signification*. They are 'elements that, when transformed, will have a place in the constituted school apparatus but which do not anticipate it, and only represent it in retrospect'.[37] It is only retroactively that the constitutive elements of the school can be said to be so, that is to say, they can be considered constitutive *only from the point where they are to be reunited in a unified apparatus*, only when considered from the vantage point of what is already materially constituted. Through the absolute erasure of the cause-effect relationship, the school is, so to speak, the 'cause' of its own beginnings – which, being irreducible to points of Origin (the history of the school is not an expression of some teleological perfectibility of the elements of its constitution: 'they are not elements

---

36   Ibid.
37   ALT2. A14-02.05 (C), p. 25.

of schooling'),[38] cannot be reduced even to mere anticipations (since its constituent elements are relative to different MPs).[39] Or again, its simple existence makes its constituent *elements* be *its* elements.

Here, then, we are offered a general outline of the constitution of the school system: 'I. The development of its elements. II. A progressive autonomy of these elements from their original terrain. III. Their reunion into a specific unified apparatus'.[40] We could even risk reformulating the famous Kantian formula – once again, if we are careful to expunge any teleological connotation, if it has any – and say that 'constitutive elements without the school are blind, but school without the constitutive elements is empty'. The school system is constituted by these elements, but to make them factors of its Origin or its anticipations would mean, as we have already seen, *substituting a logic of backwards causation for a logic of positioning*. This is crucial, for this explains why 'bourgeois historians propose a whole series of more or less illusory periodisations'.

Thus, when commenting on Henri-Irénée Marrou's 1948 *Histoire de l'éducation dans l'Antiquité*, Baudelot and Macherey write that 'the school finds its origin and exists in a fully developed form as early as the Hellenistic period',[41] and that 'during this period the cultural content (*paideia*) and the form of the public school institution are given; there is therefore from antiquity a completed school-form, which defines a tradition in dependence of which we find ourselves'.[42] On the other hand, Durkheim, (here they are commenting his 1938 *L'évolution pédagogique en France*), 'privileges the Carolingian school', so that 'the idea of education is related to Christianity'.[43] In this case, as in the first one and in all those that follow, 'one form is privileged as the original form, i.e., as the essential reference point against which to think about the current situation of the education system'. Armando Sapori too argues that what is at stake is the notion of origin. It is situated 'in the thirteenth century' and 'it coincides with a strengthening of the role of the merchant in medieval society and the development of communes and communal life'.[44] The school was born ('against the church') as a communal public school and has as its purpose the transmission of 'elements of knowledge necessary for the merchant's professional practice:

---

38   Ibid.
39   On this topic cf. Althusser 2005, p. 57 n. 16: 'In the theory of sources it is the origin that measures the development. In the theory of anticipation, it is the goal that decides the meaning of the moments of the process'.
40   ALT2. A14-02.05 (C), p. 5.
41   Ibid.
42   ALT2. A14-02.05 (C), p. 6.
43   ALT2. A14-02.05 (C), p. 7.
44   ALT2. A14-02.05 (C), p. 8.

writing, arithmetic, history, geography'. It is in this context that two antagonistic forms of popular schooling face one other: one organised by the Church – which is intended for teaching in the countryside and in which 'one learns to read: its main function is ideologising' – and the communal, secular one, in which 'students learn to write (scripts: chancellery scripts, notarial scripts, commercial scripts) and to count. In the latter, the material learning function is dominant'.[45] For Ariès too (in his 1960 *L'enfant et la vie familiale sous l'ancien régime*), the theoretical framework of the original periodisation remains intact. Here, in fact, 'the appearance of the school-form as we know it today must be related to a third historical moment, which corresponds to the rise of the bourgeoisie in a period spanning the sixteenth and seventeenth centuries', since this is the period when, according to a well-known thesis, 'a new representation of culture and of childhood' appears and develops.[46] Finally, for Antoine Prost (the text quoted from is probably *L'Enseignement en France (1800–1967)*, published in 1968) 'the history of the school begins this time with the French Revolution of which it is a product: the public school or state school'.[47]

These are five possible origins which correspond (except for Sapori and Ariès' periodisation) to 'some political events' (Alexander's empire for Morrou, the Carolingian Renaissance for Durkheim, the French Revolution for Prost) and to five dates ('300 CE, 800, [1200], 1500–1700, 1800'). The point here is to emphasise that the heterogeneity of these dates depends on their *addressing a false problem*: the school, in fact, 'did not suddenly appear, ready-made, with its current characteristics, at a given moment in history'. These five temporal coordinates do not take into account that the school 'has been built up gradually (within the history of other ideological apparatuses)', since 'it depends on the history of the CMP' being an effect 'of the of the classes'. Thus, this means that if every mode of production has a certain dominant mode of ideology, then what all those periodisations ultimately have in common is 'the flaw of not involving (and for good reason ...) the concepts of mode of production and mode of ideologisation'.[48] Having forsaken these two concepts, the beginnings necessarily appear as points of Origin, or anticipations. But what was considered as 'the origin of the school, is actually the impact of certain political events on the development of elements that will be integrated into the school apparatus at the time of its constitution'.[49] Presupposing the validity of the

45   Ibid.
46   ALT2. A14-02.05 (C), p. 9.
47   ALT2. A14-02.05 (C), p. 10.
48   ALT2. A14-02.05 (C), p. 14.
49   ALT2. A14-02.05 (C), p. 11.

'principle of contemporaneity' as a fundamental principle of the CBS forma-tion process – that is, presupposing that *the only possible periodisation* will be guided 'by the distinction of modes of ideologisation'[50] – we arrive at a simple theoretical proposition: 'the school does not have an Origin; it has beginnings'.[51]

It is thus possible to supplement the formula given in §2: CBS = CAS(tr.), SS(sup.) ∈ CMP – which expresses the heterogeneous forms of the CBS as an apparatus belonging to the CMP – with the following: AF ∈ AMP, FMP // CBS = CAS(tr.), SS(sup.) ∈ CMP, which amounts to a formalisation of the historical pro-cess of formation (which necessarily entails the first one), according to which the constituent elements of the CBS belong, at the stage of their specific devel-opment, to other MPs (ancient: family; feudal: Church) than the capitalist one, so as to represent, of its specific mode of ideologisation (of the CBS as a theor-etical indicator of the CAS(tr.) and of the SS(sup.)), simple *antediluvian forms* (AF). So, once again, if it is true that in the modes of ideologisation of the 'mode of production prior to the CMP', the CBS 'does not exist as such', then it is also true 'that the development of elements of schooling on the terrain of the dom-inant ideological apparatus, will take their place, transformed, in the school apparatus, once this is constituted'.[52] Constituent elements which represent those very *formes antédiluviennes* about which, on the basis of this assumption, in the second chapter of *Écoles*, Balibar argued that 'cannot by themselves per-mit the understanding of the *form* [school] proper' and that, 'despite appear-ances, i.e., despite retrospective illusions', 'are not processes of school-form'.[53]

Thus, it is possible to integrate the periodisation outlined above (develop-ment of the elements; their progressive emancipation; and merging into a spe-cific apparatus) with this:[54]

---

50   ALT2. A14-02.05 (C), p. 14.
51   Ibid. Cf. Althusser 2005, p. 198: 'what Marxism refuses is the (ideological) philosophical pretension to coincide exhaustively with a "root origin", whatever its form (the tabula rasa; the zero point in a process; the state of nature; the concept of the beginning that for example, Hegel sees as being immediately identical with nothingness; the simplicity that, for Hegel once again, is the starting-point – and restarting-point, indefinitely – for every process, what restores it to its origin, etc.); it rejects, therefore, the Hegelian philosophical pretension which accepts this original simple unity (reproduced at each moment of the process) which will produce the whole complexity of the process later in its autodevelop-ment, but without ever getting lost in this complexity itself, without ever losing in it either its simplicity or its unity – since the plurality and the complexity will never be more than its own "phenomenon", entrusted with the manifestation of its own essence'.
52   ALT2. A14-02.05 (C), p. 15.
53   ALT2. A14-02.04, p. 55 and cf. above, Chapter 3, §2.
54   Baudelot and Macherey write: 'to take this periodisation and its terminology as definitive'. ALT2. A14-02.05 (C), p. 16.

1.   'Prehistory of the school apparatus. Antediluvian forms of schooling'
2.   'Transitional phase. Within the CMP. In this phase, we are dealing with elements of schooling developed within the Church and family apparatus, whose organisational process will produce the school apparatus. At the end of this phase, the school apparatus will be constituted as an autonomous apparatus'
3.   'Process of development of the class-based school within the CMP. The history of the capitalist school apparatus as determined by the forms of the class struggle'
4.   'The supreme form of the capitalist class-based school, the form it leans towards: the single school'[55]

Baudelot and Macherey's analysis stops at the second moment of the periodisation (but the third moment – referring to the forms of class struggle as specific stories located within the framework of the CMP – seems to allude to the historical-geographical part, given that the heterogeneity of the historical-geographical situations is dictated by the heterogeneity of the bourgeois processes of democratisation).

Let us now explore these antediluvian forms.

••

There are a number of *institutions* which fall under this label: 'the ancient schoolmaster: grammatical; the ecclesiastical school [*école presbytérale*]; the medieval university, the public writer'; as well as a number of *practices*: 'material learning of reading, writing, counting, practices of ideologisation, family practices of education ...', and a number of *philosophies of education*: mostly Plato and Montaigne 'which prepare the ground for the pedagogy of the class-based school' (but these philosophies of education – we are now familiar with this theoretical move – 'are pedagogical only at the level of a retrospective interpretation').[56] As in the case of a retrospective interpretation, the elements of institutions and practices themselves appear to belong to the school system, since they 'appear within the framework of other ideological apparatuses': in the middle ages 'the forms of schooling are instruments at the service of the ideological apparatus of the church (the apparatus which has a monopoly on ideologisation in the feudal mode of production)'; in antiquity, the 'future' elements of the school system developed 'as an extension of the family and at its service'. In the AMP, as well as in the feudal mode of production, although ways

---

55   ALT2. A14-02.05 (C), p. 17.
56   ALT2. A14-02.05 (C), p. 17.

of ideologising functional to the formation (of the labour-force) do exist, there is no school (they are disparate elements since 'no principle unifies them' and, therefore, do not 'constitute an autonomous apparatus') because there is no education (hence the rectification of the 'principle of contemporaneity', which 'is specific to a particular mode of production: the CMP').[57]

Originating in specific contexts, the antediluvian forms are meant for specific functions. Indeed, in all class societies, 'the functioning of the ideological and state apparatus', whatever these are, requires 'specialised personnel who are trained on the spot'.[58] Hence the existence of 'schools' (corresponding to the institutions mentioned above) 'that are part of the apparatus they are used to reproduce' and which serve, more precisely, to recruit the operators of these apparatuses. If every apparatus, in every mode of production, is instrumental to ideologisation (i.e., to the formation of labour power), then every apparatus, in every mode of production, needs to train those who are assigned to the process of ideologisation. This is this sense in which the 'schools' that are not schools emerge (and what their antediluvian forms comprise) – 'Brahmin schools, Mandarin schools, rabbinical schools, scribal schools, vestal schools, the Carolingian school (which trained the clergy and civil servants of the nascent state), theological and law schools'[59] – necessary spaces (that is to say necessarily formed) which provide the 'education of the functionaries of ideology. The clerks, improperly known as intellectuals'.[60]

---

57   ALT2. A14-02.05 (A), p. 1.
58   ALT2. A14-02.05 (C), p. 18.
59   Ibid.
60   On the question of the intellectual, and on whether the functionaries of the MPA or of feudal ideology (but, during a certain period, also of the capitalist one) are improperly called, cf. Michel Tort's thesis contained in ALT2. A14-02.01, pp. 4–5: 'Theses on the ideological state personnel (intellectuals). 1 – Teachers, professors, engineers and technicians constitute a large part of the "intellectuals". 2 – The "intellectuals" represent the form of the state ideological personnel in the imperialist phase. The determining categories of state ideological personnel vary in the course of the imperialist phase (cf. the decline of the schoolteachers, charged with transmitting imperialist bourgeois ideology, and the promotion of technicians-engineers-cultural luminaries of all kinds). 3 – Ideological state personnel, in the form of intellectuals, is an indispensable element of imperialism (precisely as neo-colonialism): cf. The transition from the export of the mercenary + missionary couple to the engineer + teacher couple. The importance of the world market for ideological personnel as intellectual mercenaries should not be overlooked. 4 – The control of the social process (reprod. of the relations of production); from a certain stage onwards, is no longer adequately ensured by the traditional vehicles. This control must be "scientific": hence the systematic training of reproducers/operators of social controls in the School itself, together with the development of appropriate ideological techniques: introduction of sociology + psychology into the School training of sociologist-

In some cases, moreover, the ancient or feudal ideological apparatus present practices which, aimed at securing ideologising function, will appear 'as schools' only 'in retrospect': 'for example, one can observe in the functioning of certain devices a specialisation of educational tasks'.[61] In the context of the ancient family there arises (retroactively) the idea that the pedagogue is a profession starting from 'the allocation of training or educational tasks to specific members'.[62] In the context of the Church educational functions also seem to arise (retroactively), which are then taken up by the university ('and by its essential part: the Faculty of Arts'), along with 'the very early appearance of monastic centres specialising in cultural dissemination (which developed literary studies as a prerequisite to religious training)'.[63]

Even the material education of subjects assigned to certain activities of production (which does not necessarily correspond to that of the functionaries of ideology) gives rise 'to the existence of certain elements which, transformed, will be integrated into the school-form'. For example, 'apprenticeship [*apprentissage*]' which, far from being something separate if not before the development of the CMP (indeed, 'it is directly linked to production'), is implemented through forms that will later be taken up by the CBS: 'the master-apprentice relationship, and the notion of the masterpiece [*chef d'œuvre*], which will permeate classical and modern pedagogy'.[64]

Finally, linked to this last type of training, the elements that will be integrated into the school-form are placed in the framework 'of the development of the market economy'. Pertaining to the material education of individuals responsible for the circulation and distribution of goods, they give rise to 'the learning of writing and arithmetic (not reading) by the public writer [*maître-écrivain*] linked to the development of trade and the expansion of the commercial professions'.[65] What must be emphasised here is that this kind of teaching, although constituting until the seventeenth century a 'corporate and specialised' activity that triggered a conflict with the Church ('who have a monopoly on education to maintain their privilege of learning to write and calculate'),[66] is the primary factor for the development of a specialised process of education.

---

psychologist-psychosociologists-sociopsychologists etc. The formula towards which the ideological composition of the state ideological staff tends in the present phase of the decline of imperialism is: Culture + technology of social relations'.

61   ALT2. A14-02.05 (C), p. 18.
62   ALT2. A14-02.05 (C), p. 19.
63   Ibid.
64   Ibid.
65   Ibid.
66   ALT2. A14-02.05 (C), p. 22.

It could be said that, just as every form of ideologisation requires the training of its operators, so the development of commercial capitalism since the end of the Middle Ages requires training of specific operators (traders) through specific institutions ('the master writer (France) or communal and shop schools (Italy)').[67]

As noted, the inculcation of these particular forms of knowledge (linked to 'a specialised practice: that of commerce') takes place out of ecclesiastical control (it is 'controlled by the corporations'), and indeed in conflict with it ('the church claiming to retain a monopoly on the training of the youth of France'), which leads to an institutionalised *separation* (a 'state guarantee') of the proper functions of religious schools, on the one hand, and vocational schools, on the other. Concurrently with the development of the latter (secular schools that secularise a part of the old 'education'), there is also the beginning of 'a pragmatic critique of the traditional institution (the church)' which pertains, essentially, to the question of time (and its use): '*Time is money* is opposed to the Christian conception of eternity according to which *time is God* (*time is gold ≠ time is God*). Hence the development of original forms of education within these new institutions: rationalisation and organisation of time'.[68]

With the constitution of the CBS, the Church will recover its monopoly by combining the (temporal) organisational structure that had been opposed to it by the secular schools (in particular with the counter-reformation school programme aimed at 'adapting educational tasks to the demands of the time')[69] with its traditional functions, thus realising 'the first form of schooling organised around the production of a double effect: a material training dominated by an ideological subjection. All in a separate place'.[70] And yet, we encounter a 'fundamental historical paradox' here: those elements – previously developed in alternative forms of material transmission that the Church combines with its own specific and traditional functions – *are elements that, with this combination, work towards its (the Church's) weakening and erasure*. If the Church re-hegemonises its function through the re-signification of (previously) antagonistic practices, the (re-actualised) elements of those practices, starting from their combination, become the conditions for the overcoming of the apparatus that mobilises them: 'the church thus directly ensures the conditions for its own erasure'.[71]

---

67   ALT2. A14-02.05 (C), p. 20.
68   Ibid.
69   Ibid.
70   ALT2. A14-02.05 (C), pp. 20–1.
71   ALT2. A14-02.05 (C), p. 21.

Here is an example of an antediluvian form: the university.

In certain respects, the university as it functions today is a trace of the feudal ideological system: it has retained functions (training of clerics), and practices (programmes, institutions, rituals) which already existed and made sense in the feudal ideological system. Nothing is gained by grouping these elements under the idealistic concept of survival: the University, a sclerotic institution which, by its very inertia, would have succeeded in perpetuating itself and which would represent the past within the present. Such a representation is meaningless: the university, in the heterogeneity of its components, some of which have their antecedents in very different previous periods, exists in the present and must be understood in its real complexity.[72]

The representation according to which certain elements of present-day university ('certain functions (training of clerks) and practices (programmes, institutions, rites)') have survived the mode of (feudal) ideologisation in which they were born is meaningless (*the concept of survival is an idealist concept*, like that of anticipation). Once again, although as constituent elements of the feudal university, they are materially identical to those of the capitalist university, they are only antediluvian forms: *the material equality of the antediluvian elements of the constitution is not equivalent to the substantial equality of what is already constituted.* The Faculties of Law and Letters, for example, 'are not fundamentally different (in terms of their institutional status, the content of their teaching) from the law faculties and the faculties of arts that operated in the 14th century'. And yet, the 'principle of contemporaneity between modes of ideologisation and modes of production' *places that indifference in a relationship of absolute inequality.* Indeed, those elements, although materially identical, 'are profoundly transformed because their function and operation have been displaced'.[73] One reason for this is that the university, as a specific apparatus of the CMP, is at the *end* of a course of study, indeed appearing as its crowning achievement.[74] Another reason is that, as a specific apparatus of the CMP, it abandons all those elements of vocational training that once essentially defined it. Finally, in the university, as a specific apparatus of the CMP, what once was the Faculty of Letters now becomes the Faculty of Letters and

---

72   ALT2. A14-02.05 (C), p. 22.
73   ALT2. A14-02.05 (C), p. 23.
74   This completely transfigures its function. Recall the image of the line above in Chapter 3, Introduction and §1.

Human Sciences, and the Faculty of Law now becomes the Faculty of Law and Economic Sciences. Heterogeneous elements whose addition is determined by the development of capitalism, assigning them – and to materially identical ones, arising in a different mode of production and ideologisation – 'a completely different status'.[75]

4   The Transition Phase: A Look at the French Case

> We have just described antediluvian forms: that is to say, elements which, when transformed, will have a place in the constituted school apparatus, but which do not anticipate it and represent it only in retrospect. In other words, they are not elements of schooling.[76]

Things are different for the transitional forms of the CBS which are placed in the transitional phase (TP) we are discussing here (and that, please note, do not correspond to the CAS as this, as we have seen, is *already* representative of the CBS: the CAS is indeed a transitional form, but it is the transitional form of the SS as the supreme form of the CBS). They certainly have a non-correspondence with the CBS as such in common with the antediluvian forms (for 'in both cases, they are singular and dispersed forms'); but the latter, unlike the former, are *internal to the CMP* and can already be considered, by the CBS, as *real anticipations* (hence an important clarification: 'in this case, the term '*already*' does not have the meaning of a retrospective fiction'). Thus, the identification of FAs has both a foundational expositional role and a critical one (being critical of periodisations that do *not* make use of the notions of mode of production, of mode of ideologisation, and of their specific relationship): once the CMP is posited, a certain number of *rassemblements* come into being, consisting of (antediluvian) elements 'inherited from earlier periods'. Constitutive elements (if starting from a logic of retroaction) are assembled in *primitive forms of organisation* that, although still dispersed, represent the prehistory of the schooling processes (according to what is already a positioning logic). We are not yet in the CBS as such (it is only a transitional phase and it is only 'at the end of this phase' that 'the School apparatus will be constituted as an autonomous apparatus')[77] – and yet we are in *the conflictual phase of its real anticipation* ('it is in these forms that the class-based school is tendentially realised: however, it

---

75   ALT2. A14-02.05 (C), p. 23.
76   ALT2. A14-02.05 (C), p. 25.
77   ALT2. A14-02.05 (C), p. 17.

will only materially exist at the end of a process of transformation produced by the combination of these forms (their articulation, disjunction, conflict)').[78]

Therefore, this is the final integration: if $AF \in AMP$, FMP and $CBS = CAS(tr.)$, $SS(sup.) \in CMP$, and if TP is posited as a phase in which $AF \in AMP$, FMP are assembled into forms of organisation that, belonging to CMP, anticipate $CBS = CAS(tr.)$, $SS(sup.) \in CMP$. Then we have: $AF \in AMP$, $FMP // TP$, $CBS = CAS(tr.)$, $SS(sup.) \in CMP$.

∴

We can thus briefly examine the transitional phase. Baudelot and Macherey's analysis focuses on the case 'of French social education', characterised by the formation of a number of primitive organisations (A) and their transformation (B).

A. Primitive forms of organisation.

1. They are constituted by 'the meeting or cohabitation (gathering)' of pre-viously separate and independent antediluvian practices. In 'colleges and small schools', in the early modern period, there was a *merging* of (ideo-logical) principles formerly belonging to religious schools, on the one hand, and secular schools (principles of material learning), on the other: 'reading and singing (practices of religious origin) + writing and counting (specialised material training provided separately by a corporation spe-cialised in these two practices)'.[79]

2. for the first time they involve, in different ways, *some* members of *all* social classes: each social class is involved with heterogeneous schooling prac-tices, but this happens 'in a scattered manner: by different educational institutions and personnel'.[80] For the first time 'all social classes from the nobility to the beggars are involved in the operation of specialised educa-tional practices'. And yet, this universalism is factually realised in contin-gent forms (the orders of the Church, for example, 'appear and disappear according to the precise need that gave rise to them'), since it does not yet compose a unified form of organisation (as the CBS will, as a generalised form), 'nor to a unified functioning of parallel elements, which will, on the contrary, clash and are displaced'. The 'constitution of the school sys-

---

78   ALT2. A14-02.05 (C), p. 25.
79   Ibid.
80   ALT2. A14-02.05 (C), p. 26.

tem'[81] will depend precisely on this conflictual relationship. *Only 'some' members of the social classes are involved in the educational process*: far from implying a unified form of organisation, primitive forms do not even entail a unified form of teaching, which would address all members of a social class. 'the generalisation of schooling is therefore only partial: no class is enrolled in its entirety'.[82]

3. they necessarily appear within the framework of the existing ideological apparatuses (family and Church), since the CBS as such does not yet exist. And yet, as transitional forms (and not simple FAs), they give rise to a 'characteristic phenomenon of this period': *the progressive schooling of existing ideological apparatuses*. On the one hand, 'the whole church tends to become a school (development of religious instruction: catechism)'; on the other hand, the aristocratic family starts to delegate its educational functions to 'inter-family exchanges (the trip abroad, the internship, the page)' and 'specialised institutions (military academy)',[83] as well as hiring specialised personnel 'who makes it a kind of school institution (tutor, governor who add to the nanny and extend the material training with a spiritual education)'.[84]

B. Transformation of the primitive forms.

1. The organisational forms are embodied in three types of institutions, 'which are exact contemporaries'[85] and are meant for different social categories: the 'small schools', which are 'for the poor, dedicated to popular education'; 'the colleges', meant for the bourgeoisie and the upper bourgeoisie (*noblesse de robe*); the 'military academies', meant for the military aristocracy (*noblesse d'épée*).[86] These are separate forms of education, which 'are not an extension of each other'. However, their contemporaneity produces 'paradoxical' effects that transfigure their original (social) vocation. In medieval times, colleges – institutions originally intended to give hospitality to poor students – were later colonised by wealthy students 'because the quality of their teaching was superior'. In the same way, new organisational forms 'will be diverted from their original purpose': bearers of innovative pedagogical practices that break with tradi-

---

81   Ibid.
82   Ibid.
83   ALT2. A14-02.05 (C), p. 27.
84   Ibid.
85   Ibid.
86   Here we find an interesting handwritten *marginalium*: *Castes?* Cf. below.

tional ones, *petites écoles* and *collèges* are invaded 'by social categories for which they were not explicitly intended' – the former, originally devoted to popular education, are later colonised by the bourgeoisie and the petty bourgeoisie (and 'make the poor and the rich live together, if not on the same benches, at least within the same walls'); the latter, originally meant for the education of the bourgeoisie and the *noblesse de robe*, are later colonised by the petty bourgeoisie and the great nobility. Note, however, that *these blendings are not yet unifications*, since 'the classes remain ostensibly separate and even opposed'.[87] And yet – this is an historically crucial point since it is here that the truly germinal form of the future class-based schooling network can be discerned – they are opposed 'within a common educational institution'. Moreover, here we see how, at least in the French case,[88] the primitive forms of schooling do not require the functioning of the CAS ('this is not a caste school'): like a sudden glow (the glow of the original vocations, immediately shattered by their colonisation by other social classes), it 'disappears as soon as it is born and remains only in a thin fringe, that of the military academies which will soon wither away'.[89] In contrast, for example, to the English case, already at this stage in France 'the school-form cannot be used to set up institutions reserved for one class, aimed at protecting it from contact with other classes'. With one characteristic feature: this form begins to develop by leaving the popular classes behind (first accepted in *petites écoles* and then immediately rejected). Their place, in fact, is the factory. Seen in its historical-geographical context, therefore, the (French) scholastic form takes shape out of the alliance ('which is not without conflict and which presupposes the existence of schooling networks') between the aristocracy and the bourgeoisie and, above all, between the bourgeoisie and the petty bourgeoisie. It can therefore be understood that, when the popular classes enter the process of schooling, the scholastic form conveying this process *will remain substantially the same*: 'it will simply be a matter of adding an extra piece: the primary school'. In the fourth point, below, I will return to the meaning of this addition.

2.   The historical articulation of the TP has determinate effects. The first pertains to the antagonism between the city and the countryside: the latter 'is emptied of its educational institutions whose development is reserved

---

87   ALT2. A14-02.05 (C), p. 28.
88   Cf. above, §1.
89   ALT2. A14-02.05 (C), p. 28.

for urban centres: in order to learn, you must go to the city'.[90] An emptier countryside corresponds to a weakened Church (we have already seen how, for Ariès, in the previous period religious schools, unlike secular ones, were located precisely in the countryside) that loses 'its place as the dominant ideological apparatus' by means of the *external* opposition of the ruling classes. In France, this leads to a massive secularisation of the educational institutions by the bourgeoise and petty bourgeoise through an 'anticlerical ideology of the public'.[91] This point should be stressed: the rather early appearance of the school's monopoly (dictated by its growing hegemony as a single apparatus) coincides, according to a law of inverse proportionality, with *the actual deschooling of the popular classes*, so that 'the progress of enlightenment is the progress of illiteracy'. We will explore this again below, for now suffice it to say that the second effect of the TP lies in the emergence of 'the idea of compulsory education'.[92]

3.   A prime example of a scholastic institution produced in the TP is the Napoleonic University. Far from being an innovative institution ('a break, or a beginning'), it is rather the result of a process that, proper of the CMP, originated in the seventeenth century: 'the *lycées* are colleges in the sense that the Jesuits gave to this term'. It simply merges and organises, under a single jurisdiction, 'the various elements that have been gradually brought together in the classical school'. Its main feature concerns the *exclusivity of secondary education* which, controlled by the state – because it is the state (the ruling class) that is educated in the university – causes the absolute exclusion of the popular classes 'who are redistributed towards other works'. Crucially, this is the first time that, in France (and the whole French school system has its origin here), *the schooling process turns out to be an autonomous process, detached from other systems* ('that which the bourgeoisie reserves for itself'),[93] *and operated by specialised personnel.*

4.   From 1750–1830, the schooling of the ruling classes corresponded, as we have already mentioned, to a massive de-schooling of the dominated classes. Let us examine this phenomenon further. This is a determining factor for the entire history of the CBS in France and (even more crucially) in England, where the CAS prevails. An inverse proportionality that seems to contradict the very existence of the CBS, that is, a generalised apparatus

---

90   ALT2. A14-02.05 (C), p. 28.
91   ALT2. A14-02.05 (C), p. 29.
92   Ibid.
93   ALT2. A14-02.05 (C), p. 30.

of ideologisation – meant for the formation of labour power – that is specific to the CMP. In other words, it seems to contradict the thesis that 'the history of educational institutions is ultimately determined by the problem of the schooling of workers'.[94] In fact, the first development of capitalist production ('industrialisation, concentration, machinery, factories ...') coincided with *the non-schooling of the proletariat*: 'non-workers were the first to experience a form of schooling'. Indeed, the first laws regulating labour in France, forced by the workers' demands, were established in 1830, and only then can we start talking about the schooling of the working class and, therefore, about a generalised form of schooling typical of the CBS. And yet, at least in the French case, the primitive forms of TP schooling are already embryonic and anticipatory forms of CBS: in 1. we have seen how it suffices to add elements functional to the education of the new popular classes to the primitive school-form. This thesis is restated here:

> hence a (class-based) school which presents itself as a school for one class (the dominant one), and which will be perfected by adding new elements destined for other classes: hence the history of French schooling, presenting itself as the successive addition of complementary and autonomous units to an initial unit (the Napoleonic *lycées*).[95]

It could be said, therefore, that if the TP is the phase of the *rassemblements* constituted by the AF, then these *rassemblements*, effectively produced by the ruling classes, are not meant (at least at the initial state of development of big industry) 'for all classes: on the contrary, the constitution of the school-form has divided them'. More precisely, the working class is excluded for two fundamental reasons. The first is of political nature: 'it is dangerous to educate the people because to educate them is to give them weapons'.[96] The second is economic: 'there is no free time for schooling in the organisation of the working day'.[97] This leads to the increase of illiteracy and a de-qualification of workers – due to the lack of an education that would adapt them to technically and technologically developed means of production – as well as to the development of a (sub) proletarian culture 'which is initially constituted on its own background (the experience of work and the first struggles, the working class history that

---

94   Ibid.

95   ALT2. A14-02.05 (C), p. 31.

96   ALT2. A14-02.05 (C), p. 32.

97   Indeed, at this stage, the process of schooling is not yet a factor in the enhancement of labour power (see the third chapter of 'Schools').

only the working class really knows)'.[98] From this starting point, the will
of the working class to have its own education is manifested, in a first
phase, through demands of a multipurpose training – scientific and technological – which is dispensed *in the workplace* and *conditioned by the
production process itself*. Hence the contradictory character of popular
education: if, for the proletariat, it is a question of educating itself 'by its
own means', the bourgeoisie considers education *to be placed at its service*, an 'instrument of propaganda intended, through the intermediary of
knowledge of nature, to subjugate proletarian ideology to the bourgeois
order'.[99] If before 1830 the organisation of time in the factory erased all
other forms of time ('what is a working day? Twenty-four full hours'), then
after 1830, thanks to the working class's social pressure, capitalists were
forced to reduce the working hours.[100] This was an historical landmark,
for we are now abandoning the field of TP: the concession is only partial;
the time 'stolen' from production is not free time – i.e., time freely usable
by the worker for his own education – but rather it is 'school time, where
labour power is 'qualified' under the control of the ruling class, so as to
reinforce the subjection of the dominated class'.[101] *The compulsory education of the proletariat is an effect of the shortening of the working day*. In
the first phase of child labour, which precedes this obligation, the factory
already functions as a school ('the organisation of the working day has, for
the worker, the function of the timetable in the school life of the bourgeois
schoolboy').[102] This is a thoroughly ideological equivalence: this fictitious
merging of production and education does not lead to the possibility of
dislocating, within the same unit of production, the labour power of the
worker on the basis of the technological and practical-theoretical knowledge which was acquired during production (which would lead to the
suppression of the old division of labour).[103] The time of school is subservient to education, the time of the factory is subservient to production:
different times, of course, but both are meant to educate. Doesn't the
factory also have a moral function? It 'enables the children of the people
to be rescued from the dangers and temptations of the street; it trains
them in its own way, which is not that of the school but which takes its

98   ALT2. A14-02.05 (C), p. 32.
99   Ibid.
100   ALT2. A14-02.05 (C), p. 33.
101   Ibid.
102   ALT2. A14-02.05 (C), p. 36.
103   On this topic cf. above, Chapter 3, note 229, 243.

place'.[104] It also fosters discipline, because labouring in the production process entails punishment and 'this penal regulation makes the factory a school, or rather temporarily allows the factory to do without a school'.[105] And yet, as mentioned, this is only an ideological equivalence, since the overlap between education and work, far from heralding their unification, simply refers to a process of 'disguising [*travestissement*] production as education'.[106] But now, with the introduction of mandatory schooling, there is a change in the mode of domination. Lower-class children get in and out of the factory, just as they get in and out of the school. The working class is finally a formed class. An accomplishment, to be sure, for the school time is now removed from capitalist exploitation (moreover, 'school work is less tiring than production work'), and it is reclaimed. But that education goes also (and above all) to the advantage of the bourgeoisie. Compromises must be made, for I said that the concession is only partial: 'the proletariat', in fact, 'will only find liberation in the forms provided by bourgeois freedom, which will inevitably tend to turn against it'.[107]

5.   One last feature. As mentioned, the earliest laws regulating labour and the organisation of elementary education were the effect 'of an economic and political struggle'.[108] The former, aiming at regulating the working hours in factories, was conducted 'by the working class against capital'. The latter was fought on two levels. The first is that of the working class against the bourgeoisie. There's no need to chronicle the events that led to the appearance, on the political scene, of the first workers' organisations (a spectre is haunting Europe ...). Suffice it to say that under the influence of these political struggles the proletariat changed its profile in the eyes of the dominant ideology. Now it is neither a helpless class in need of assistance, nor one to be exploited. Rather, 'it represents an immediate danger against which one must protect oneself'. In this sense, mandatory education and its perfectioning are, precisely, 'means invented by the bourgeoisie to defend itself against the working class'. The second level is that of a clash internal to the ruling classes, produced by struggle between workers and capital, where bourgeois politics and petty bourgeois politics find themselves on different sides, corresponding to two ideologies,

---

104   ALT2. A14-02.05 (C), p. 36.
105   ALT2. A14-02.05 (C), p. 37.
106   ALT2. A14-02.05 (C), p. 36.
107   ALT2. A14-02.05 (C), p. 33.
108   ALT2. A14-02.05 (C), p. 38.

'that of order and that of progress, that of the conservatives and that of the liberals'. What is at stake in this clash is the very idea of schooling, and it concluded around 1880 with the triumph of the petty bourgeois line (promoting the idea that schooling is 'beneficial') over the bourgeois one (according to which the schooling of the working class is 'dangerous'). On the one hand, therefore, there is a 'negative' ideology, that is, 'an ideology of denigration of educational institutions' that finds its origin in Rousseau's *Emile*: what's better than a natural education, without schools? Work in the factory, the bourgeois would answer; it is there that the beautiful soul of the young worker will have neither the time nor the occasion to pervert their nature. On the other hand, there is a 'positive' ideology that finds its origin in Smith's *The Wealth of Nations*. It is there that, according to Baudelot and Macherey, three theses are developed that function as an ideological justification of a generalised educational practice, functional to the formation of labour power. It is with their identification that these notes end and, with them, my analysis. These theses certainly do not over even the smallest part of the articulation of the theoretical system elaborated in 'Schools'. However, they are some of the most fundamental theoretical nodes of the familiar argument according to which:

a) the educational system must be developed for the people and is only indirectly of interest to the idle classes; b) the process of schooling of the people is dominated by its function of ideological subjugation (the people must go to school to learn to live in a democracy); material learning will take place at the place of production and has nothing to do with schooling (this is identified in Smith's critique of feudal apprenticeship, which hinders the free movement of labour power); c) schooling takes place thanks to a legal sanction: the certificate.[109]

---

109   ALT2. A14-02.05 (C), p. 39.

Afterword

What happened in May 1968? Can Althusser's pragmatic analysis give us any clue about the indispensable conditions for the transformation of the class-based school, as it was defined in 'Schools'? Although this historical phase represents only a sketch of a '"concrete analysis" of the "concrete situation"', Althusser's letter to Maria Antonietta Macciocchi, dated 15 March 1969 (one month before the composition of the first chapter of 'Schools'), is the most important theoretical document on these issues.[1]

Althusser opens his letter with the observation that 'ultimately, what played the absolutely *decisive* role in the events of May was the general strike of 9 million workers'.[2] This claim is far from accommodating since it collides with what, among those events, *presented* itself and still *presents* itself in his own memory. Indeed, both the denial of a certain subordination and the overthrow of a certain order were exhibited. Even if the massive participation 'of university students, high school students and young intellectual workers' had been a powerful phenomenon, the point remains that from an historical point of view, this was *subordinated* 'to the movement of class economic struggle'.[3] This is a thesis which, in accordance with the Marxist thesis on the 'revolutionary character of the working class *alone*', reveals, against all immediate representations, a real disposition that can be summarised by what is both a simple slogan and a crucial theoretical claim: *the primacy of the general strike over student actions.*

On the one hand, there is the role of the working class as determining in the last instance; on the other, there is the subordinate role of those who are still part of the educational process. Clearly, the text suggests an order and a taxonomy: when we speak of May 1968, we are actually dealing with *two* separate events, and the origin of the political failures of the student movement is precisely related to a certain mystification of this overdetermined duality – i.e., to a mystification of its disposition.[4]

This mystification is not simply motivated by 'all bourgeois and petty-bourgeois publications' but, more worryingly, can also be detected in the 'majority of publications of the Student Movement'. Certainly, they were guided by different reasons, but the point stands that all interpretations share the same perspect-

---

1   Macciocchi 1969, p. 338.
2   Macciocchi 1969, p. 339.
3   Macciocchi 1969, p. 340.
4   On the plurality of 'Mays', see also Badiou 2018. On May '68 in general, see Badiou 2009.

ive (everything, here, depends on a 'knowing how' to look at things) according to which 'the general strike takes second place: *nobody talks about it anymore'*. What gets obscured, then, is the order and the arrangement of the two 'May 1968s'. 'The mass of students lives in a dream', a dream from which those who uncritically believe in what happens before one's eyes can hardly awaken.[5] Indeed, both the subordination of student actions and the primacy of the general strike, as acknowledged by theory, do not belong to the order of their empirical givenness. Could it be that, once again, the distinction between true-factual propositions and theoretical propositions is at stake here? Althusser observes that 'under the pretext (and this is a historical-chronological fact) that the savagely repressed "barricades" served as a "detonator" for the general strike, the mass of students think they were in the vanguard of May, in workers' vanguard'. Such distortion ('it is obviously an illusion') of the real order between the determining and the subordinate instance, then, arises from the immediate confusion (immediate like its experiential grip) of the historical level with the chronological level, of the level of determination in the last instance – that is, the level of overdetermination – with the causal level, that is, the level of mere factual succession. The order of time is not necessarily the order of significa-tion (the primacy of the strike is the determining condition of the name: 'May 1968') – what happens at a given moment of time may be late with respect to its value.

This reversal of the order of things, therefore, is dictated by a grave mis-understanding ('the clash of May 13th ... is, *essentially*, left without a tomor-row').[6] Indeed, it is from here that the student movement, disregarding a delay that takes its own struggle for an anticipation, misses the opportunity of an encounter that could have produced a merging.[7] 'What goes under the name of "the events of May '68" was the result of the objective *clash* of two orders of action'.[8] An encounter

---

5   Macciocchi 1969, p. 341.
6   Macciocchi 1969, p. 343.
7   This theme can be further analysed by means of a reading of Althusser's 'The Underground Current of the Materialism of the Encounter' in which the notion of an 'encounter' (and of 'rain', of the 'swerve', of the 'take') – and therefore of the aleatory and contingency – serves, among other things, to identify an unknown (and not simply forgotten) materialist 'tradition' in the history of philosophy. I hypothesise – and this hypothesis would deserve a detailed ana-lysis – that the question of the 'encounter' as well as the 'void', which I will mention later, have found space in his thought already starting from the political analyses of the events of May '68, although they found a more solid theoretical elaboration almost fifteen years later, in the three-year period from 1982 (year of publication of 'The Underground Current') to 1985 (year of publication of 'The Only Materialist Tradition'). A crucial analysis of the notions guiding the work of so-called 'late Althusser' can be found in Morfino 2022.
8   Macciocchi 1969, p. 344.

may or may not occur. It can be a brief 'encounter', *relatively* accidental, which does not result in a *merging*. This is the case of May, the meeting of workers/wage earners-students, high schoolers, and young intellectual workers, was a brief encounter that did not result ... in a *merging*.[9]

This thesis is important and needs to be clarified. In this context, the term 'merging' indicates neither an *erasure* of the (actually) subordinate term, nor a *mutual* recognition for what pertains to action – it is neither an erasure of a duality in favour of unity, nor a positing of unity through duality. Althusser is not suggesting that the political demands of students should be made *invalid*, and subordinated to those of labour power, as if the primacy of the general strike should have an exclusionary function. Neither does he want to argue that, between the two orders of actions, there must be a dialectical relationship of positing, as if the agents of those actions could be only recognised and identifiable, in their respective manifestations, through a process of *mutual* recognition. The working class, in fact, has 'essentially solved its own problems: first of all, the problem of its demands; then also, in some cases, the problem (then absolutely secondary from the point of view of the existing conjuncture) of its relations with its leaders'.[10] There is no reciprocity: the problem, in fact, is only for the students: a confusion (a misunderstanding of a primacy and a subordination) which is the radical opposite of a merging. To speak of a 'merging' here means recognising that (and, therefore, practicing) the political demands of the student movement are, in the last instance, overdetermined by those of the working class (hence their failure), although the demands of the working class are not linked to those of the student movement (hence the non-reciprocity):[11] 'It is necessary for the students to imprint this elementary truth in their heads, even if it is hard for them to understand it'.[12]

---

9   Ibid.
10   Macciocchi 1969, p. 348.
11   'As a general rule, the working masses did not respond to the enthusiastic invitation of the students. Clearly there was a discrepancy and a misunderstanding between the utopian (ideological–'political') hopes of the students, and the workers' demands. Some students have too simplistically identified the reason for this in the 'betrayal' of the leaders of the CGT and the PCF. A little too simplistically: because when a mass movement of this magnitude is at stake, it is not a Marxist-Leninist explanation to believe in *the decisive role of leaders*. In truth, the working class as a whole was not at all willing to 'follow' the students in their goals, made more of dreamed experience than of known reality. The working class felt, in view of the students' manifest inexperience with the class struggle, that they risked being drawn into what must be called, in the absence of another word, the unknown of an adventure'. Macciocchi 1969, p. 347.
12   Macciocchi 1969, p. 348.

Althusser's argument should not surprise us. Indeed, it is nothing but the political translation of what the educational apparatus turned out to be when considered from a theoretical point of view. It suffices to recall what was said about the students' interrupted paths: they 'are interrupted paths from the point of view of the myth of the Unity and Continuity of the School.[13] *But they are not at all interrupted from the point of view of production and the labour market*'.[14] This claim led us to a concatenation of fundamental theses: the truth of the process of schooling does not pertain to knowledge but to labour. It does not pertain to the technical division but rather the social division. It is not internal but external, for that is where the real outcomes of production lay. In short: precisely because the truth of the school is not knowledge but labour, the criterion of fairness for the student's political practice needed to merge with the political practice of the working class, although the latter did not need the former.[15]

It is clear that, for Althusser, the demands arising from the political struggle of the student movement were, in essence (and in spite of itself: 'I know that some students do not fall into this bourgeois trap'),[16] ideologically character-ised: although it consisted of several layers (and this is why it could not be considered a 'real Movement, that is, a *united* Movement',[17] because it is the merging of a single social class 'and of the only *objectively revolutionary class*'),[18] 'this great diversity had at least one thing in common, an ideological common ground that dominated this mass of petty-bourgeois origin: *it was dominated by petty-bourgeois ideology*'.[19] This refers to another familiar thesis: if the misun-

---

13   Cf. above, Chapter 3, §1.

14   ALT2. A14-02.03, p. 38.

15   Badiou writes that 'a very important part of the student movement, from a numerical point of view, consisted of endless general assemblies intended in principle to transform the University, to create "working groups", to contest the exams, to criticise the master courses, to change the programs in other second-order occupations, even if full of good-will', Badiou 2018, p. 30.

16   Macciocchi 1969, p. 341.

17   Macciocchi 1969, p. 351.

18   Macciocchi 1969, p. 350.

19   Cf. again Badiou 2018, p. 27: 'When we speak of "students" we are referring to a very small and privileged fraction of the youth as a whole, a fraction strongly separated from the mass of the popular youth. This may explain why, during May '68, an important part of the youth movement was animated by boys and girls belonging to the bourgeoisie, or even the upper bourgeoisie. This phenomenon illustrates how weak the ideological coherence of the movement was: in fact, since the end of the seventies, an extraordinary move-ment of denial decimates the militant camp, especially among those who played a leading role. Many intellectuals beat their breasts abjuring Maoism, Trotskyism, Stalinism, and

derstanding of primacy and subordination has simply produced an encounter that did not result in a merging – because it implies the denial of the priority of production – then every slogan, like that of the student movement, which is oriented to transform the outline of the educational process on the assumption of that misunderstanding and denial, will simply reaffirm the (ideological) logic and the course of that process. This is what Balibar suggests at the beginning of the first chapter of 'Schools':[20]

> More often than not, even among those who, like some of the 'enraged' French academics of May–June 1968, no longer talk about transforming it but about destroying it, recognise and denounce its role in a system of class exploitation. For most of them remain more or less willing prisoners of illusory representations that are at one with the very object they criticise. And so all 'reforms' are actually *reinforcements* of the existing state of affairs, while revolutionary 'destructions' are in practice impotent *denials* of religious dreams of sudden 'annihilation'. This is because all the spontaneous representations of the school, even when they are 'critical', which are currently dominant, remain fundamentally *internal* to the functioning mechanisms and practices of the school, which have a vital need to represent themselves to all under the disguise of an ideology of the school.[21]

---

adhering *en masse* to "democracy", "human rights" and "Western civilisation". This curious phenomenon becomes clear when we remember that the student youth of May '68 came from the ruling bourgeoisie.'

20   Cf. above, Chapter 3, §1.

21   ALT2. A14-02.03, p. 2. Given Balibar's reference to 'mai–juin 1968', see also Balibar 2018. Althusser, in 'Sur le phénomène actuel de la "Mode"', an unpublished text to which we will refer again soon, probably written in 1971, is even more explicit. It was included in a dossier dedicated to May '68 which, along with the letter addressed to Maria Antonietta Macciocchi, contained 'Du mouvement étudiant', from 1969 (ALT2. A15-02.01), 'Notes sur le Parti communiste français et le mouvement étudiant', from 1970 (ALT2. A15-02.02), a letter from Althusser to Emmanuel Terray dated 27 January 1969 (ALT2. A15-02.04) and a different version of 'À propos de l'article de Michel Verret sur "Mai étudiant"' titled 'Réponse à l'article de Michel Verret "Mai étudiant, ou les substitutions"' from 15 March 1969 (ALT2. A15-02.05). The text on fashion, theoretically akin to the letter we are examining (fashion is, precisely, a form of revolt that goes to replace the failed politics of 1968: it is a 'compensation for the failure of political forms') was published in *Décalages*, 1 (2014): 4. Here is the passage I want to highlight: 'What does the shaking of the school system mean? Experience shows that these apparatuses possess extraordinary resistance, and extraordinary resources of permanence and recovery, as well as prodigious capacities for disguising their preservation under the guise of renewal (cf. Faure's Orientation Law). In other words, the revolution against the IEAs is exercised in ways which, despite the extremism they display,

The student movement should have filled a *void* – or better, it should have filled it in the *correct way*.[22] Once again what is at stake is an encounter between anti-imperialist struggles,[23] or, more precisely, the effect they had 'on student youth', and the 'events that punctuated the years from 1930 to 1960',[24] that is, the role that they played in undermining bourgeois ideology '*to the point of making it extremely fragile and vulnerable*'. On the one hand, under the effect of the first sequence of events, the spontaneous petty-bourgeois forms of student politics as 'generally utopian-leftist forms'; on the other hand, under the effect of a second sequence, the *fundamental* fact that the space of traditional bourgeois ideology has been progressively emptying itself. The defeat of the dominant ideology, in fact, 'is a defeat that extends *over the entire world*'.[25] It has 'opened a void, a wide-open door that makes the Marxist-Leninist ideology virtually hegemonic, even if the petty-bourgeois layers in revolt somehow try to catch up with it, taking the form of ideologies that are still "childish", utopian'.[26]

---

only succeed with infinite difficulty in breaking the "umbilical cord" which links them to the ideology in question. I pointed out that it took many years for the process of undermining the IEAs to produce visible effects. We might add that even when these effects become visible, they conceal other effects, this time of conservation. If the IEAs in question really are the immediate environment in which young people live, it is their ideology that weighs on them, including the forms of their revolt, including the meaning of their revolt. A simple comparison would enable us to take the measure of the facts in question'. ALT2. A18-03.10, pp. 8–9.

22   I use the term in the Althusserian sense. The term 'correct' [*juste*], for example, as used in Althusser 2017, p. 229, is 'the adjective corresponding not to justice [*justice*], a moral category, but to correctness [*justesse*], a practical category that refers to the adaptation of means to ends as a function of the class character of the one pursuing those ends'. A more detailed analysis of this notion can be found in Althusser's *Philosophy and the Spontaneous Philosophy of the Scientists* in Althusser 1990.

23   'The Algerian War, the Cuban Revolution, and the South American guerrilla war itself ... the prodigious and victorious struggle of the Vietnamese people against the aggression of the world's greatest military power, the Chinese Cultural Revolution, the violent revolts of Black Americans in the great cities of the United States, the Palestinian resistance, etc.' Macciocchi 1969, p. 352.

24   'Mussolini's fascism, Hitler's Nazism, the Spanish war and the defeat of the Republicans under the blows of international fascism, the great World War, the revolutions that followed in Central Europe, but especially in China, the political and sometimes social liberation of the countries of the "Third World", the "victories" as well as the defeats (Korea, Vietnam!), the direct political and military interventions of the US which, became due to the weakness and contradictions of its "allies", the only international gendarme of imperialism'. Macciocchi 1969, pp. 352–3.

25   Macciocchi 1969, p. 353.

26   Ibid.

The name May '68 was therefore informed by a historical conjuncture that functioned as an open door, determined by an empty space whose proper filling was only virtual because not yet justly actualised. We talk once again of justice – there was, in fact, a way of filling that space which was undoubtedly progressive ('the worldwide ideological revolt of student youth is objectively and definitively *progressive* ... of course at its level and within its limits').[27] And yet, for a political practice aimed at transforming the features of a specific social institution (being the 'assault of the petty-bourgeois youth against certain capitalist state apparatuses, first of all its apparatuses of ideological indoctrination'),[28] it proved to be ineffective because it was produced and provoked by a misunderstanding of an order and of a disposition, that is, by the misunderstanding of an *essential* exteriority: '*under what conditions and in what time, at the end of what trials*', Althusser asks, '*will the student movement be able to reach the workers' movement once and for all, and finally merge with it?*'[29]

The historical conjuncture of May 1968 was both unprecedented and propitious, for it saw the mobilisation of an economic class struggle (historically decisive, in the last instance), and of a scholastic class struggle (which precedes the former, although only chronologically). That is, the two groups that animate what has been called the 'principle of contemporaneity' – the working class (for the modes of production) and the students (for the school as a specific way of ideologisation). Through a merging it would have been possible to hegemonise a vacuum, by means of the invention of a new institution. This did not take place. What did take place was an educational process subsumed under an apparent (ideological) principle of interiority that establishes its own self-subsistence and stability.

For the student movement it was a matter of coming to terms with the fullness and the emptiness of a historical situation, on the assumption of recognising the 'historical order of things' (as well as 'the international and national causes that are at the origin of [their] *ideological revolt*').[30] It was a question of coming to terms, that is, with *a theoretical practice that dictated the line of a correct political practice*. This is something which, in conclusion, gives meaning from a political point of view to the analysis conducted in 'Schools':

---

27   Macciocchi 1969, p. 355. Montag emphasises this progressive side of the student uprising
        in his introduction to the English translation of Althusser's 'À propos de l'article de Michel
        Verret sur "Mai étudiant"' (Montag 2018) and Legrand 2009.
28   Macciocchi 1969, pp. 353–4.
29   Macciocchi 1969, p. 355.
30   Macciocchi 1969, p. 356.

The only way to know the reality of the school, and therefore to forge certain means indispensable to its transformation, is *to get out of the school,
to get out of the ideology of the school, and to get out of the dominant bourgeois ideology*, in which the school, as we shall see, occupies a decisive
place. To get out of it means, in fact, to find oneself already installed,
at least partially, *elsewhere, outside* the school, an outside that is not a
vacuum. This other place, where one must stand, from which one must
draw the instruments of a critique and a knowledge, has a double reality:
the reality of the class struggle, and the reality of the Marxist scientific
theory of social formations.[31]

It is this analysis that I have tried my best to fully reconstruct in this book,
accounting for its complexity.

---

31   ALT2. A14-02.03, pp. 2–3.

References

Unpublished writings (IMEC, Caen, Fonds Althusser)

ALT2. A2-03.03: « Le communisme et les étudiants ».

ALT2. A3-02.01: « Technocratie et Humanisme ». Version complète, fragments, notes, documents réunis par Louis Althusser dans une chemise intitulée « Τέχνη ».

ALT2. A14-01.01: Feuillet d'un ouvrage inédit de Louis Althusser sur le Livre I du *Capital* (1969), annonçant la parution prochaine d'un livre intitulé *Écoles* dans la collection « Théorie ».

ALT2. A14-01.02: « Additifs » de Renée Balibar.

ALT2. A14-01.03: Notes diverses. [The subdivision of the dossier into ALT2. A14-01.03 (A), ALT2. A14-01.03 (B1), ALT2. A14-01.03 (B2), ALT2. A14-01.03 (B3) is mine and is for clarity of exposition].

ALT2. A14-01.04: « Les mythologies scolaires ». Texte de Pierre Macherey. 10 mars 1968. [The subdivision of the dossier into ALT2. A14-01.04 (A), ALT2. A14-01.04 (B) is mine and is for clarity of exposition].

ALT2. A14-01.05: « Pratiques littéraires et pratiques scolaires » (à propos du texte de Pierre Macherey: « Mythologies scolaires »). Texte de Michel Tort.

ALT2. A14-01.06: Texte de Michel Tort. 23 juillet 1968.

ALT2. A14-01.07: État du projet au 9 septembre 1968. Texte d'Étienne Balibar.

ALT2. A14-01.08: Sur les « Grandes illusions de l'École ». Texte de Louis Althusser. [Automne-hiver?] 1968.

ALT2. A14-02.01: [1) Sur les effets de répression et d'idéologisation et leur rapport]. Texte sans titre de Michel Tort. 16 mars 1969.

ALT2. A14-02.03: Projet de livre collectif « Chapitre I. Quelques représentations idéologiques bourgeoises de l'École ». Texte d'Étienne Balibar. 28 avril 1969.

ALT2. A14-02.04: Projet de livre collectif. Première Partie. Introduction et chapitres II et III.

ALT2. A14-02.05: 4 textes de Christian Baudelot et Pierre Macherey. Octobre-novembre 1969. [The subdivision of the dossier into ALT2. A14-02.05 (A), ALT2. A14-02.05 (B), ALT2. A14-02.05 (C) is mine and is for clarity of exposition].

ALT2. A15-02.01: « Du mouvement étudiant ». [1969?].

ALT2. A15-02.02: Notes sur le Parti communiste français et le mouvement étudiant. Avril 1970.

ALT2. A15-02.04: Lettre de Louis Althusser à Emmanuel Terray. 27 janvier 1969.

ALT2. A15-02.05: Réponse à l'article de Michel Verret « Mai étudiant, ou les substitutions » (*La Pensée* n°143, février1969). 15 mars 1969.

ALT2. A18-03.10: « Sur le phénomène actuel de la 'Mode' ». Sans date.

ALT2. A40-03.01: Introduction de Louis Althusser au séminaire Bourdieu-Passeron. 1963–1964.

ALT2. A40-03.04: « Question posée au cours du séminaire du 10.1.1964 ».

ALT2. A40-04.03: Polémique entre Louis Althusser et Bruno Queysanne. Correspondance de Louis Althusser avec Bruno Queysanne et Georges Lapassade. [The subdivision of the dossier into ALT2. A40-04.03 (A), ALT2. A40-04.03 (B), ALT2. A40-04.03 (C), ALT2. A40-04.03 (D) is mine and is for clarity of exposition].

ALT2. C1-05: Louis Althusser à Pierre Bourdieu. [The subdivision of the dossier into ALT2. C1-05 (A), ALT2. C1-05 (B) is mine and is for clarity of exposition].

872ALT/142/6: Louis Althusser à Bruno Queysanne.

Coll. La contemporaine, 4Delta 1183/8. Georges Lapassade: Eloge du révisionnisme: À propos de la lettre d'Althusser à Queysanne, et des problèmes posés par le travail du C.E.R.S.

Published Texts by Althusser

Althusser, Louis 1990, *Philosophy and the Spontaneous Philosophy of the Scientists and Other Essays*, London: Verso.

Althusser, Louis 1954, 'L'enseignement de la philosophie', *Esprit*, 6.

Althusser, Louis 1964, 'Problèmes étudiants', *La Nouvelle Critique*, 152.

Althusser, Louis 1971, *Lenin and Philosophy and Other Essays*, New York: Monthly Review Press.

Althusser, Louis 1995, *Sur la reproduction*, Paris: PUF.

Althusser, Louis 1996, *Psychanalyse et sciences humaines: deux conférences (1963–64)*, Paris: Stock/IMEC.

Althusser, Louis 2002, *Lenin and Philosophy and Other Essays*, New York: Monthly Review Press.

Althusser, Louis 2003, *The Humanist Controversy and Other Writings (1966–67)*, London: Verso.

Althusser, Louis 2005, *For Marx*, London: Verso.

Althusser, Louis 2011, 'Student Problems: Dossier: The Althusser–Rancière Controversy (with an introduction by Warren Montag)', *Radical Philosophy*, 170.

Althusser, Louis 2014, *On the Reproduction of Capitalism. Ideology and Ideological State Apparatuses*, London: Verso.

Althusser, Louis 2017, *Philosophy for Non-Philosophers*, London: Bloomsbury.

Althusser, Louis 2018, Letter on the 'May Events', *Verso Blog*, 25 May, https://www.versobooks.com/en-gb/blogs/news/3851-louis-althusser-s-letter-on-the-may-events?srsltid=AfmBOopt_do-kJiraL94qUdxglni4PJmjXfs_cZptlcoz4znflIQA47u.

Other Texts

Anonymous [Etienne Balibar] n.d., 'Les Héritiers, par P. Bourdieu et JC Passeron, notes de lecture', *Cahiers marxistes-leninistes* 3, 28–48, https://adlc.hypotheses.org/archive s-du-seminaire-marx/cahiers-marxistes-leninistes/cahiers-marxistes-leninistes-n3 -iii.

Anonymous [Louis Althusser] n.d., 'Sur la révolution culturelle', *Cahiers marxistes-Leninistes*, 5–16, https://adlc.hypotheses.org/archives-du-seminaire-marx/cahiers-marxistes-leninistes/cml14-sur-la-revolution-culturelle.

Anrich, Ernst (ed.) 1964, *Die Idee der deutschen Universität*, Darmstadt: Wissenschaftliche Buchgesellschaft.

Badiou, Alain 2009, *The Communist Hypothesis*, London: Verso.

Badiou, Alain 2018, *On a raison de se révolter ... L'actualité de Mai 68*, Paris: Librairie Arthème Fayard.

Balibar, Étienne 1995, *The Philosophy of Marx*, London: Verso.

Balibar, Étienne 2006, 'Sub specie universitatis', *Topoi*, 25: 3–16.

Balibar, Étienne 2018, 'Scattered Notes on "May 68" and its Interpretations', *Crisis & Critique*, 5, no. 2: 53–83.

Balibar, Renée 1974, *Les Français fictifs: le rapport des styles littéraires au français national*, Paris: Hachette.

Barthes, Roland 1977, *Writing Degree Zero*, New York: Hill and Wang.

Baudelot, Christian and Roger Establet 1971, *L'école capitaliste en France*, Paris: Maspero.

Benelli, Graziano 1981, *La nouvelle critique. Il dibattito critico in Francia dal 1960 ad oggi*, Bologna: Nicola Zanichelli.

Bertani, Corrado and Maria Antonietta Pranteda (eds.) 2003, *Kant e il conflitto delle facoltà. Ermeneutica, progresso storico, medicina*, Bologna: Il Mulino.

Bettelheim, Charles 1966, *Problèmes théoriques et pratiques de la planification*, Paris: François Maspero.

Bonvecchio, Claudio (ed.) 2012, *Il mito dell'Università*, Milano-Udine: Mimesis Edizioni.

Bourdieu, Pierre 1966, 'La transmission de l'héritage culturel', in *Le partage des bénéfices*, edited by Darras, Paris: Les Editions de Minuit.

Bourdieu, Pierre and Alain Darbel 1991, *The Love of Art: European Art Museums and their Public*, Cambridge: Polity Press.

Bourdieu, Pierre and Jean Claude Passeron 1979, *The Inheritors: French Students and their Relation to Culture*, Chicago: University of Chicago Press.

Bourdieu, Pierre, Jean Claude Passeron, and Monique de Saint-Martin 1965, *Rapport pédagogique et communication*, Paris: Mouton.

Clemente, Giacomo 2016, 'Il centro e la circonferenza. La questione della totalità in Lo scopo ultimo del pensiero umano di K.P. Moritz', *Rivista di Filosofia Neo-Scolastica*, 3: 627–47.

Dolar, Mladen and Giacomo Clemente 2017, 'Interview on Beyond Interpellation and Related Questions', *Quaderni Materialisti*, 15.

Establet, Roger 1966, 'Culture et idéologie', *Cahiers marxistes-léninistes*, 12–13.

Ferry, Luc, Jean-Pierre Pesron, and Alain Renaut (eds.) 1979, *Philosophies de l'Université: l'idéalisme allemand et la question de l'Université*, Paris: Payot.

Freinet, Célestin 1968–69, *La méthode naturelle, 2 voll*, Neuchâtel: Delachaux et Niestlé.

Freinet, Célestin 1969, *Pour l'école du peuple*, Paris: François Maspero.

Freinet, Elise 1969, *Naissance d'une pédagogie populaire*, Paris: Maspero.

Gorz, André 1973, *Socialism and Revolution*, Garden City, NY: Anchor Press.

Hallward, Peter and Jacques Rancière 2012, 'Only in the Form of Rapture. Paris, France, 2 May 2008', in *Concept and Form, Volume Two: Interviews and Essays on the Cahiers pour l'Analyse*, edited by Peter Hallward and Knox Peden, London: Verso.

Illetterati, Luca (ed.) 2007, *Insegnare la filosofia. Modelli di pensiero e pratiche didattiche*, Novara: De Agostini Scuola.

Kant, Immanuel 1979, *The Conflict of the Faculties*, New York: Abaris Books.

Kravetz, Marc 1964, 'Naissance d'un syndicalisme étudiant', *Les Temps Modernes*, 213: 1454–5.

Landolfi Petrone, Giuseppe 1997, *L'ancella della ragione. Le origini di* Der Streit der Fakultäten *di Kant*, Napoli: La Città del Sole.

Legrand, Stéphane 2009, 'Louis Althusser: Mai 1968 et les fluctuations de l'idéologie', *Actuel Marx*, 1, no. 45: 128–36.

Macciocchi, Maria Antonietta 1969, *Lettere dall'interno del p.c.i. a Louis Althusser*, Milan: Feltrinelli.

Macherey, Pierre 1966, 'À propos de L'amour de l'art (Bourdieu et Darbel)', *Cahiers marxistes-léninistes*, 12–13: 8–13.

Macherey, Pierre 1978, *A Theory of Literary Production*, London: Routledge & Kegan Paul.

Macherey, Pierre 2011, *La parole universitaire*, Paris, La Fabrique éditions.

Maltese, Pietro 2014. *L'università postfordista. Nuovi modi di produzione e trasmissione della conoscenza*, Pisa: Edizioni ETS.

Manacorda, Mario Alighiero 1971a, *Marx e la pedagogia moderna*, Rome: Editori Riuniti.

Manacorda, Mario Alighiero 1971b, *Il marxismo e l'educazione, 3 vols*, Rome: Armando Editore.

Manifeste POUR UNE RÉFORME DEMOCRATIQUE DE L'ENSEIGNEMENT SUPERIEUR 1964, https://www.institut-tribune-socialiste.fr/wp-content/uploads/1964/11/64-09_manifestenseig.pdf.

Marx, Karl 1992, *Capital: A Critique of Political Economy*, London: Penguin.

Marx, Karl and Friedrich Engels 1965, 'Briefe Januar 1868–Mitte Juli 1870', in *MEW: Marx-Engels-Werke, Bd. 32*, Berlin/DDR: Dietz Verlag. Translation available at: https://www.marxists.org/archive/marx/works/1868/letters/68_07_11-abs.htm.

Milbergue, Jean-Paul 1965 'La signification politique des rapports pédagogiques dans l'Université française', *Les Temps Modernes*, 227.

Milner, Jean-Claude 2021, *A Search for Clarity: Science and Philosophy in Lacan's Oeuvre*, Evanston: Northwestern University Press.

Montag, Warren 2018, 'Introduction', available at: https://www.versobooks.com/blogs/ 4187-louis-althusser-michel-verret-s-article-on-the-student-may

Morfino, Vittorio 2002, 'Il materialismo della pioggia in Louis Althusser. Un lessico', *Quaderni materialisti*, 1: 95–122.

Moritz, Karl Philip 1962, 'Gesichtspunkt für die mythologischen dichtungen', in *Schriften zur Ästhetik und Poetik: Kritische ausgabe*, edited by H.J. Schrimpf, Tübingen: Max Niemeyer Verlag.

Pippa, Stefano 2019, *Althusser and Contingency*, Milan: Mimesis International.

Rancière, Jacques 1973, 'Sur la théorie de l'idéologie. Politique d'Althusser', *L'Homme et la société*, 27.

Rancière, Jacques 1974, 'On the Theory of Ideology (the Politics of Althusser)', *Radical Philosophy*, 7.

Rancière, Jacques 1991, *The Ignorant Schoolmaster: Five Lessons in Intellectual Emancipation*, Stanford: Stanford University Press.

Rancière, Jacques 2011, *Althusser's Lesson*, London: Continuum.

Rancière, Jacques 2012, *La leçon d'Althusser*, Paris: La Fabrique.

Rigobello, Armando 1997, 'L'orizzonte tematico e il suo sviluppo storico', in *L'unità del sapere. La Questione Universitaria nella Filosofia del XIX Secolo*, edited by A. Rigobello, G. Amati, A. Bausola, M. Borghesi, M. Ivaldo, and G. Mura, Rome: Città Nuova.

Roggero, Gigi 2009, *La produzione del sapere vivo. Crisi dell'università e trasformazione del lavoro tra le due sponde dell'Atlantico*, Verona: Ombre Corte.

Schlegel, A.W. 1963, *Vorlesungen über schöne Literatur und Kunst*, Stuttgart: W. Kohlhammer Verlag.

Tessitore, Fulvio 1995, *Contributi alla storia e alla teoria dello storicismo II*, Rome: Edizioni di Storia e Letteratura.

Tort, Michel 1974, *Le Quotient intellectuel*, Paris: Maspero.

Willis, Paul 1977, *Learning to Labour: How Working Class Kids Get Working Class Jobs*, Saxon House: Columbia University Press.

Index

academic labour   27, 45, 47, 50, 52
analogical mechanism   89–90, 92–93, 100–101
antediluvian forms   156, 168, 217, 230, 231–232, 235–236
  of schooling   167, 231
  of modern capital   167
  of education   216
Alain [Émile-Auguste Chartier]   1
Ariès, P.   86, 229, 240
assimilation   101, 143, 152, 170, 206
  of knowledge   22, 45–47, 55, 101, 194
  of culture   153
  subject of   154, 160

Badiou, A.   102, 108n132, 248n15
Balibar, E.   VIII, XIV–VI, XIX–XX, 6, 10–11, 68, 86, 102, 108n132, 123n170, 150–1, 153–8, 160–3, 165–9, 171–4, 178, 180–90, 192–5, 197–202, 204–5, 207–12, 214, 216, 219n9, 230, 249
Balibar, R.   112, 126n179
Balzac, H.   102, 124–7
Barthes, R.   123n171
Baudelot, C.   VIII, XIX, XXIII–VII, 6, 74, 150, 163, 214, 216, 220, 224, 228, 230n54, 231, 237, 244
Bergson, H.   1
Bidet, J.   68–9, 80
Bourdieu, P.   VIII, XI, XIV, XX, 5, 21, 26–8, 30–2, 34–5, 37n77, 48, 85–86, 94, 96–7, 102–8, 110, 112, 114, 123n170, 207n243
  The Love of Art (with Darbel, A.),   104, 106–7
  The Love of Art (with Darbel, A.),   104, 106–7
  Rapport pédagogique et communication (with Passeron, J.-C., de Saint-Martin, M.),   6, 28
Brunschvicg, L.   1–2

caste school   130, 221–225, 239
childhood   102, 143, 152–153, 157–158, 229
class-based school   5–6, 130–131, 133–136, 156, 173–174, 203n229, 214, 219–221, 223–224, 226, 231, 236

class division   XII, XV, 18, 20, 22–25, 70, 94–95, 118, 125
concealment   79, 82–84, 91, 94, 125, 138, 176n155, 184, 200
cultural field   51, 109

Darbel, A.   102
dehumanisation of the Human Sciences   28
depolitizisation   81–82, 88
dialectical materialism   10
dissimulation   82, 90, 118, 126
Dolar, M.   19
dominant culture   109–110
Duroux, I.   108n132
Durkheim, E.   XX, 228–9

education
  costs of   49, 178, 185
  level of   106, 136, 167
  mode of   72–73, 83, 94, 96–100, 116, 128–131, 156, 166–167, 214, 216–217, 219
  ownership of   186, 189, 194
Engels, F.   10n21, 206–7n243
Epicurus,   11
Establet, R.   VIII, XIX, XXIII–VII, 6, 68, 102–11, 113–21, 123, 136–7, 157
exchange value   45–47, 146–149, 171, 190–193

Ferry, J.   VIII
Feuerbach, L.   11
For Marx (Althusser, L.),   7n18, 10n21, 11, 13, 19
form of value   147–150, 191, 196
formal equality   21, 42, 45
Foucault, M   XIII, XXI
Freinet, C.   VIII, XX, 176n
Freinet, E.   VIII
Freire, P.   VIII
Freud, S.   19

Galileo, G.   19
Godelier, M.   31
Gorz, A.   VIII, XII, 43, 48–53, 54, 69, 203

Hallward, P.   26
Hegel, G.W.F.   IX, 11, 19, 11, 113, 144n25, 230n51

historical materialism 10, 62, 104, 107
Homer 127n179

ideological representation 12, 151, 153–154, 159, 163–164, 178, 205, 212
image of the pyramid 143, 145, 158–160
imaginary level 82, 90, 92, 125–126
intellectual labour VIII, XXI–XXII, XVII, 17, 26–27, 36, 43, 51, 69, 71–72, 80, 94, 99–100, 116, 121, 135, 138, 162, 164

Kant, I. 30–1, 76, 144n25, 162n109, 169
know-how 70, 153, 155, 166
Kravetz, M. 23
Krupskaya, N. VIII, XX, XXIII, 71

labour power 4, 45, 47, 49–53, 68, 73, 139, 148–150, 165–166, 169, 170, 175, 178–201, 205, 209n250, 212, 215, 217–219, 222, 232, 241–242, 244, 247
Lapassade, G. 32
L'enseignement de la philosophie (Althusser, L.), 1, 7
Lenin, V.I. XXII–III, 36–7, 69, 71–3, 75, 102, 119
literary production 102, 122, 124–125, 127

Macherey, P. VIII, XIII, XIX, 6, 8–9, 11, 68, 72, 74–84, 86–9, 91–7, 99, 101–2, 104, 107–9, 111, 114, 116–23, 125–9, 135, 137–8, 142, 146, 150–1, 154, 157, 162–3, 167, 171, 175–6, 214, 216, 220, 224–5, 228, 230n54, 231, 237, 244
  A Theory of Literary Production, 75
Macciocchi, M.A. XVIII, 245, 249n21
Malraux, A. 113
Manacorda, M.A. 207n243
manual labour VIII, XX–XXIII, XXVI, 69, 71–72, 80, 94, 99–100, 116, 121, 135, 138, 162, 164
Mao, 83, 102
Marx, K. XIII, XVIII, XXI, 15, 19, 36, 71, 139, 146–50, 155, 164, 177–80, 182, 184–5, 192–4, 199, 202n229, 203n229, 207n243
Mauss, M. 31
Milbergue, J-P. 5, 32, 54–7, 59–60, 62–7
Milner, J.-C. 31, 123n171
mode of ideologisation 214–215, 217–219, 227, 229–230, 235–236

Montag, W. 251n27
de Montaigne, M. 29, 117, 231
Moritz, K.P. 78n44

non-knowledge 23, 40, 42, 54, 57–58, 142–143

On the Reproduction of Capitalism (Althusser, L.), 13–4, 68–9, 72–3, 75, 137, 154
overdetermination 74, 81, 83, 88, 246

Passeron, J.-C. VIII, XI, XIV, XV, 5, 21, 27–8, 30–2, 34–5, 37n77, 86, 94, 96–7, 102, 107n126
pedagogical
  analogy 88–89, 91, 100
  function 6, 16–17, 19, 23, 24, 27, 37, 38, 55–56, 65–67
  practice 40, 42, 54, 55, 58, 60, 62, 64–66, 89, 238
  process 95
  relationship 17n18, 24–25, 46, 55, 63, 65–67, 144
  training 15–18, 20, 22
Philosophy for Non-Philosophers (Althusser, L.), 10n21
Plato 8n19, 11, 154, 231
Plutarch 29
political practice 26–27, 35, 39, 42–43, 62–64, 104, 106, 110–111, 119–120, 248, 251
principle of contemporaneity 72, 82, 90, 96, 156, 166, 216–218, 226, 229, 232, 235, 251
process
  of production XXVII, 47, 49, 51, 53, 101, 168, 179, 181, 187, 203n229, 211–212
  of reproduction 72, 99, 118, 165–166, 182–183, 186–187, 189
  of schooling 87, 100, 152–153, 156, 165–166, 171, 173, 182–183, 205, 217, 239, 241n97, 244, 248

quality
  of knowledge 16–18, 41
  of labour power 49, 182–183, 215, 218
Queysanne, B. XIV, 5, 19, 27–8, 31–2, 34–7, 39–41, 43–4, 54, 63

Rabelais, F. 80, 82
Racine, J. 117, 124, 126n179, 127

Rancière, J.   VIII–IX, XVI–VII, 7, 14, 19, 21, 23,
      25–7, 43
   On the Theory of Ideology (Rancière, J.),
      19
real level   81–82, 88, 90, 92, 93–95, 125–126
reformism   83, 119, 142, 151, 160
representative content   79, 83, 90, 119, 125,
      129
Rousseau, J.-J.   80, 244
Roy, D.   XXVI.

Schlegel, A.W.   76
school-form   149–150, 165, 167, 169, 173–
      174, 176–177, 193, 201–202, 204, 208,
      209n250, 212, 218n8, 221, 228–230, 233,
      239, 241
scientific
   generality   6, 19, 23, 36, 56–57, 65–67, 86
   knowledge   18, 21–23, 27, 65, 103, 133, 150
   practice   X, 36–37, 41, 56, 62, 104
   theory   15, 27, 39, 43–44, 252
   validation   17, 21–22, 30, 37, 42
single school   132, 219, 221, 223–225, 231
Smith, A.   146, 154, 193, 244
social division   22–23, 43, 49–50, 53, 69, 70–
      72, 92, 94–95, 99, 160–162, 164, 167, 248
   of labour   XII, XV, XVII, XX, XXII, 14–15,
      17–20, 93, 100, 117–119, 155–156, 205
   of university labour   21, 30
Spinoza, B.   XI, XVIII, 19
Student Problems (Althusser, L.),   VIII, XI,
      XIII, XV–VII, XX, 5–6, 10, 13–5, 19–22,
      26–8, 30, 37, 40, 43, 54–5, 65–6, 68–9,
      72, 141, 171

substantial
   equality   40–41, 235
   inequality   23, 41, 45, 55, 57, 60, 67, 86,
      193
surplus
   value   XII, 140–141, 184–185, 187, 189–190,
      198–199
   labour   140, 155, 165, 190, 192–193, 198–
      200, 211–212

teaching of philosophy   1–5, 8
technical division   17–8, 22–3, 25, 37, 40, 43,
      45, 70–2, 94–5, 99, 156, 158, 161–2, 167,
      176n155, 205, 248
   of labour   XV, XVII, XX, XXII, 14–16, 20,
      69, 91, 154–155
   of knowledge   80, 93
theoretical practice   27, 35–39, 43, 57, 58,
      62–64, 120, 251
Tolstoy, L.   75
Tort, M.   VIII, XX, 6, 68, 74, 120–3, 125–9, 131,
      133–7, 150, 156, 163, 173–4, 218n8
transmission of knowledge   XII, XIII, XXI,
      XXVI, 15, 26, 58, 67, 94
true-factual proposition   11, 138–141, 144, 147,
      159, 191

unity
   of knowledge   30, 144n25
   of the school   81, 142–143, 159–160

value-form   146–149, 156

wage-form   191–201, 204–205, 209–212

www.ingramcontent.com/pod-product-compliance
Ingram Content Group UK Ltd.
Pitfield, Milton Keynes, MK11 3LW, UK
UKHW031835110526
5703IPUK00002B/32